DEMON

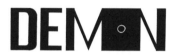

JASON SHIGA

First Second

New York

To my wife, Alina, who's threatened to divorce me if I dedicate one more book to her

First Second

Copyright © 2017 by Jason Shiga

Penciled with a Bic ballpoint on letter-size copy paper. Inked with a size 2 Windsor & Newton brush and black India ink on more copy paper. Colored digitally with Photoshop. Production help from Jackie Lo.

Published by First Second
First Second is an imprint of Roaring Brook Press,
a division of Holtzbrinck Publishing Holdings Limited Partnership
175 Fifth Avenue, New York, New York 10010
All rights reserved

Library of Congress Control Number: 2016945551

ISBN 978-1-62672-454-9

Our books may be purchased in bulk for promotional, educational, or business use. Please contact your local bookseller or the Macmillan Corporate and Premium Sales Department at (800) 221-7945 ext. 5442 or by e-mail at MacmillanSpecialMarkets@macmillan.com.

First edition 2017
Book design by John Green

Printed in China
10 9 8 7 6 5 4 3 2 1

THE STORY SO FAR

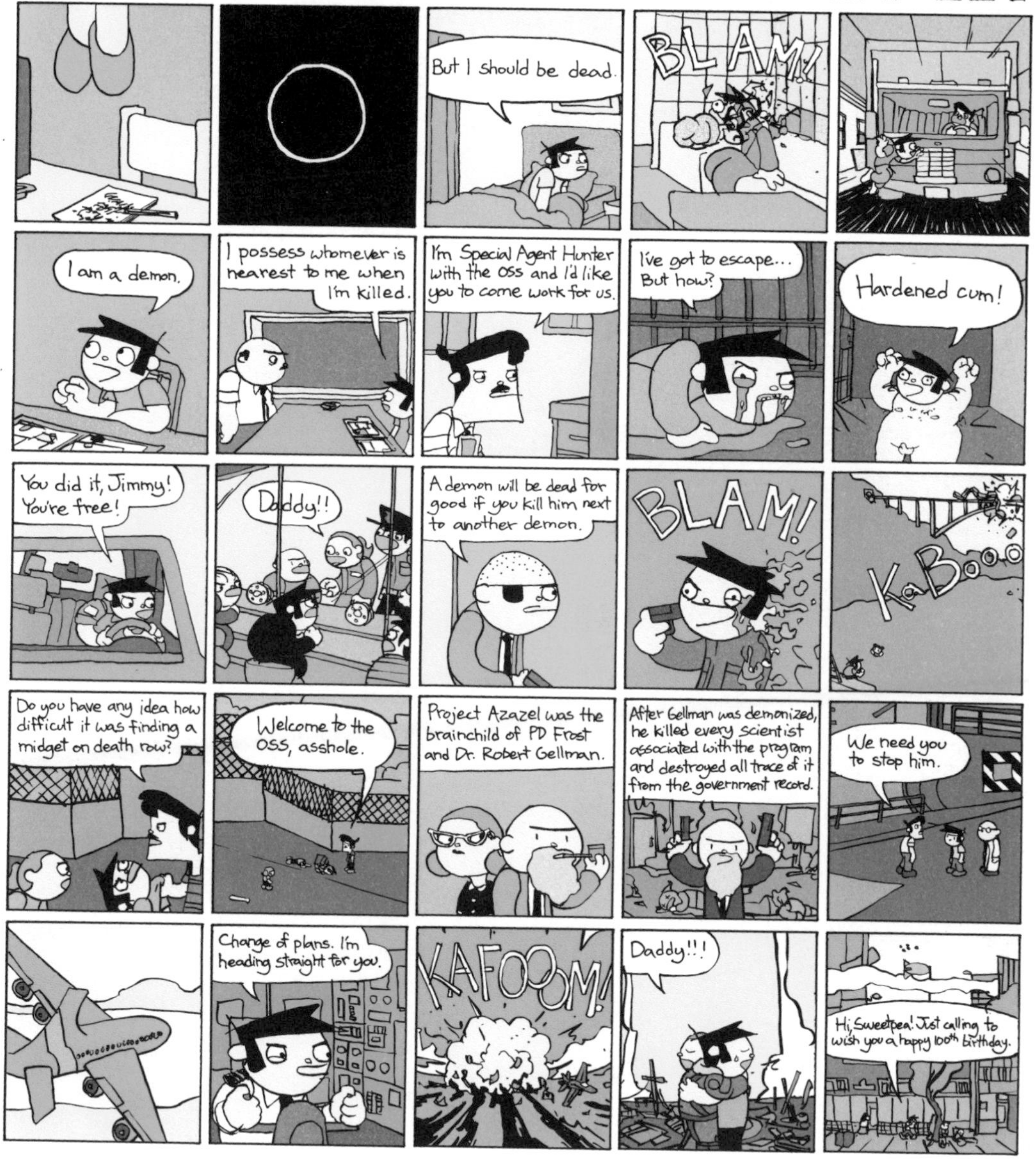

BLAM!
But I should be dead.
I am a demon.
I possess whomever is nearest to me when I'm killed.
I'm Special Agent Hunter with the OSS and I'd like you to come work for us.
I've got to escape... But how?
Hardened cum!
You did it, Jimmy! You're free!
Daddy!!
A demon will be dead for good if you kill him next to another demon.
BLAM!
KaBoo
Do you have any idea how difficult it was finding a midget on death row?
Welcome to the OSS, asshole.
Project Azazel was the brainchild of PD Frost and Dr. Robert Gellman.
After Gellman was demonized, he killed every scientist associated with the program and destroyed all trace of it from the government record.
We need you to stop him.
Change of plans. I'm heading straight for you.
KAFOOOM!
Daddy!!!
Hi, Sweetpea! Just calling to wish you a happy 100th birthday.

CHAPTER 13

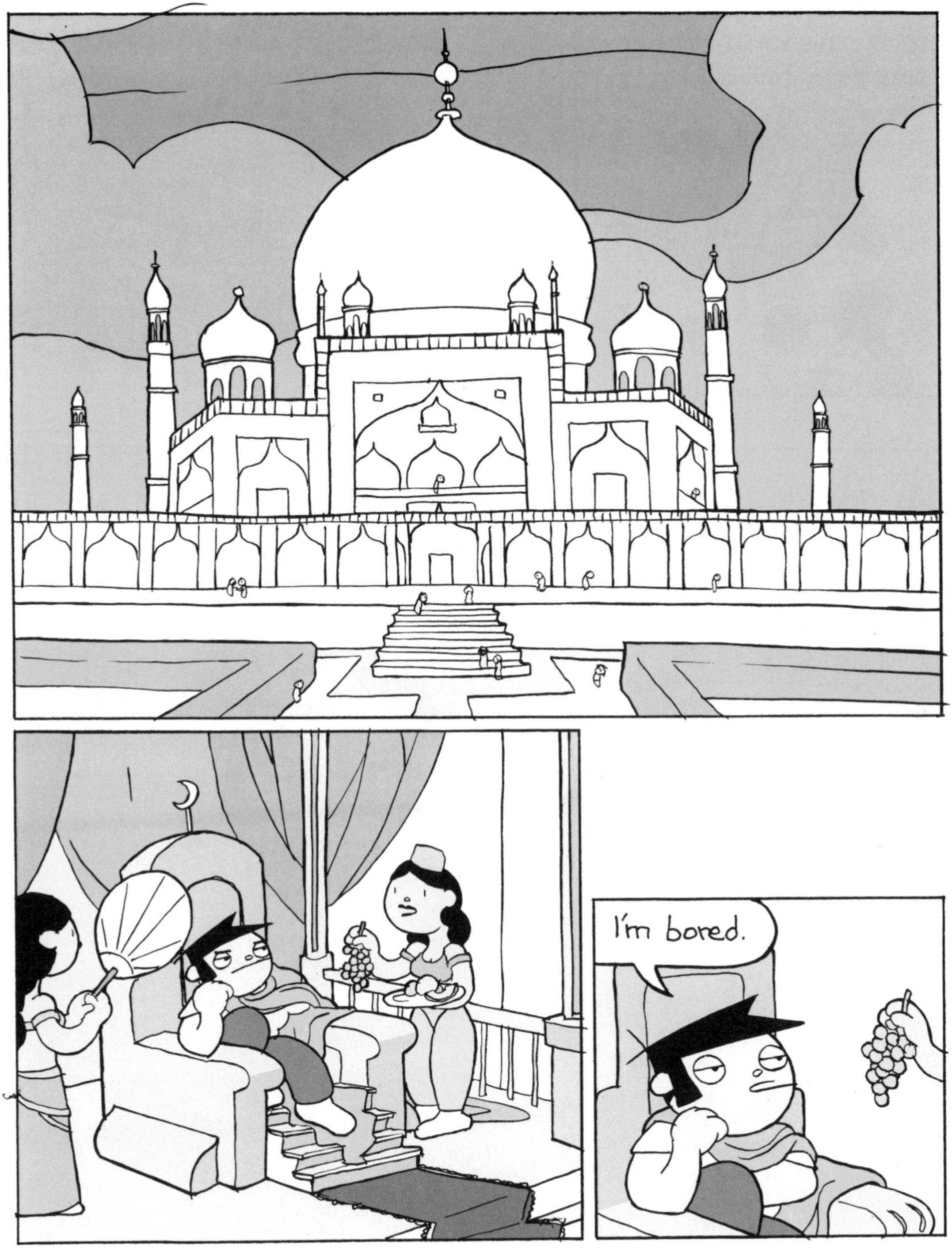
I'm bored.

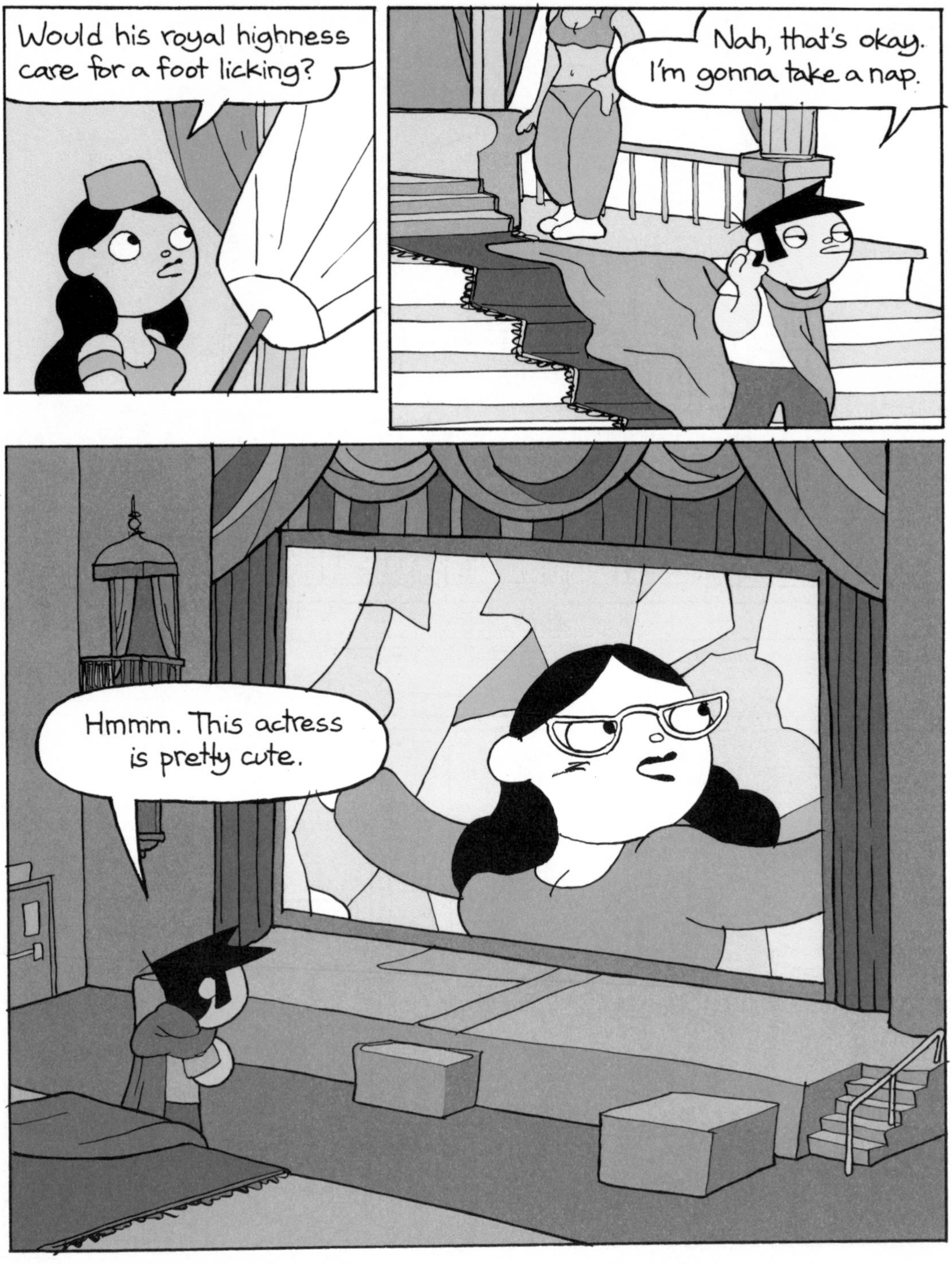
Would his royal highness care for a foot licking?
Nah, that's okay. I'm gonna take a nap.
Hmmm. This actress is pretty cute.

Could I get the latest issue of "People"?

Oh Brad!

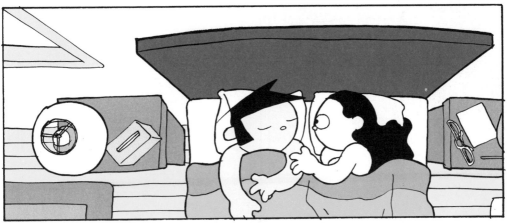

You seem different, Brad.

Gotta go!

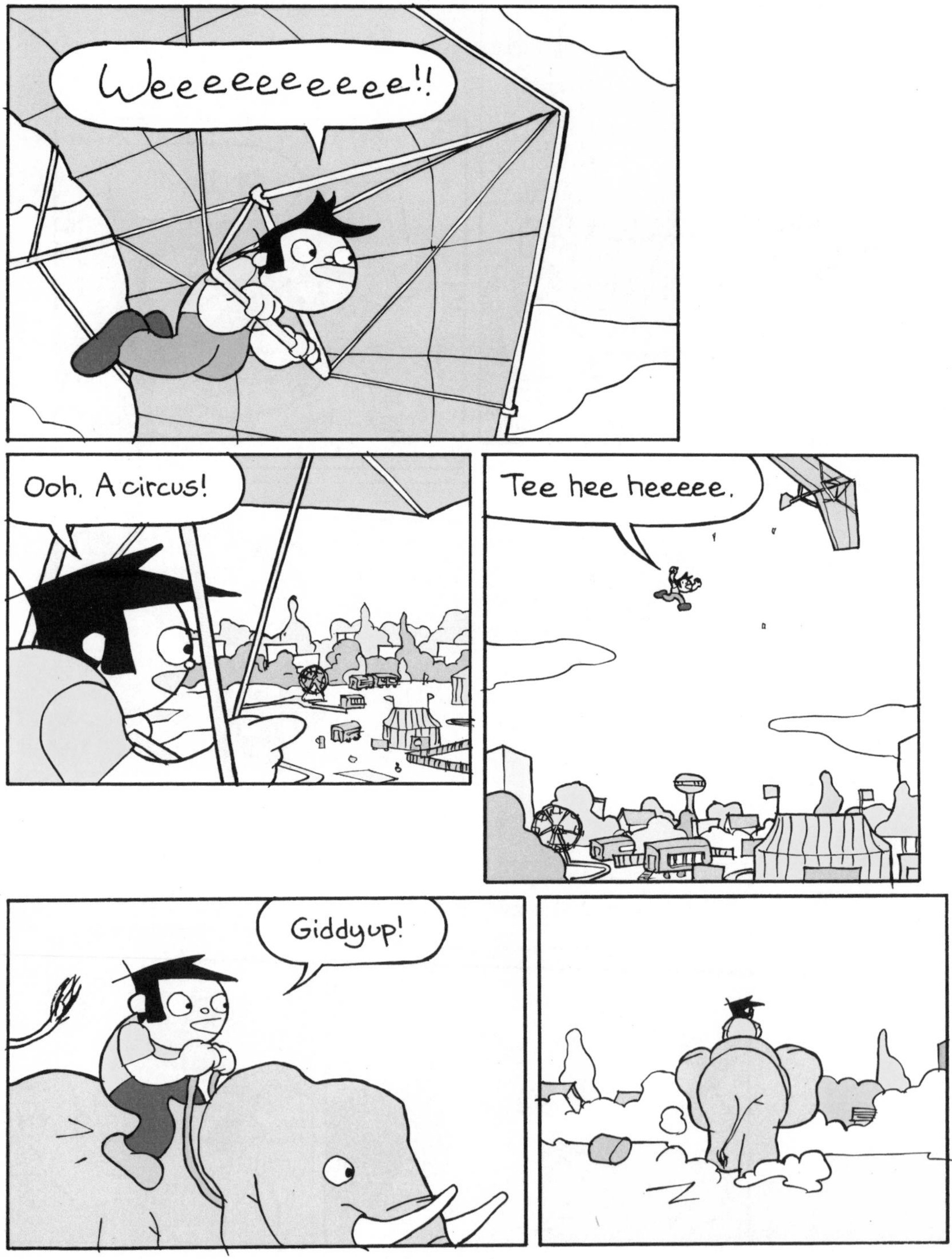
Weeeeeeeeee!!
Ooh. A circus!
Tee hee heeeee.
Giddyup!

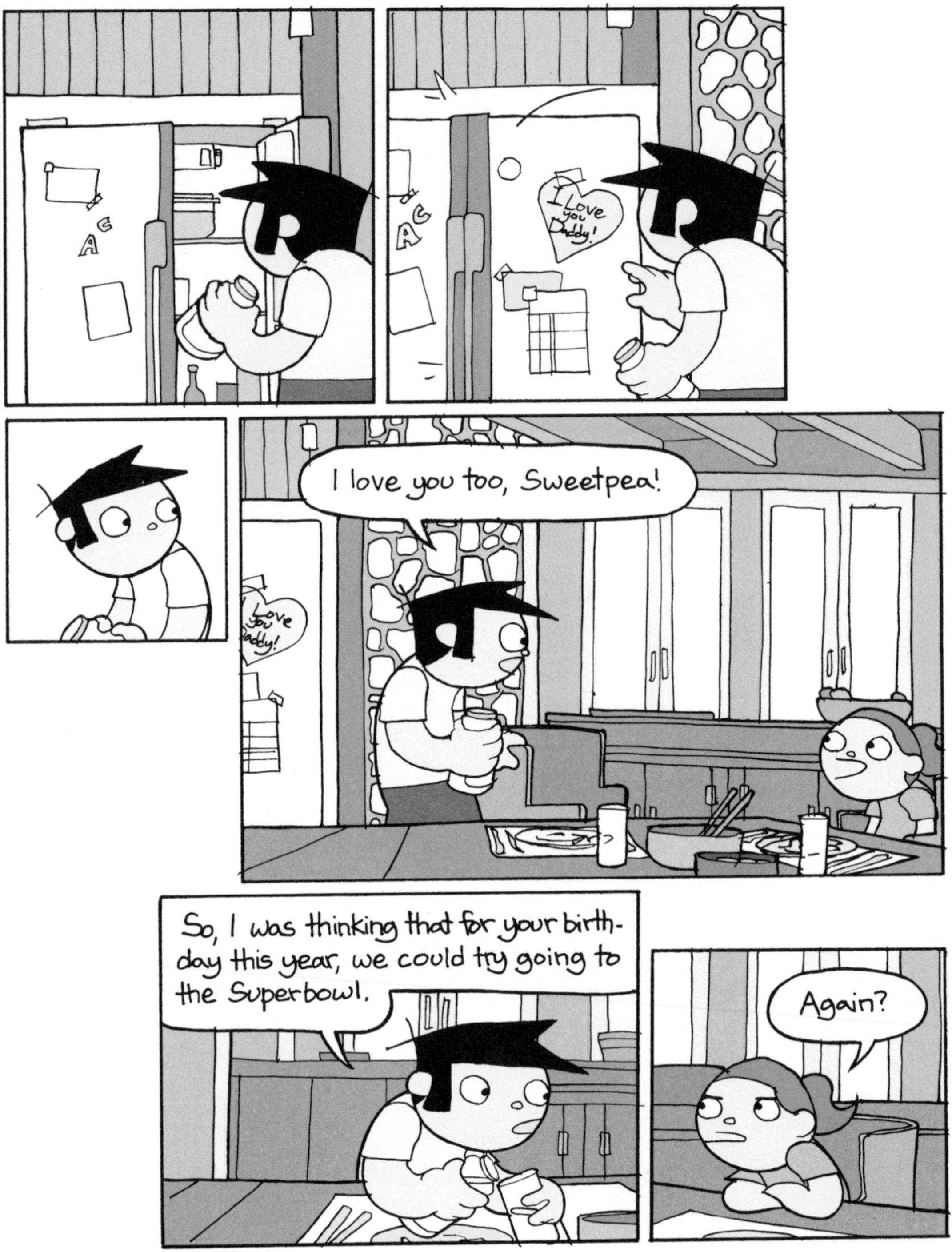
I Love you Daddy!
I love you too, Sweetpea!
So, I was thinking that for your birthday this year, we could try going to the Superbowl.
Again?

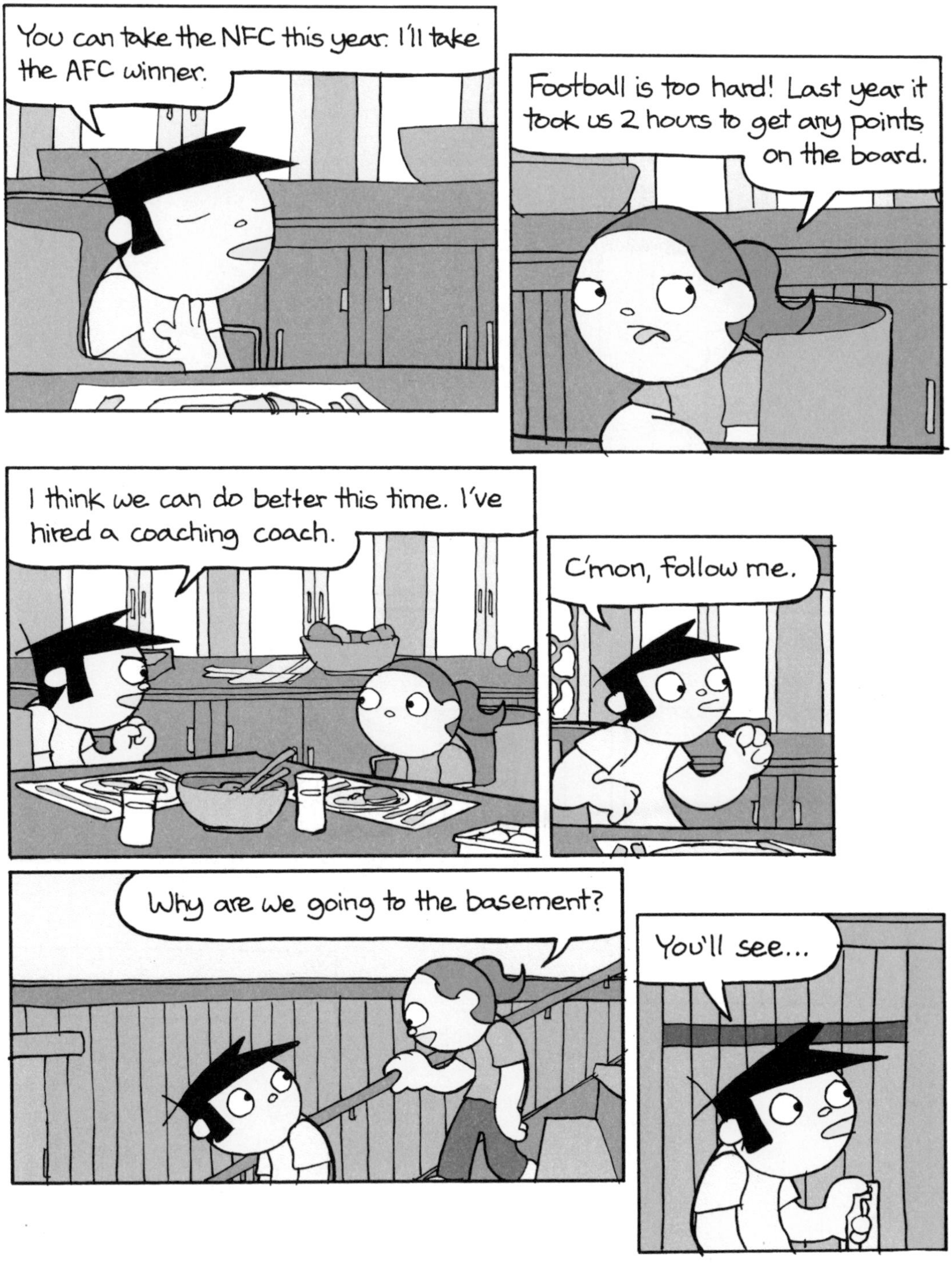
You can take the NFC this year. I'll take the AFC winner.
Football is too hard! Last year it took us 2 hours to get any points on the board.
I think we can do better this time. I've hired a coaching coach.
C'mon, follow me.
Why are we going to the basement?
You'll see...

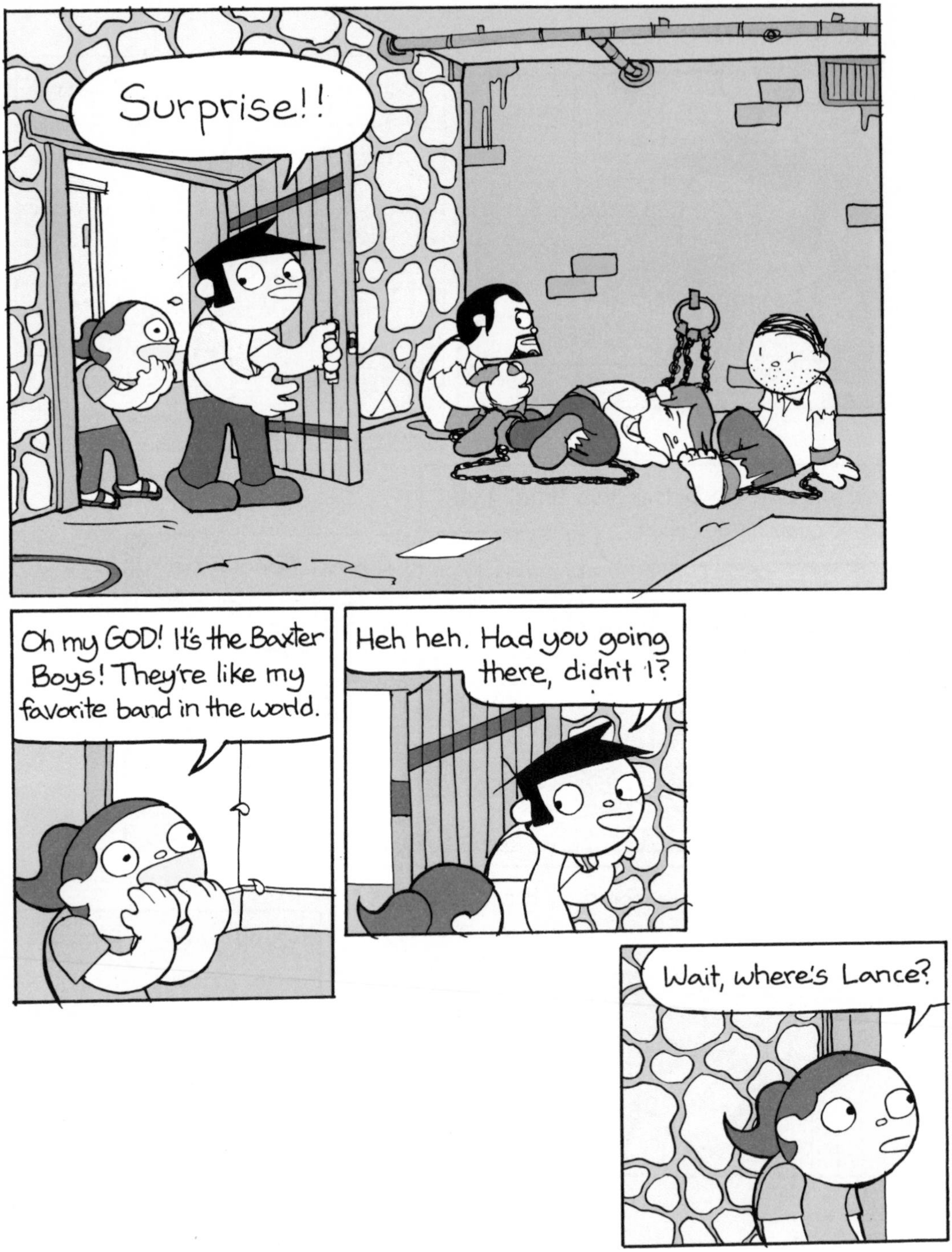
Surprise!!
Oh my GOD! It's the Baxter Boys! They're like my favorite band in the world.
Heh heh. Had you going there, didn't I?
Wait, where's Lance?

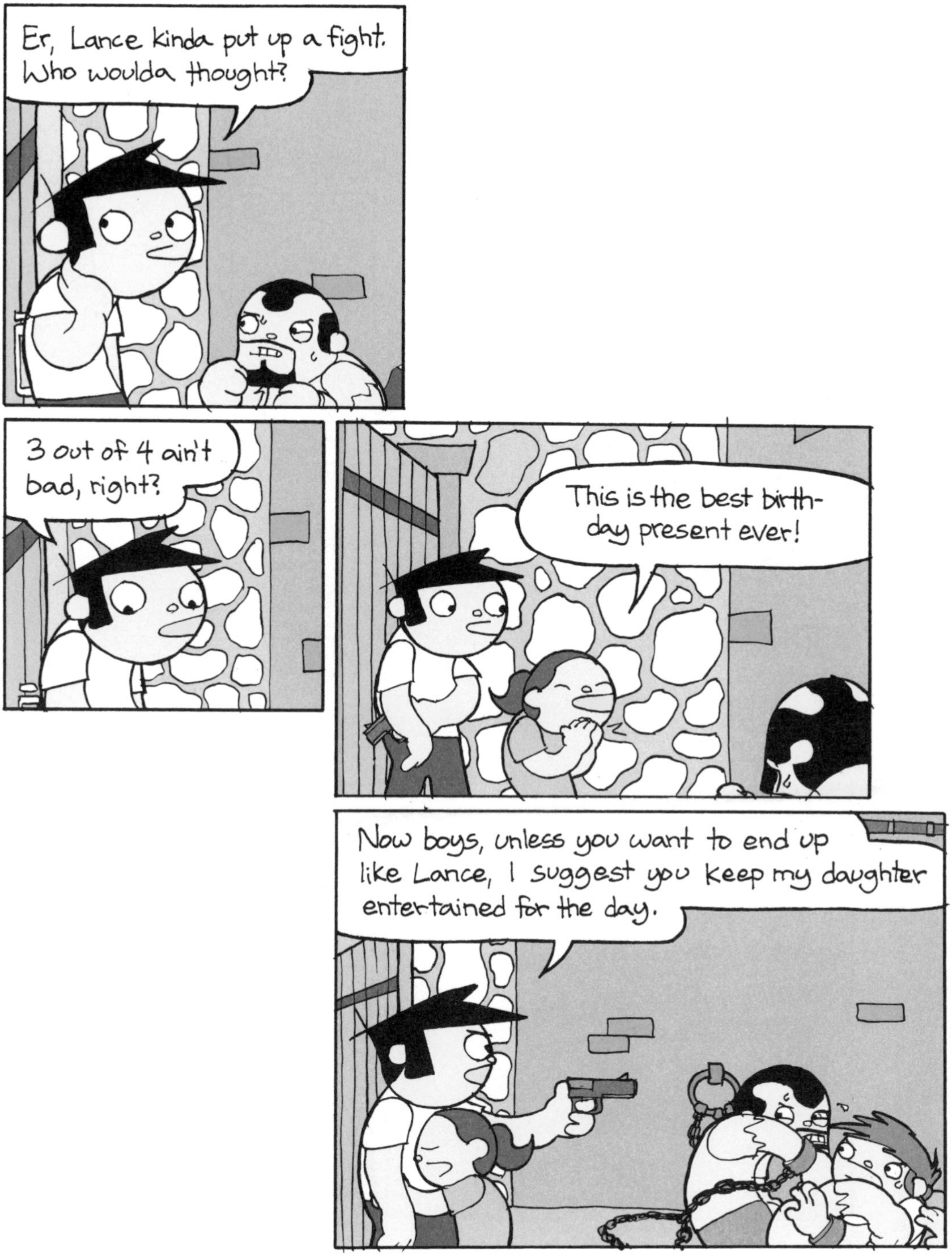
Er, Lance kinda put up a fight. Who woulda thought?
3 out of 4 ain't bad, right?
This is the best birth-day present ever!
Now boys, unless you want to end up like Lance, I suggest you keep my daughter entertained for the day.

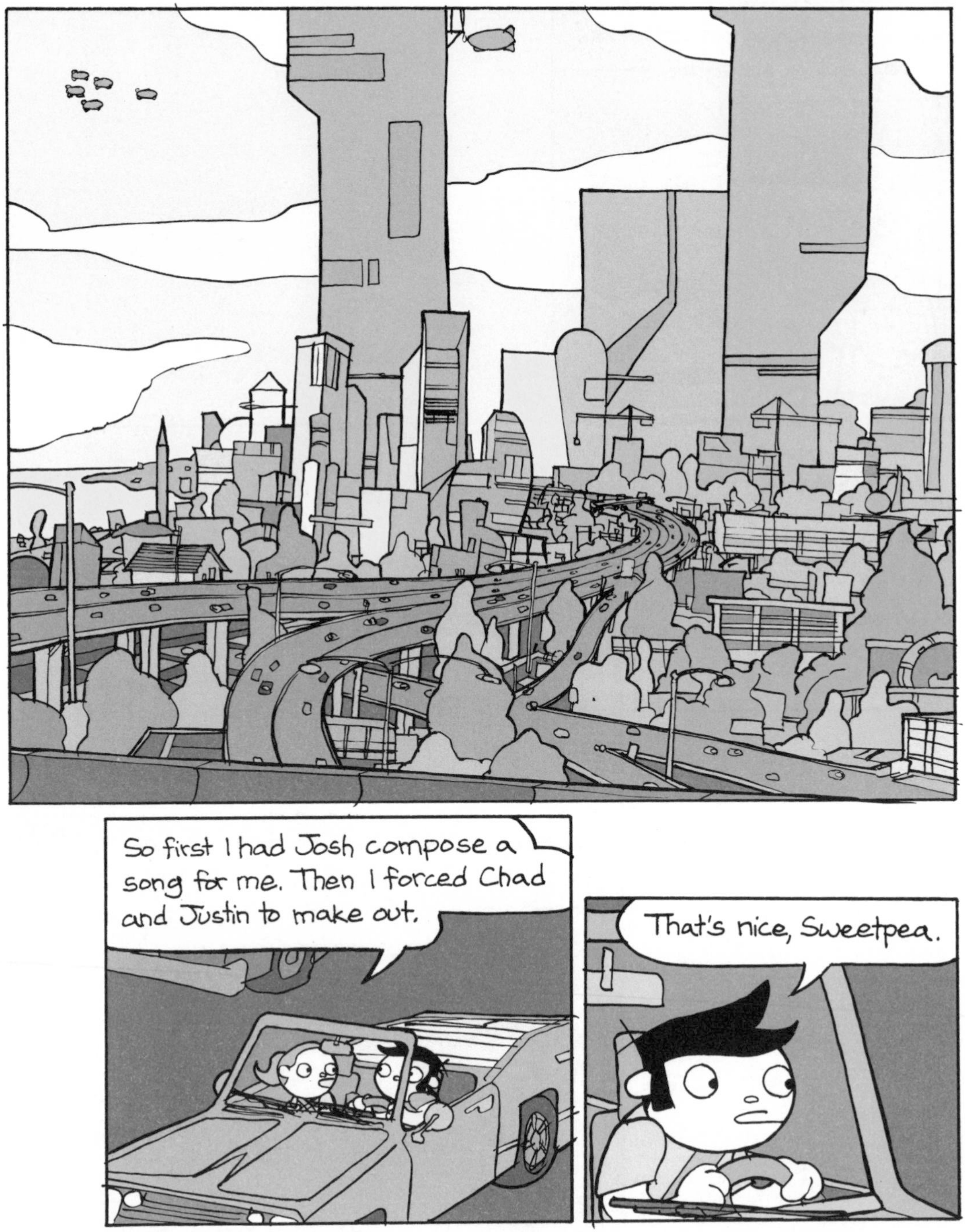
So first I had Josh compose a song for me. Then I forced Chad and Justin to make out.
That's nice, Sweetpea.

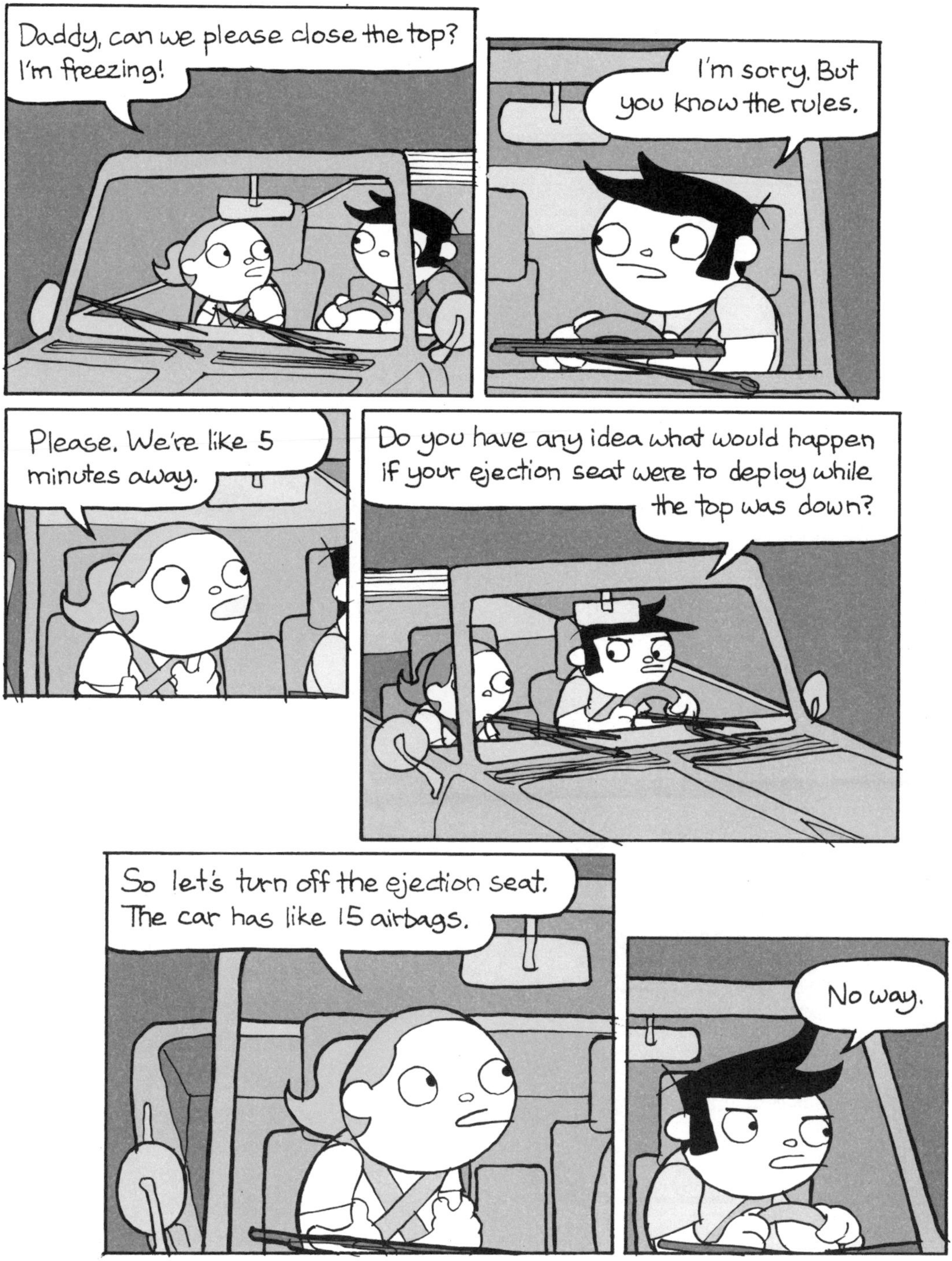

Daddy, can we please close the top? I'm freezing!
I'm sorry. But you know the rules.
Please. We're like 5 minutes away.
Do you have any idea what would happen if your ejection seat were to deploy while the top was down?
So let's turn off the ejection seat. The car has like 15 airbags.
No way.

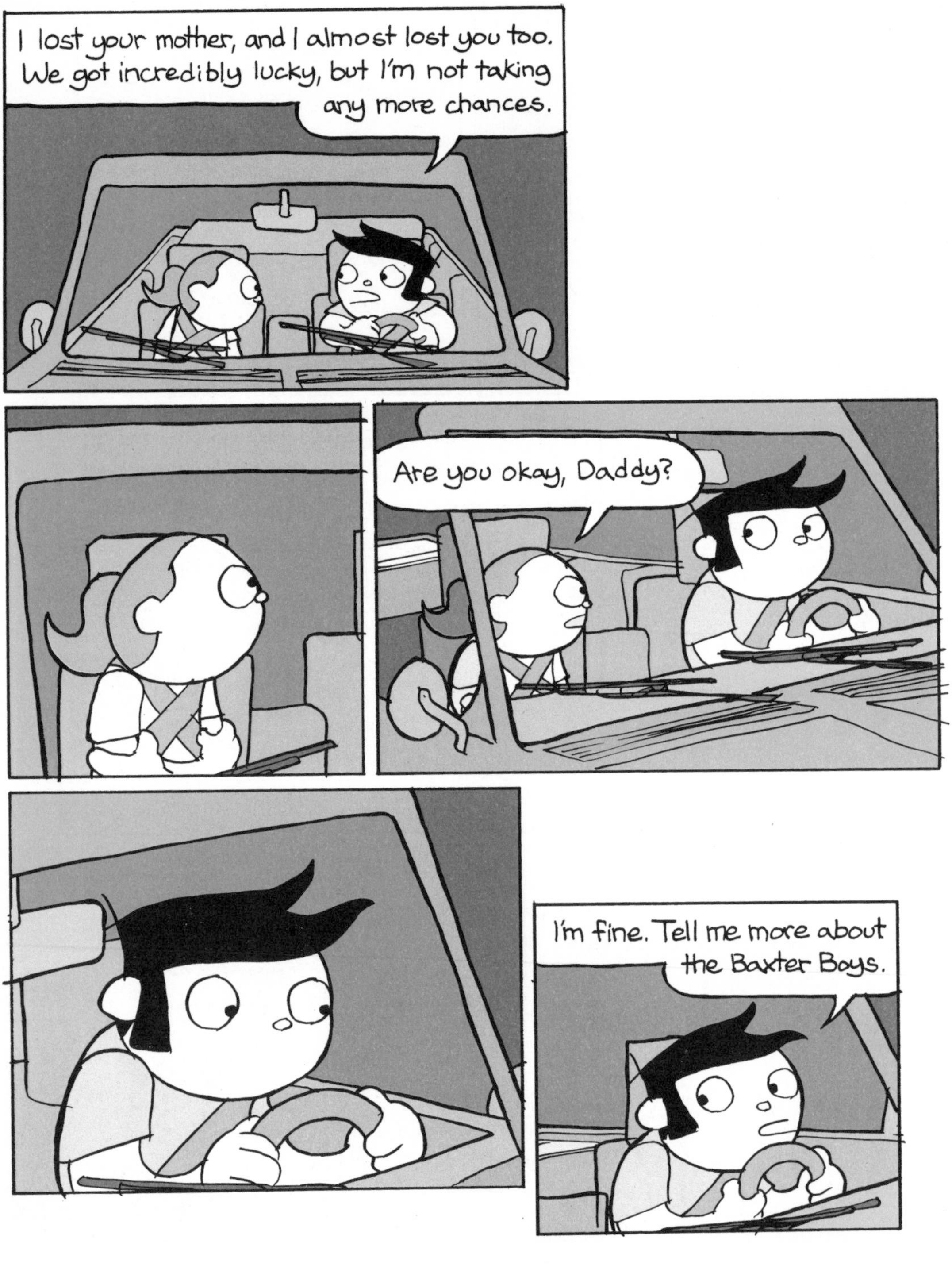
I lost your mother, and I almost lost you too. We got incredibly lucky, but I'm not taking any more chances.
Are you okay, Daddy?
I'm fine. Tell me more about the Baxter Boys.

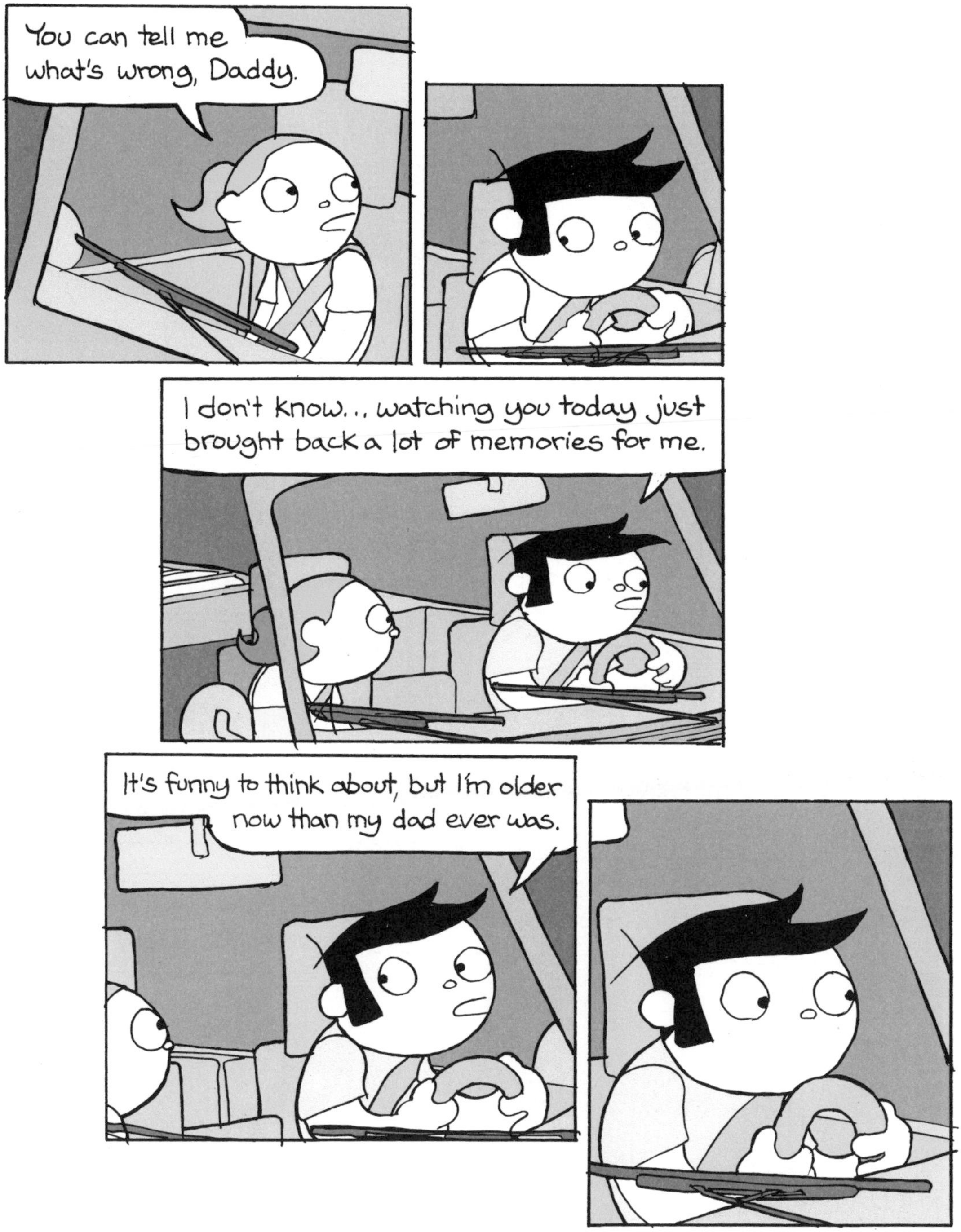
You can tell me what's wrong, Daddy.
I don't know... watching you today just brought back a lot of memories for me.
It's funny to think about, but I'm older now than my dad ever was.

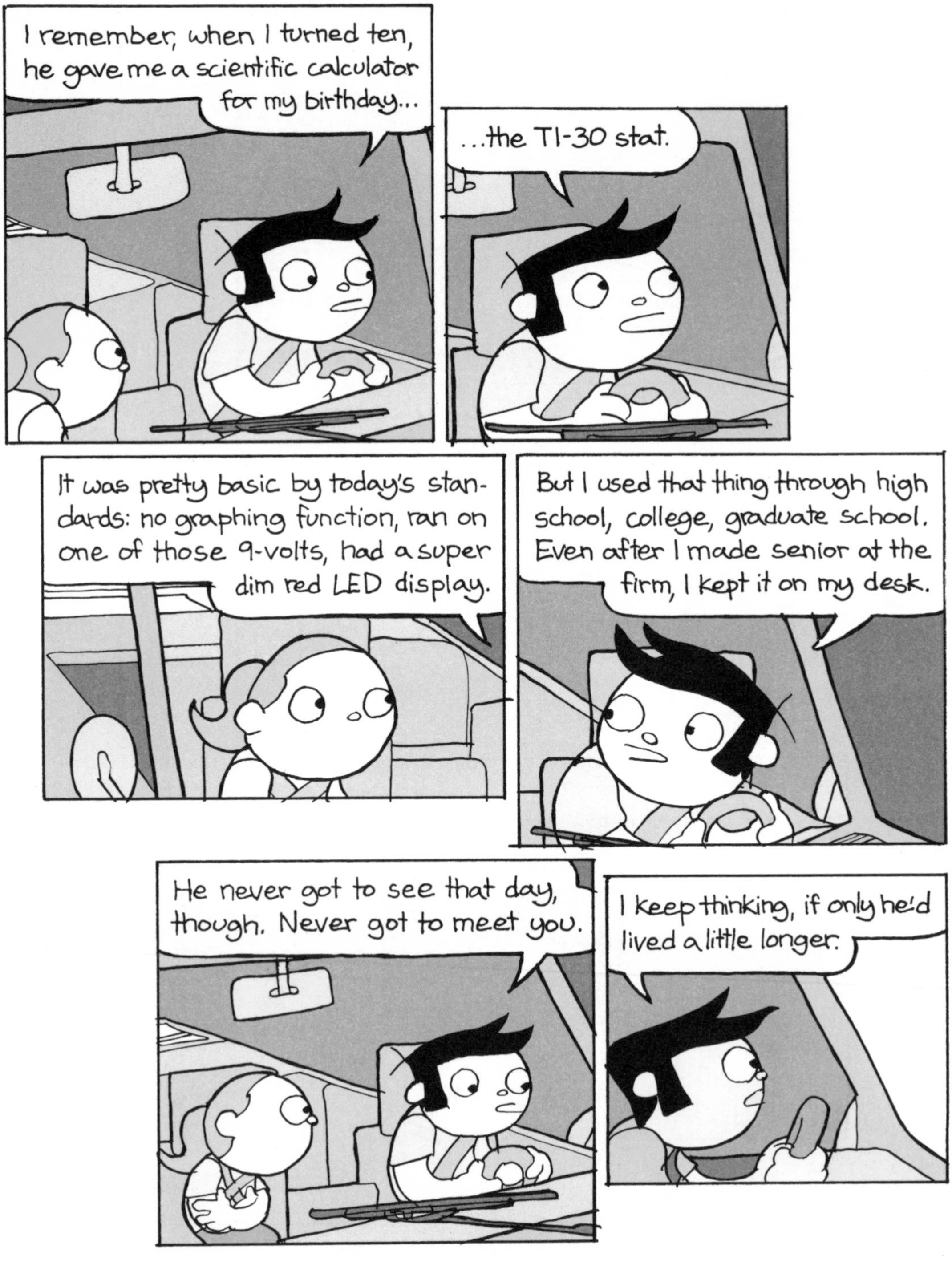
I remember, when I turned ten, he gave me a scientific calculator for my birthday...
...the TI-30 stat.
It was pretty basic by today's standards: no graphing function, ran on one of those 9-volts, had a super dim red LED display.
But I used that thing through high school, college, graduate school. Even after I made senior at the firm, I kept it on my desk.
He never got to see that day, though. Never got to meet you.
I keep thinking, if only he'd lived a little longer.

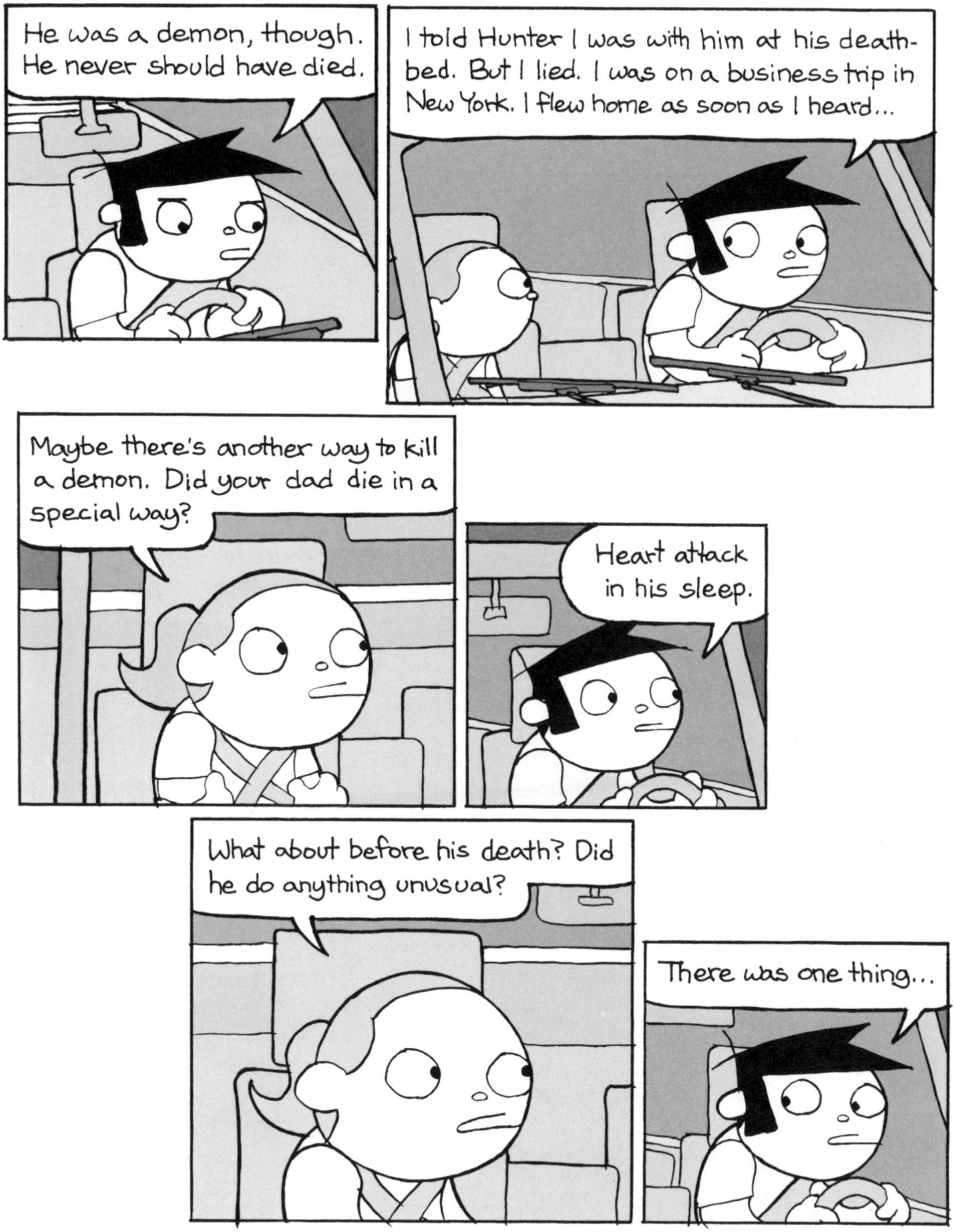

He was a demon, though. He never should have died.
I told Hunter I was with him at his death-bed. But I lied. I was on a business trip in New York. I flew home as soon as I heard...
Maybe there's another way to kill a demon. Did your dad die in a special way?
Heart attack in his sleep.
What about before his death? Did he do anything unusual?
There was one thing...

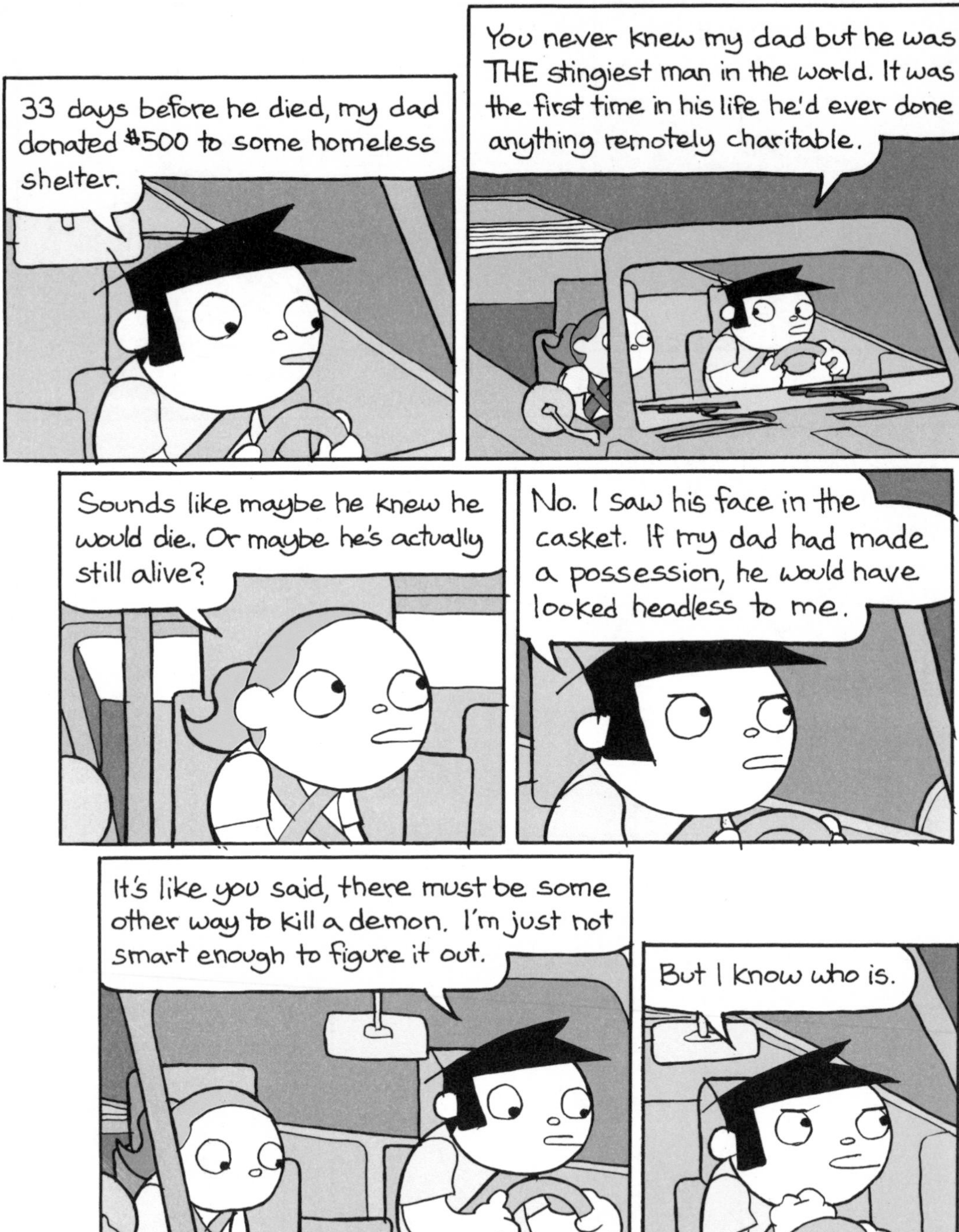
33 days before he died, my dad donated $500 to some homeless shelter.
You never knew my dad but he was THE stingiest man in the world. It was the first time in his life he'd ever done anything remotely charitable.
Sounds like maybe he knew he would die. Or maybe he's actually still alive?
No. I saw his face in the casket. If my dad had made a possession, he would have looked headless to me.
It's like you said, there must be some other way to kill a demon. I'm just not smart enough to figure it out.
But I know who is.

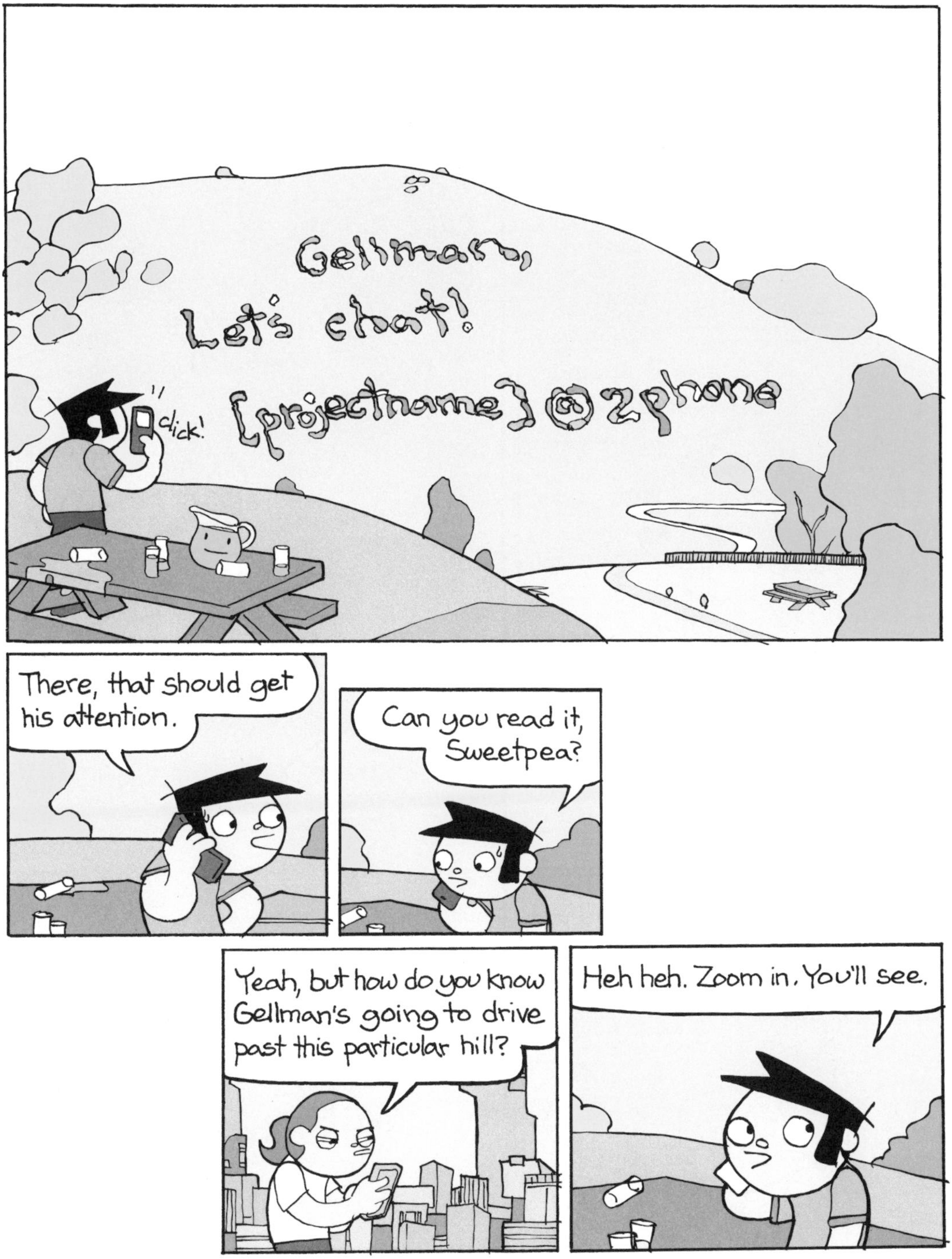
Gellman,
Let's chat!
[projectname]@zphone
click!
There, that should get his attention.
Can you read it, Sweetpea?
Yeah, but how do you know Gellman's going to drive past this particular hill?
Heh heh. Zoom in. You'll see.

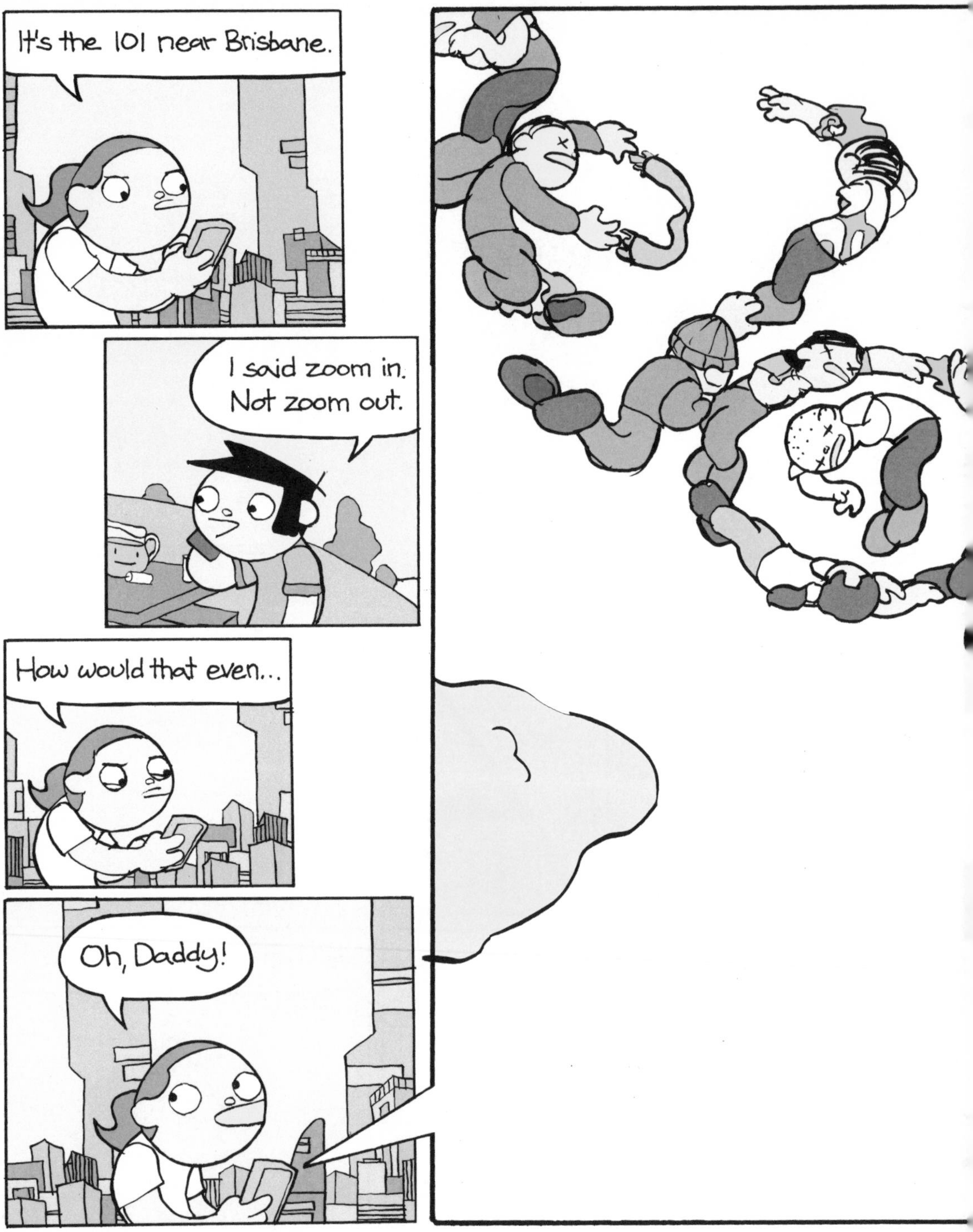
It's the 101 near Brisbane.
I said zoom in. Not zoom out.
How would that even...
Oh, Daddy!

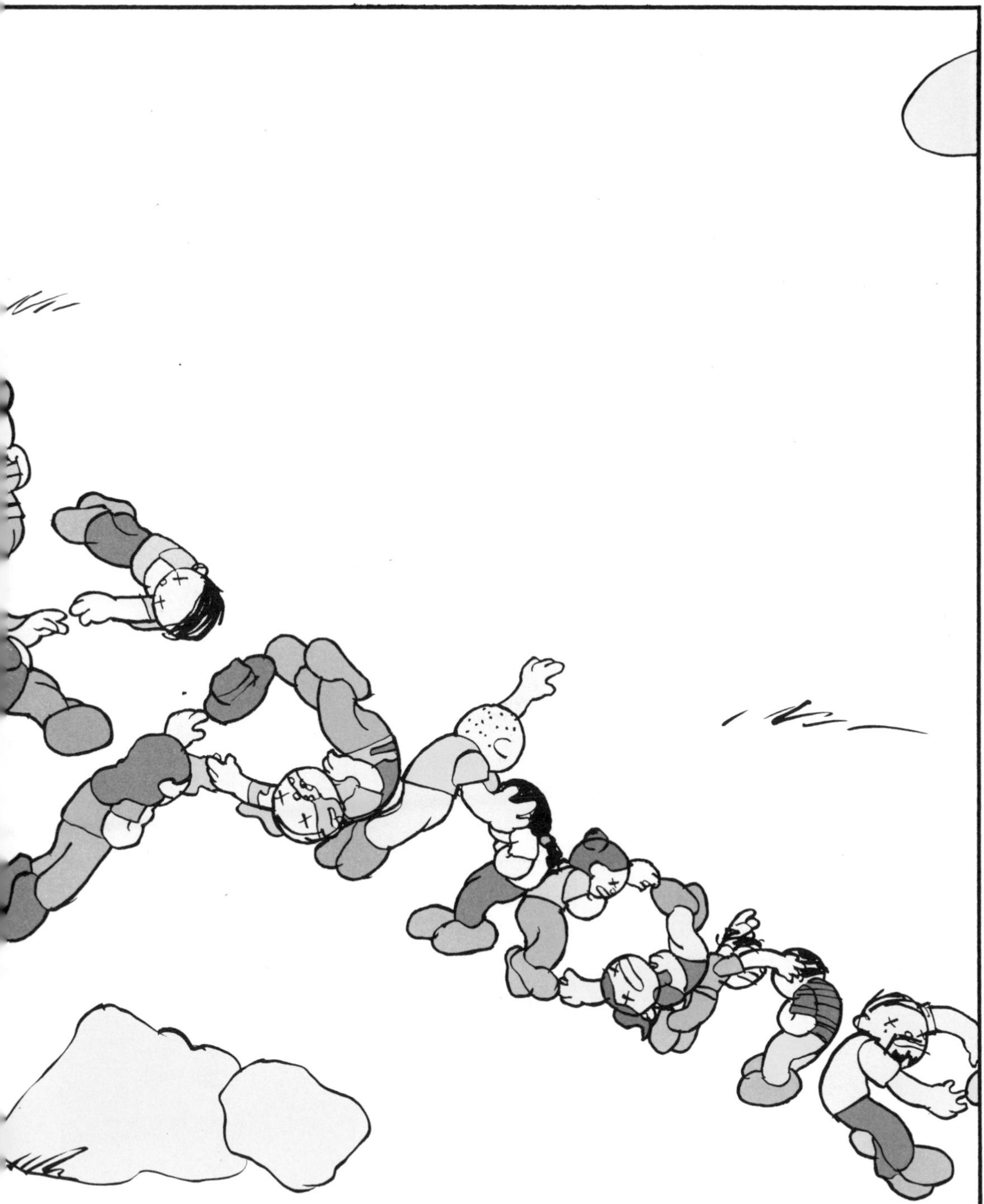

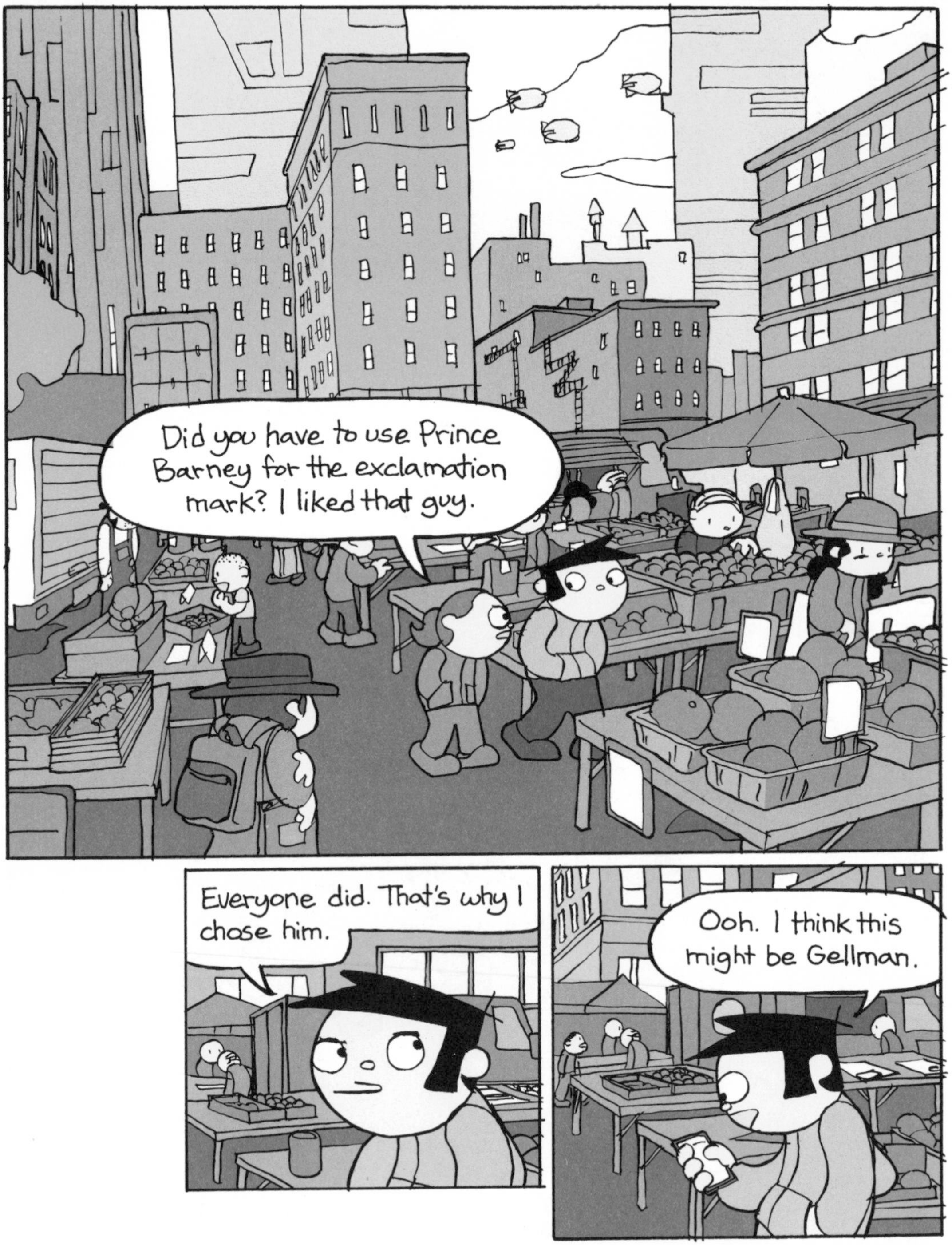
Did you have to use Prince Barney for the exclamation mark? I liked that guy.
Everyone did. That's why I chose him.
Ooh. I think this might be Gellman.

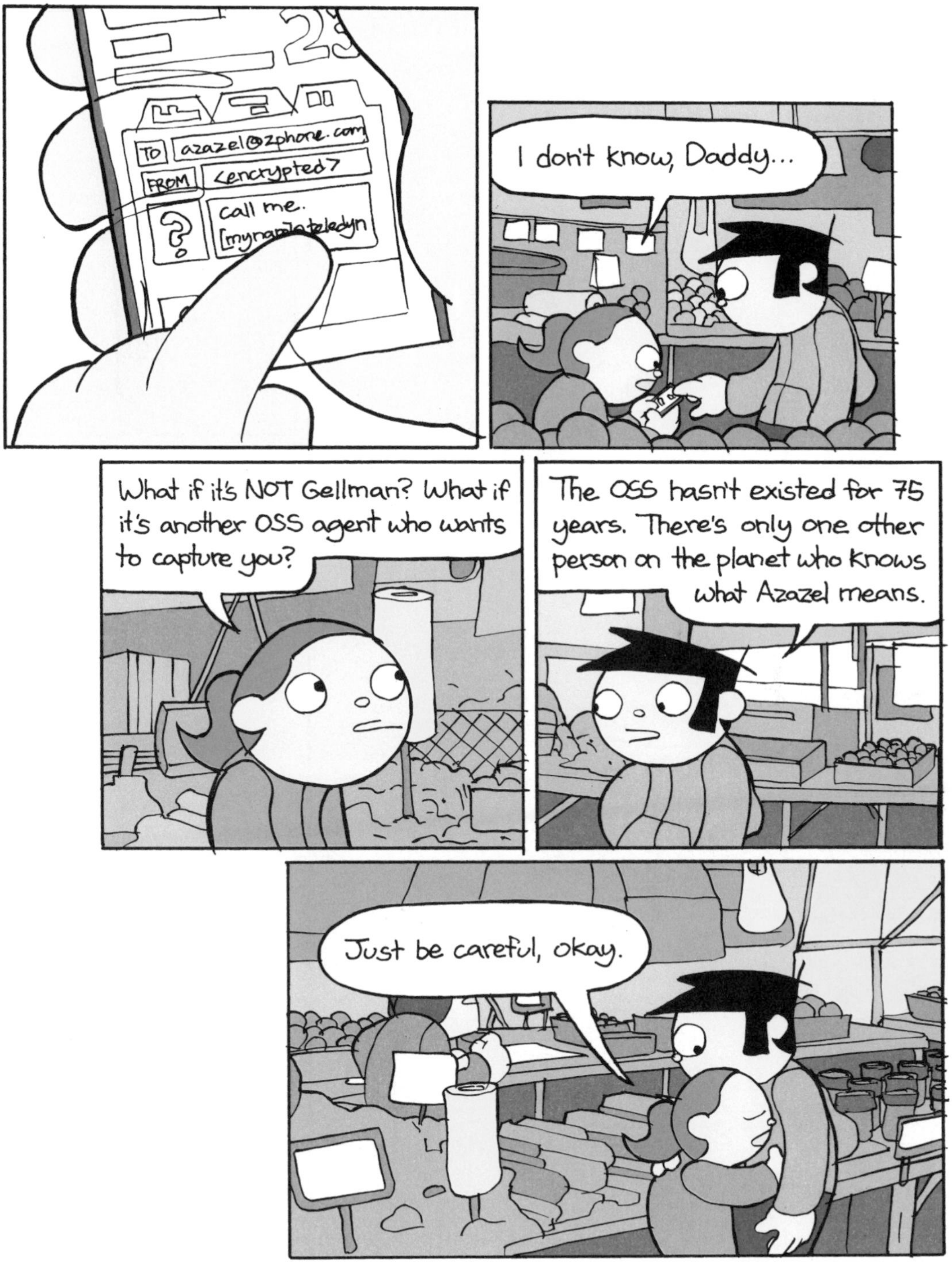
TO
azazel@zphone.com
FROM
<encrypted>
call me.
I don't know, Daddy...
What if it's NOT Gellman? What if it's another OSS agent who wants to capture you?
The OSS hasn't existed for 75 years. There's only one other person on the planet who knows what Azazel means.
Just be careful, okay.

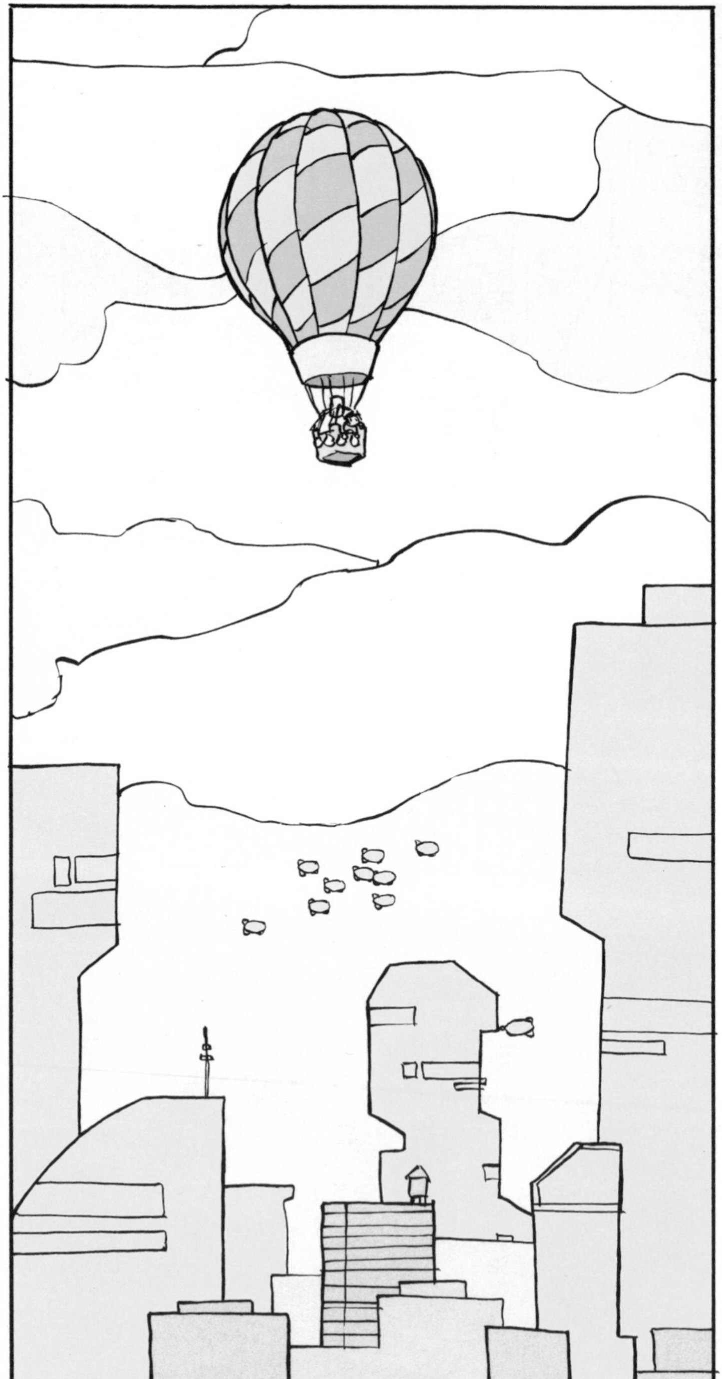

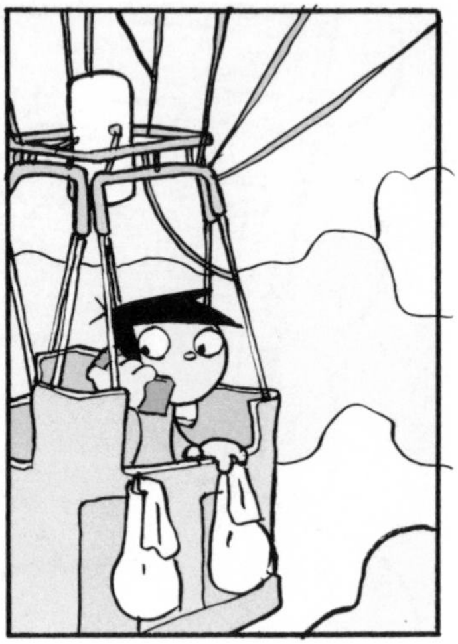

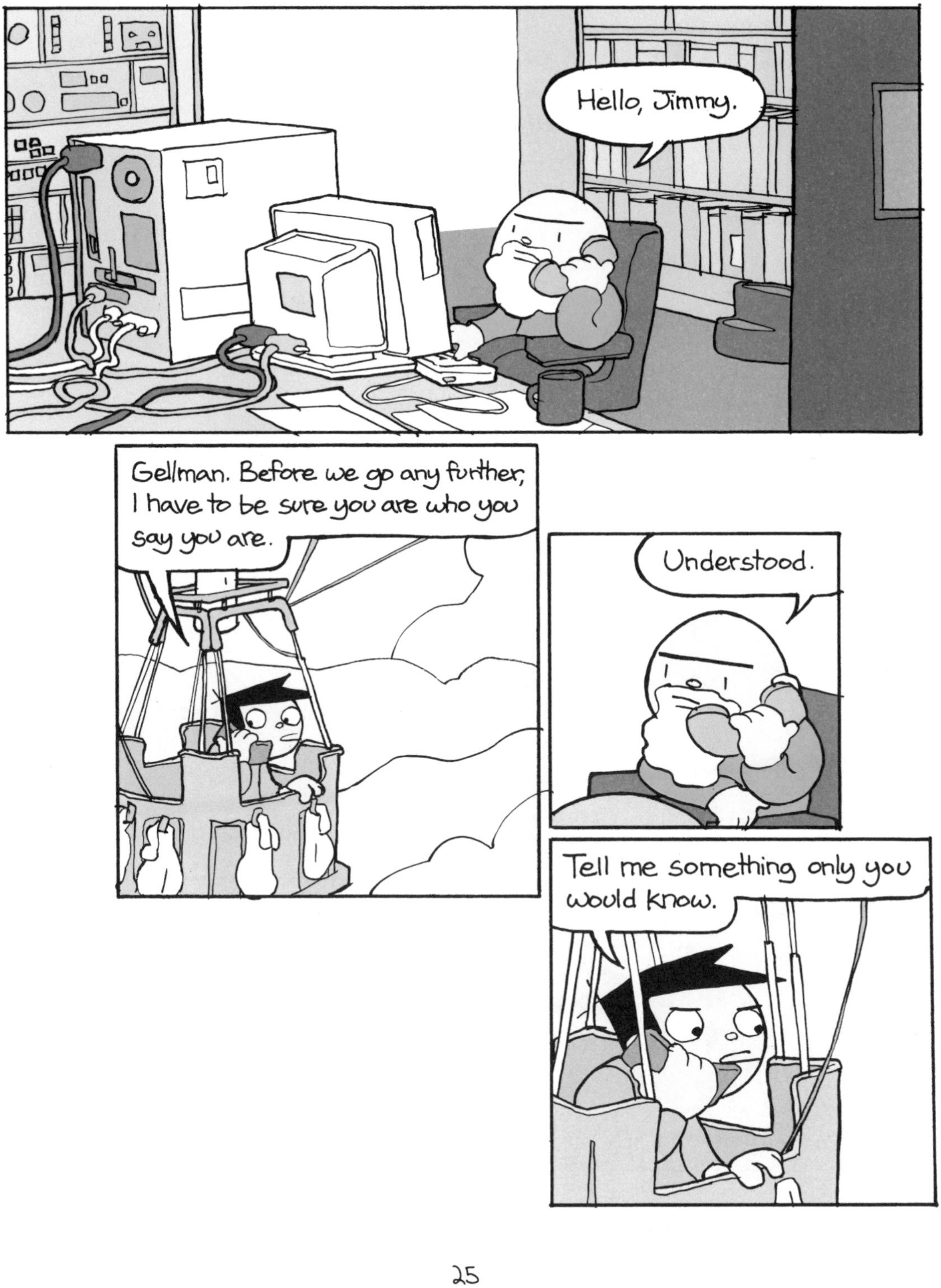
Hello, Jimmy.
Gellman. Before we go any further, I have to be sure you are who you say you are.
Understood.
Tell me something only you would know.

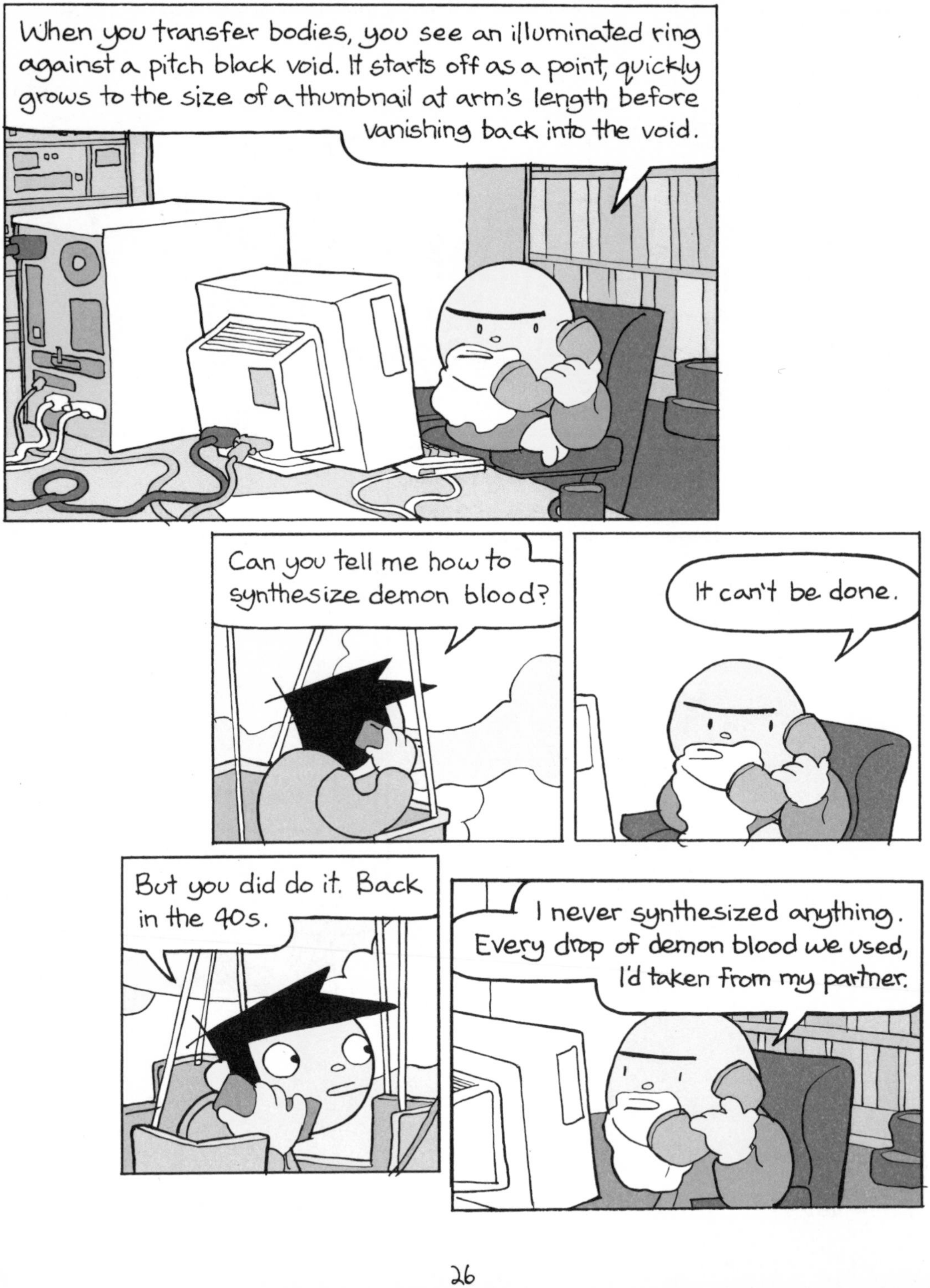
When you transfer bodies, you see an illuminated ring against a pitch black void. It starts off as a point, quickly grows to the size of a thumbnail at arm's length before vanishing back into the void.
Can you tell me how to synthesize demon blood?
It can't be done.
But you did do it. Back in the 40s.
I never synthesized anything. Every drop of demon blood we used, I'd taken from my partner.

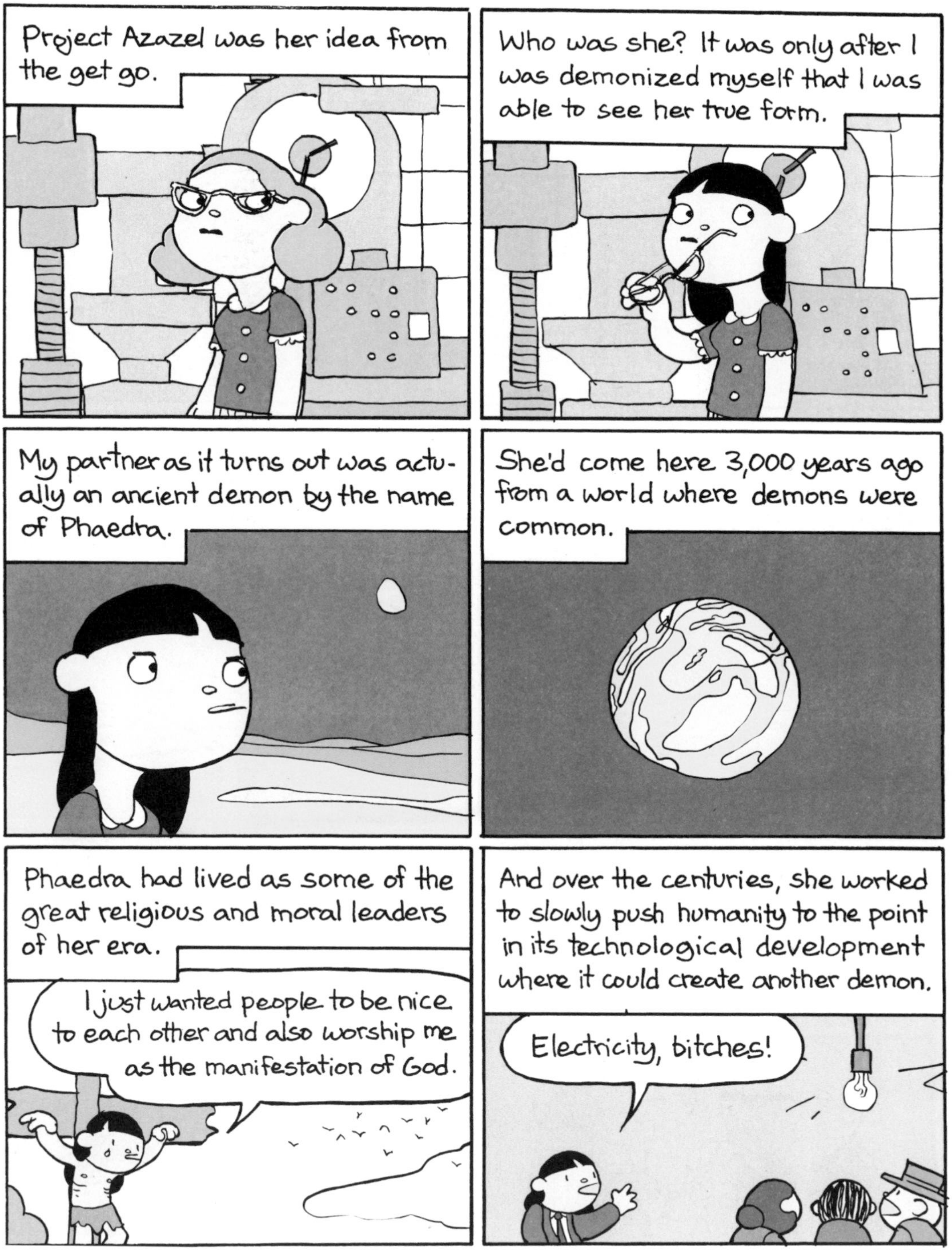
Project Azazel was her idea from the get go.
Who was she? It was only after I was demonized myself that I was able to see her true form.
My partner as it turns out was actually an ancient demon by the name of Phaedra.
She'd come here 3,000 years ago from a world where demons were common.
Phaedra had lived as some of the great religious and moral leaders of her era.
I just wanted people to be nice to each other and also worship me as the manifestation of God.
And over the centuries, she worked to slowly push humanity to the point in its technological development where it could create another demon.
Electricity, bitches!

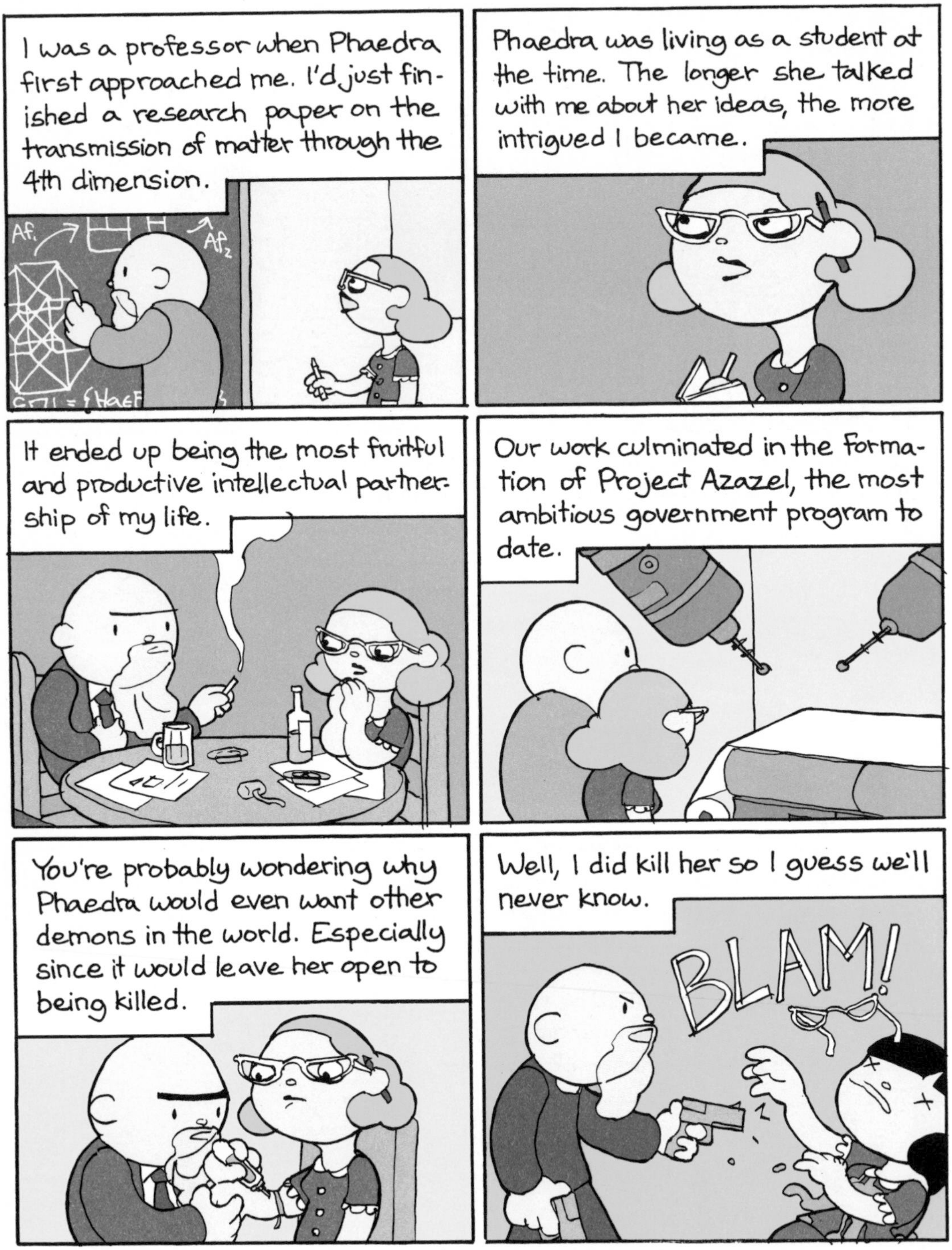
I was a professor when Phaedra first approached me. I'd just finished a research paper on the transmission of matter through the 4th dimension.
Phaedra was living as a student at the time. The longer she talked with me about her ideas, the more intrigued I became.
It ended up being the most fruitful and productive intellectual partnership of my life.
Our work culminated in the formation of Project Azazel, the most ambitious government program to date.
You're probably wondering why Phaedra would even want other demons in the world. Especially since it would leave her open to being killed.
Well, I did kill her so I guess we'll never know.
BLAM!

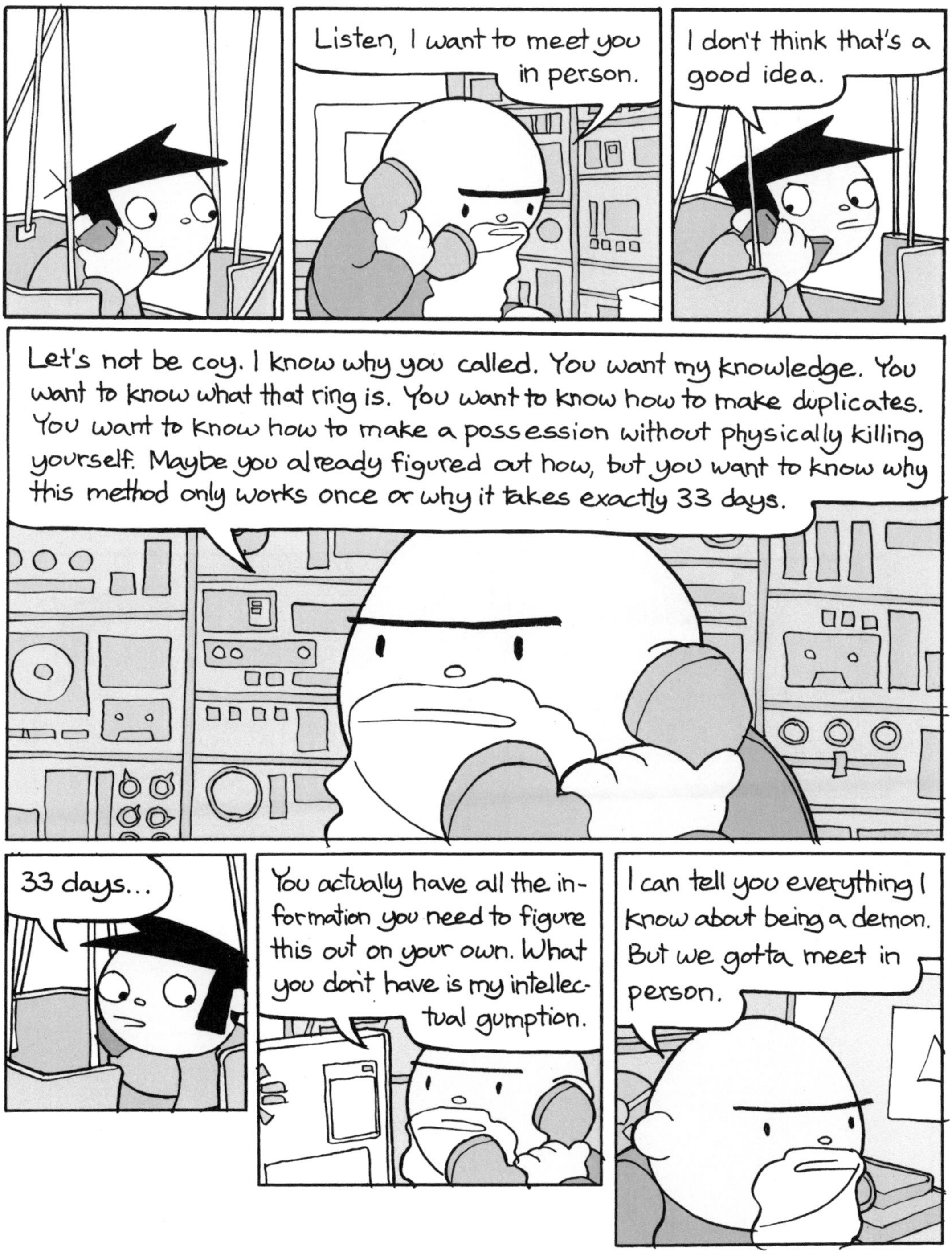
Listen, I want to meet you in person.
I don't think that's a good idea.
Let's not be coy. I know why you called. You want my knowledge. You want to know what that ring is. You want to know how to make duplicates. You want to know how to make a possession without physically killing yourself. Maybe you already figured out how, but you want to know why this method only works once or why it takes exactly 33 days.
33 days...
You actually have all the information you need to figure this out on your own. What you don't have is my intellectual gumption.
I can tell you everything I know about being a demon. But we gotta meet in person.

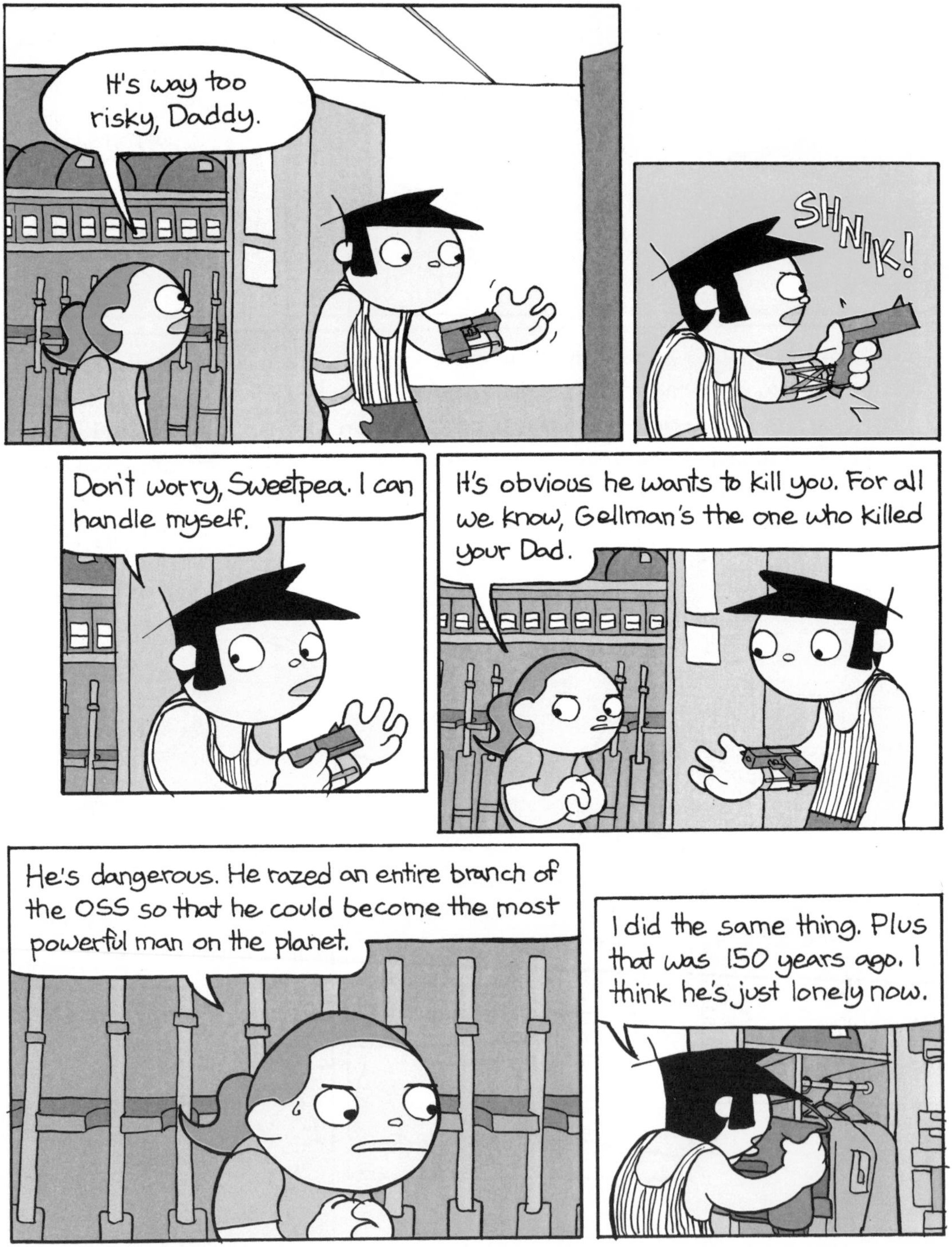
It's way too risky, Daddy.
SHNIK!
Don't worry, Sweetpea. I can handle myself.
It's obvious he wants to kill you. For all we know, Gellman's the one who killed your Dad.
He's dangerous. He razed an entire branch of the OSS so that he could become the most powerful man on the planet.
I did the same thing. Plus that was 150 years ago. I think he's just lonely now.

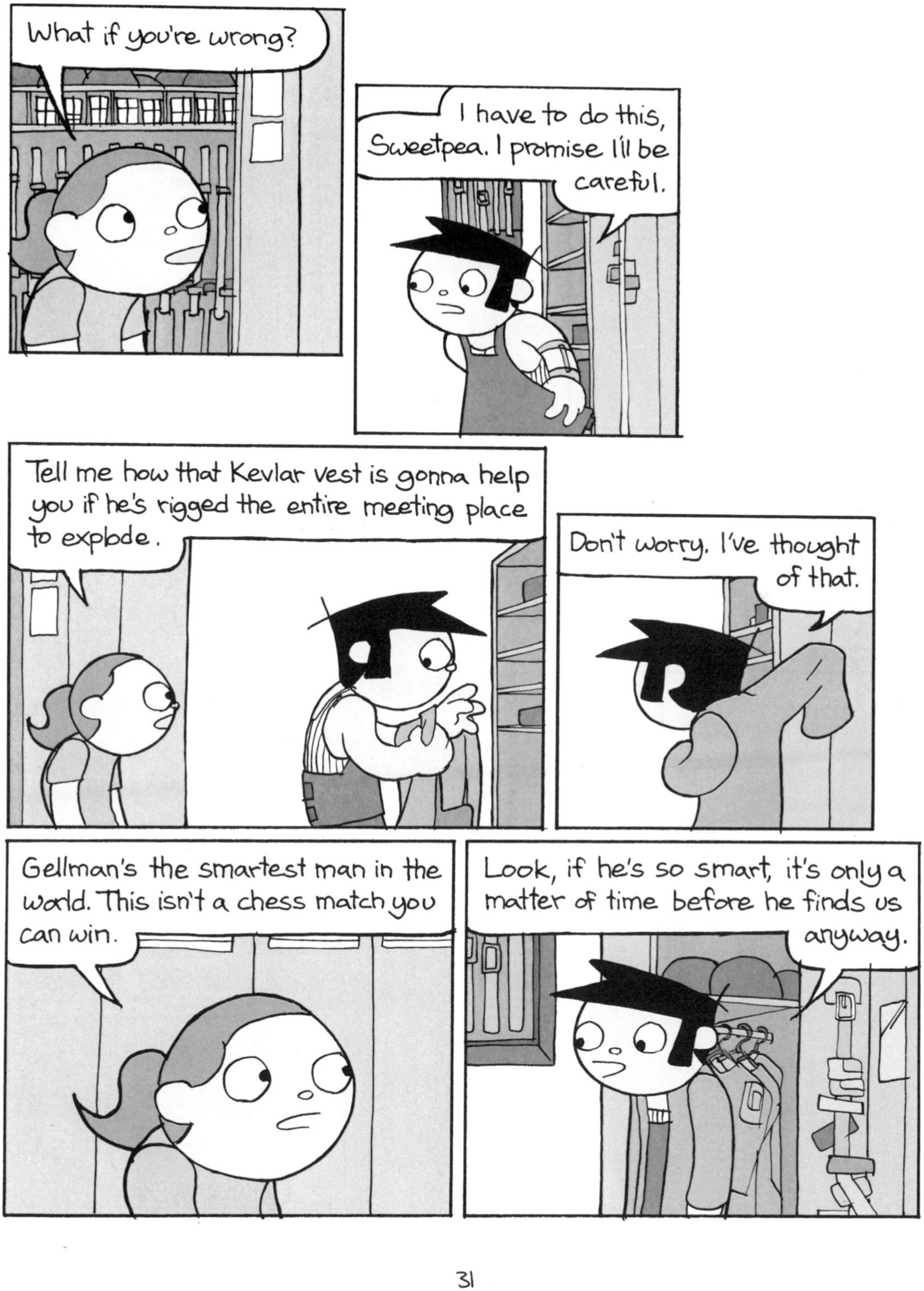
What if you're wrong?
I have to do this, Sweetpea. I promise I'll be careful.
Tell me how that Kevlar vest is gonna help you if he's rigged the entire meeting place to explode.
Don't worry. I've thought of that.
Gellman's the smartest man in the world. This isn't a chess match you can win.
Look, if he's so smart, it's only a matter of time before he finds us anyway.

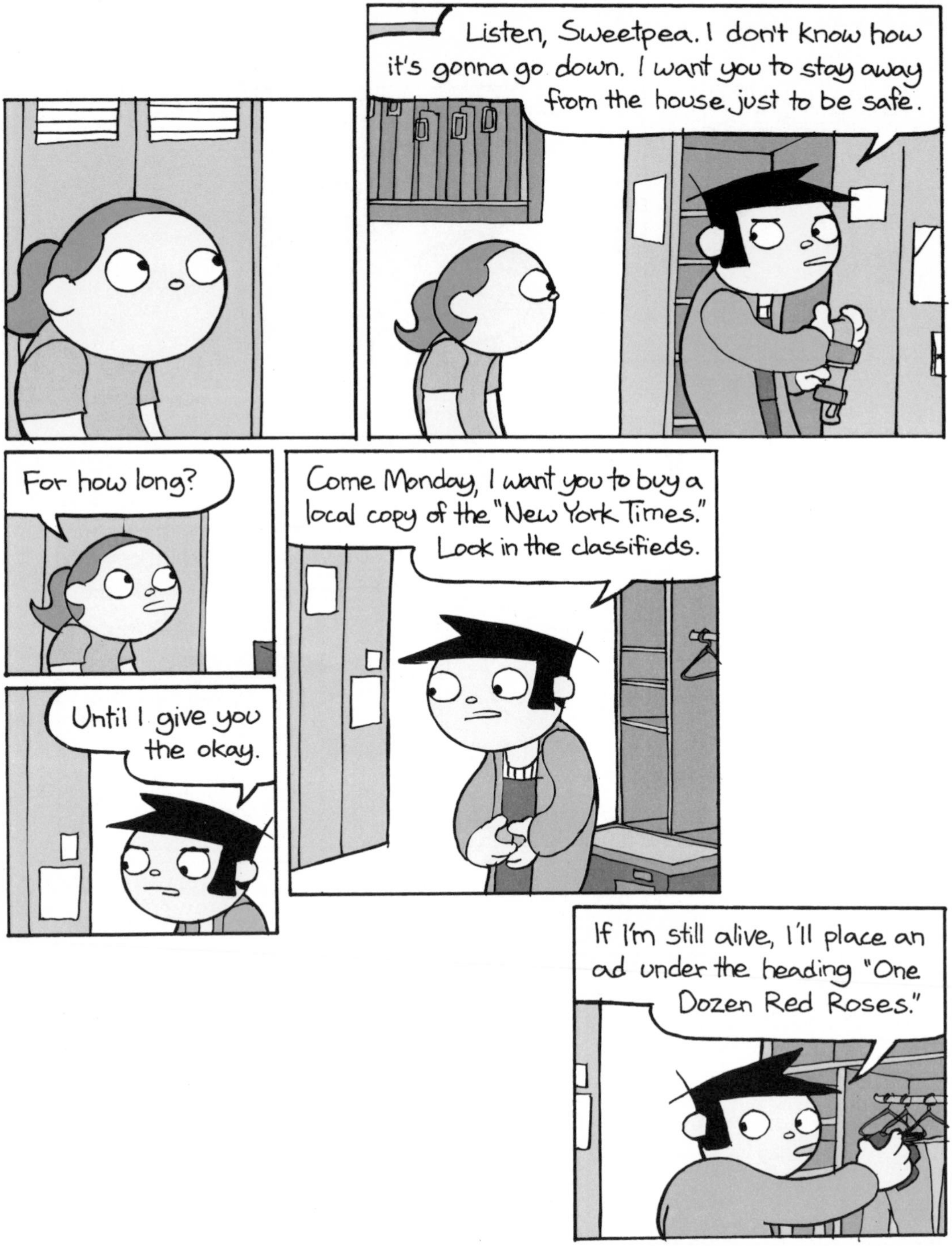
Listen, Sweetpea. I don't know how it's gonna go down. I want you to stay away from the house just to be safe.
For how long?
Until I give you the okay.
Come Monday, I want you to buy a local copy of the "New York Times." Look in the classifieds.
If I'm still alive, I'll place an ad under the heading "One Dozen Red Roses."

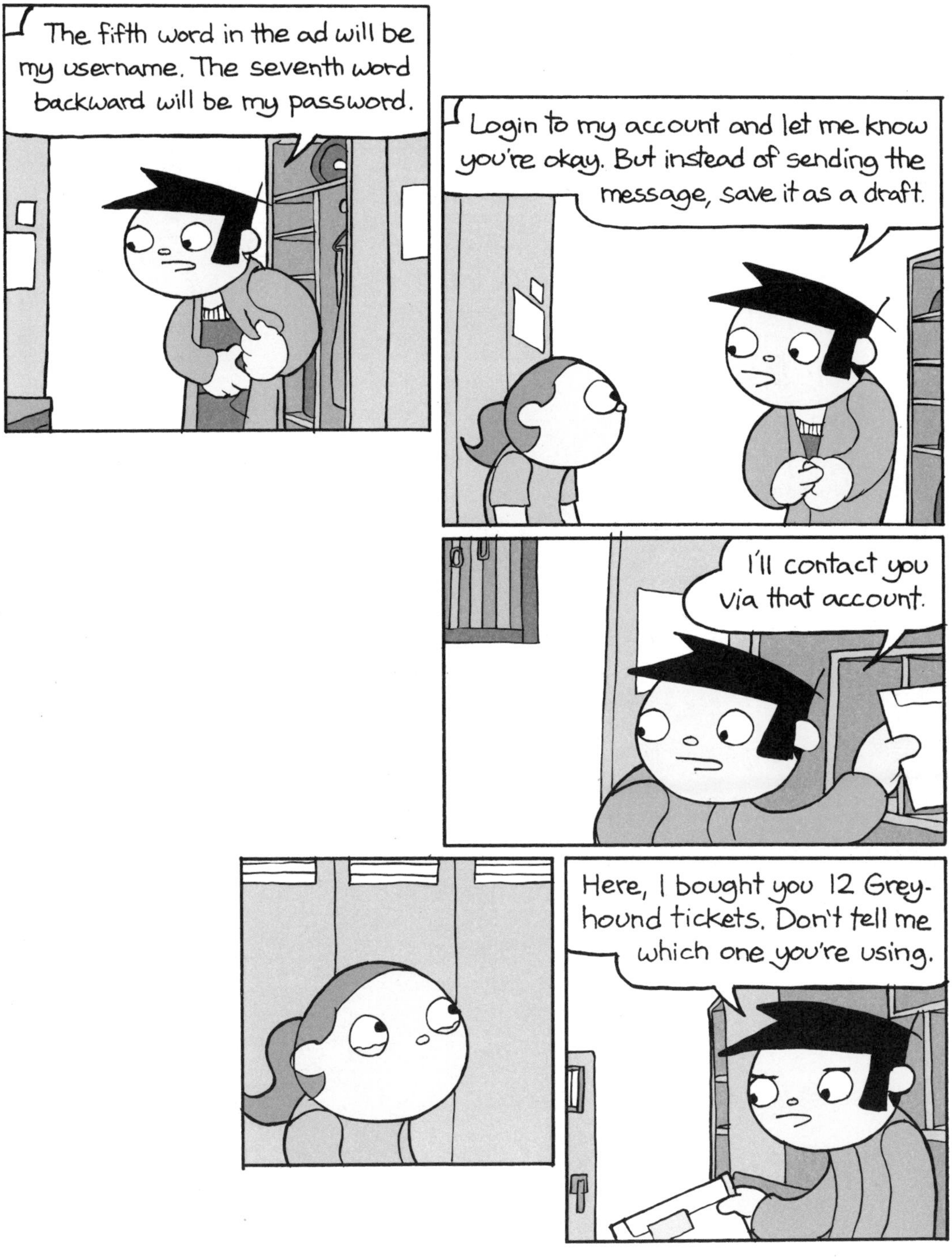
The fifth word in the ad will be my username. The seventh word backward will be my password.
Login to my account and let me know you're okay. But instead of sending the message, save it as a draft.
I'll contact you via that account.
Here, I bought you 12 Grey-hound tickets. Don't tell me which one you're using.

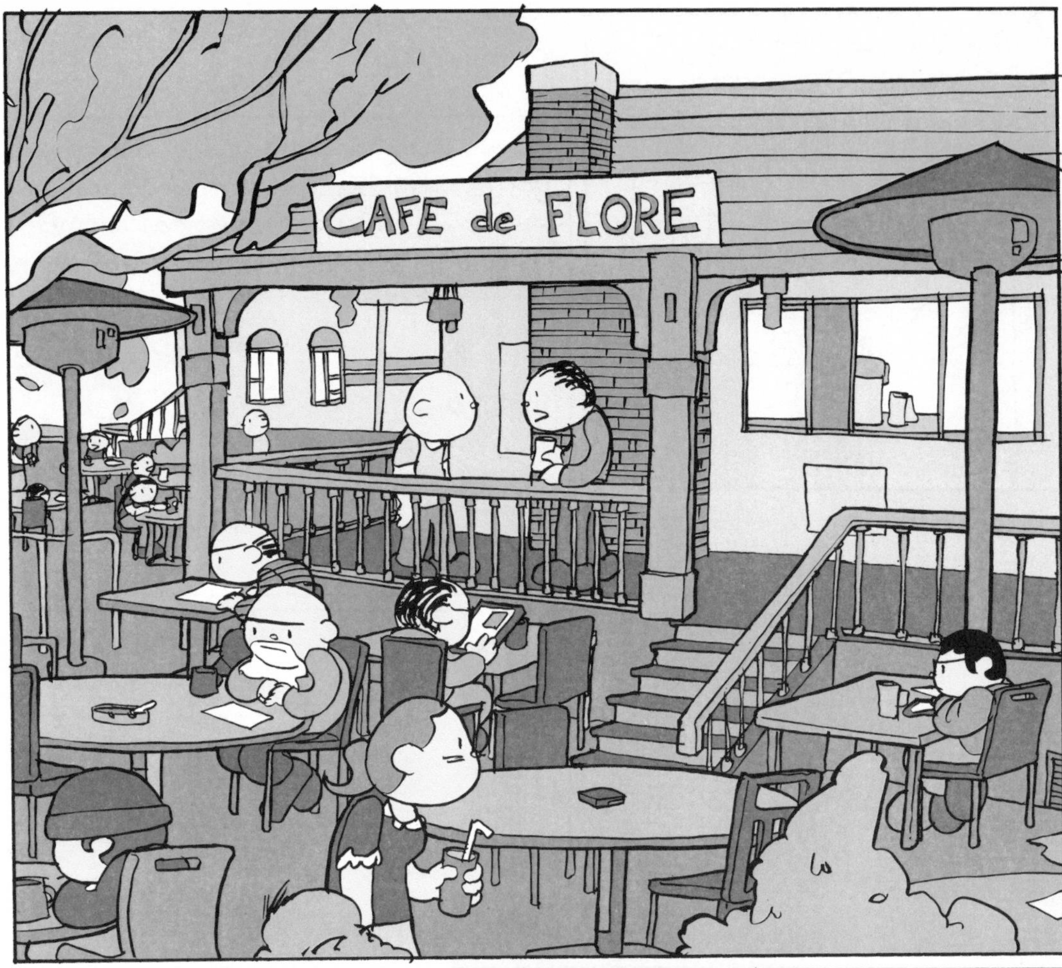
CAFE de FLORE

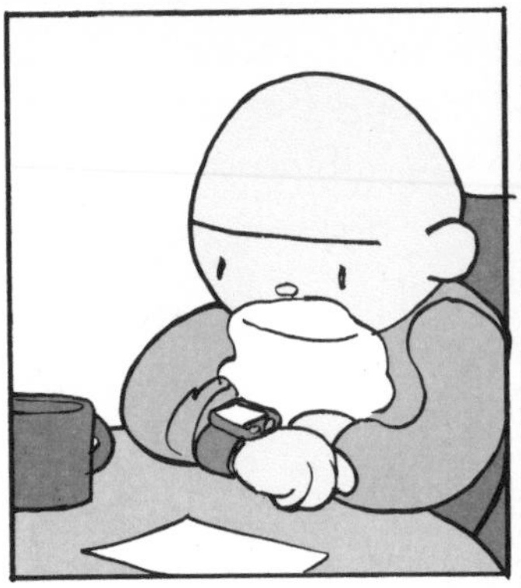

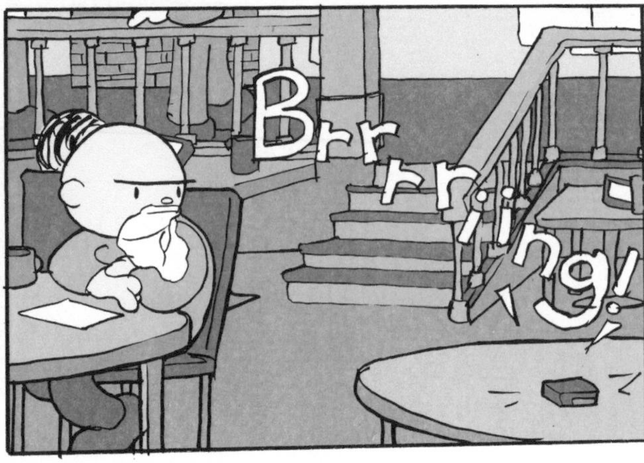
Brrrring!

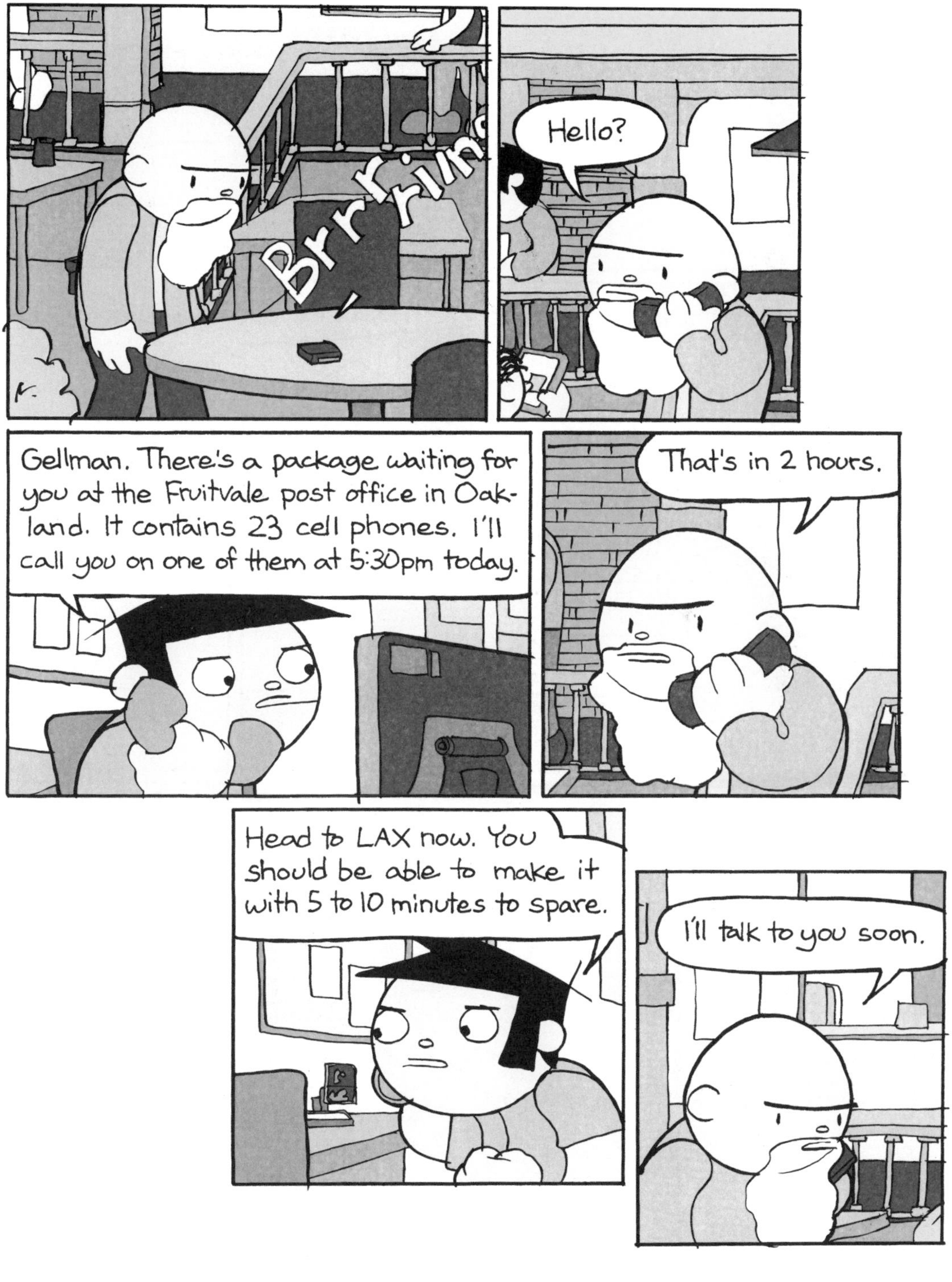
Brrring
Hello?
Gellman. There's a package waiting for you at the Fruitvale post office in Oakland. It contains 23 cell phones. I'll call you on one of them at 5:30pm today.
That's in 2 hours.
Head to LAX now. You should be able to make it with 5 to 10 minutes to spare.
I'll talk to you soon.

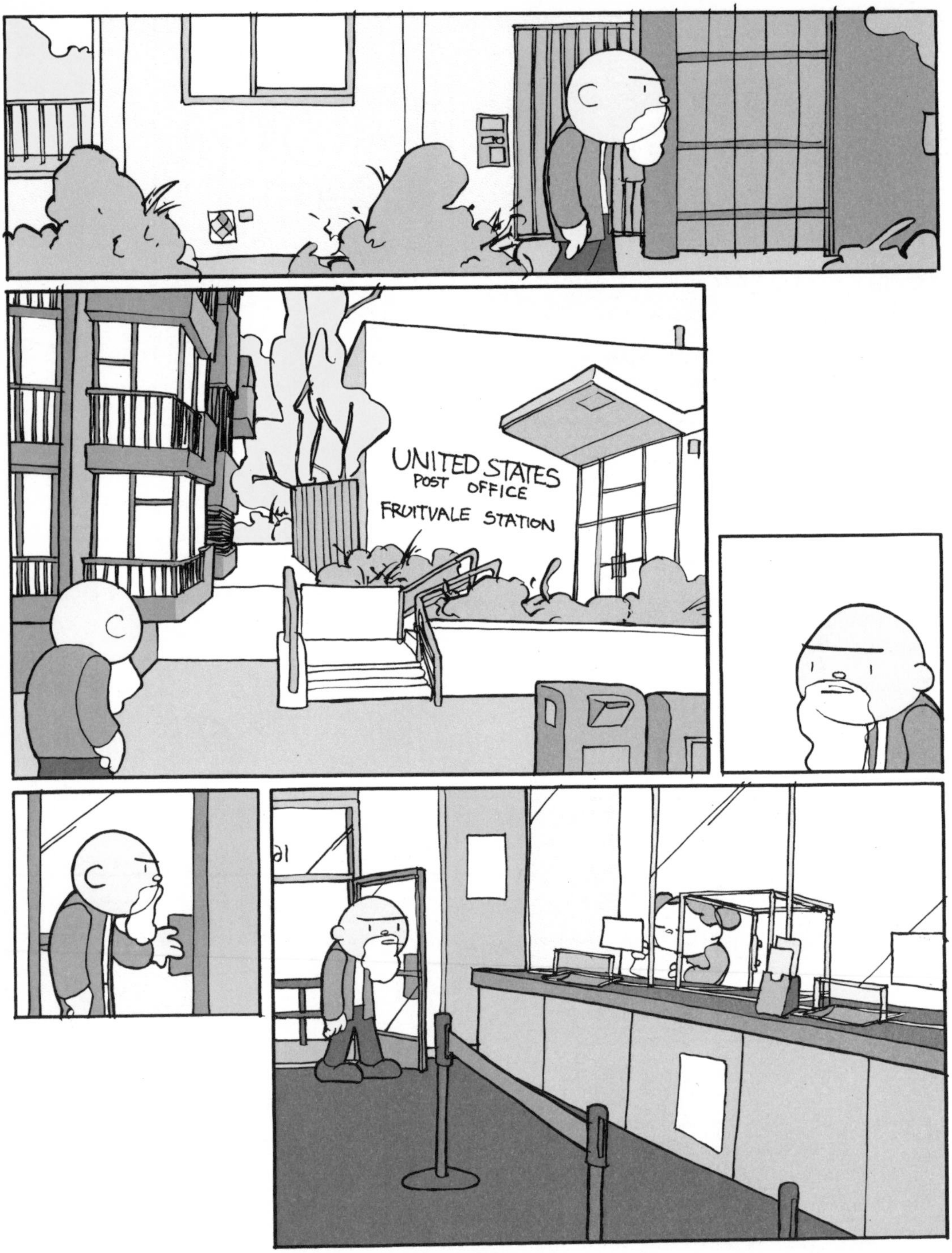
UNITED STATES
POST OFFICE
FRUITVALE STATION

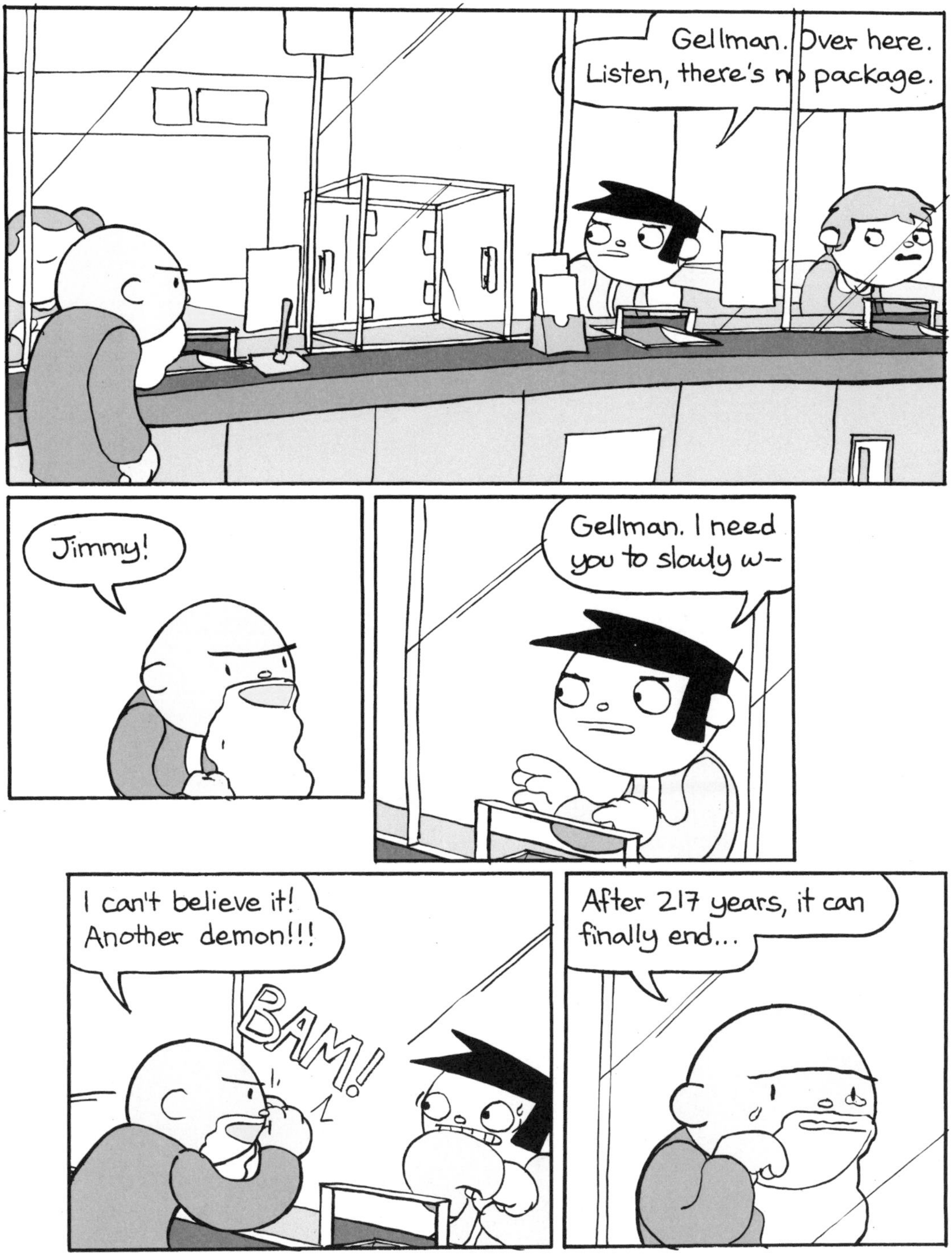
Gellman. Over here. Listen, there's no package.
Jimmy!
Gellman. I need you to slowly w—
I can't believe it! Another demon!!!
BAM!
After 217 years, it can finally end...

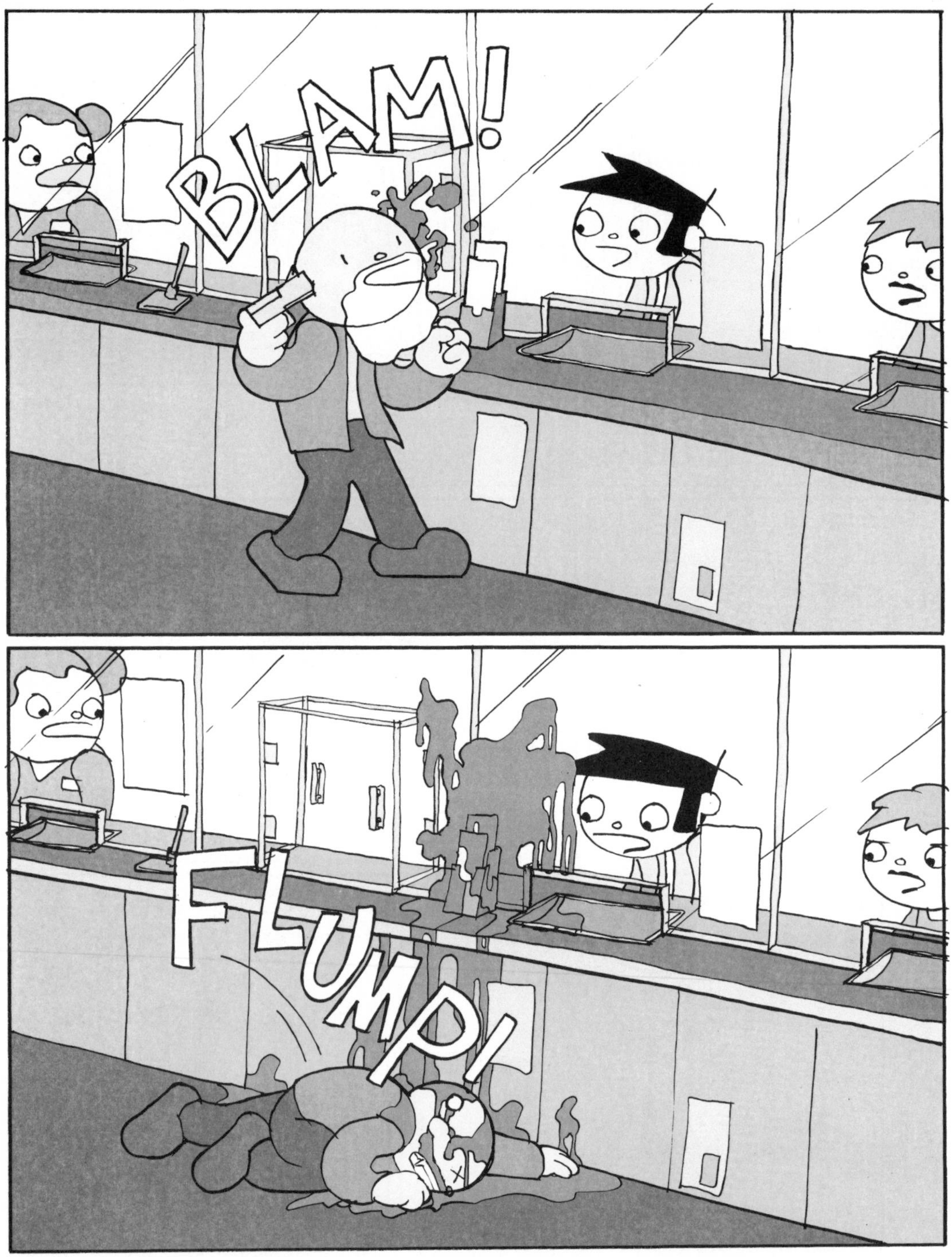
BLAM!
FLUMP!

CHAPTER 14

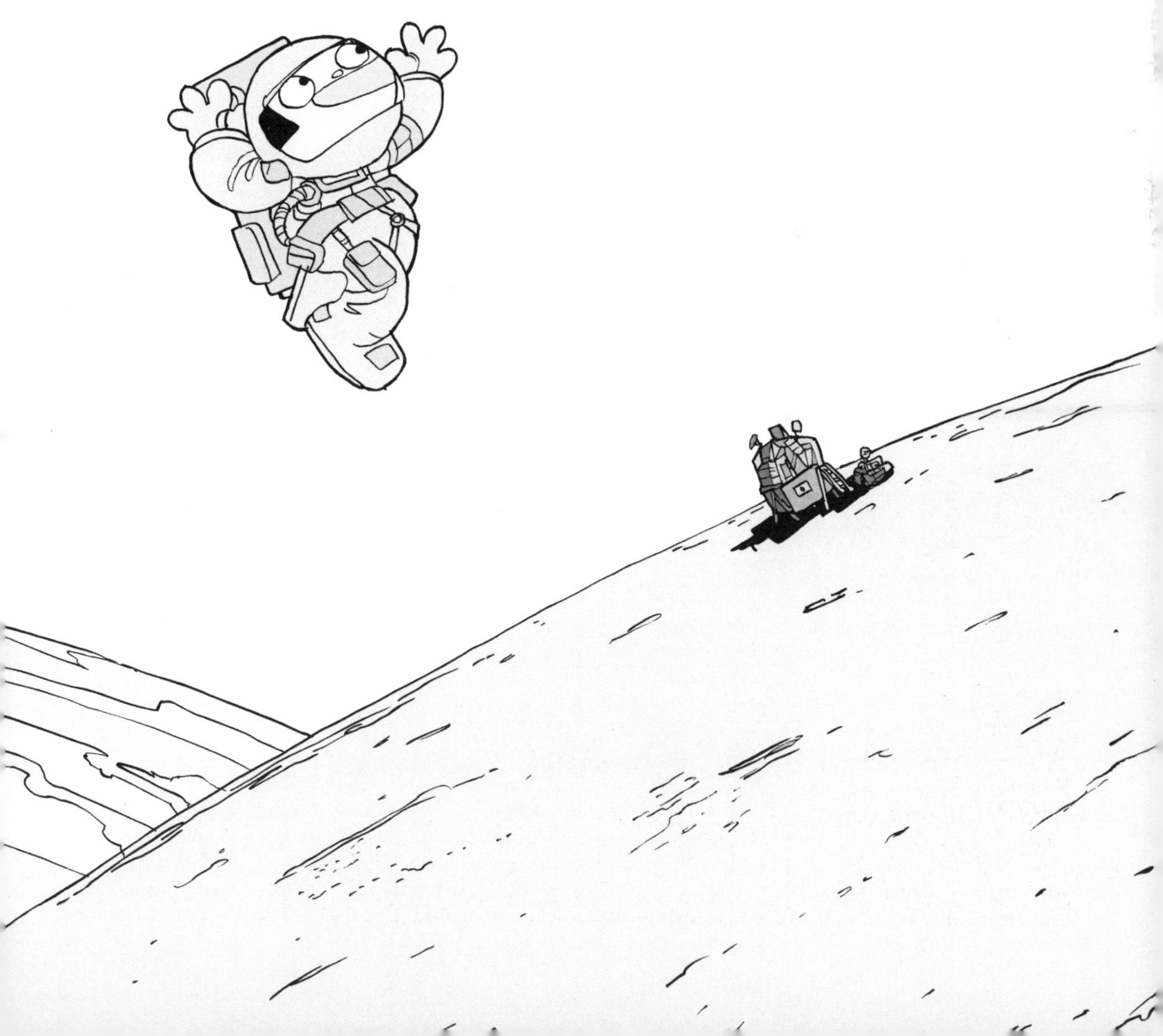

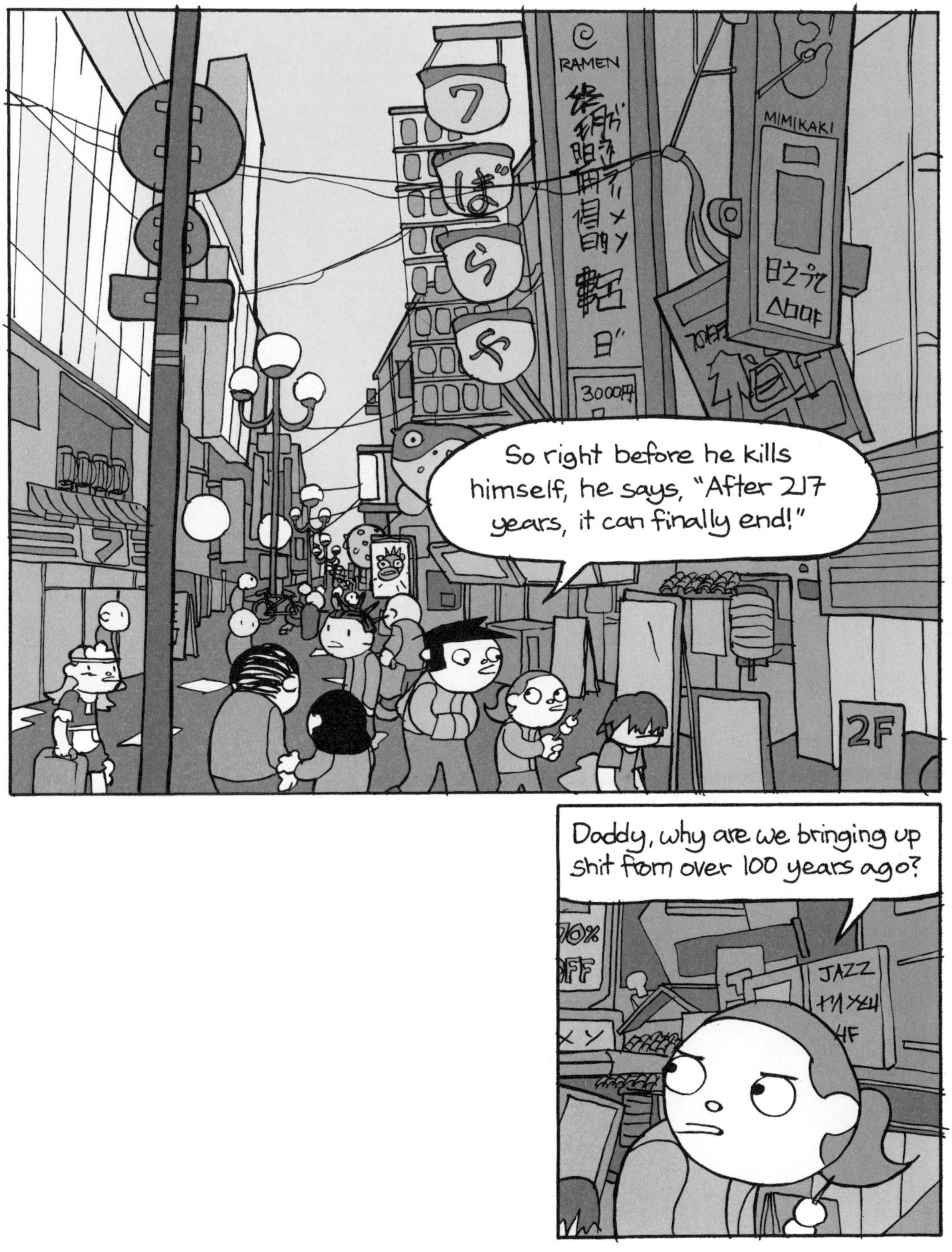
RAMEN
MIMIKAKI
So right before he kills himself, he says, "After 217 years, it can finally end!"
2F
Daddy, why are we bringing up shit from over 100 years ago?
JAZZ

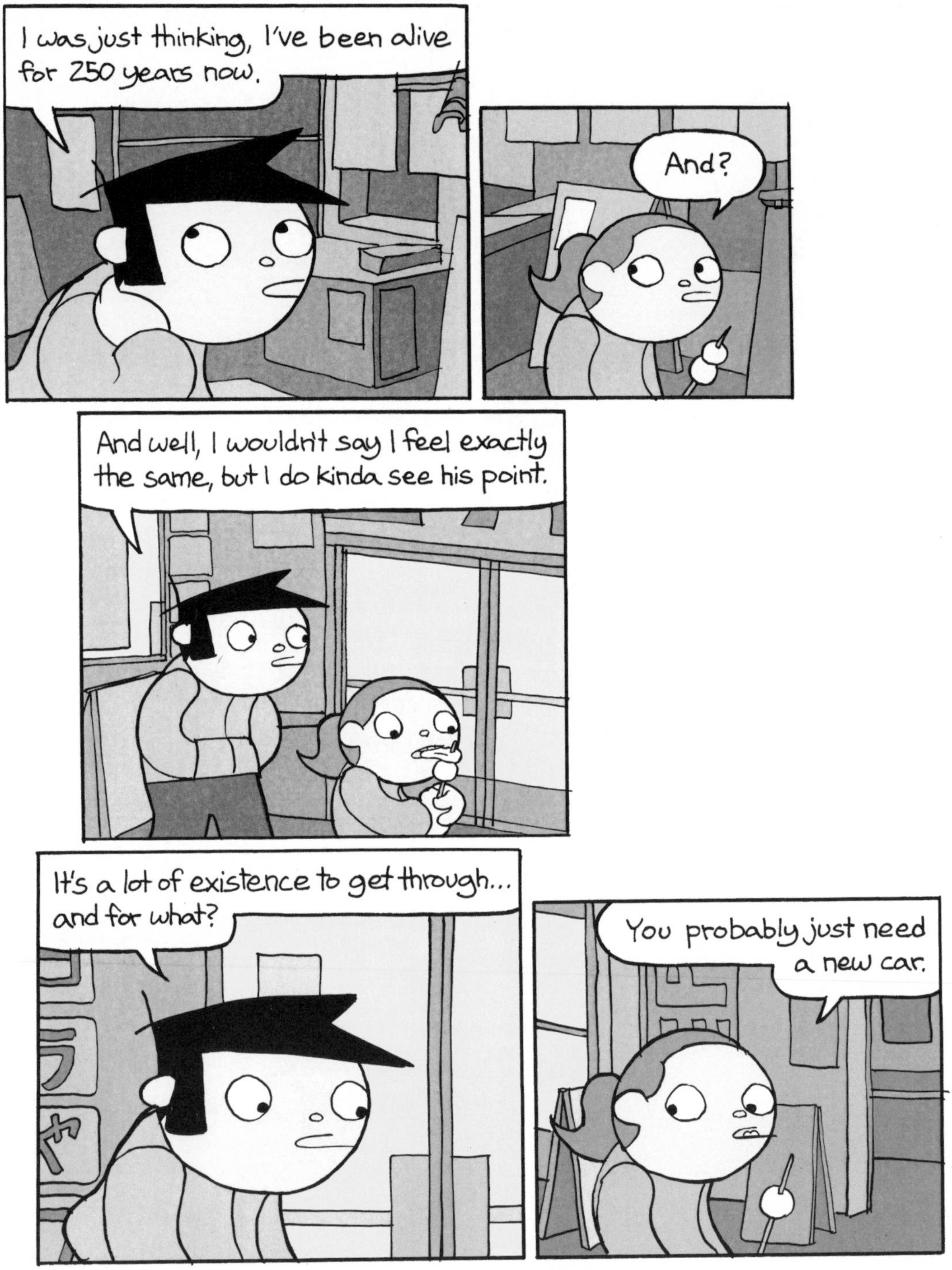
I was just thinking, I've been alive for 250 years now.
And?
And well, I wouldn't say I feel exactly the same, but I do kinda see his point.
It's a lot of existence to get through... and for what?
You probably just need a new car.

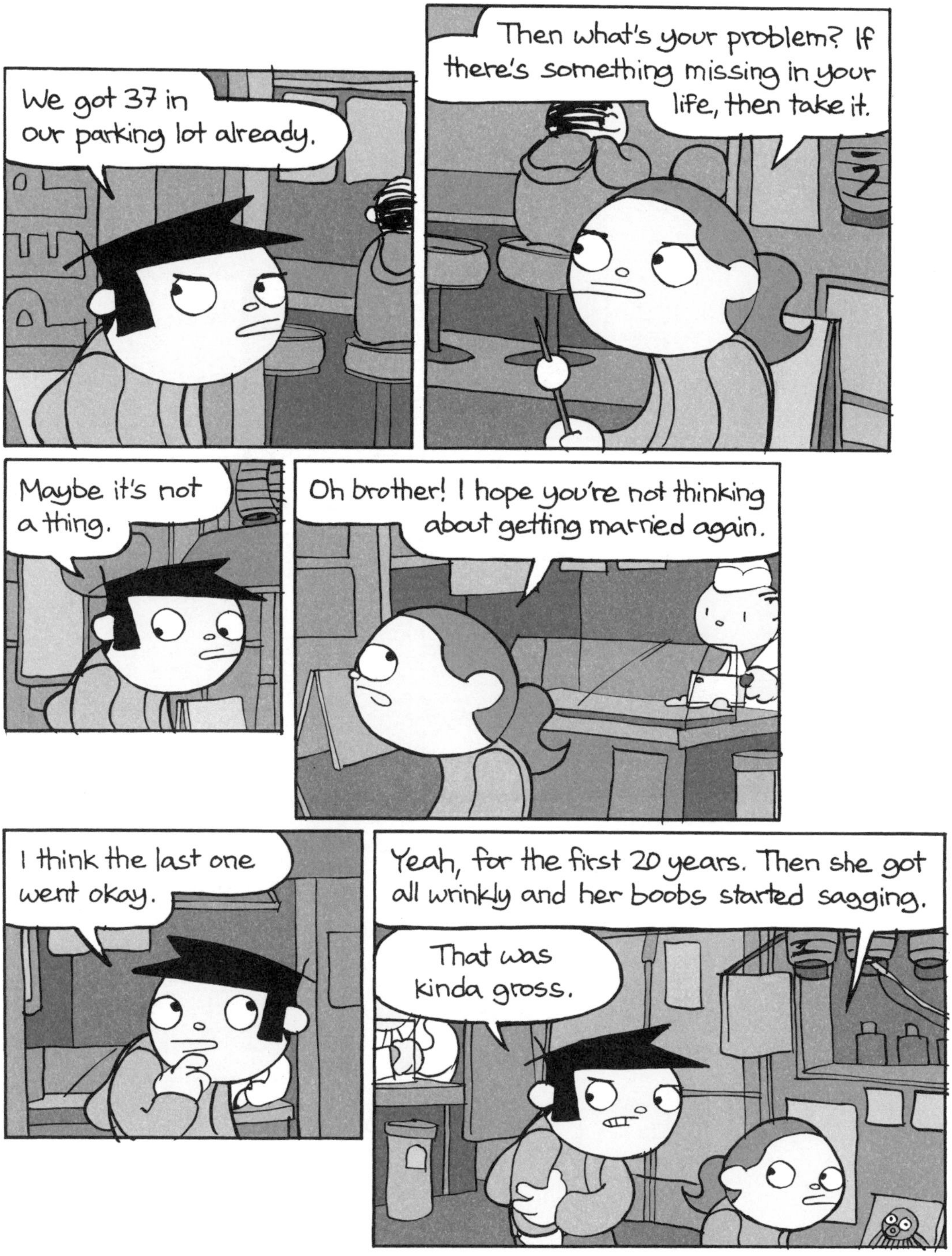
We got 37 in our parking lot already.
Then what's your problem? If there's something missing in your life, then take it.
Maybe it's not a thing.
Oh brother! I hope you're not thinking about getting married again.
I think the last one went okay.
Yeah, for the first 20 years. Then she got all wrinkly and her boobs started sagging.
That was kinda gross.

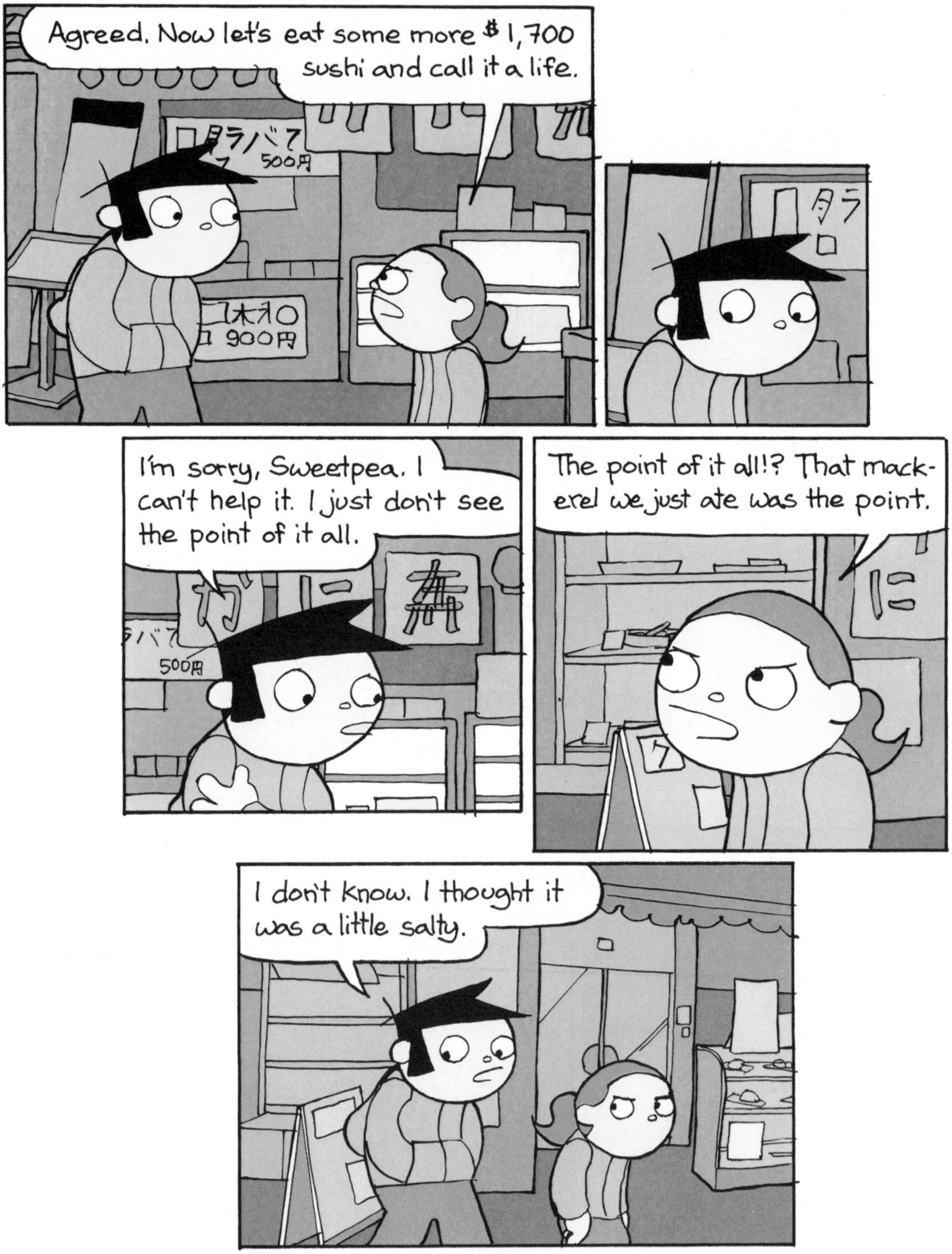
Agreed. Now let's eat some more $1,700 sushi and call it a life.
I'm sorry, Sweetpea. I can't help it. I just don't see the point of it all.
The point of it all!? That mackerel we just ate was the point.
I don't know. I thought it was a little salty.

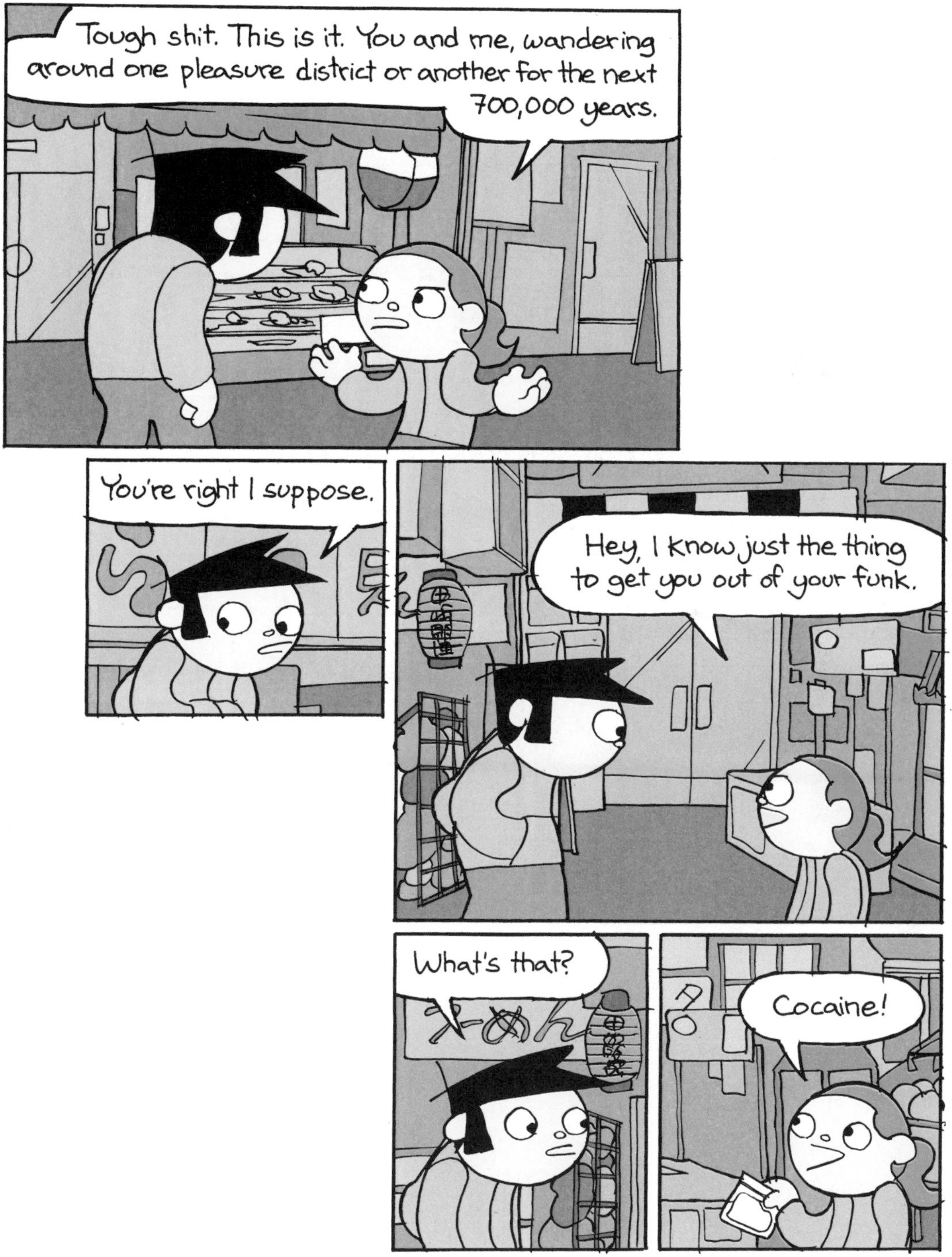
Tough shit. This is it. You and me, wandering around one pleasure district or another for the next 700,000 years.
You're right I suppose.
Hey, I know just the thing to get you out of your funk.
What's that?
Cocaine!

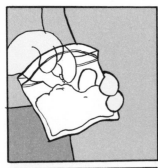

Pretty good stuff, huh?

This is better than that batch we got back in 2097,

Where'd you get it?

Vida Kwan.

The socks model?

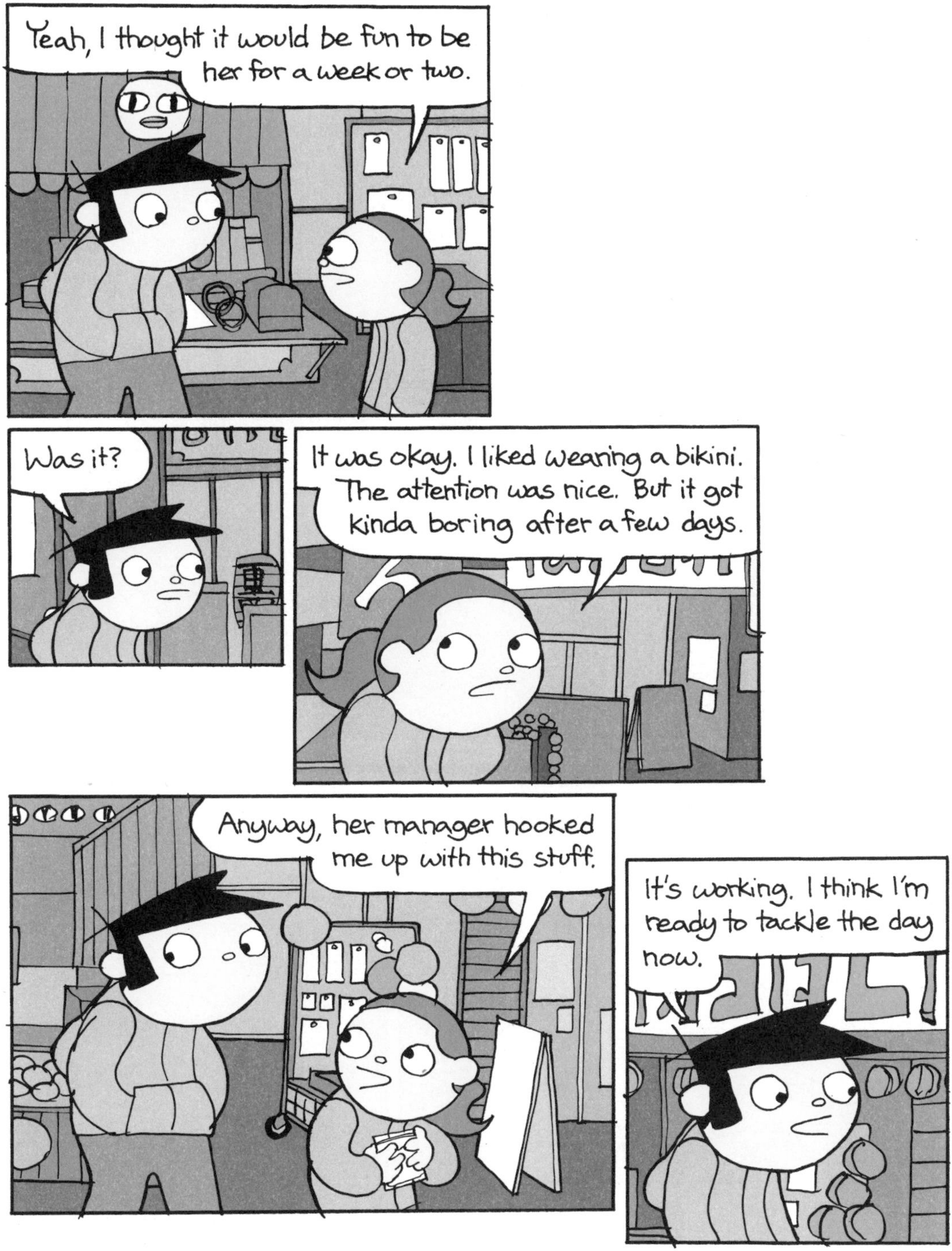
Yeah, I thought it would be fun to be her for a week or two.
Was it?
It was okay. I liked wearing a bikini. The attention was nice. But it got kinda boring after a few days.
Anyway, her manager hooked me up with this stuff.
It's working. I think I'm ready to tackle the day now.

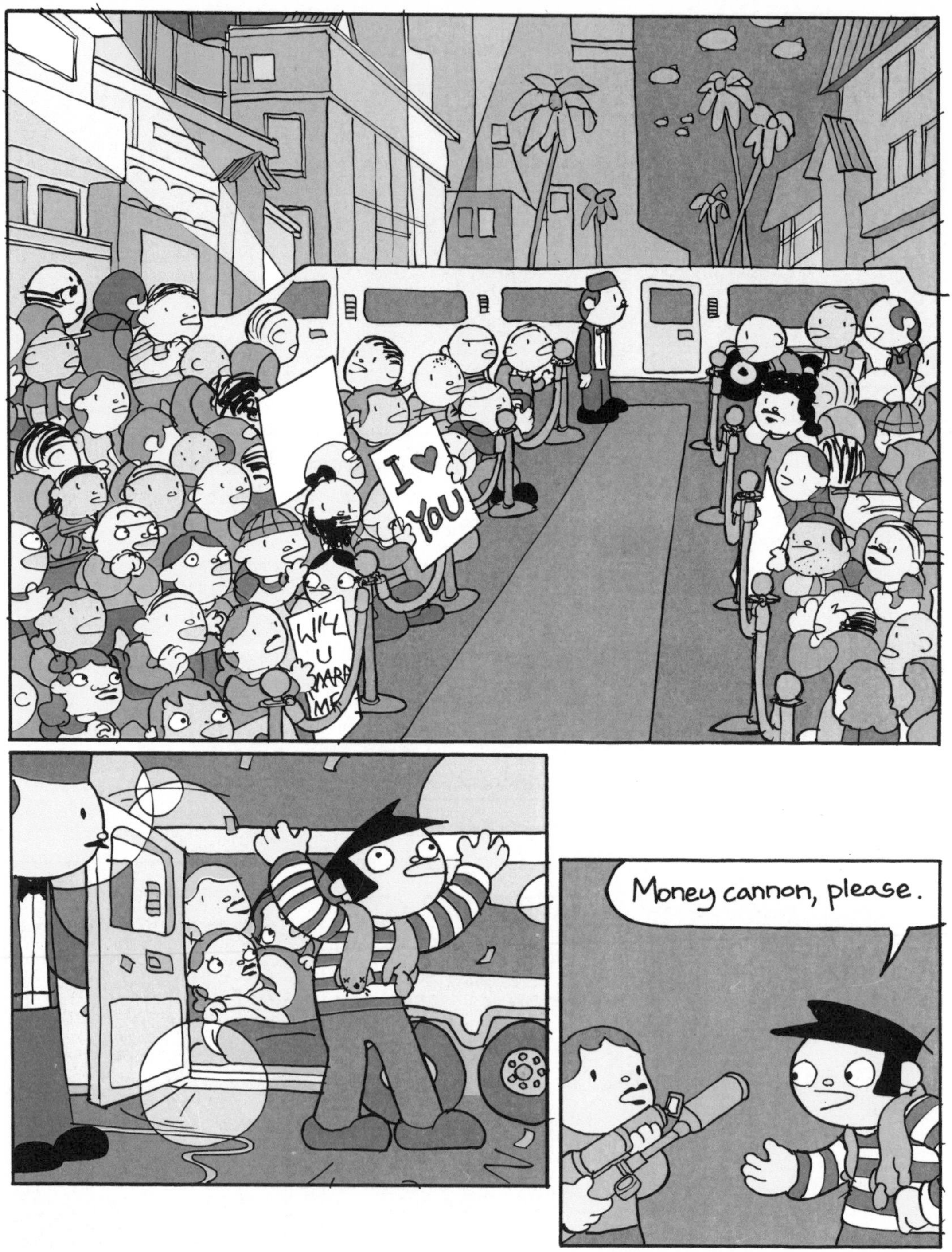
I ♥ YOU
Money cannon, please.

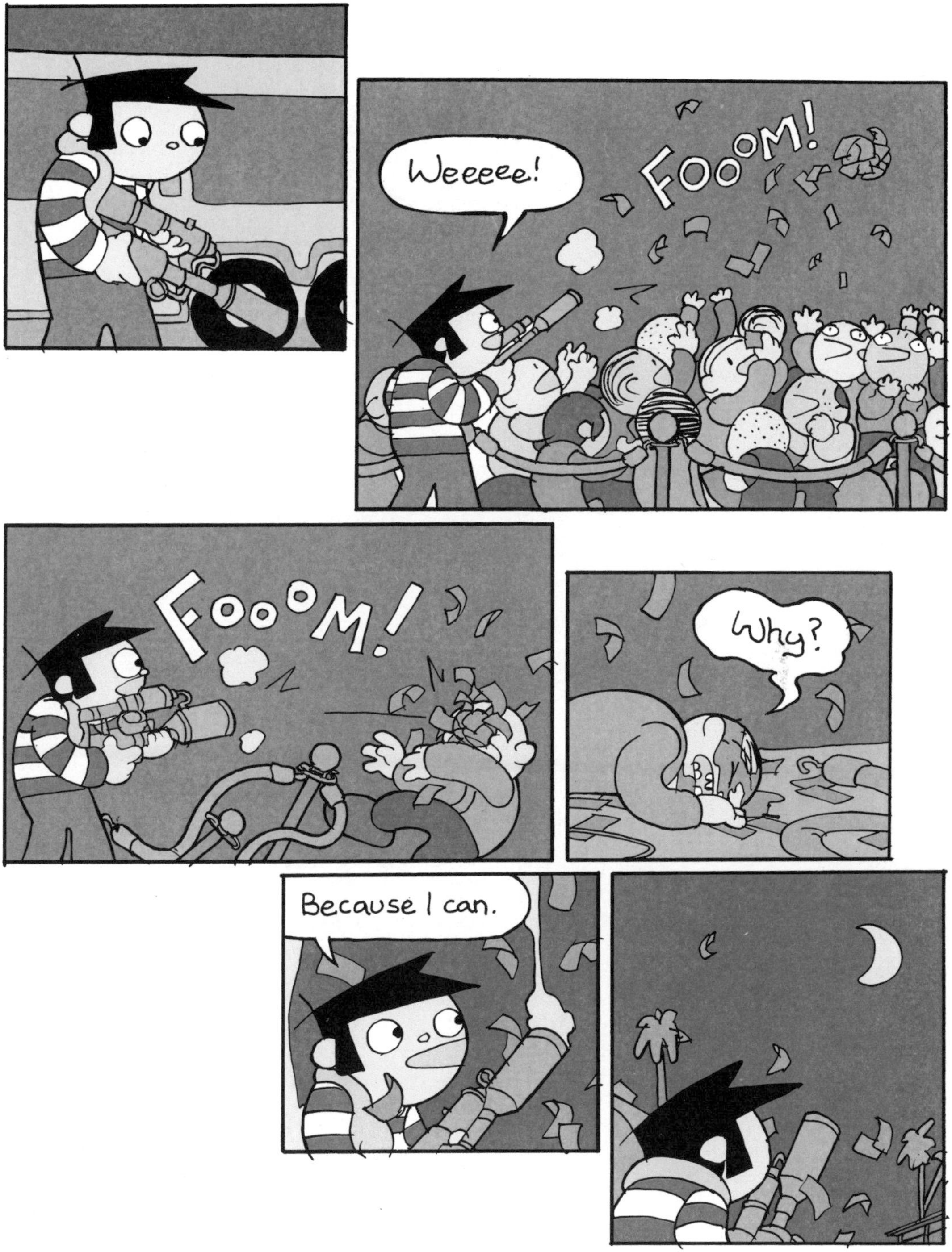
Weeeee!
FOOOM!
FOOOM!
Why?
Because I can.

JAPAN

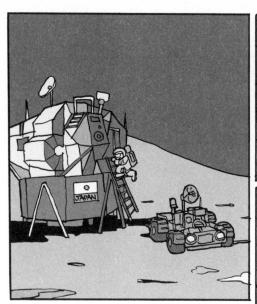

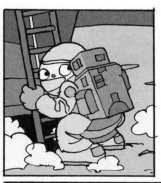

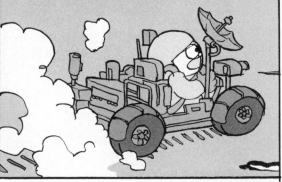

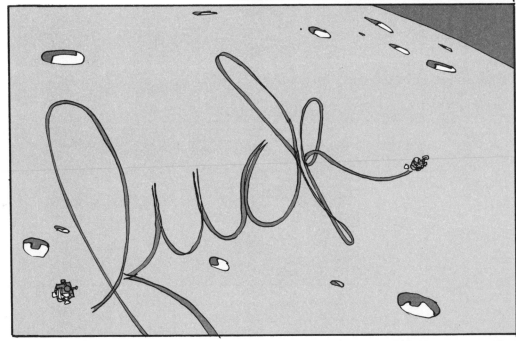

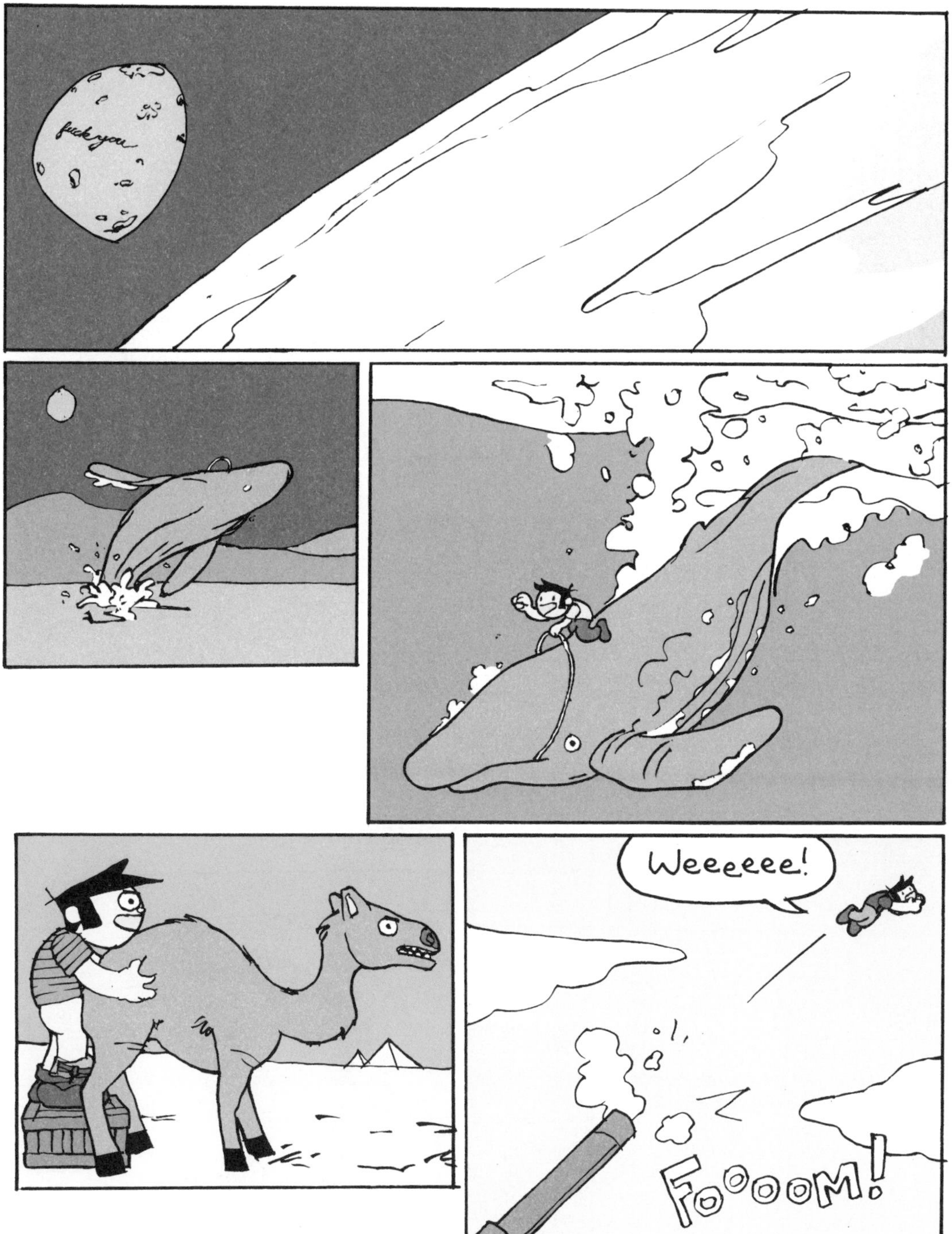
fuck you
Weeeeee!
Foooom!

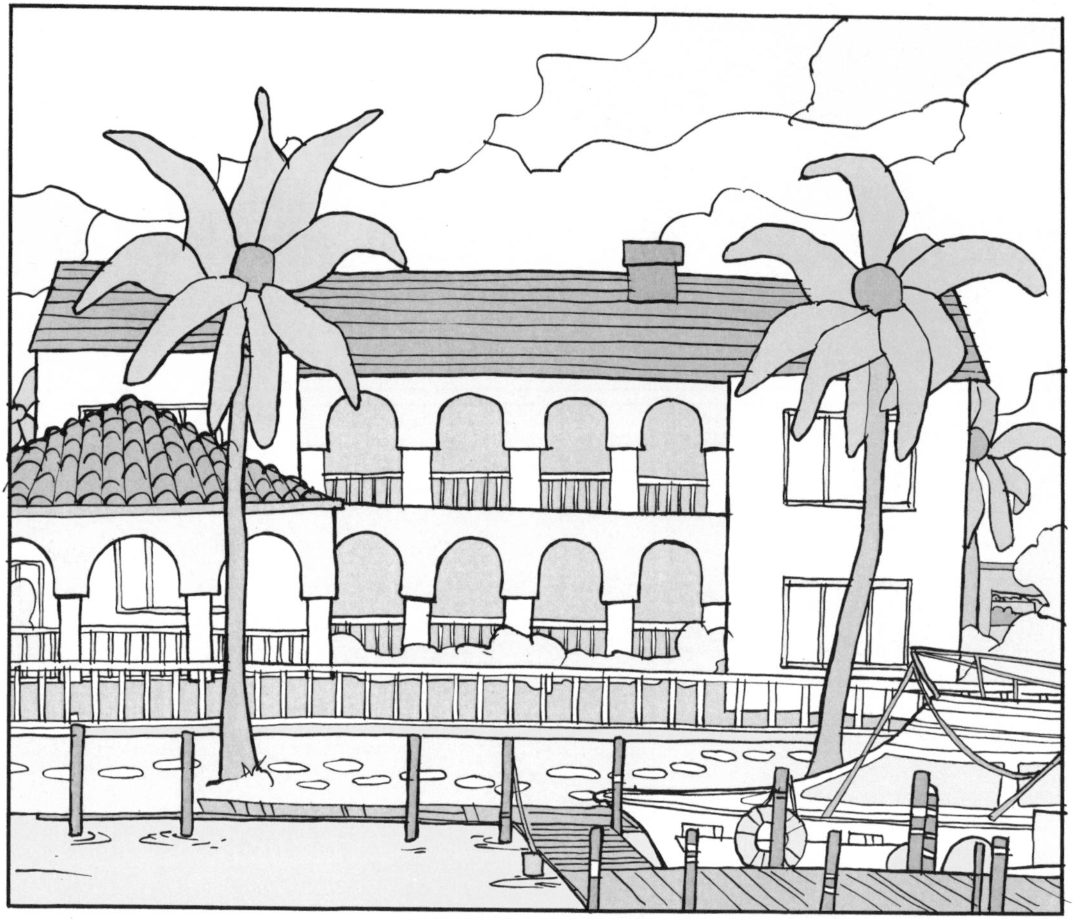

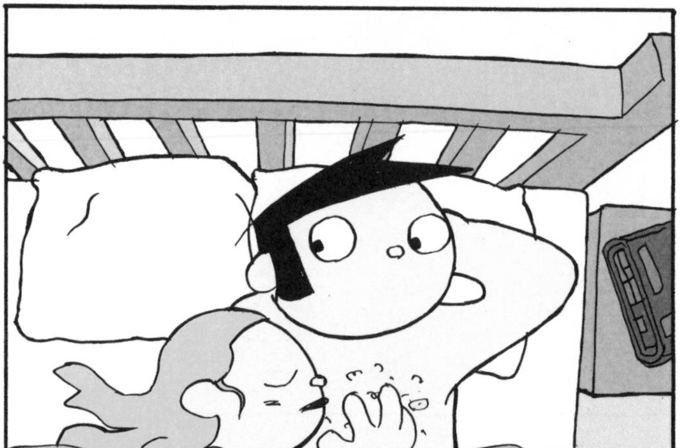

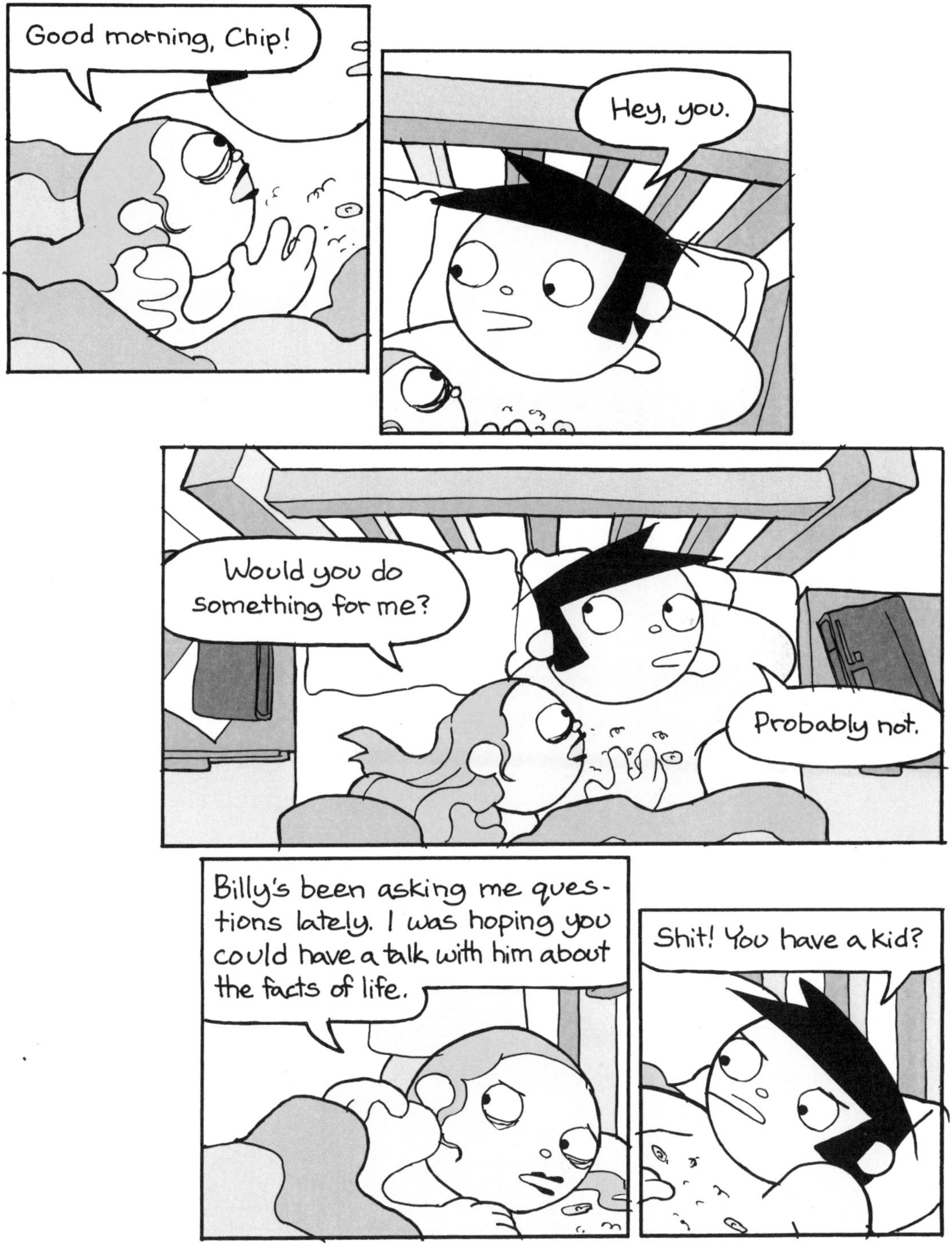
Good morning, Chip!
Hey, you.
Would you do something for me?
Probably not.
Billy's been asking me questions lately. I was hoping you could have a talk with him about the facts of life.
Shit! You have a kid?

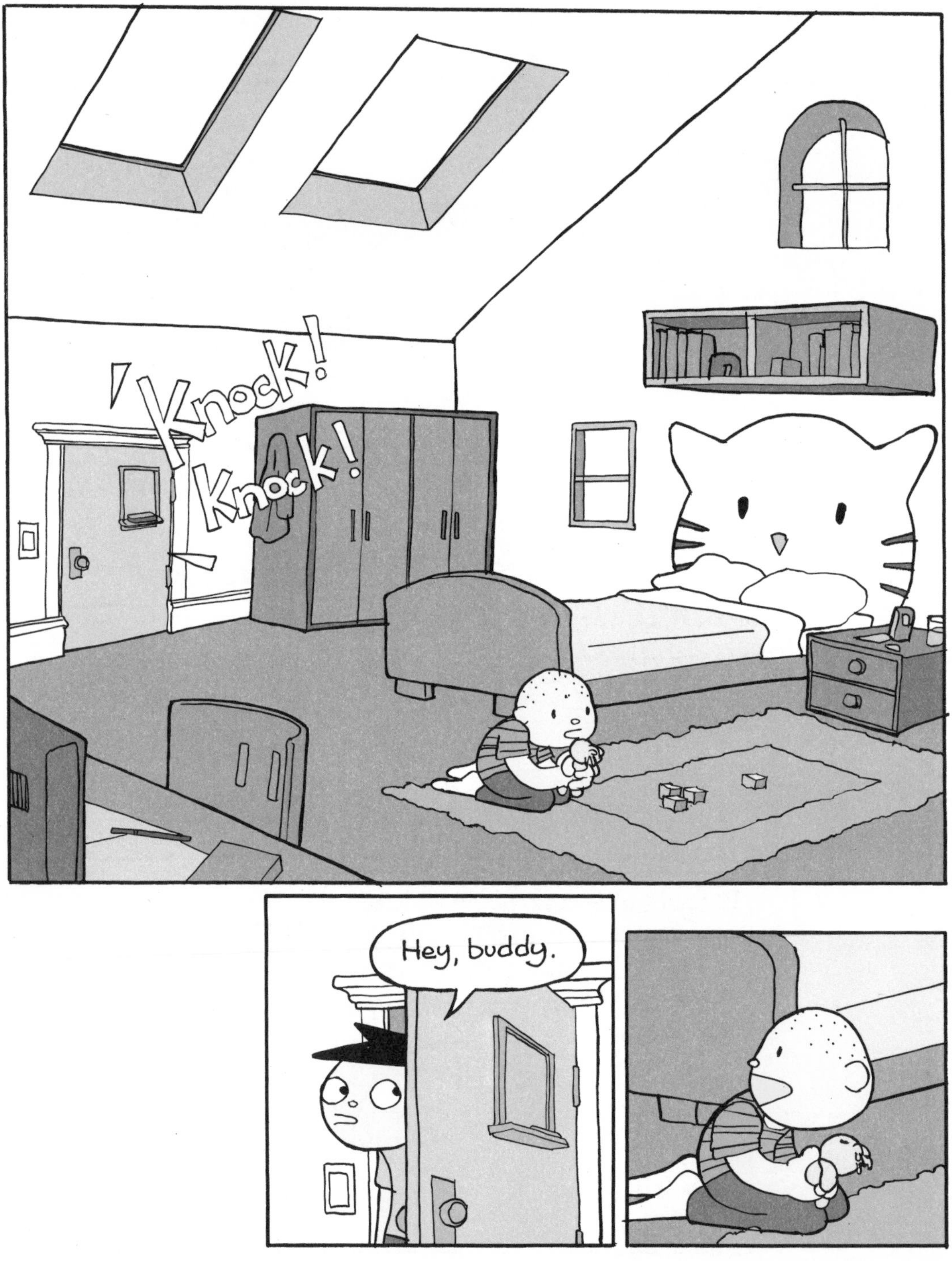
Knock!
Knock!
Hey, buddy.

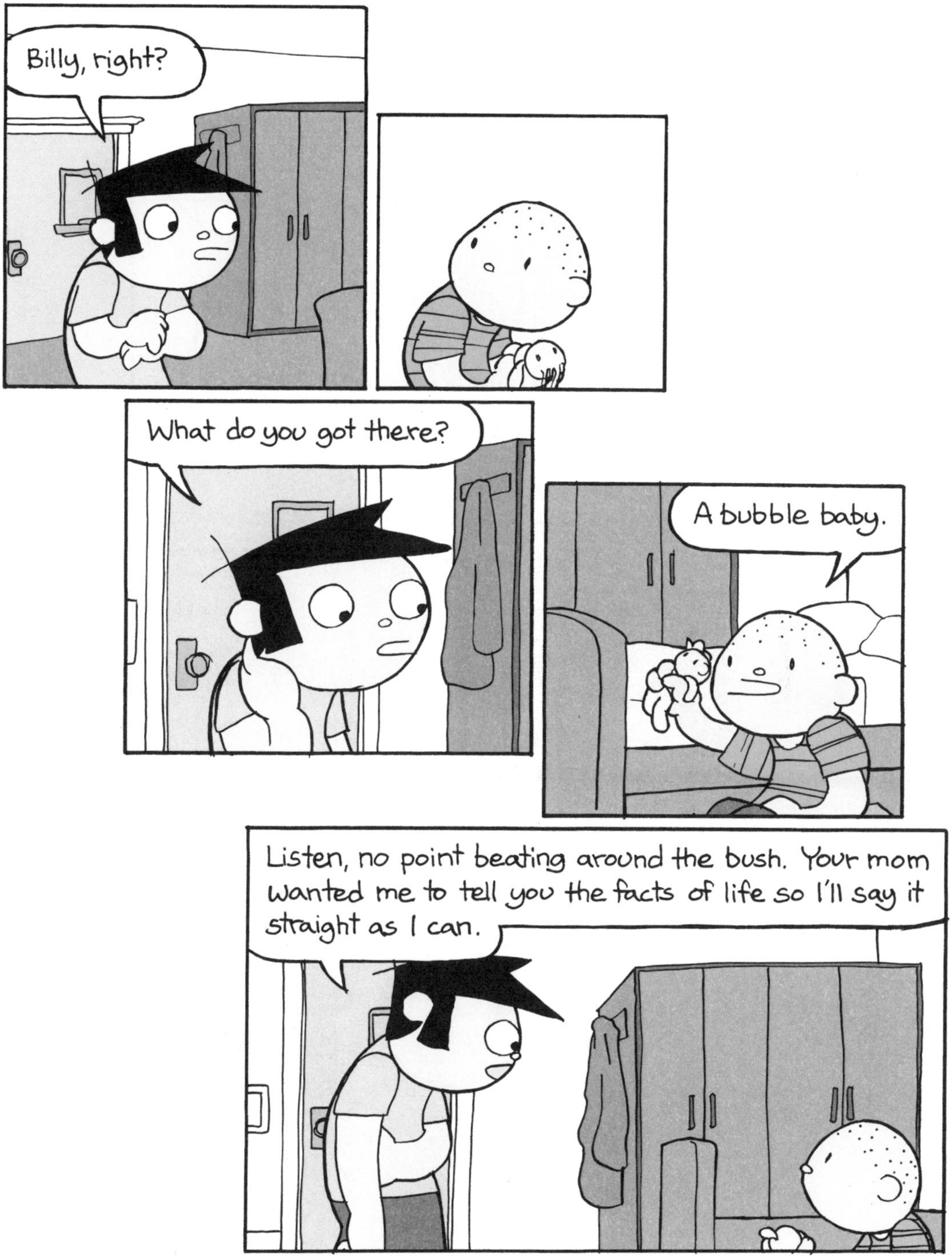
Billy, right?
What do you got there?
A bubble baby.
Listen, no point beating around the bush. Your mom wanted me to tell you the facts of life so I'll say it straight as I can.

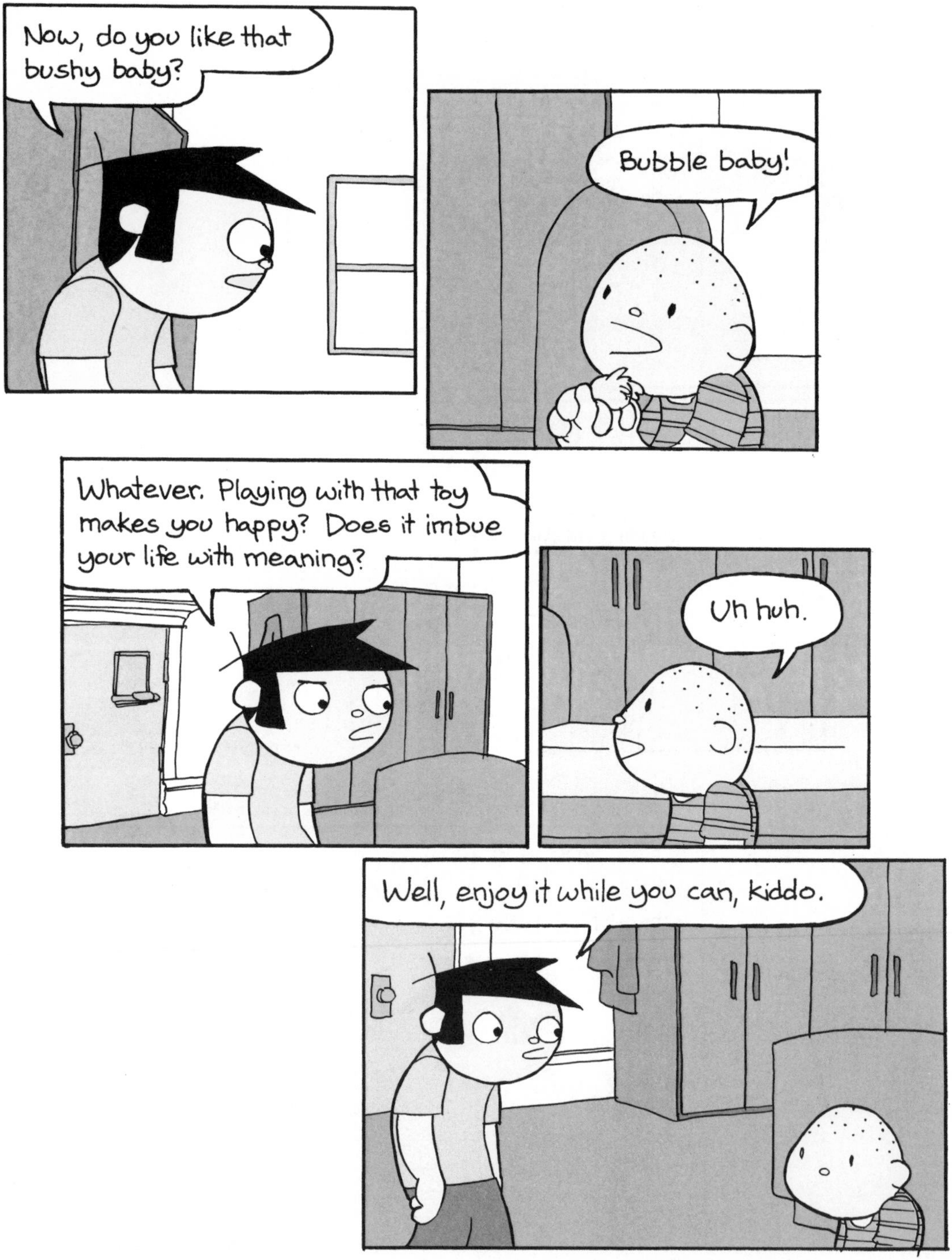
Now, do you like that bushy baby?
Bubble baby!
Whatever. Playing with that toy makes you happy? Does it imbue your life with meaning?
Uh huh.
Well, enjoy it while you can, kiddo.

You don't realize it now, but that bubble baby is a piece of shit.

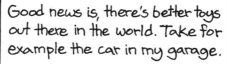

All it is is a cheap hunk of plastic with some fur glued to it.

Good news is, there's better toys out there in the world. Take for example the car in my garage.

The Aston Martin Zagato Coupe. Built on a shortened fiber carbon chassis, it's the fastest street legal car on the market today.

Now, you seem like a smart kid. I'm guessing you'll make enough money one day that you could afford one of these Aston Martins.

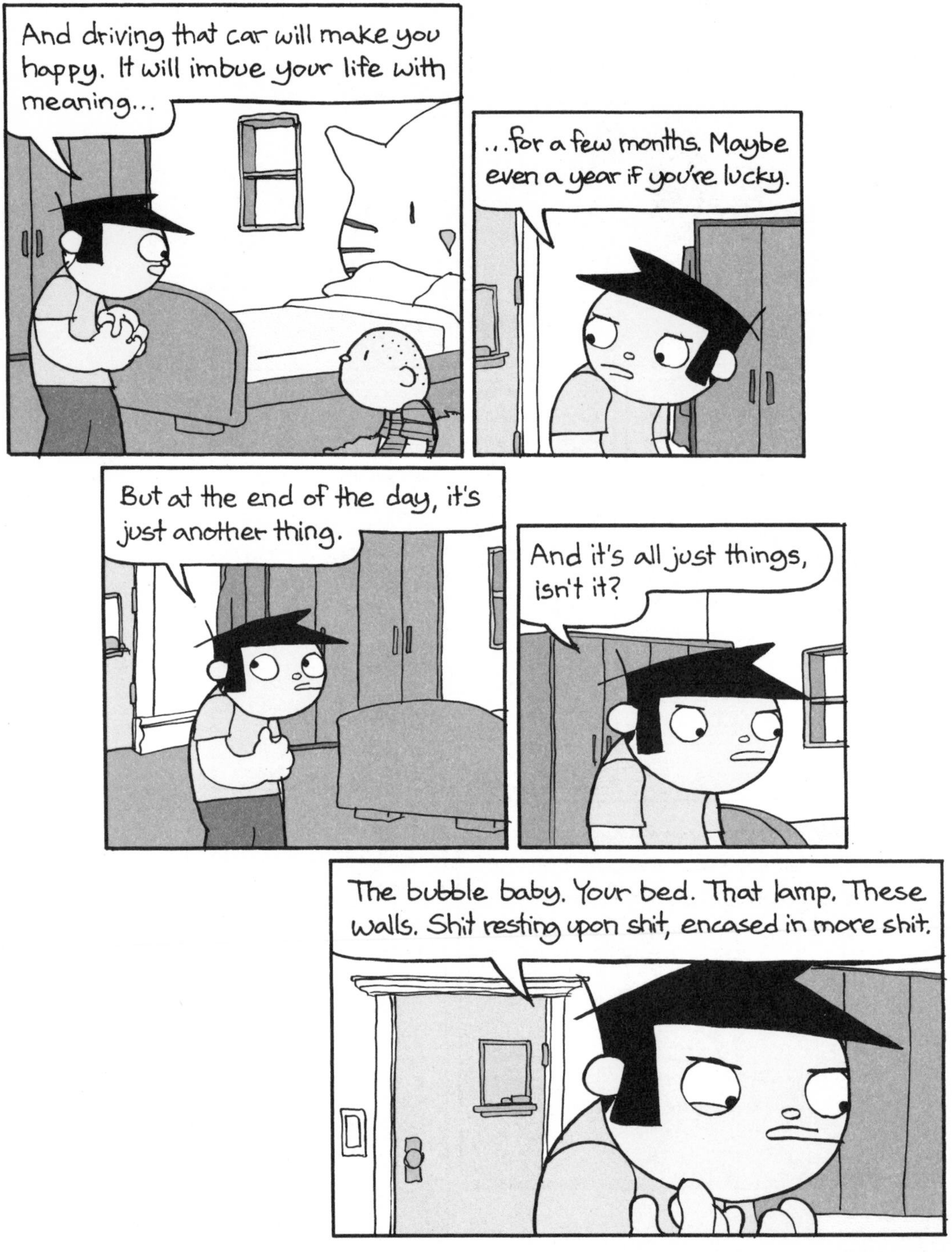
And driving that car will make you happy. It will imbue your life with meaning...
...for a few months. Maybe even a year if you're lucky.
But at the end of the day, it's just another thing.
And it's all just things, isn't it?
The bubble baby. Your bed. That lamp. These walls. Shit resting upon shit, encased in more shit.

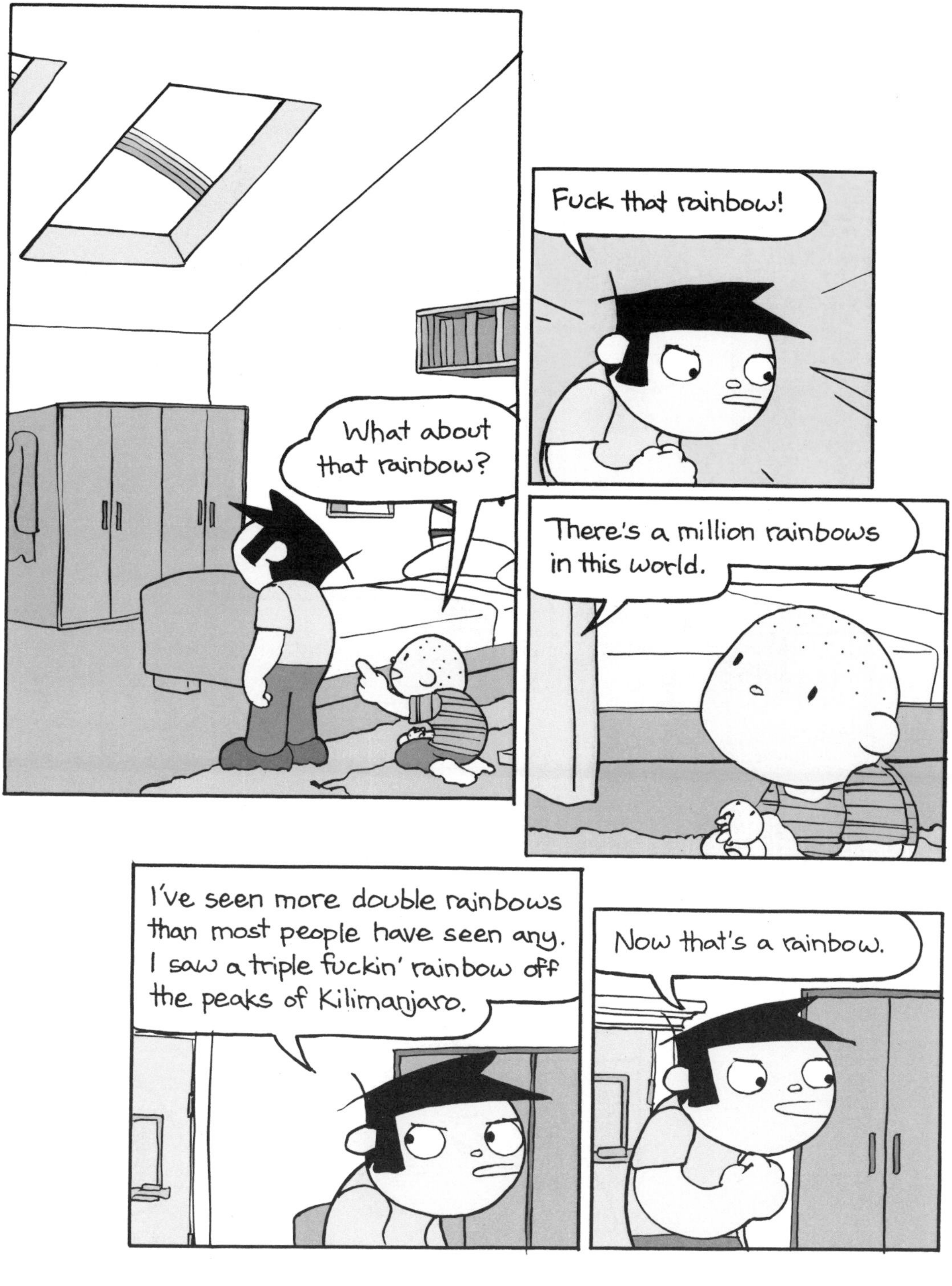
What about that rainbow?
Fuck that rainbow!
There's a million rainbows in this world.
I've seen more double rainbows than most people have seen any. I saw a triple fuckin' rainbow off the peaks of Kilimanjaro.
Now that's a rainbow.

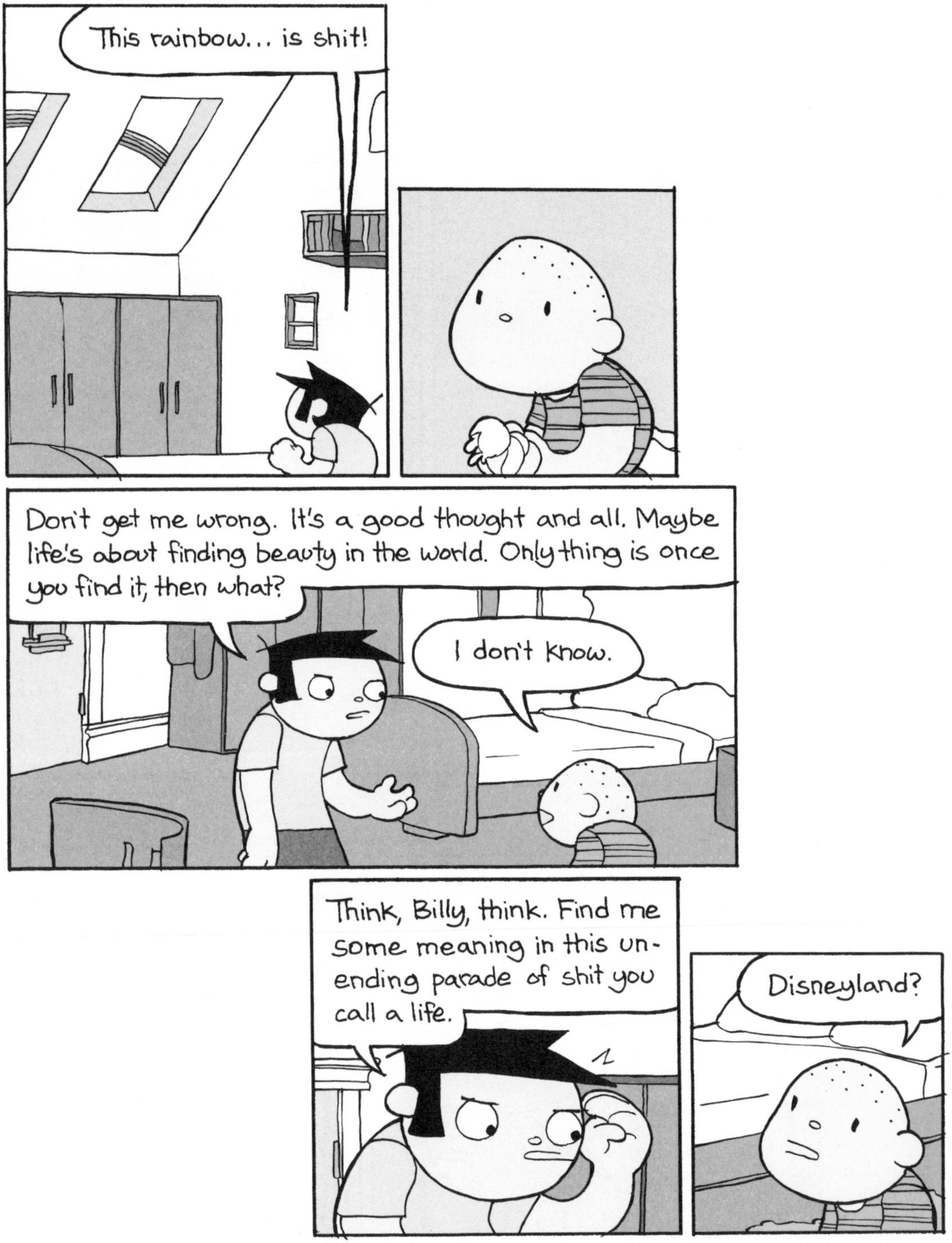
This rainbow... is shit!
Don't get me wrong. It's a good thought and all. Maybe life's about finding beauty in the world. Only thing is once you find it, then what?
I don't know.
Think, Billy, think. Find me some meaning in this un-ending parade of shit you call a life.
Disneyland?

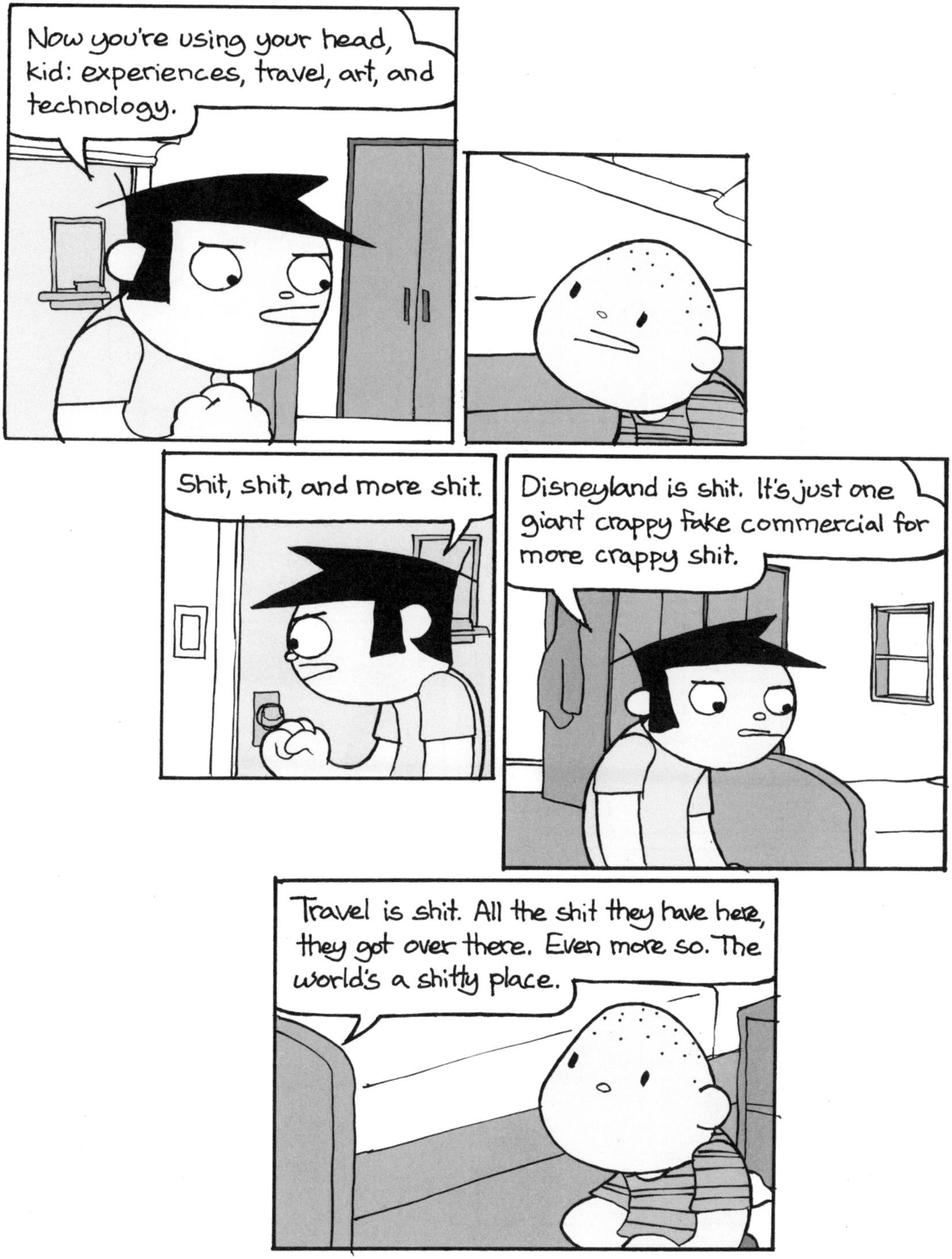

Now you're using your head, kid: experiences, travel, art, and technology.
Shit, shit, and more shit.
Disneyland is shit. It's just one giant crappy fake commercial for more crappy shit.
Travel is shit. All the shit they have here, they got over there. Even more so. The world's a shitty place.

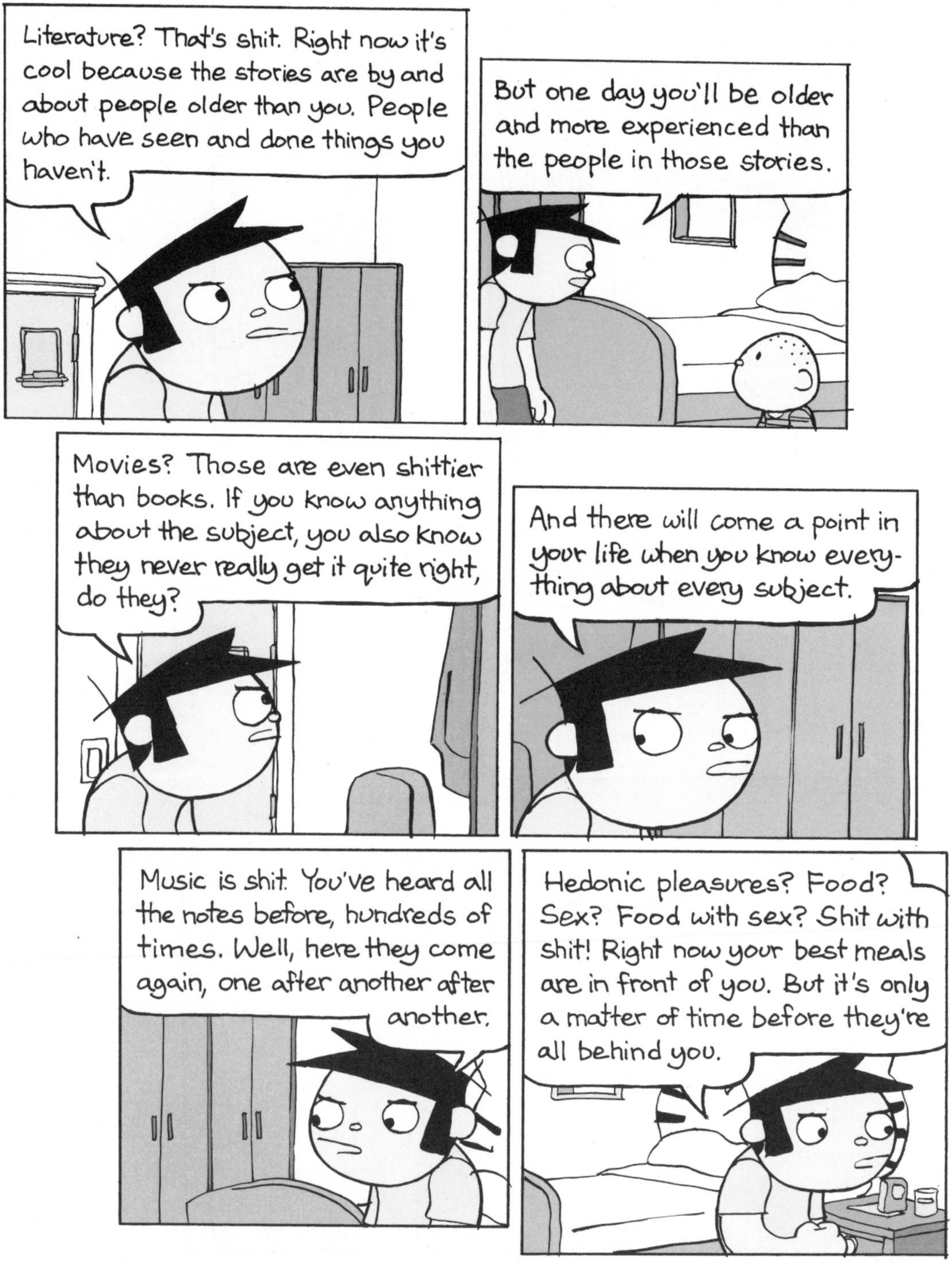
Literature? That's shit. Right now it's cool because the stories are by and about people older than you. People who have seen and done things you haven't.
But one day you'll be older and more experienced than the people in those stories.
Movies? Those are even shittier than books. If you know anything about the subject, you also know they never really get it quite right, do they?
And there will come a point in your life when you know everything about every subject.
Music is shit. You've heard all the notes before, hundreds of times. Well, here they come again, one after another after another.
Hedonic pleasures? Food? Sex? Food with sex? Shit with shit! Right now your best meals are in front of you. But it's only a matter of time before they're all behind you.

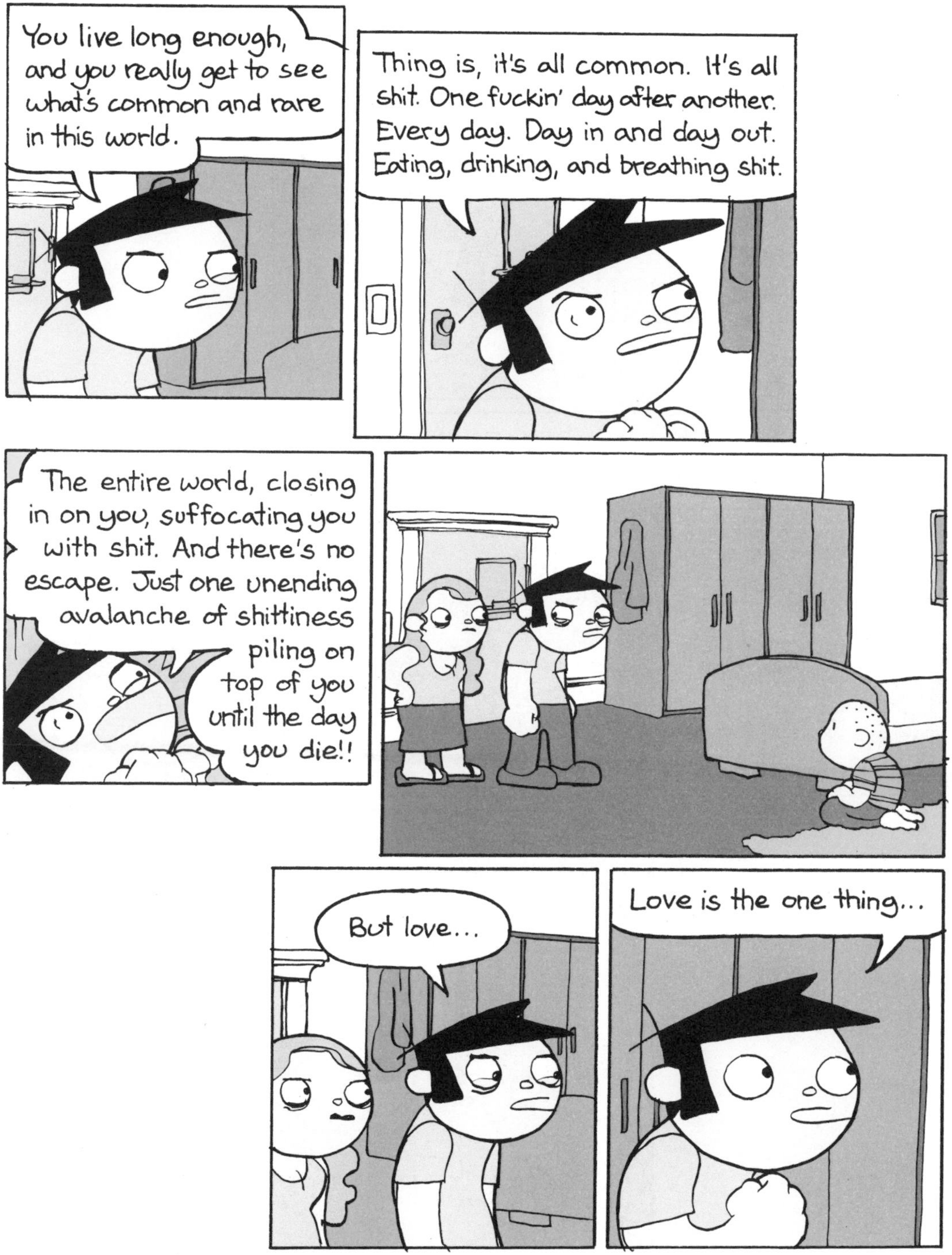

You live long enough, and you really get to see what's common and rare in this world.
Thing is, it's all common. It's all shit. One fuckin' day after another. Every day. Day in and day out. Eating, drinking, and breathing shit.
The entire world, closing in on you, suffocating you with shit. And there's no escape. Just one unending avalanche of shittiness piling on top of you until the day you die!!
But love...
Love is the one thing...

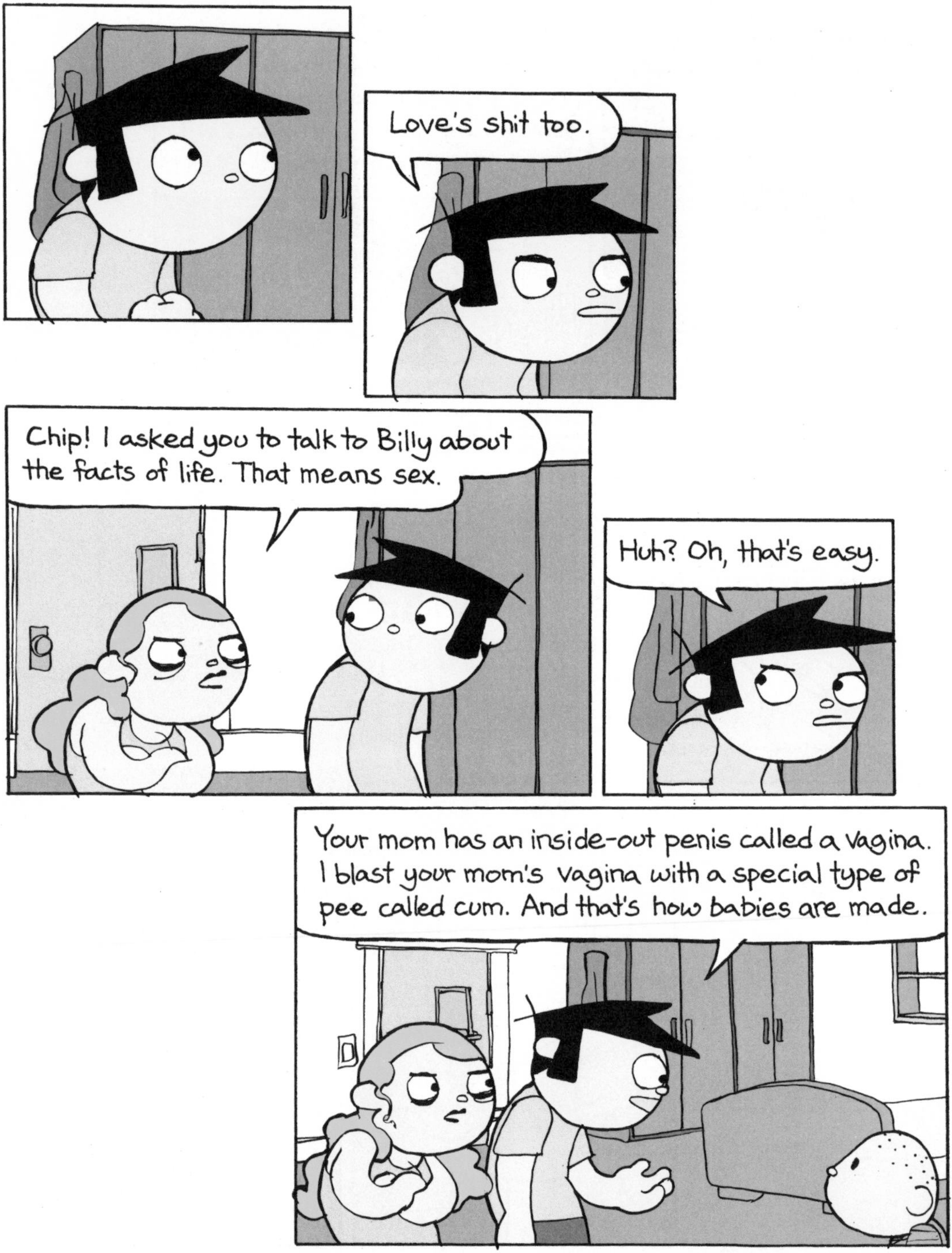
Love's shit too.
Chip! I asked you to talk to Billy about the facts of life. That means sex.
Huh? Oh, that's easy.
Your mom has an inside-out penis called a vagina. I blast your mom's vagina with a special type of pee called cum. And that's how babies are made.

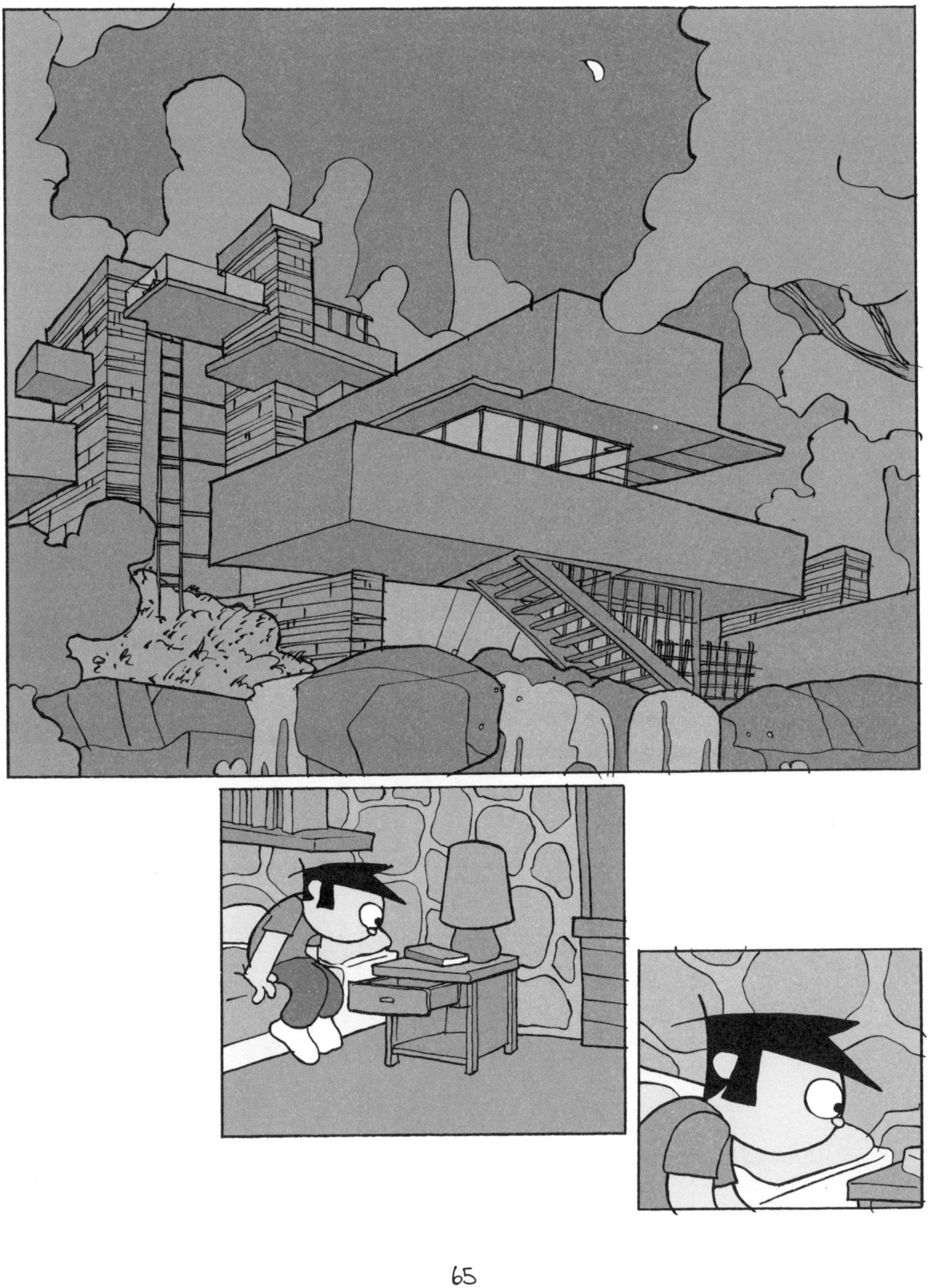

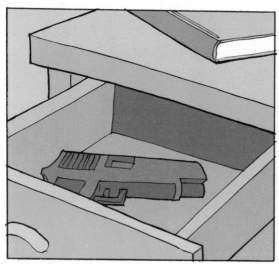

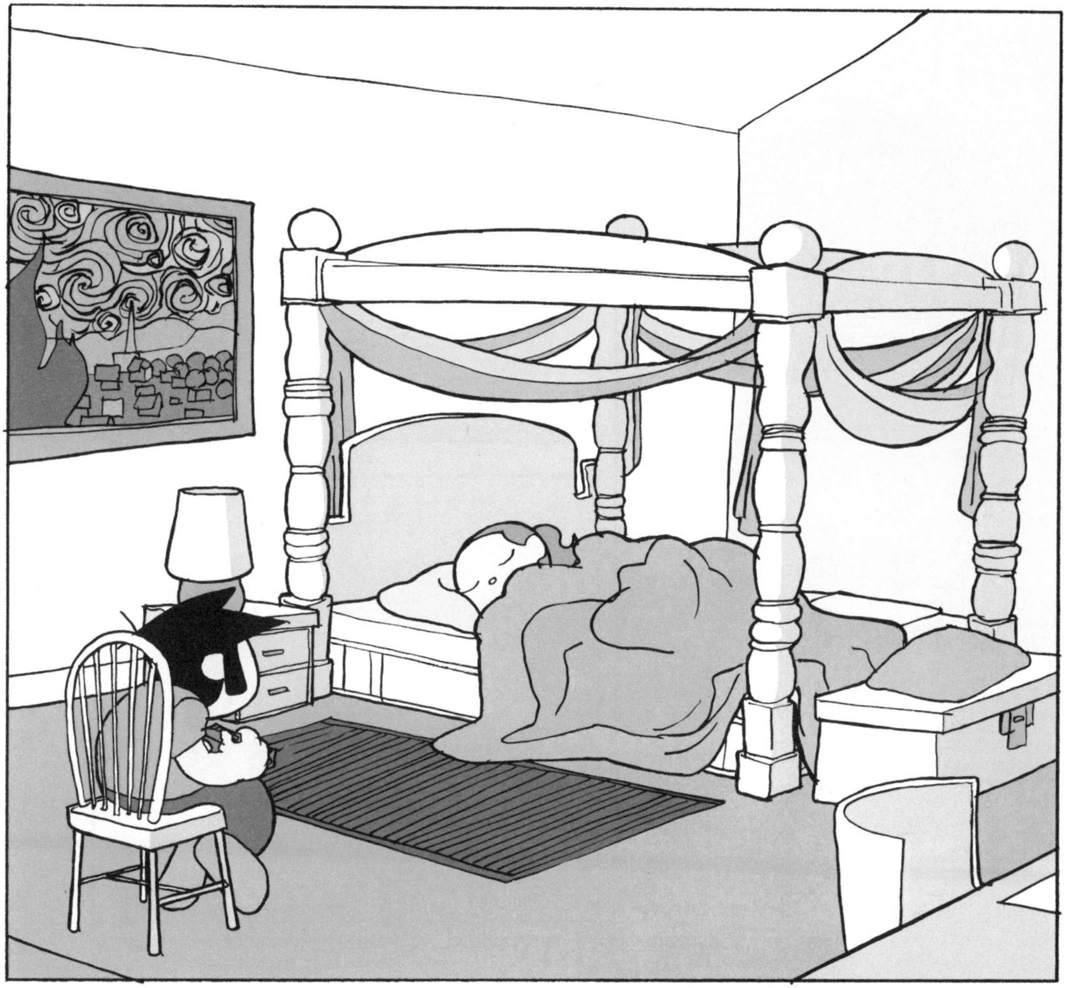

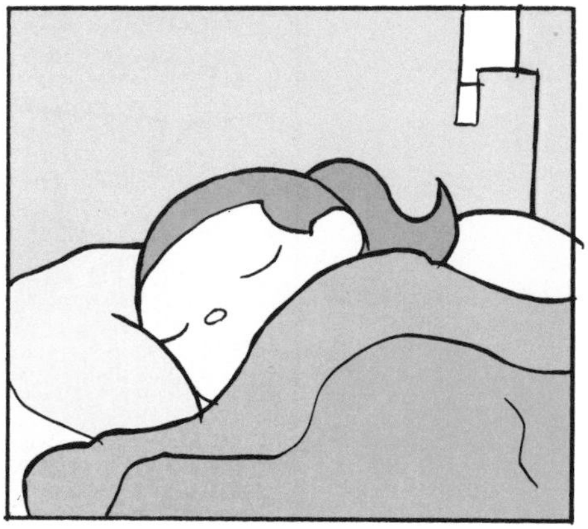

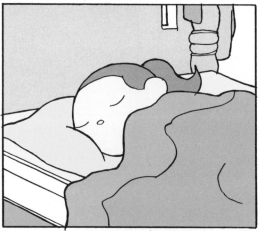

I can't... I can't do it.

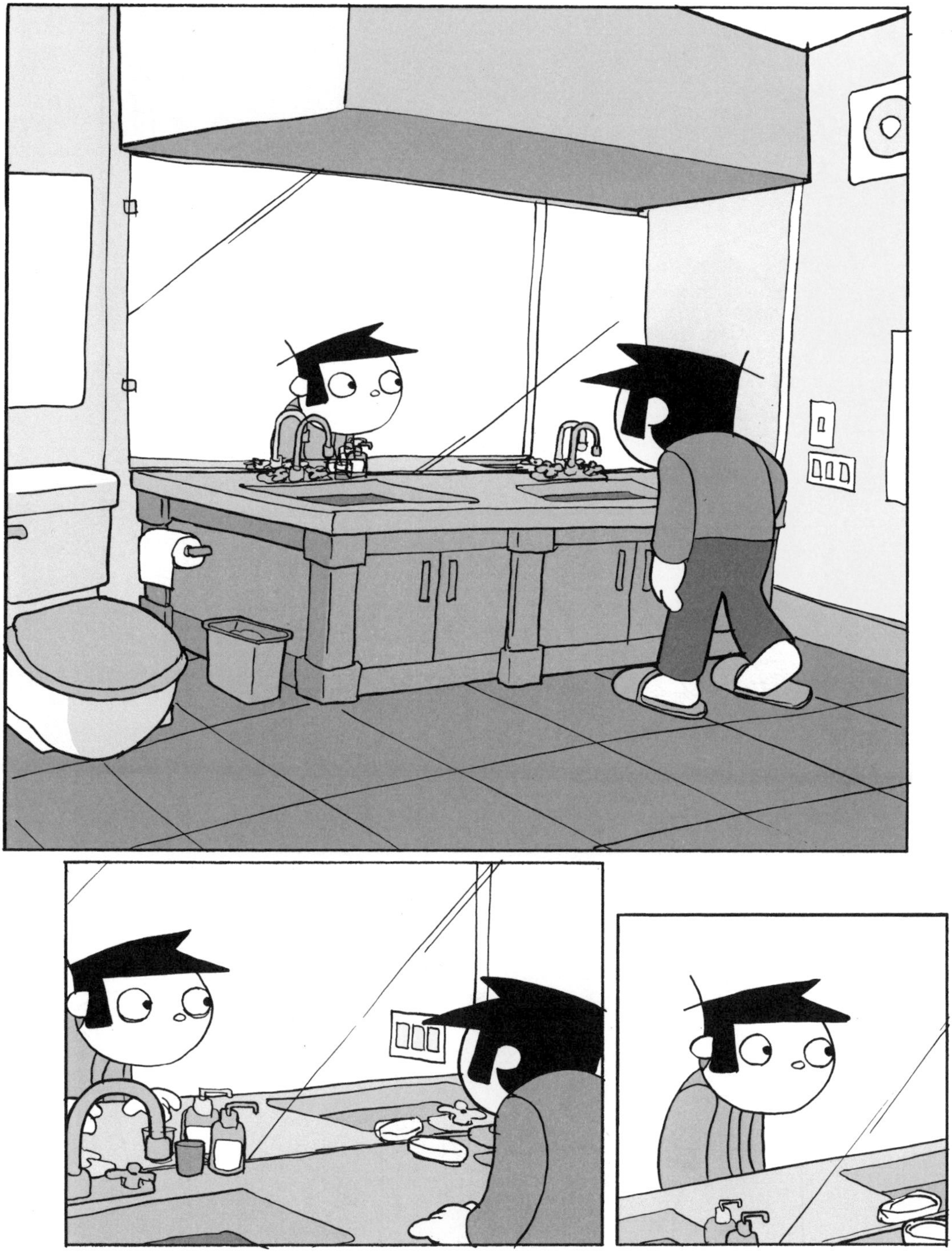

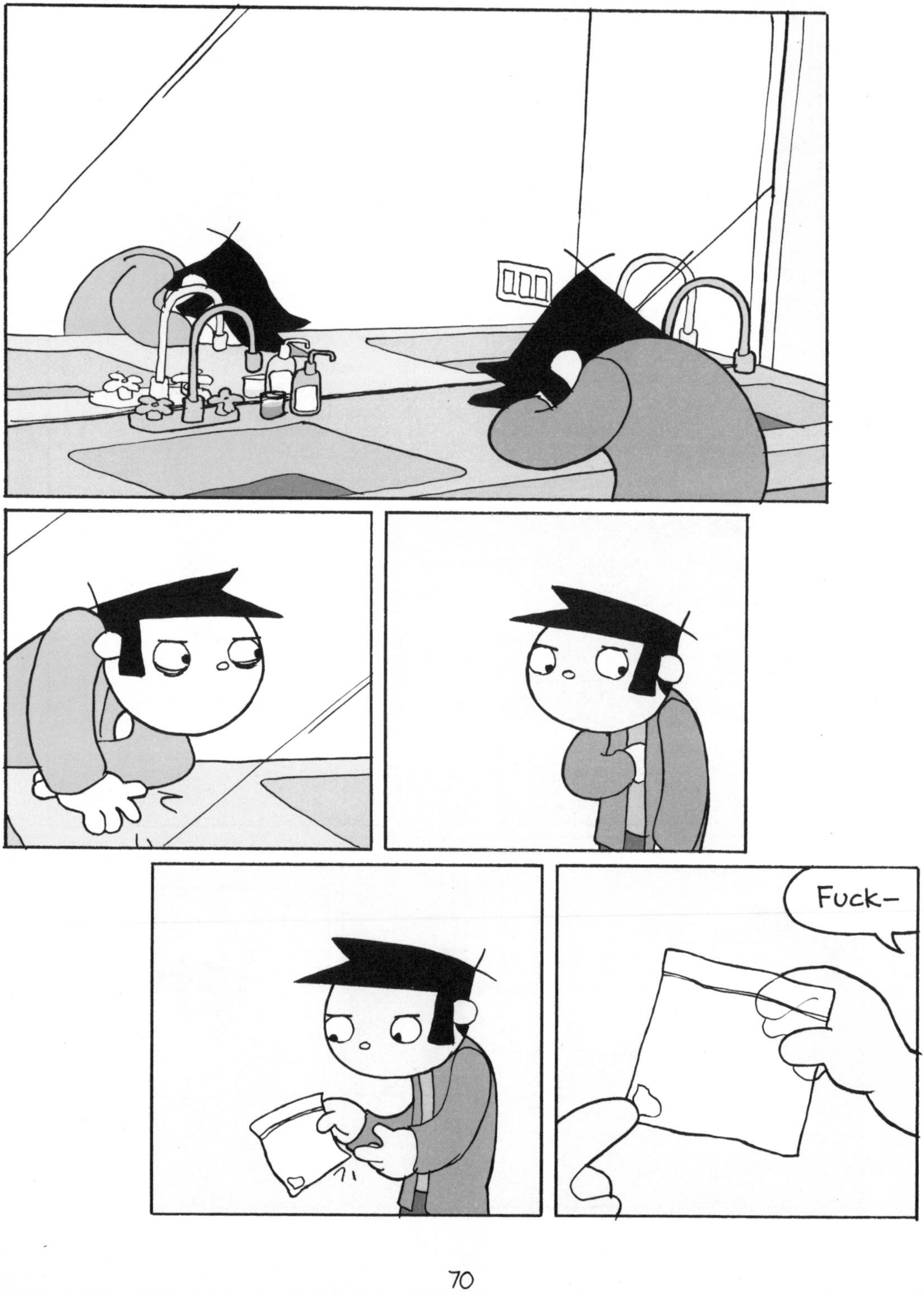
Fuck-

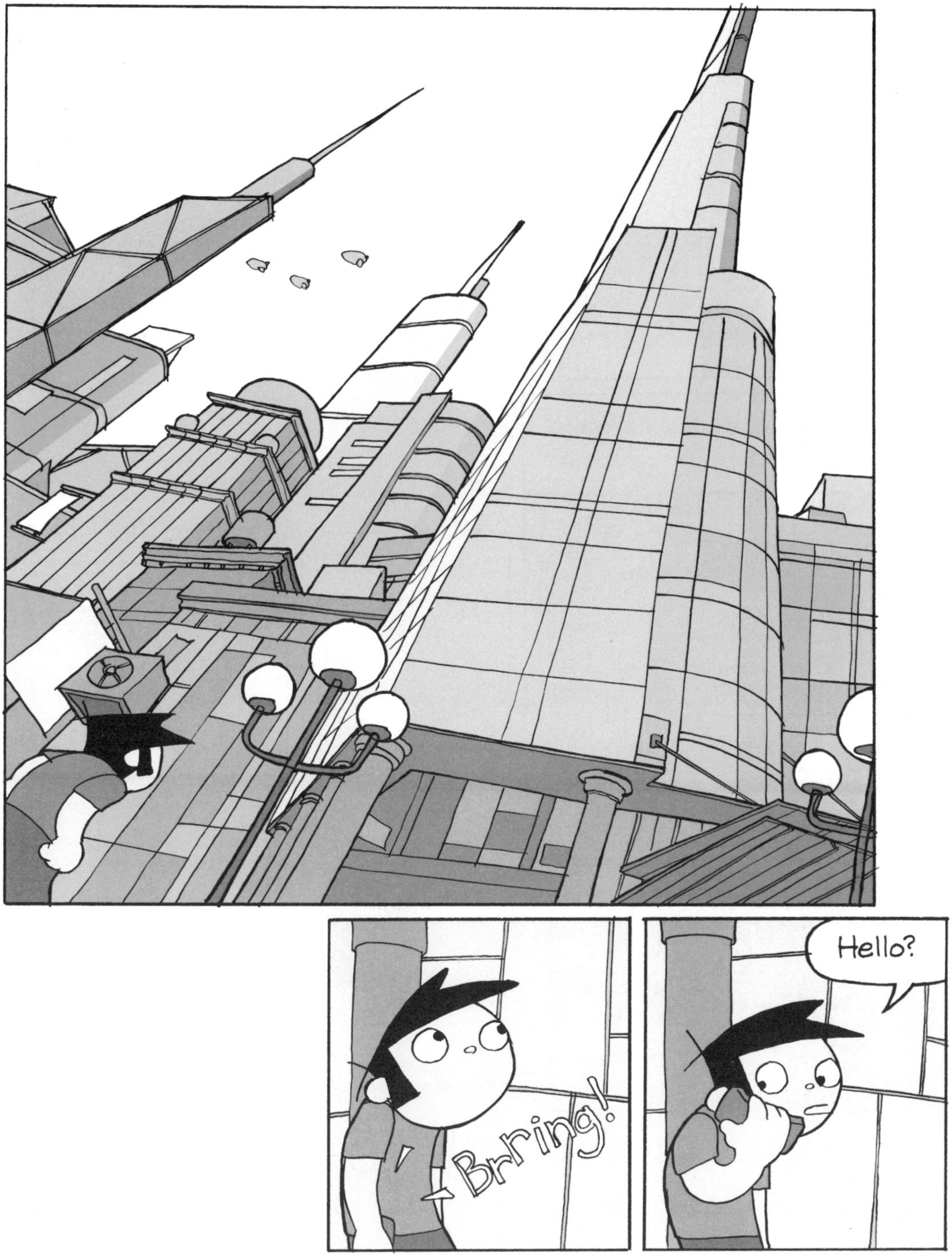
Brring!
Hello?

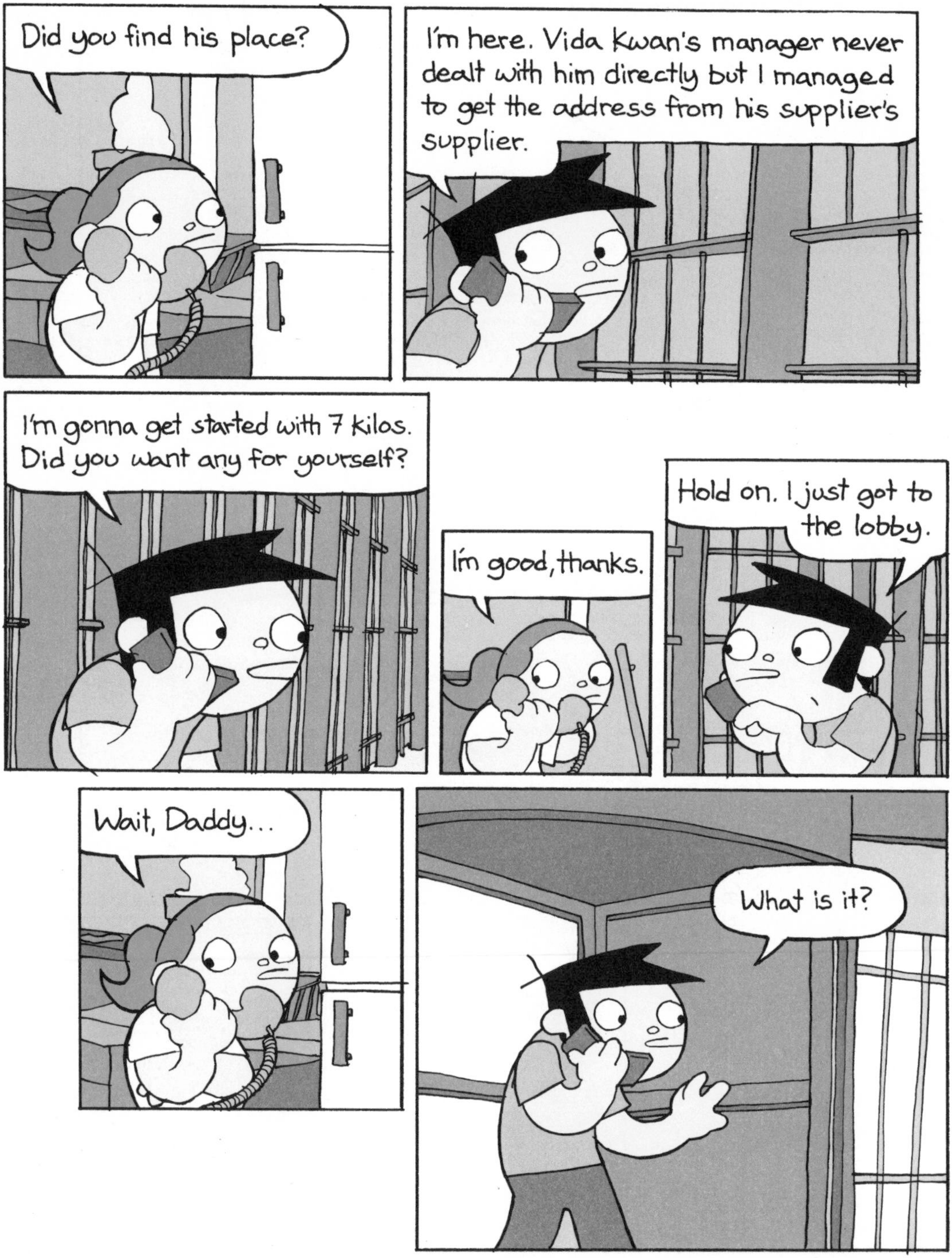
Did you find his place?
I'm here. Vida Kwan's manager never dealt with him directly but I managed to get the address from his supplier's supplier.
I'm gonna get started with 7 kilos. Did you want any for yourself?
I'm good, thanks.
Hold on. I just got to the lobby.
Wait, Daddy...
What is it?

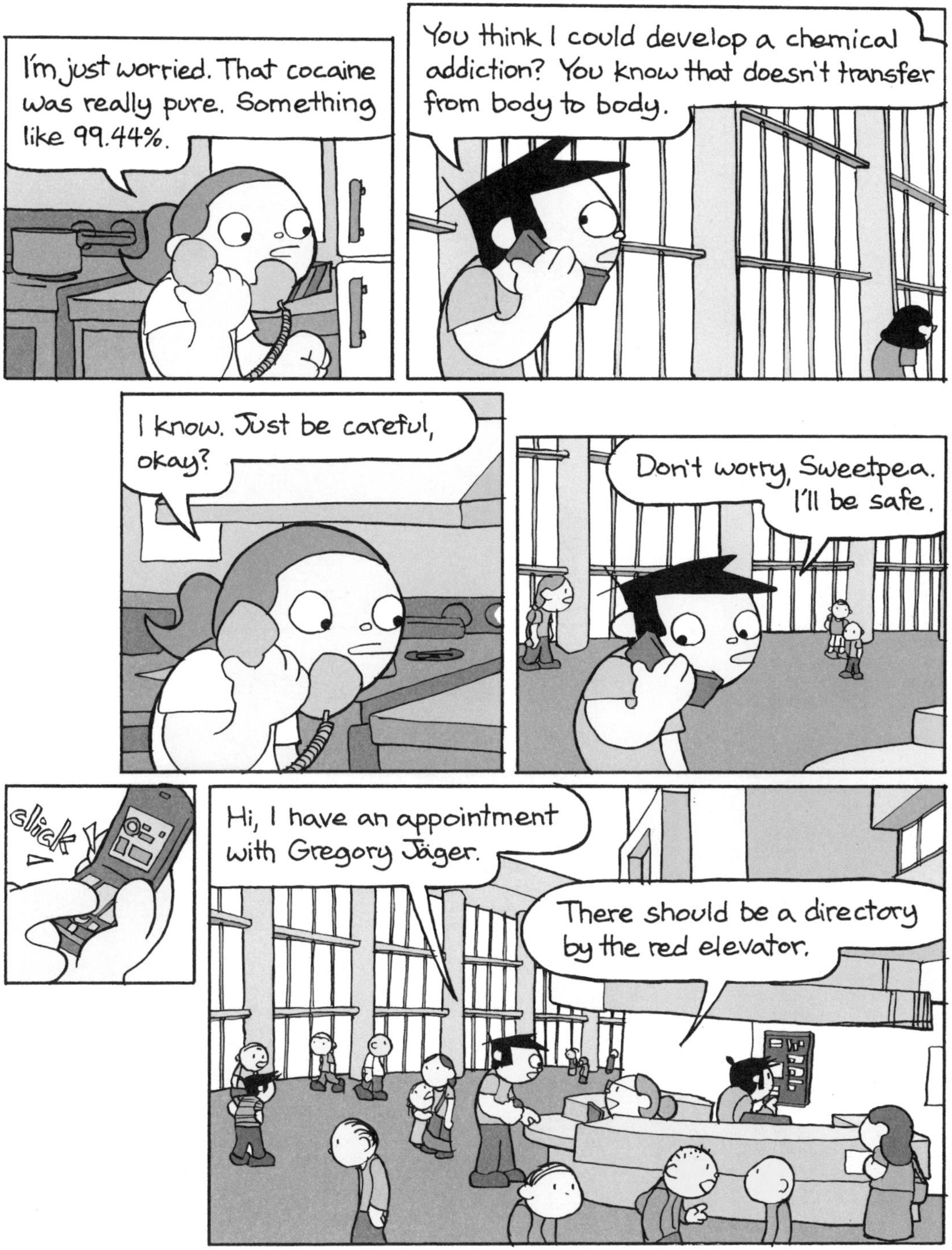
I'm just worried. That cocaine was really pure. Something like 99.44%.
You think I could develop a chemical addiction? You know that doesn't transfer from body to body.
I know. Just be careful, okay?
Don't worry, Sweetpea. I'll be safe.
click
Hi, I have an appointment with Gregory Jäger.
There should be a directory by the red elevator.

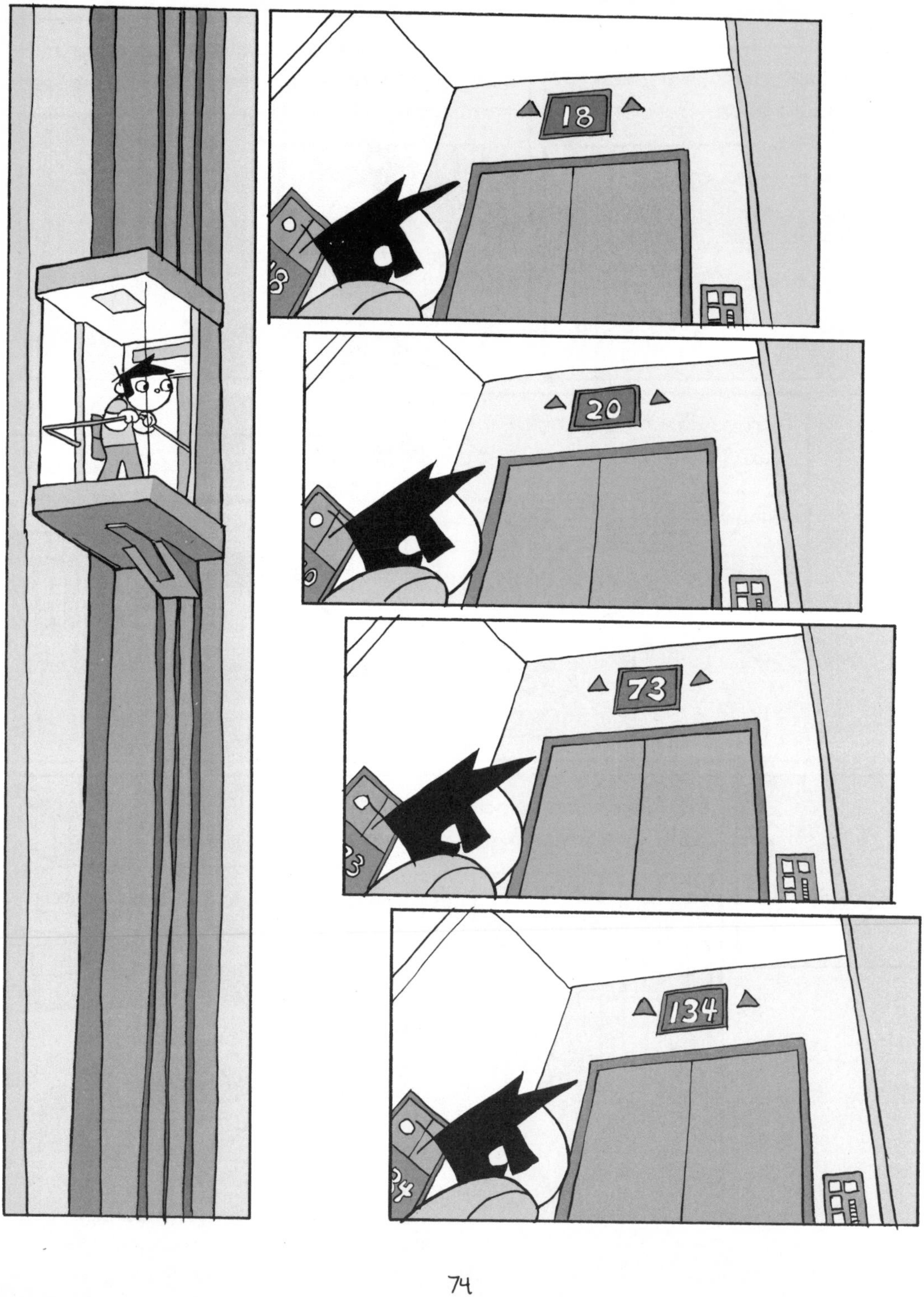
18
20
73
134

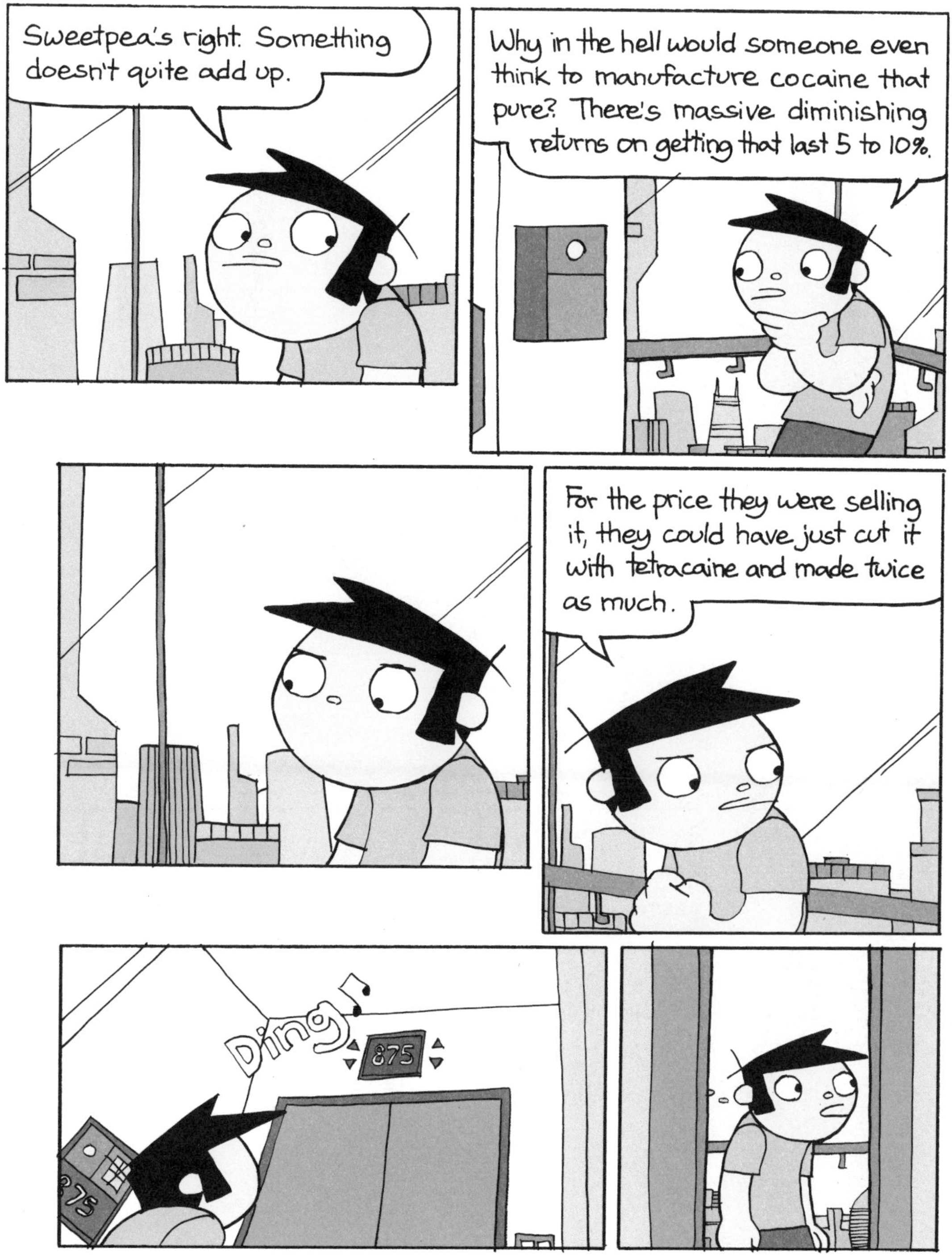
Sweetpea's right. Something doesn't quite add up.
Why in the hell would someone even think to manufacture cocaine that pure? There's massive diminishing returns on getting that last 5 to 10%.
For the price they were selling it, they could have just cut it with tetracaine and made twice as much.
Ding!
875
875

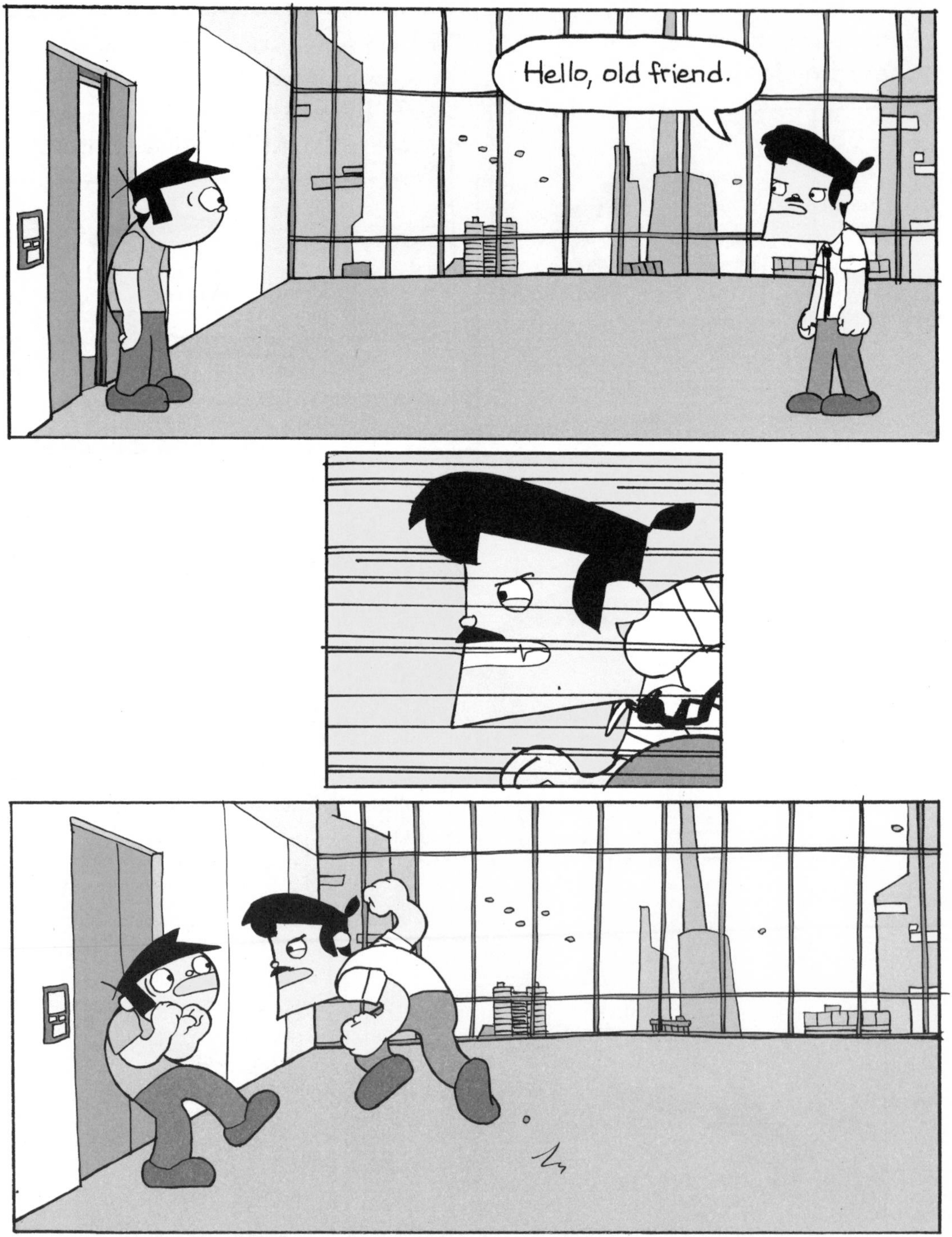
Hello, old friend.

CHAPTER 15

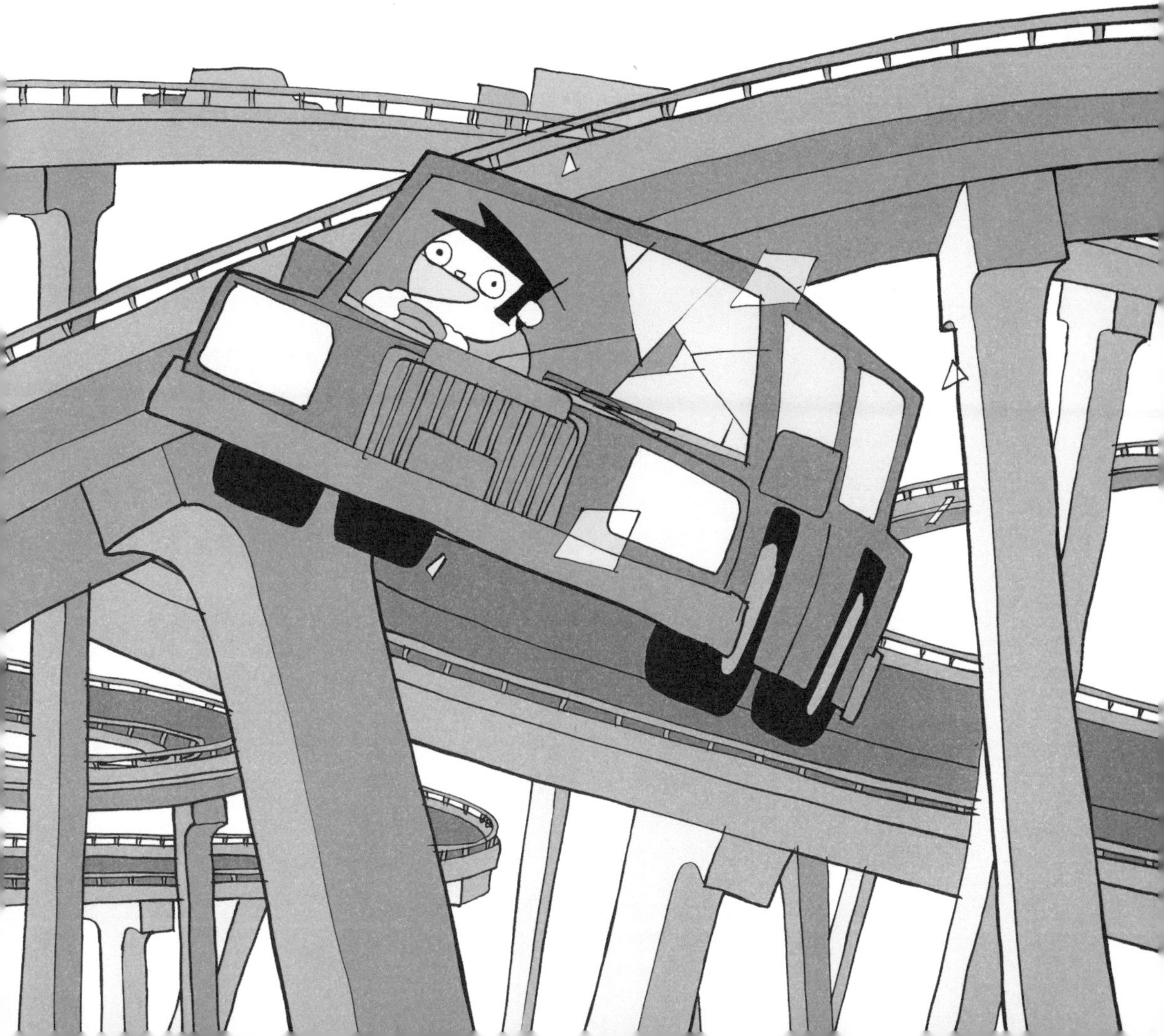

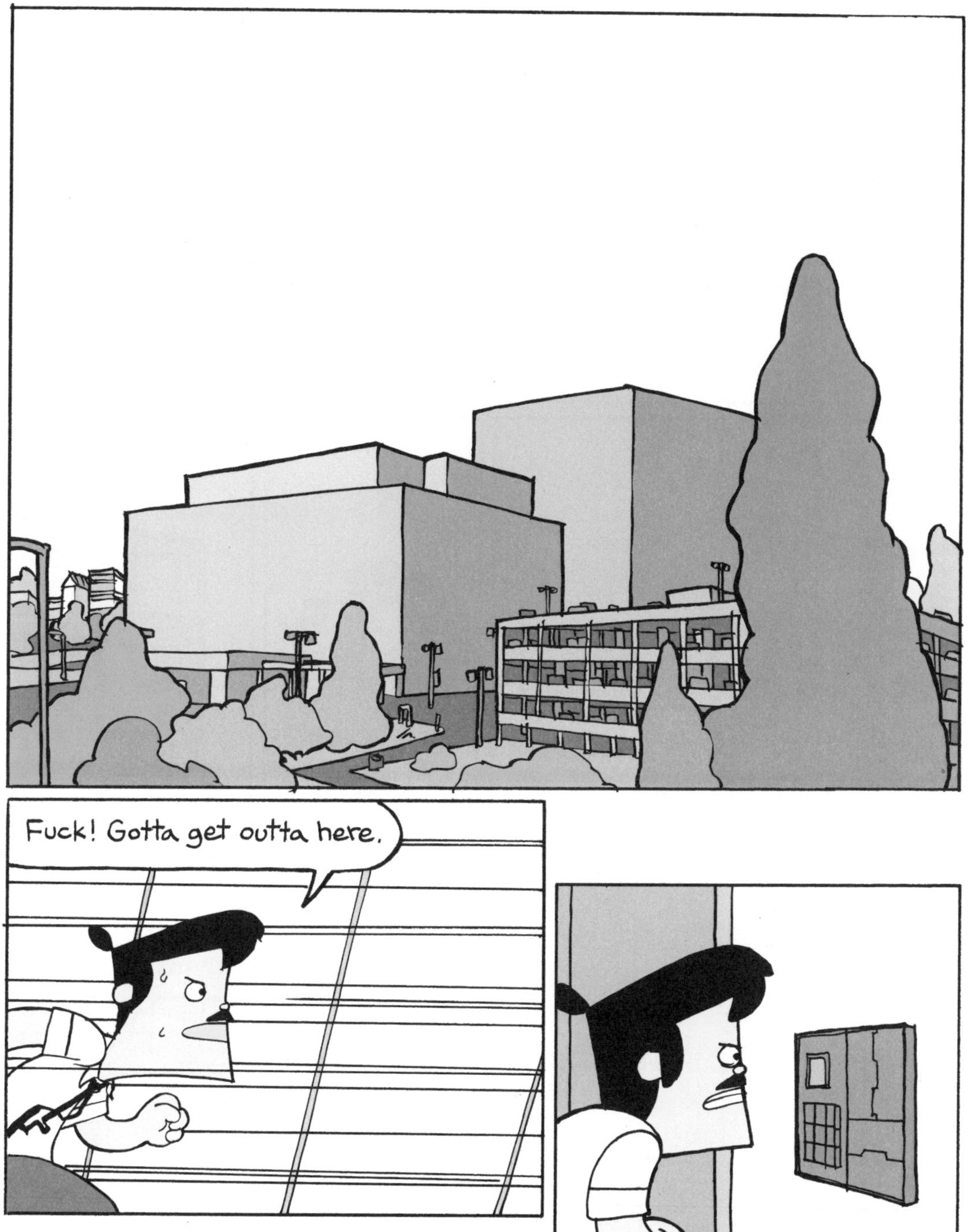
Fuck! Gotta get outta here.

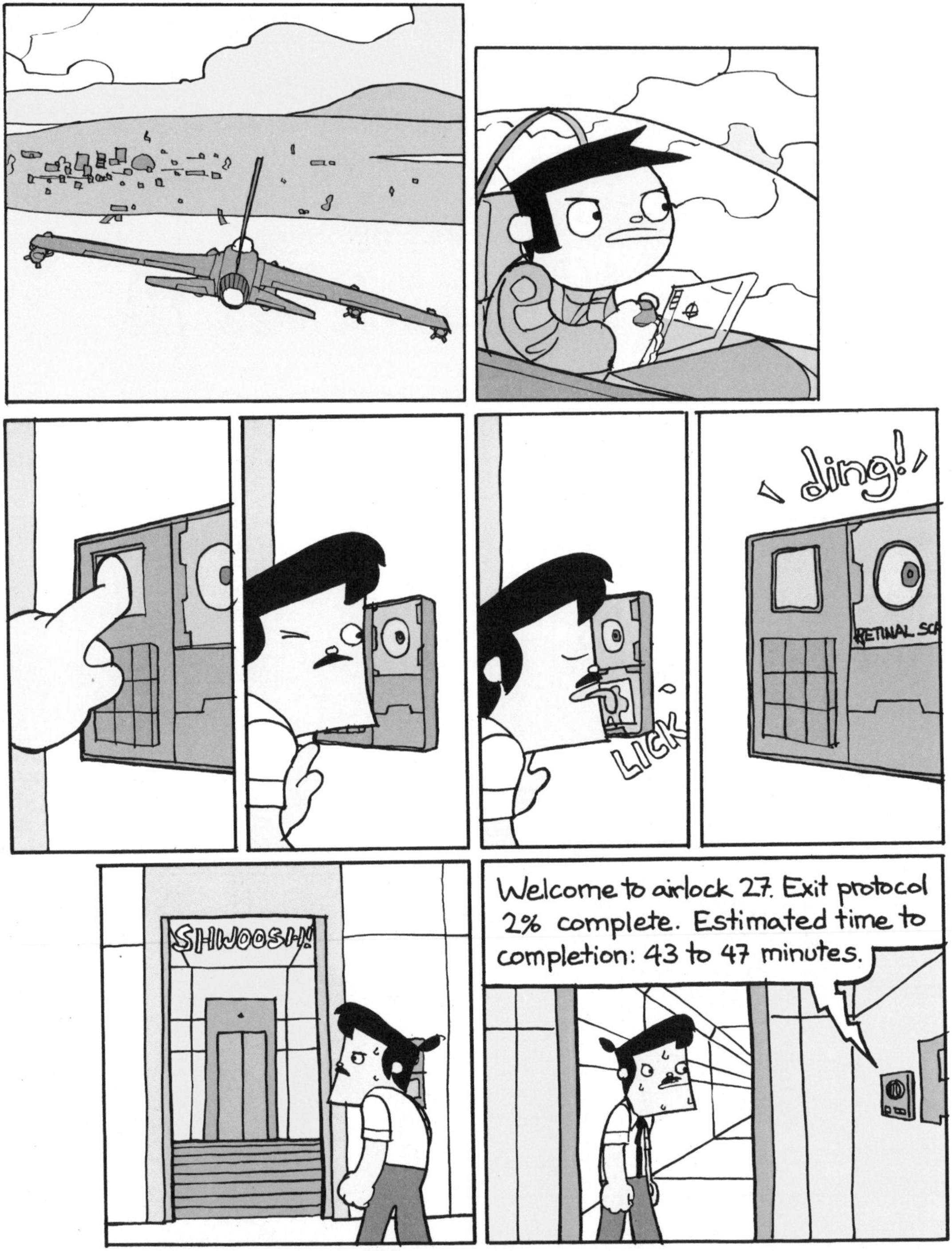
ding!
LICK
RETINAL SCA
SHWOOSH!
Welcome to airlock 27. Exit protocol 2% complete. Estimated time to completion: 43 to 47 minutes.

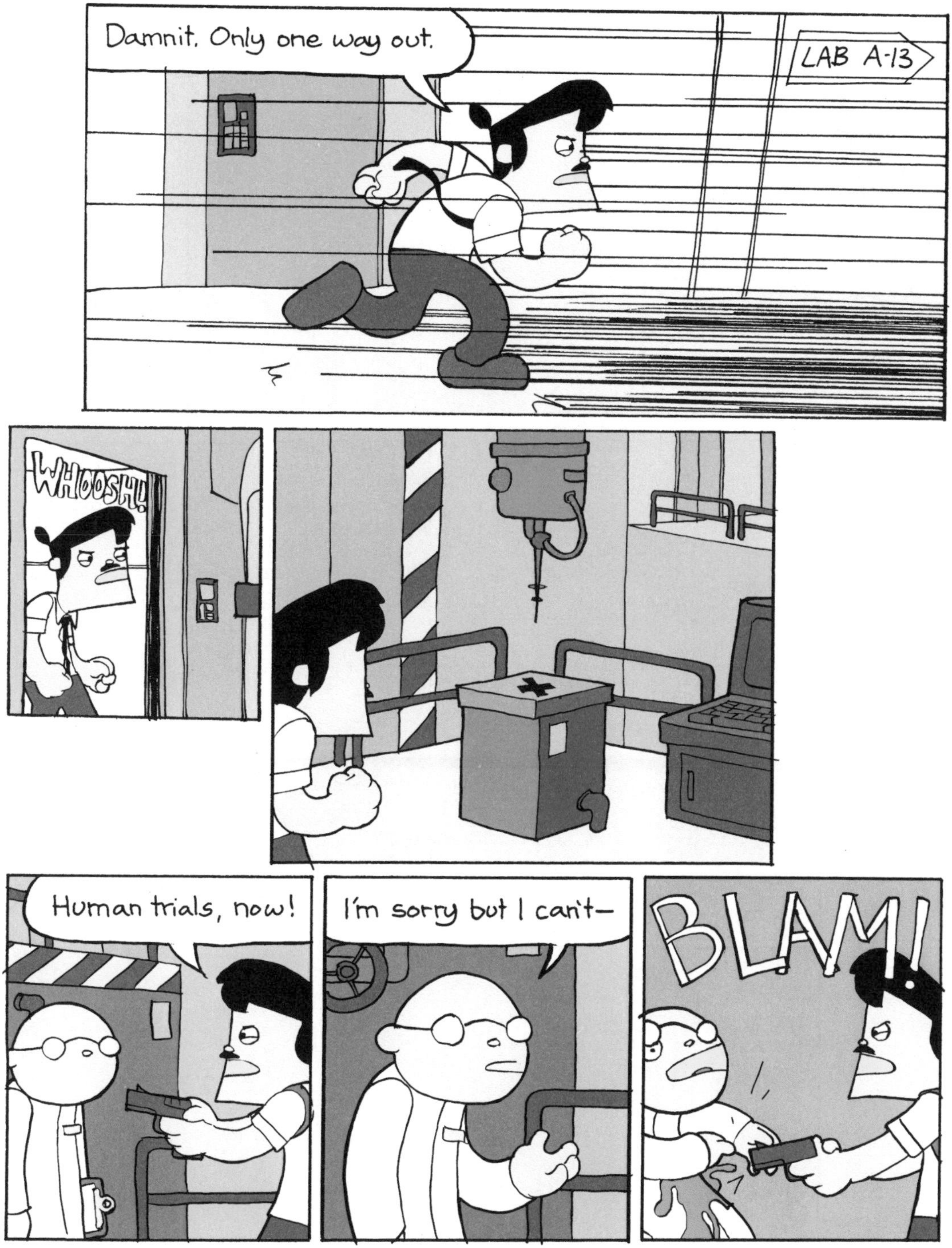
Damnit. Only one way out.
LAB A-13
WHOOSH!
Human trials, now!
I'm sorry but I can't—
BLAM!

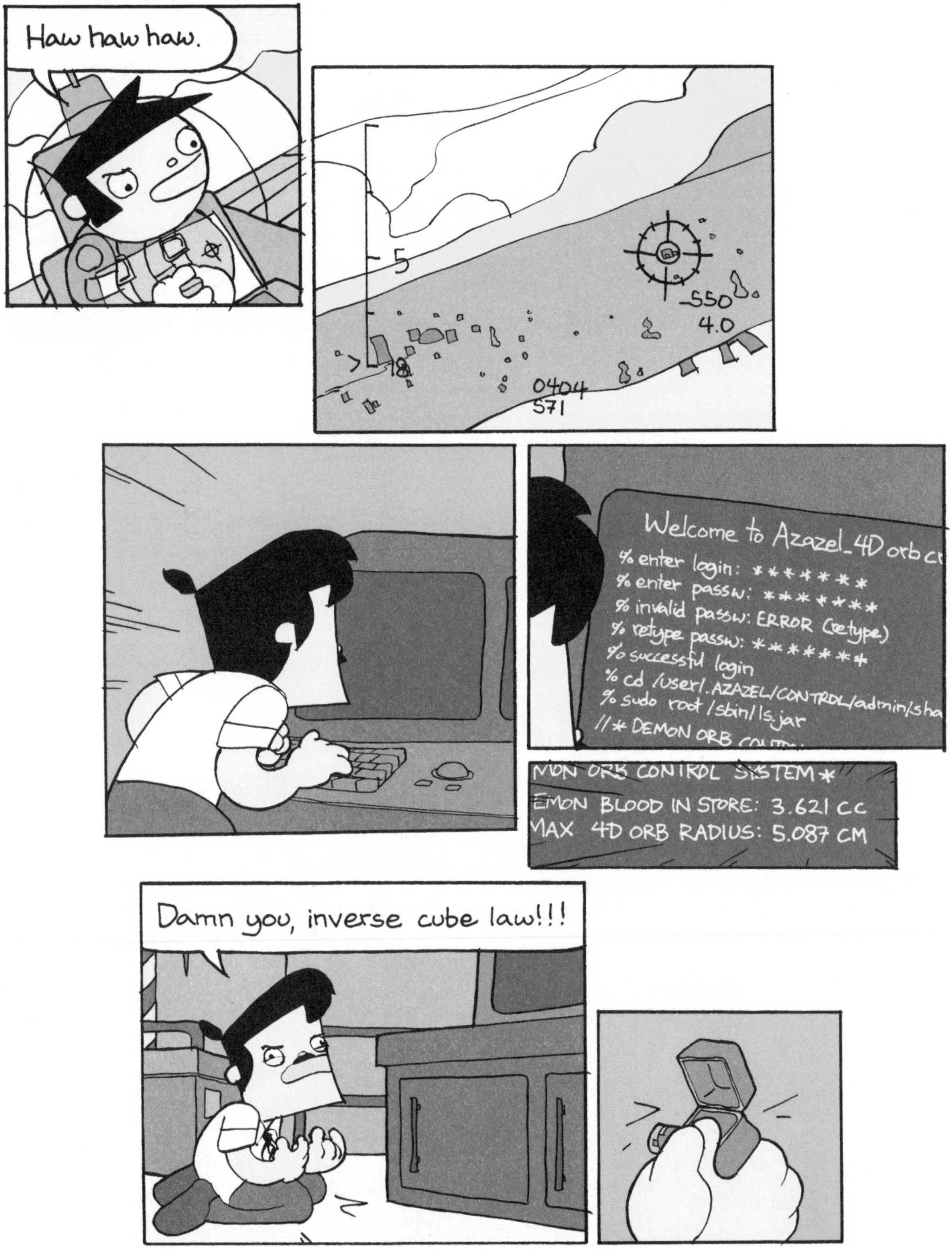
Haw haw haw.
5
550
4.0
18
0404
571
Welcome to Azazel_4D orb c
% enter login: *******
% enter passw: ********
% invalid passw: ERROR (retype)
% retype passw: *******
% successful login
% cd /user/.AZAZEL/CONTROL/admin/sha
% sudo root /sbin/ls.jar
//* DEMON ORB
MON ORB CONTROL SYSTEM *
EMON BLOOD IN STORE: 3.621 CC
MAX 4D ORB RADIUS: 5.087 CM
Damn you, inverse cube law!!!

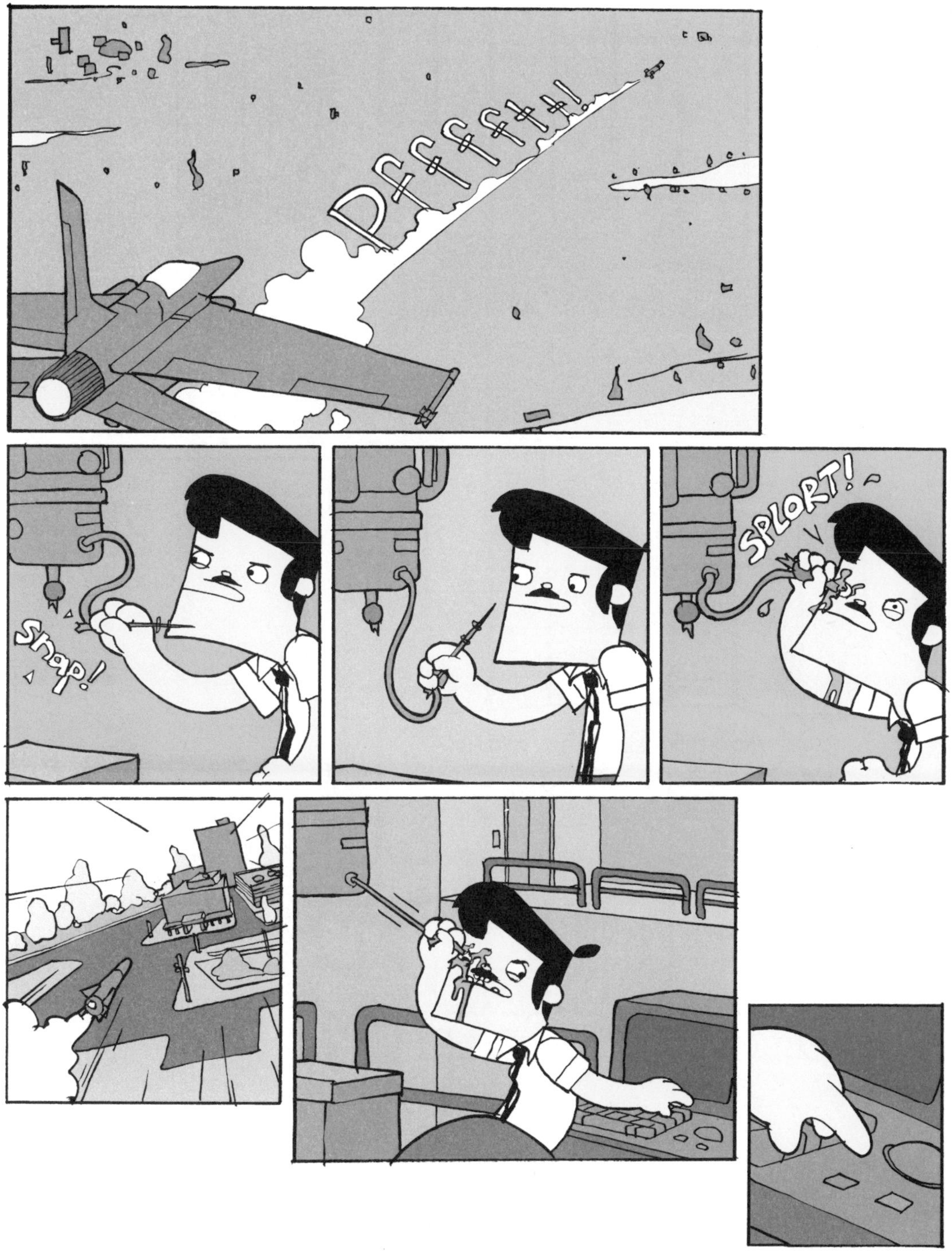
PFFFSSH!
SNAP!
SPLORT!

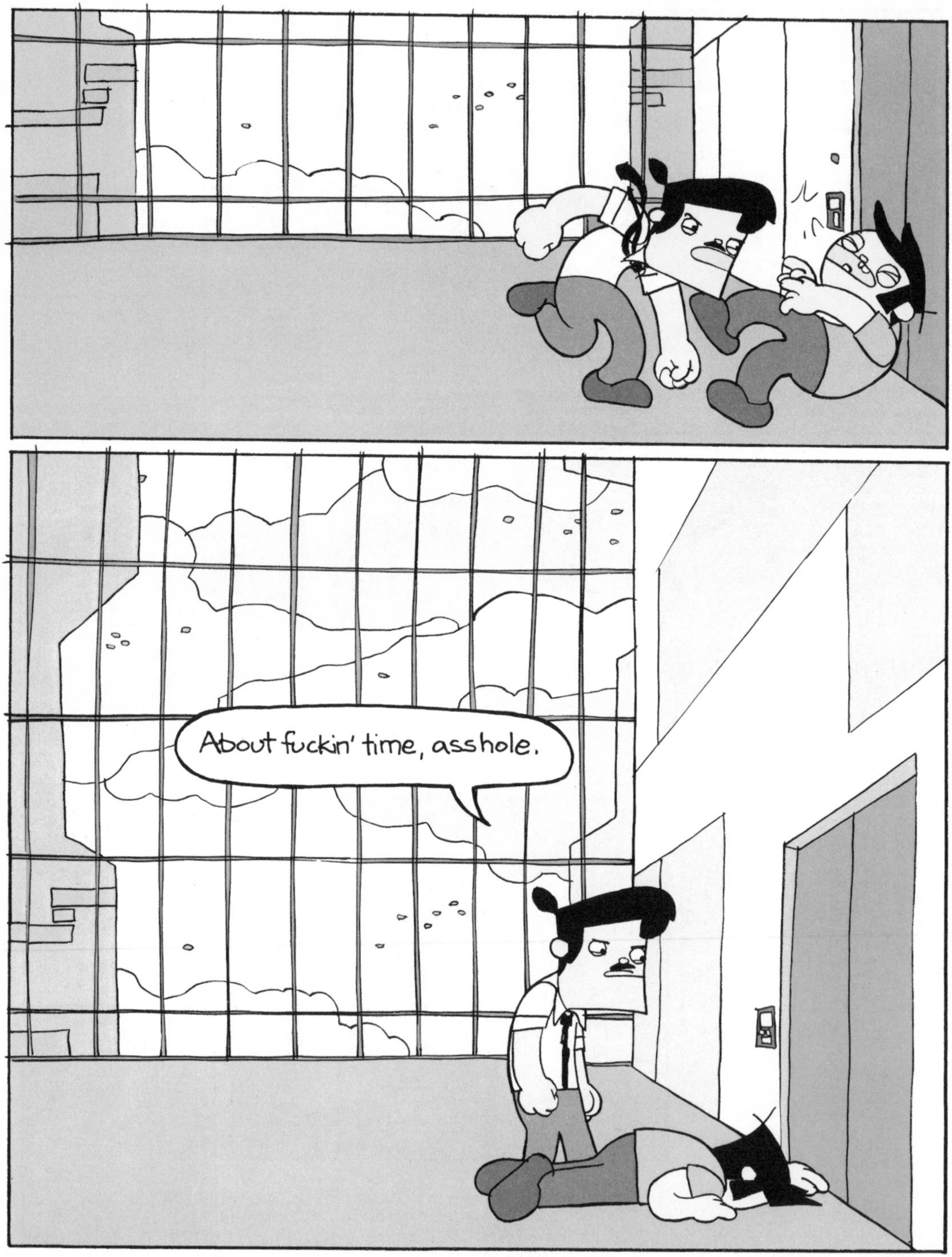
About fuckin' time, asshole.

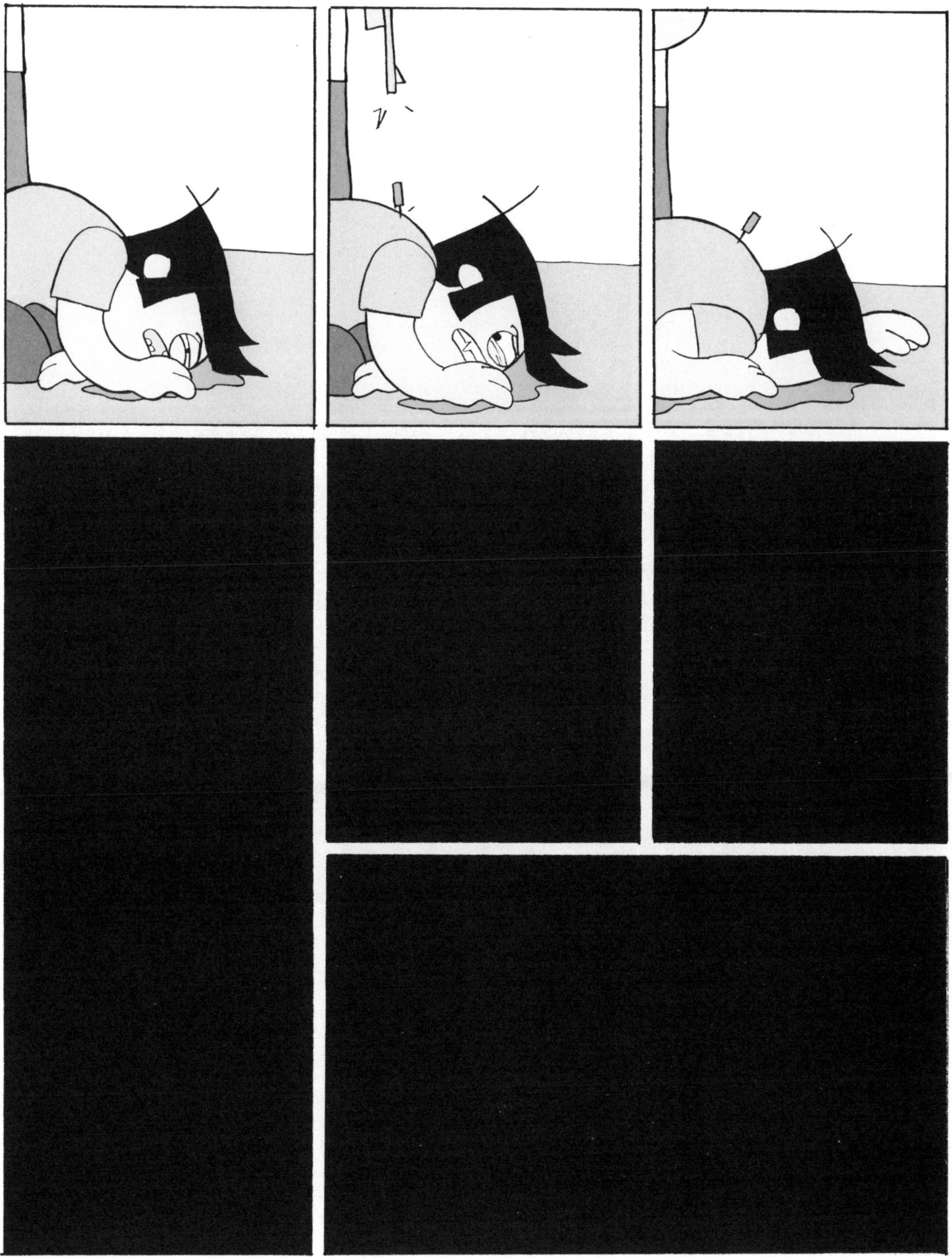

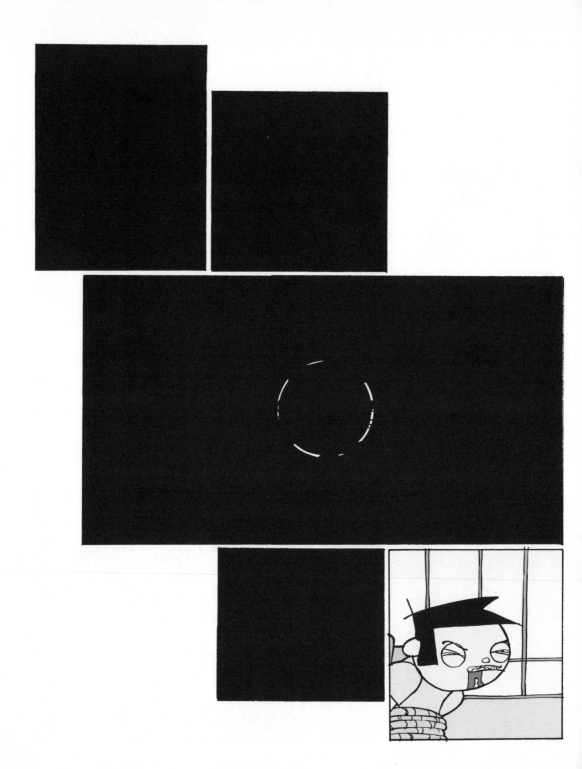

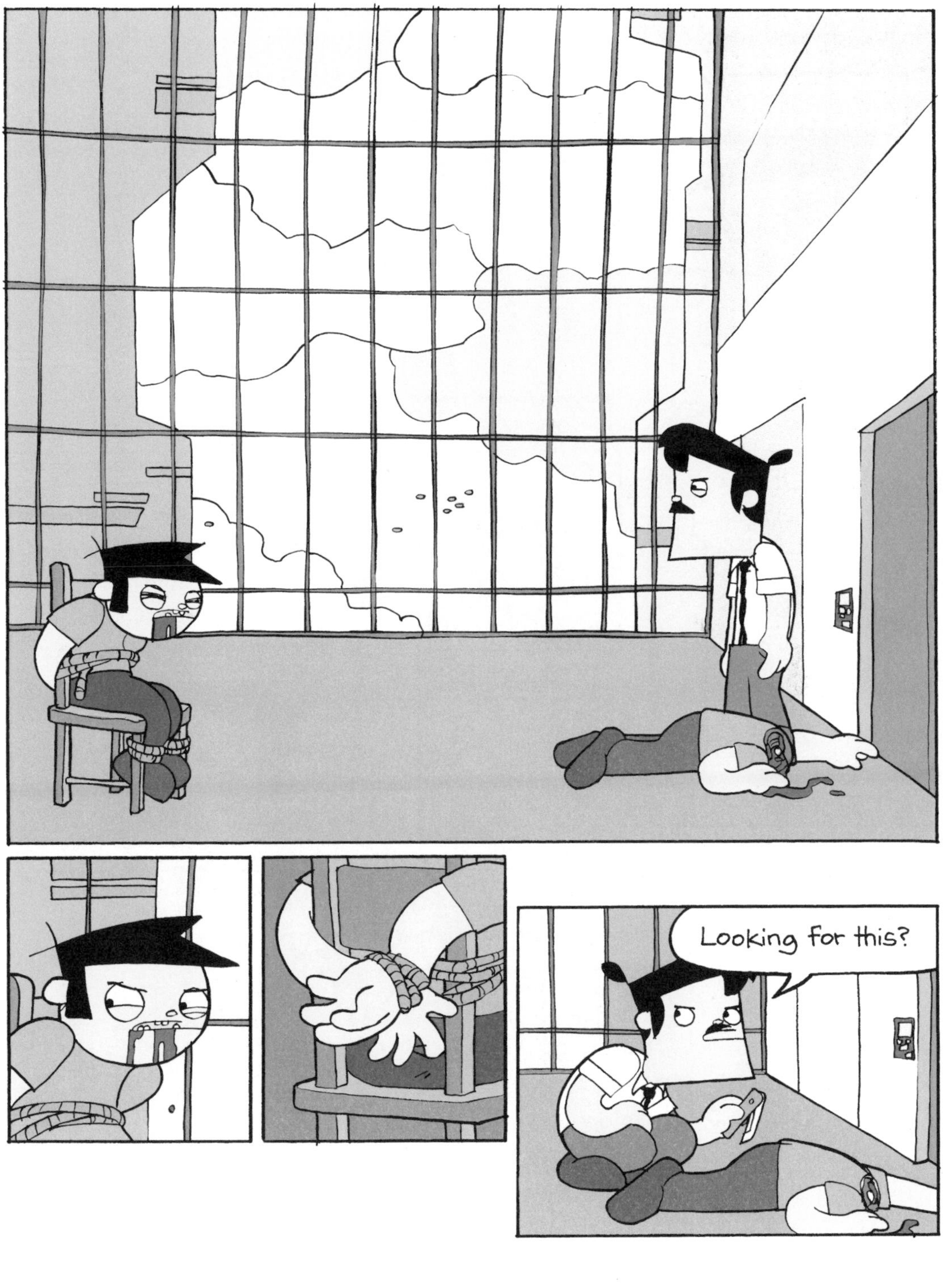
Looking for this?

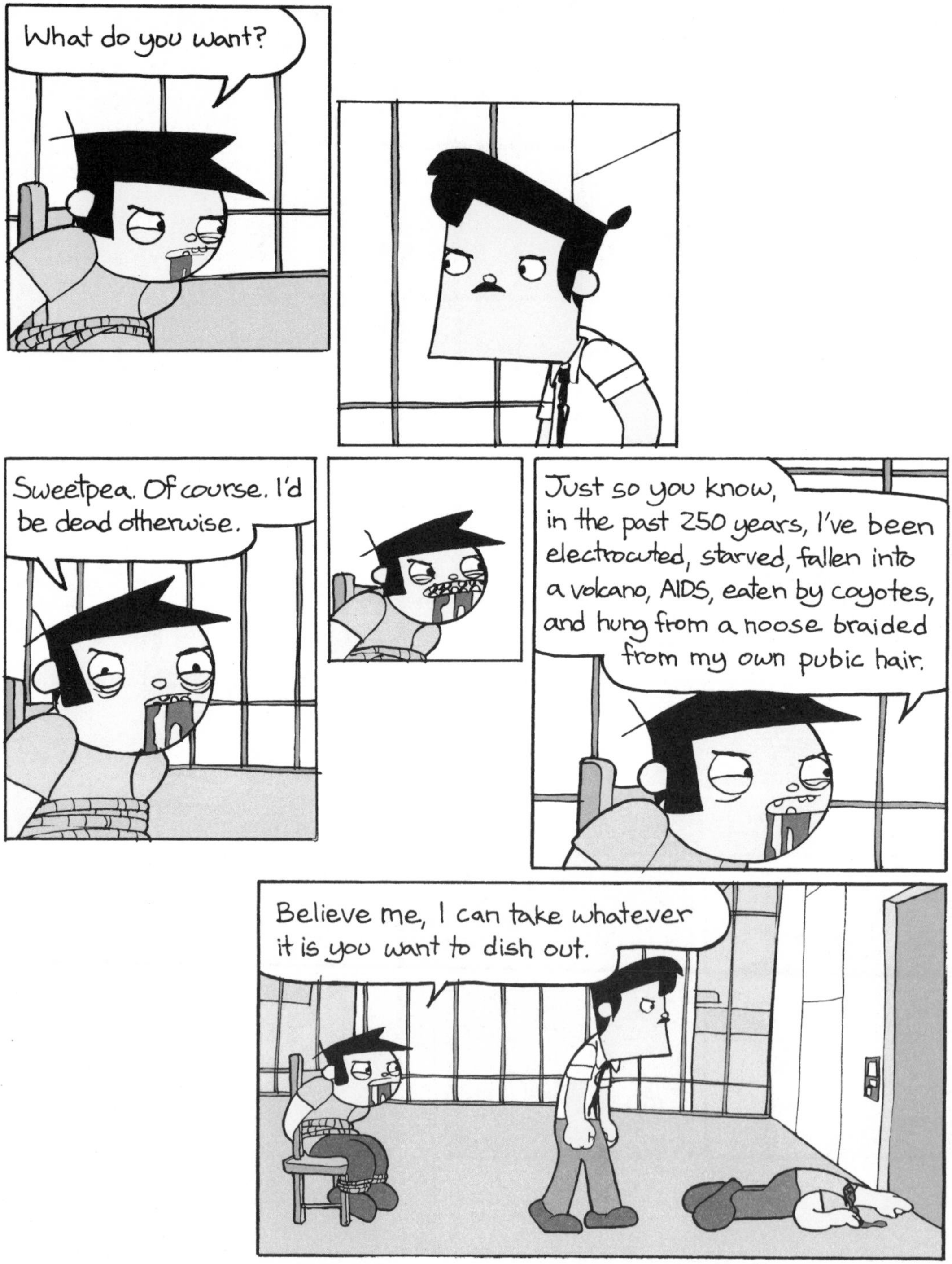
What do you want?
Sweetpea. Of course. I'd be dead otherwise.
Just so you know, in the past 250 years, I've been electrocuted, starved, fallen into a volcano, AIDS, eaten by coyotes, and hung from a noose braided from my own pubic hair.
Believe me, I can take whatever it is you want to dish out.

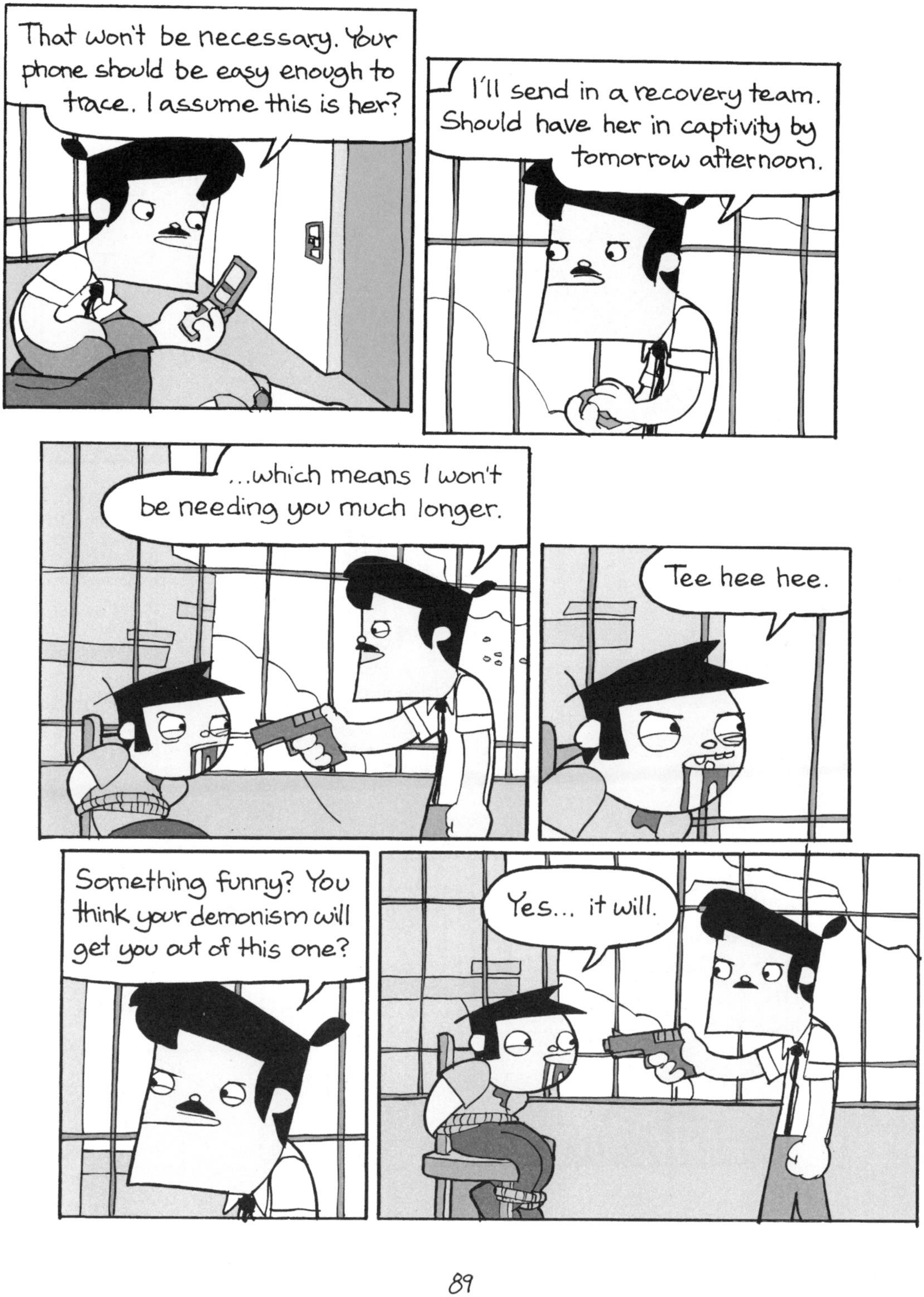
That won't be necessary. Your phone should be easy enough to trace. I assume this is her?
I'll send in a recovery team. Should have her in captivity by tomorrow afternoon.
...which means I won't be needing you much longer.
Tee hee hee.
Something funny? You think your demonism will get you out of this one?
Yes... it will.

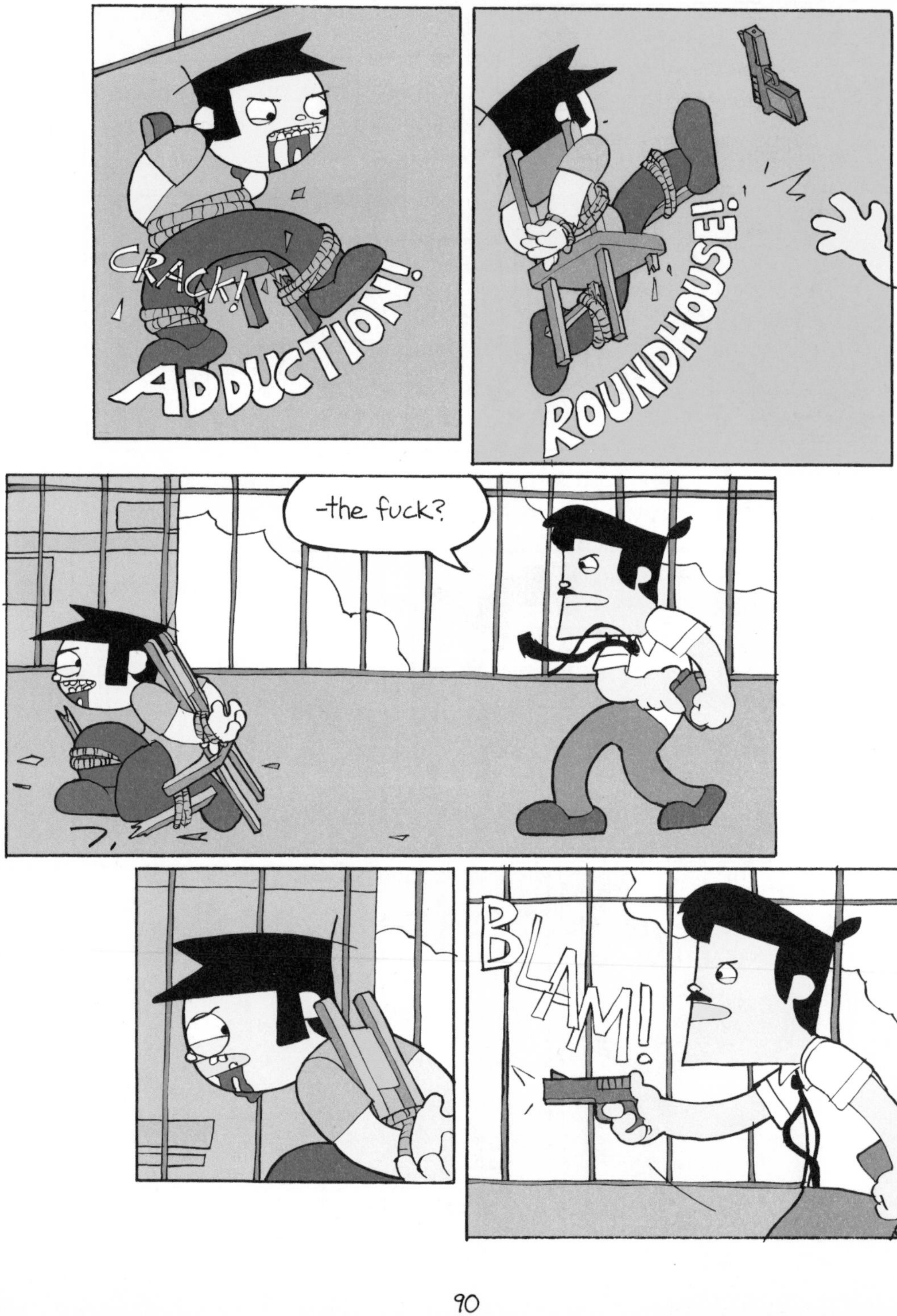
CRACK!
ADDUCTION!
ROUNDHOUSE!
-the fuck?
BLAM!

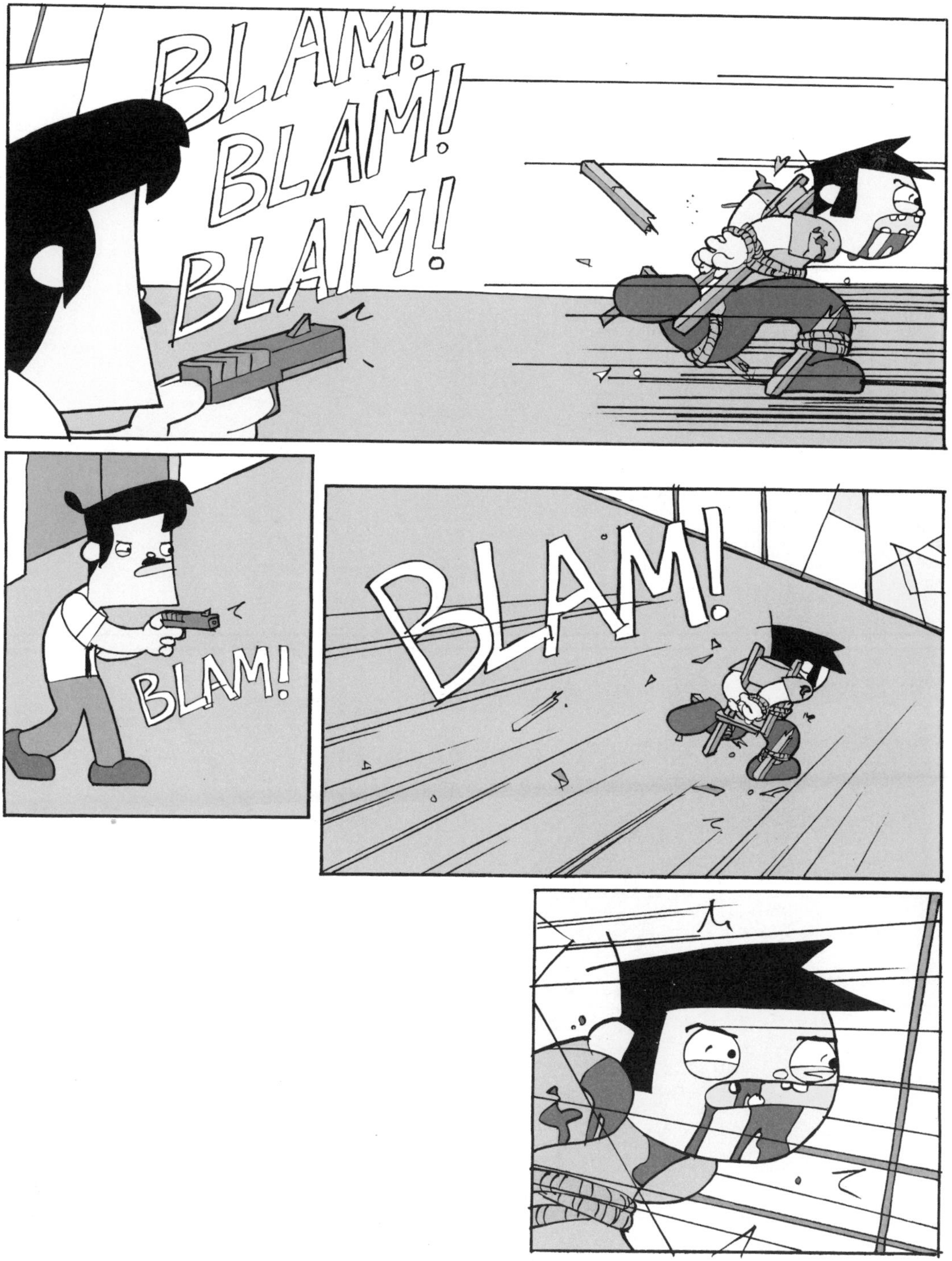
BLAM! BLAM! BLAM!
BLAM!
BLAM!

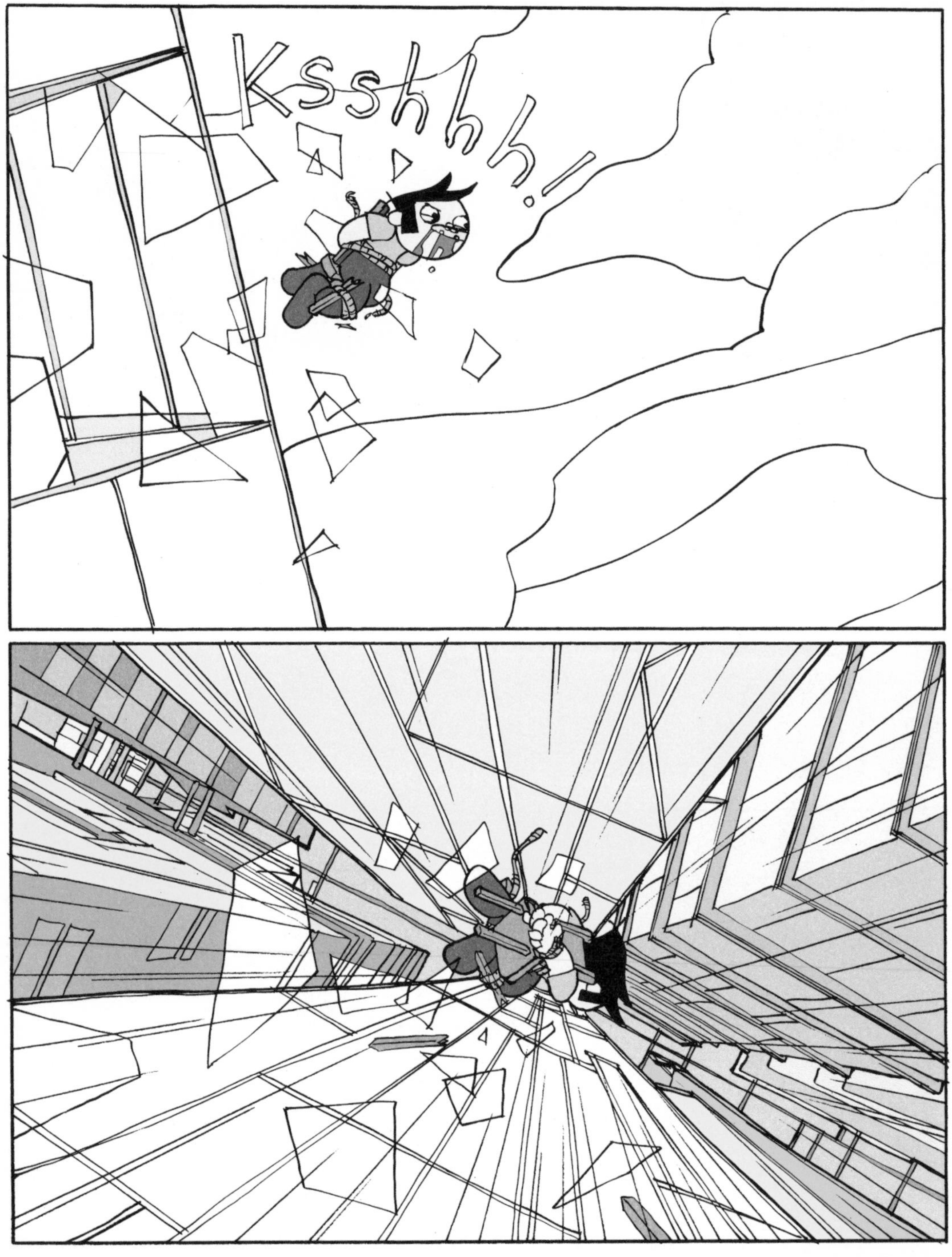
Ksshhh!!

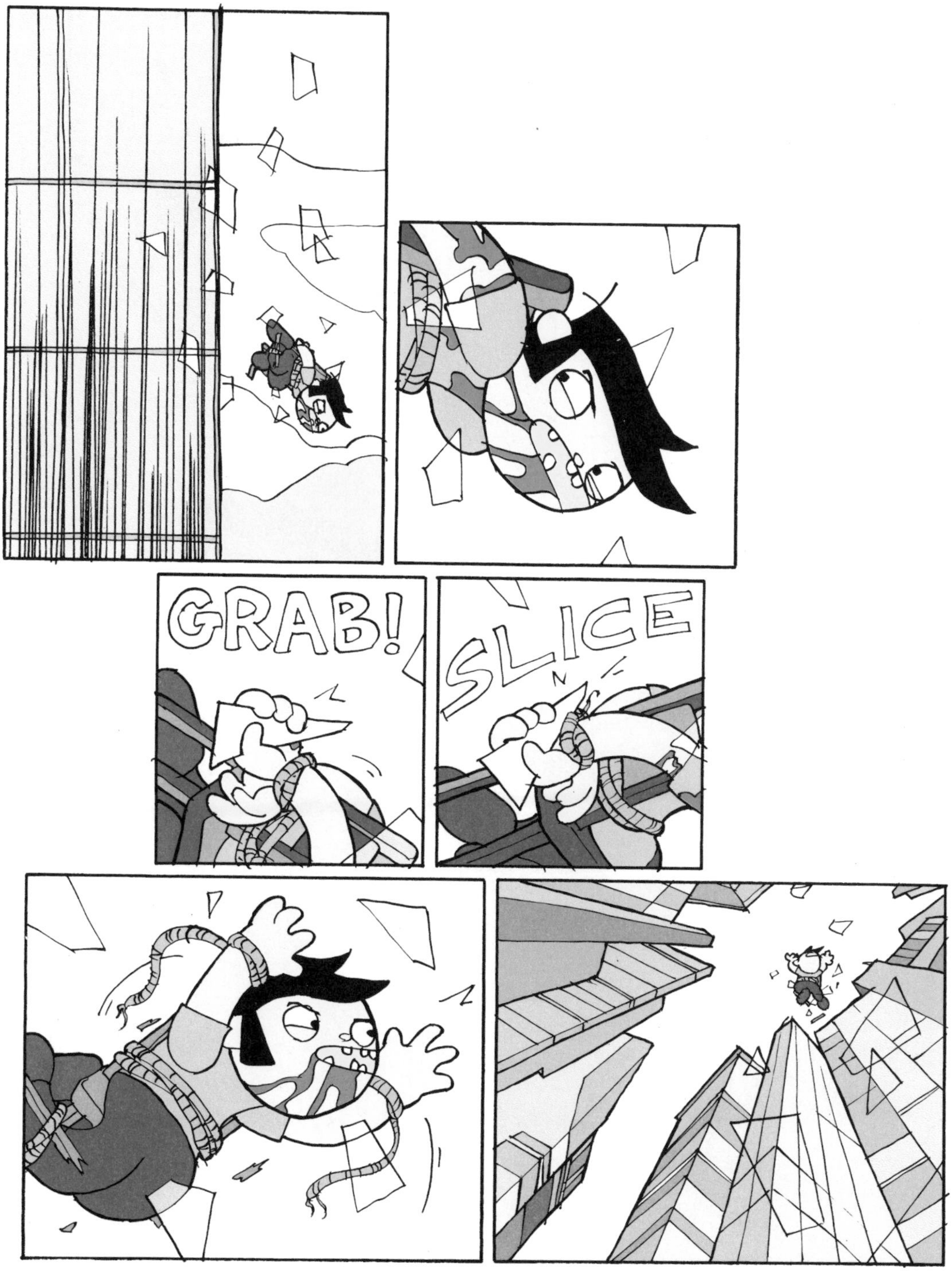
GRAB!
SLICE

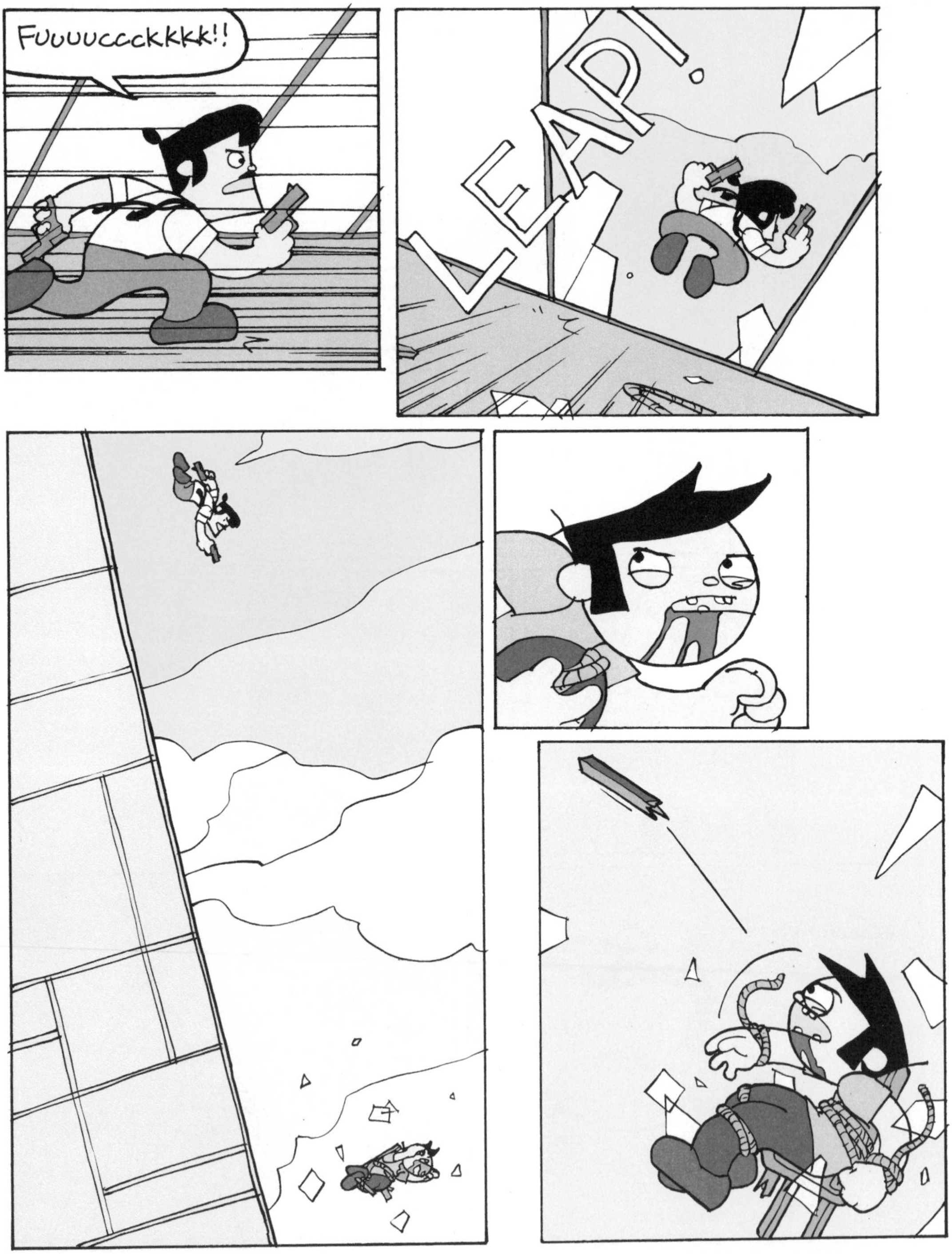
FUUUUCCCCKKKK!!
LEAP!

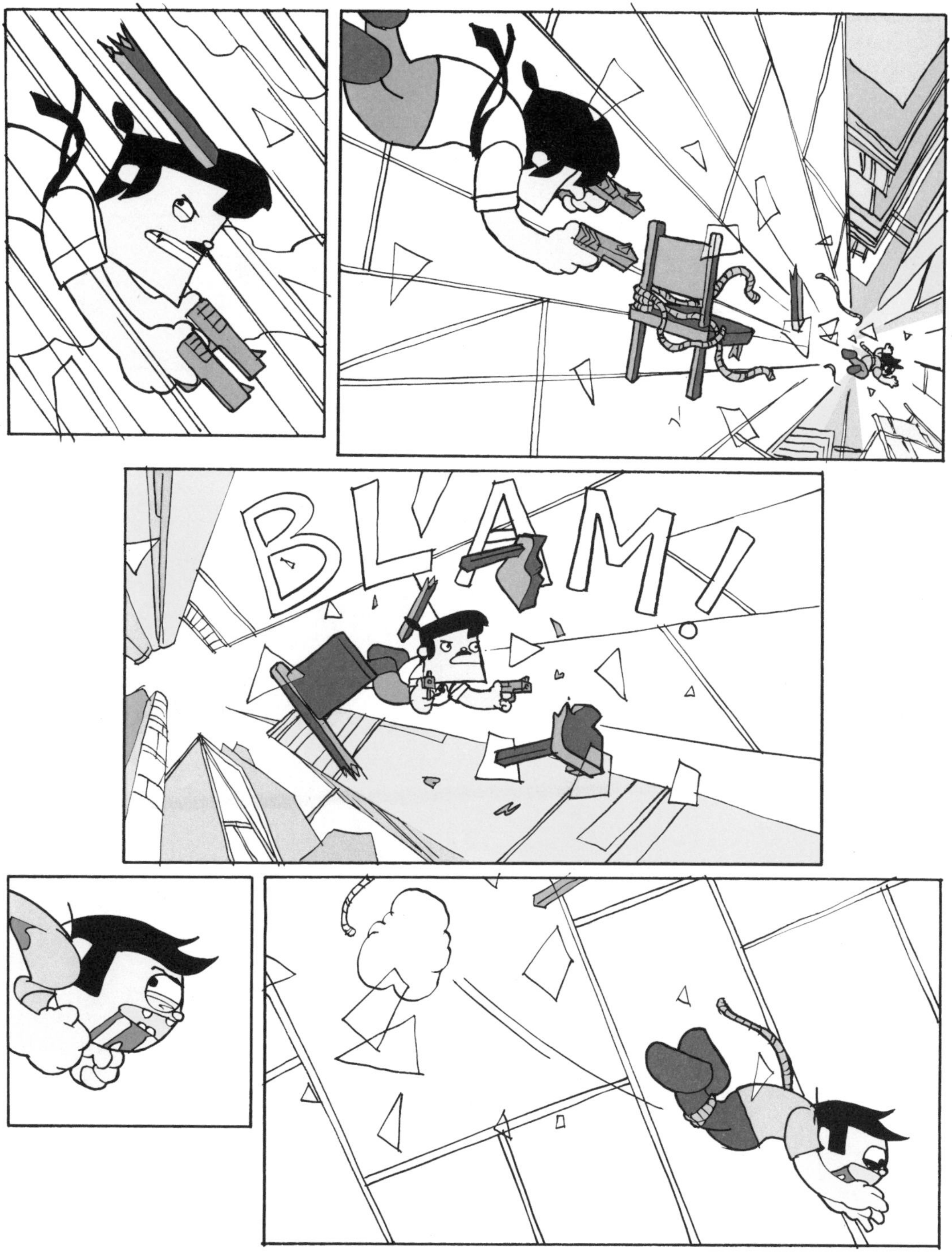
BLAM!

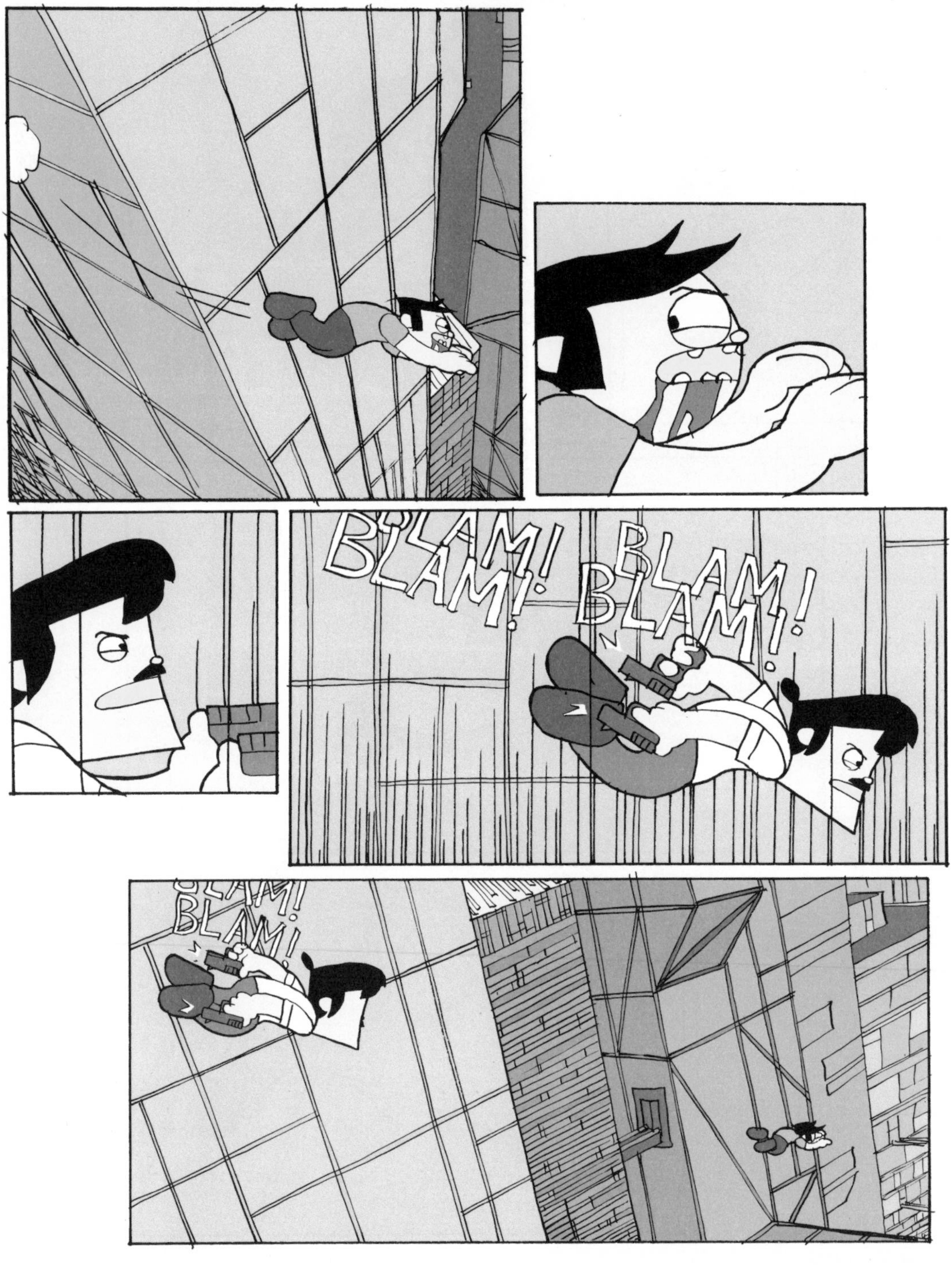
BLAM! BLAM!
BLAM! BLAM!
BLAM! BLAM!

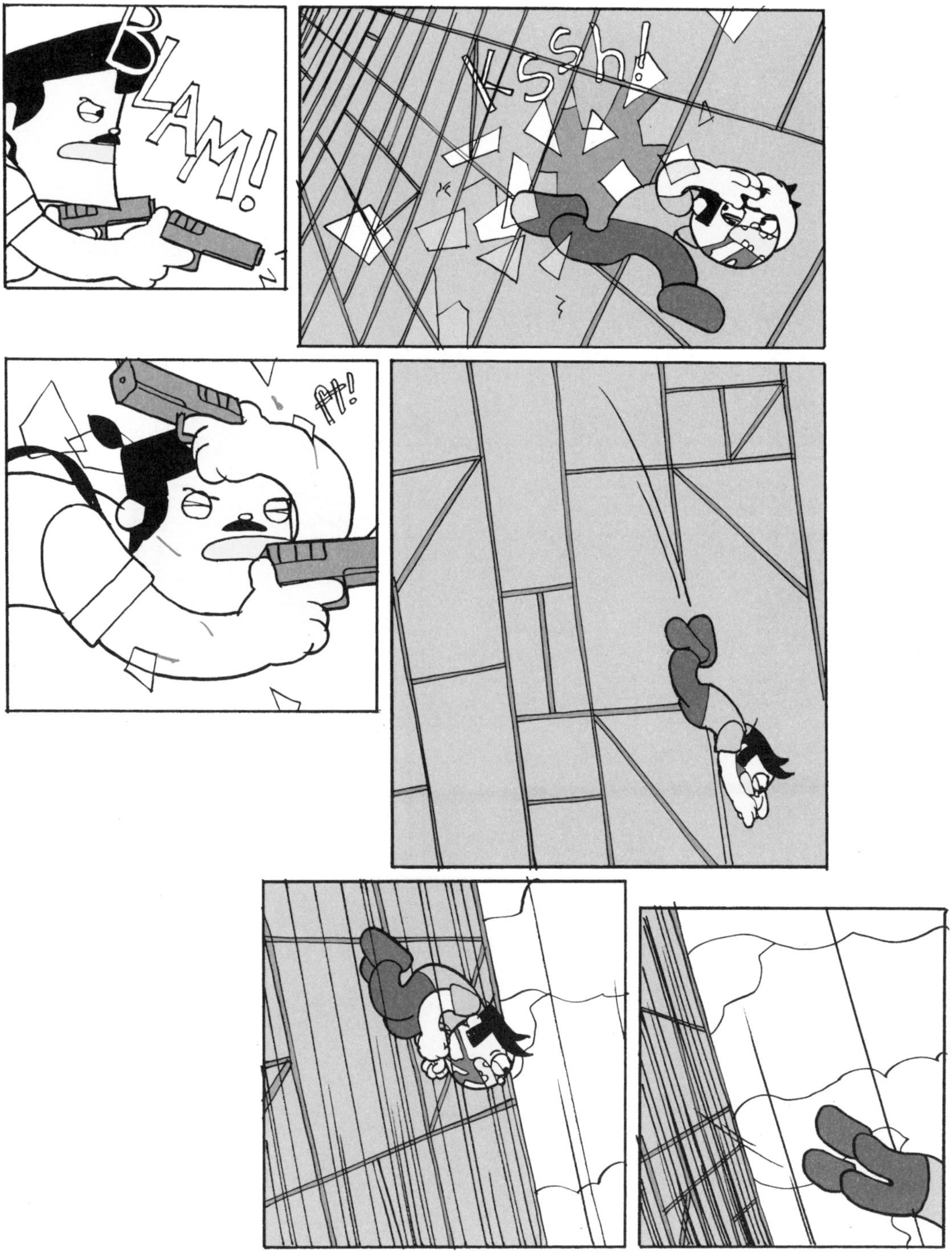
BLAM!
KSSH!
FT!

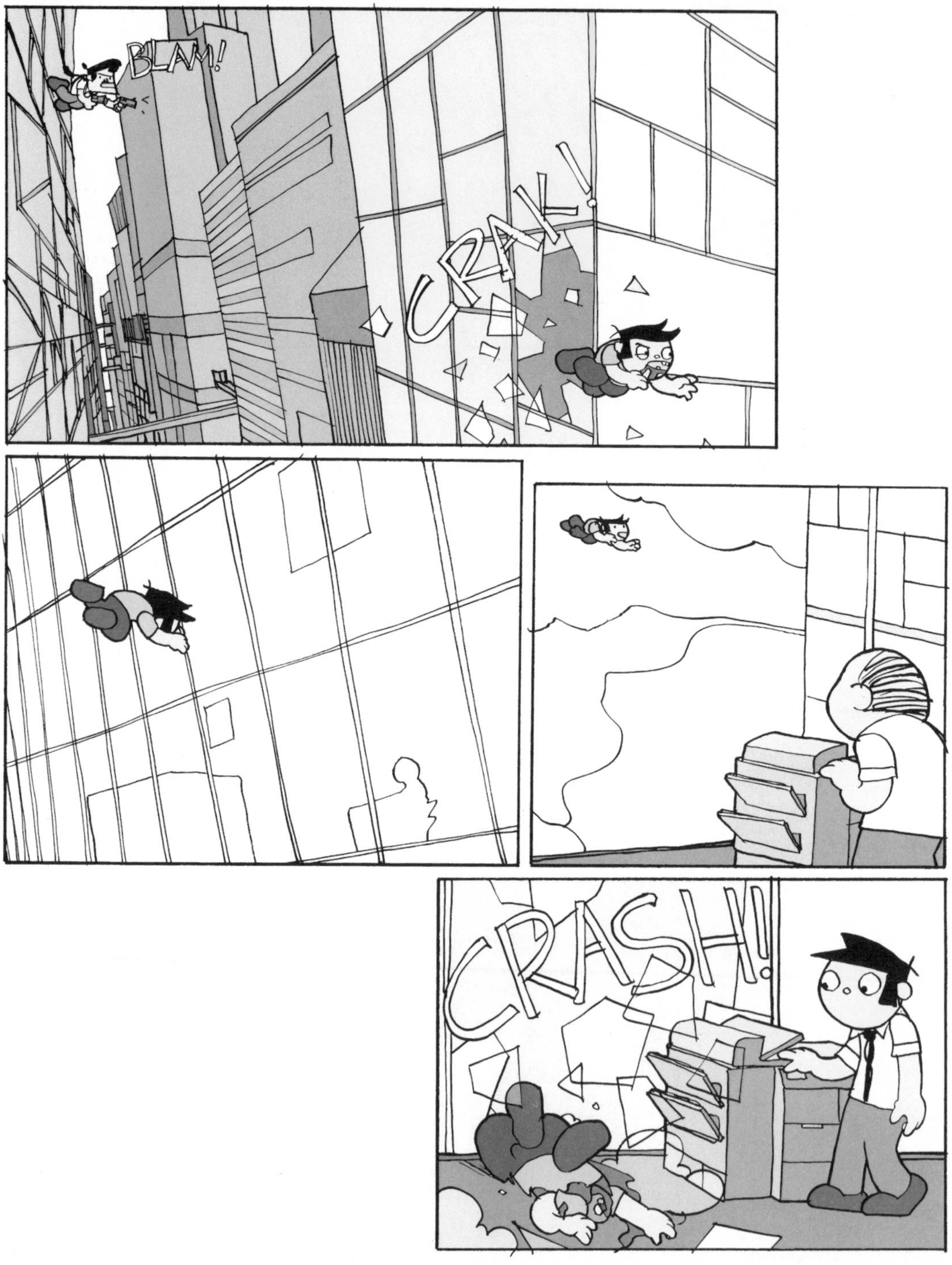
BLAM!
CRAK!
CRASH!

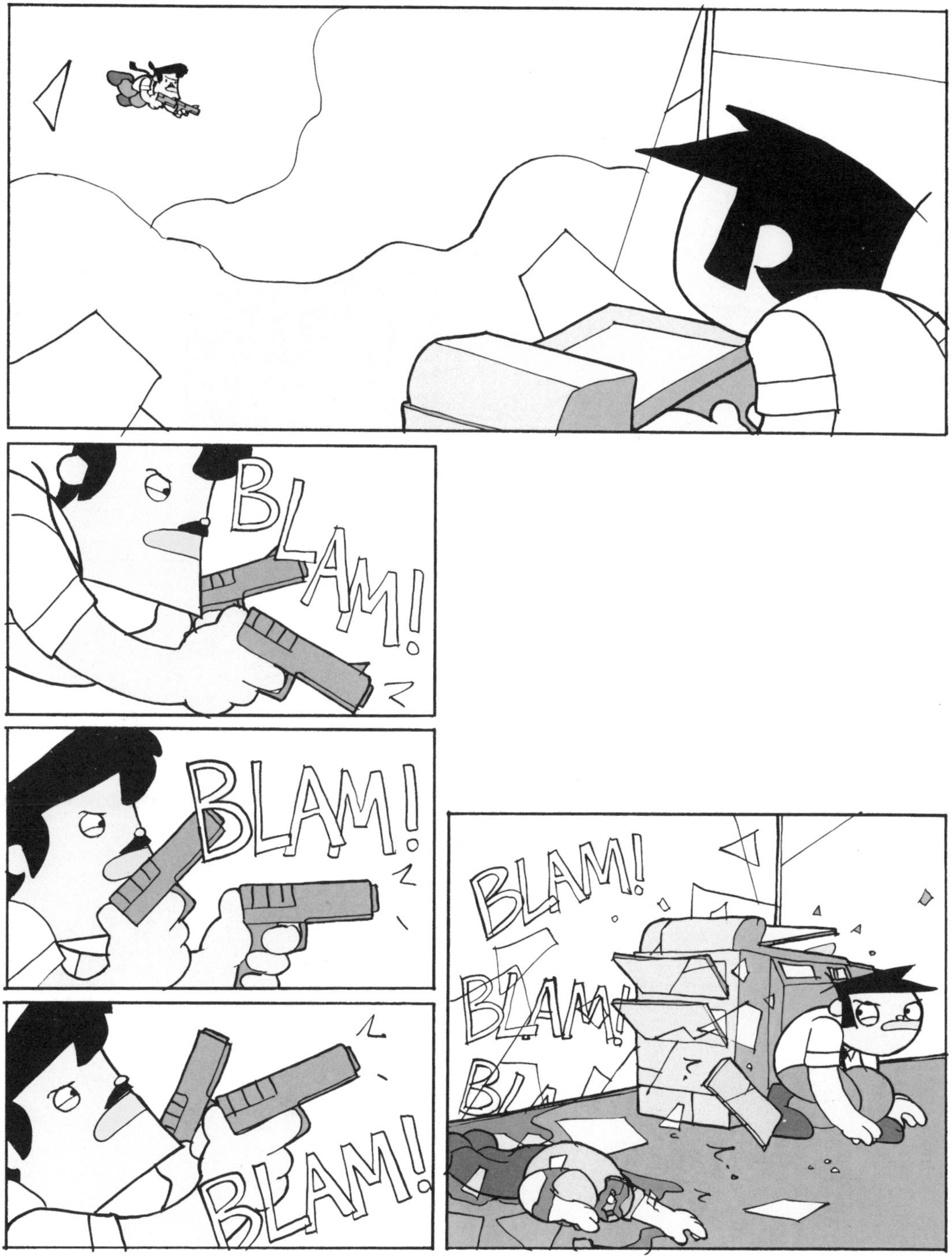
BLAM!
BLAM!
BLAM!
BLAM!
BLAM!
BLAM!

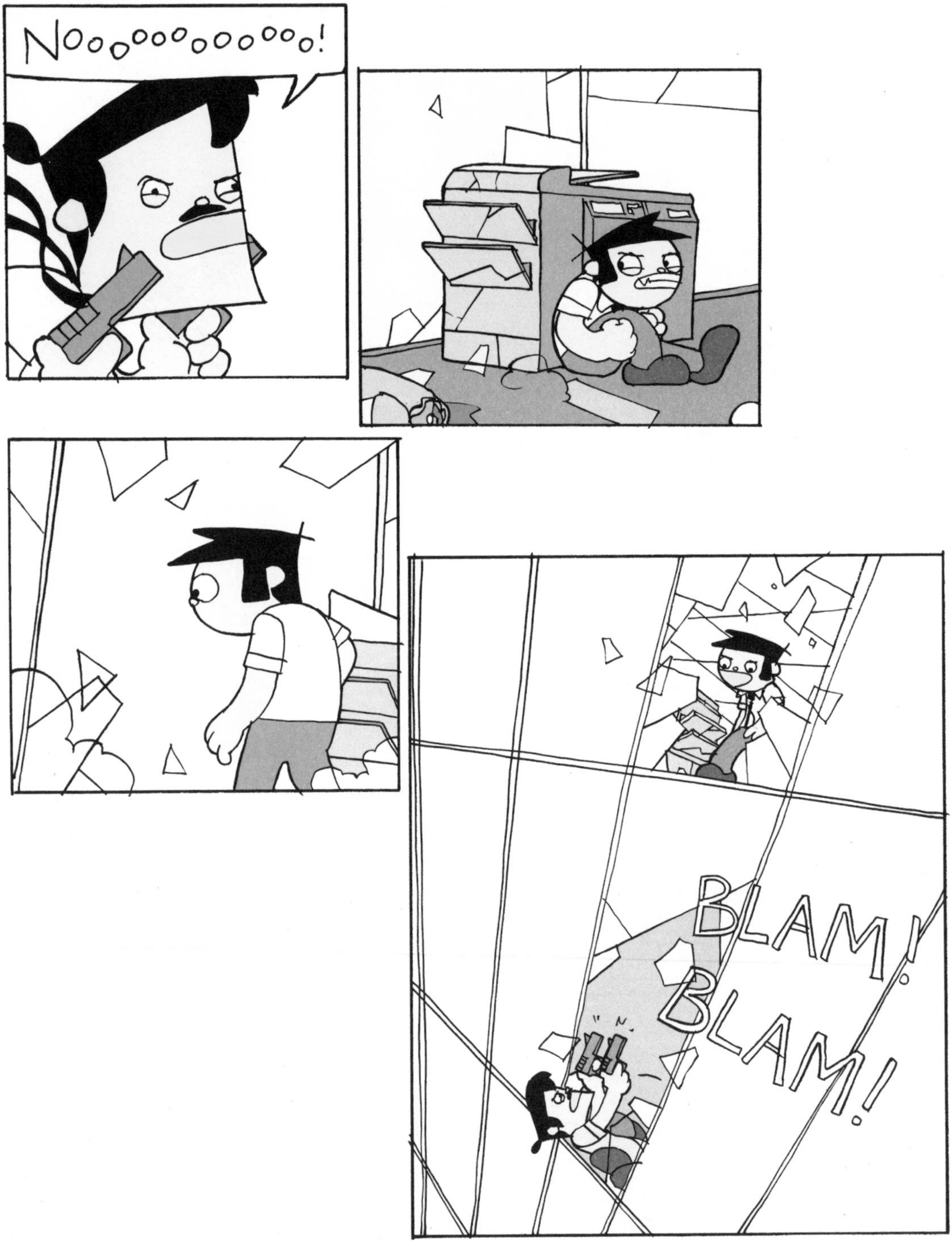
Nooooooooooooo!
BLAM!
BLAM!

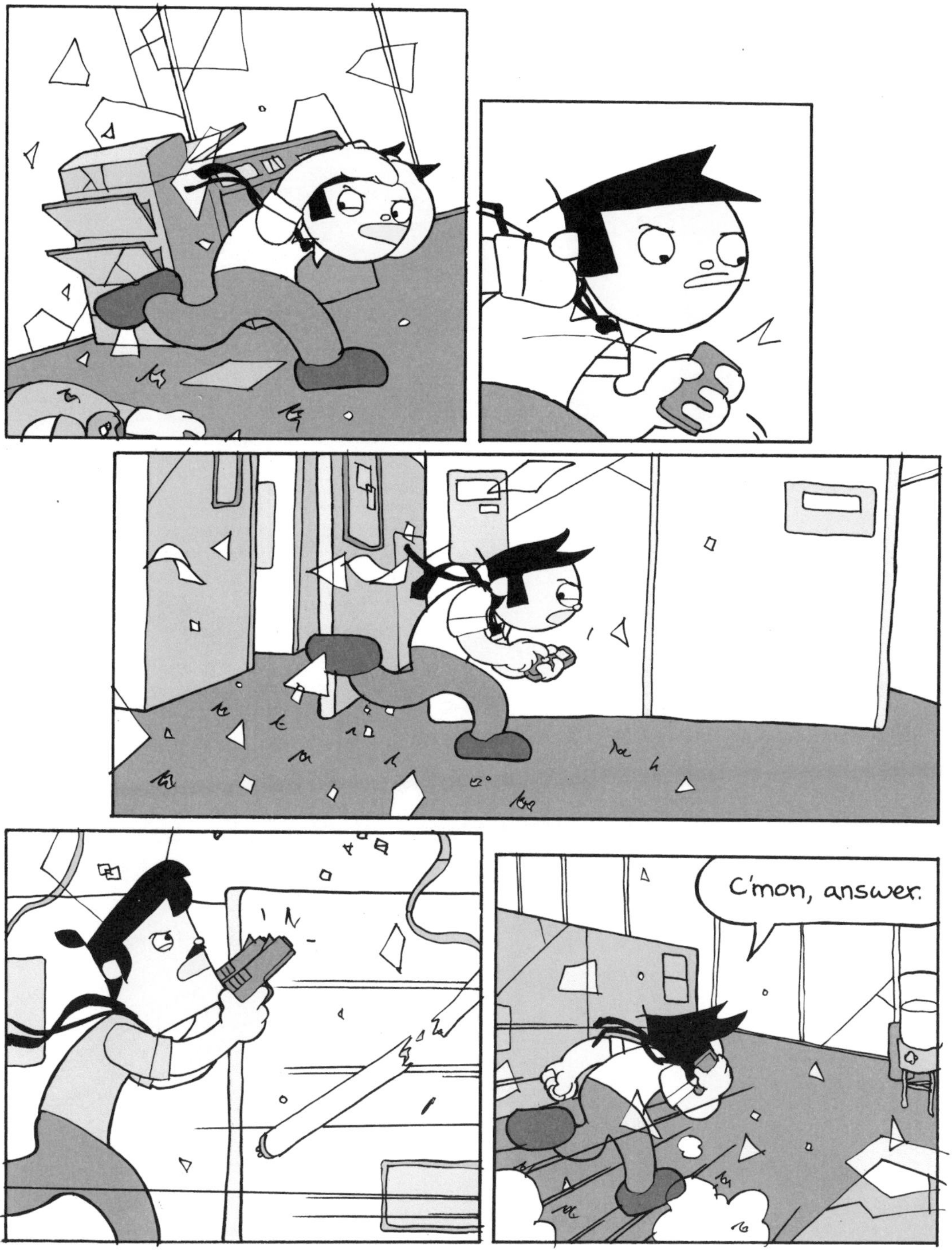
C'mon, answer.

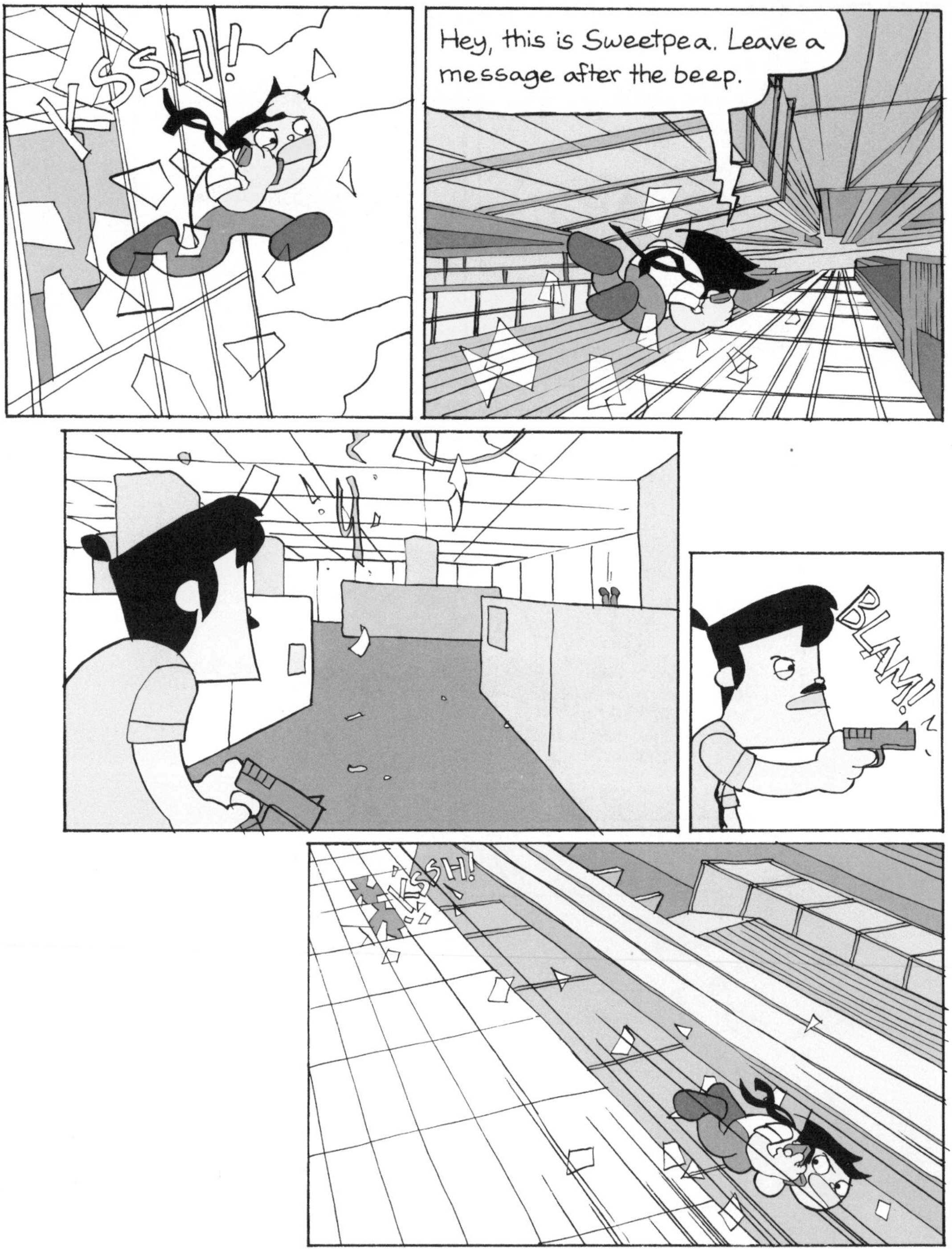

KSSH!
Hey, this is Sweetpea. Leave a message after the beep.
BLAM!
KSSH!

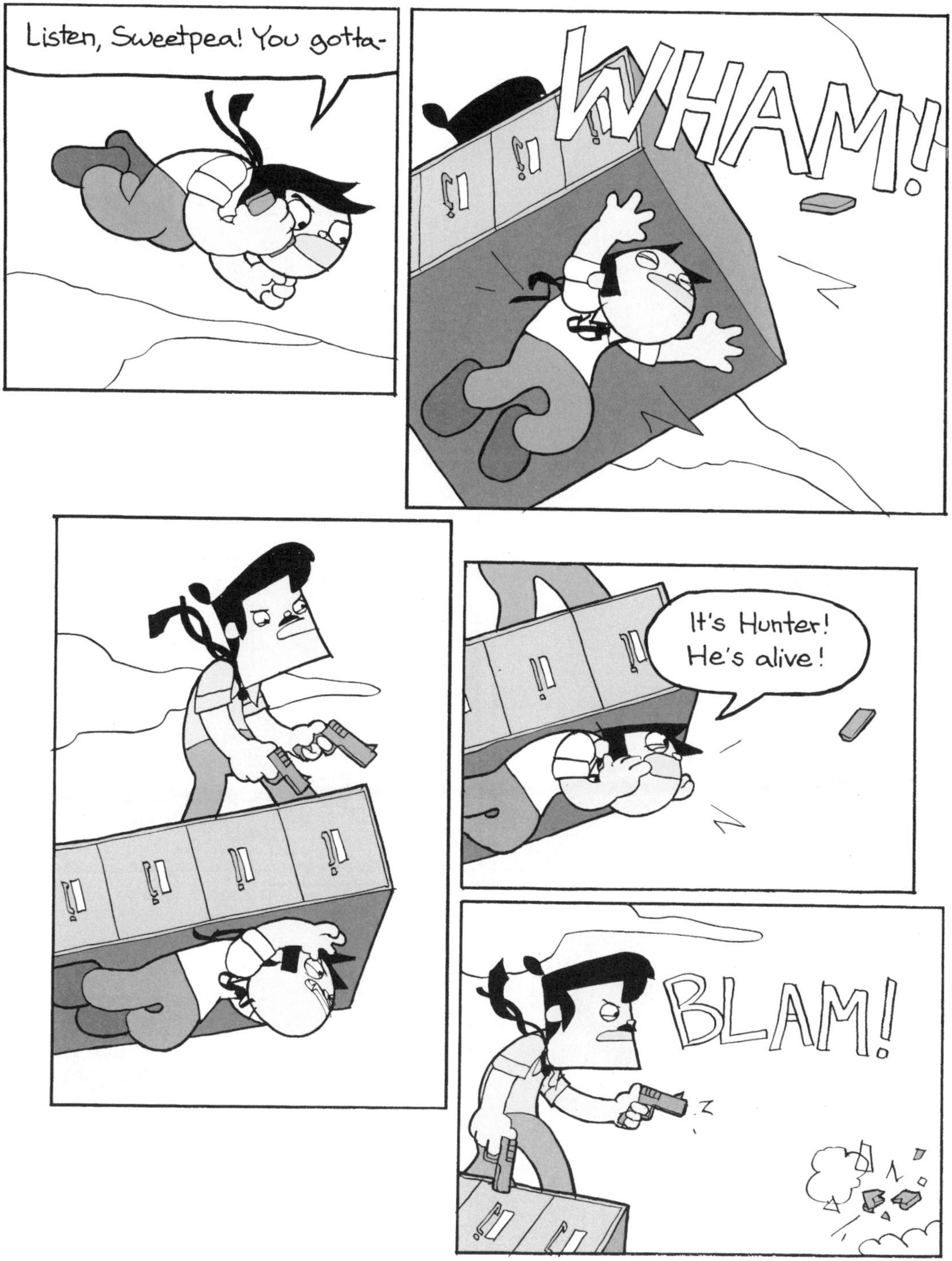
Listen, Sweetpea! You gotta-
WHAM!
It's Hunter! He's alive!
BLAM!

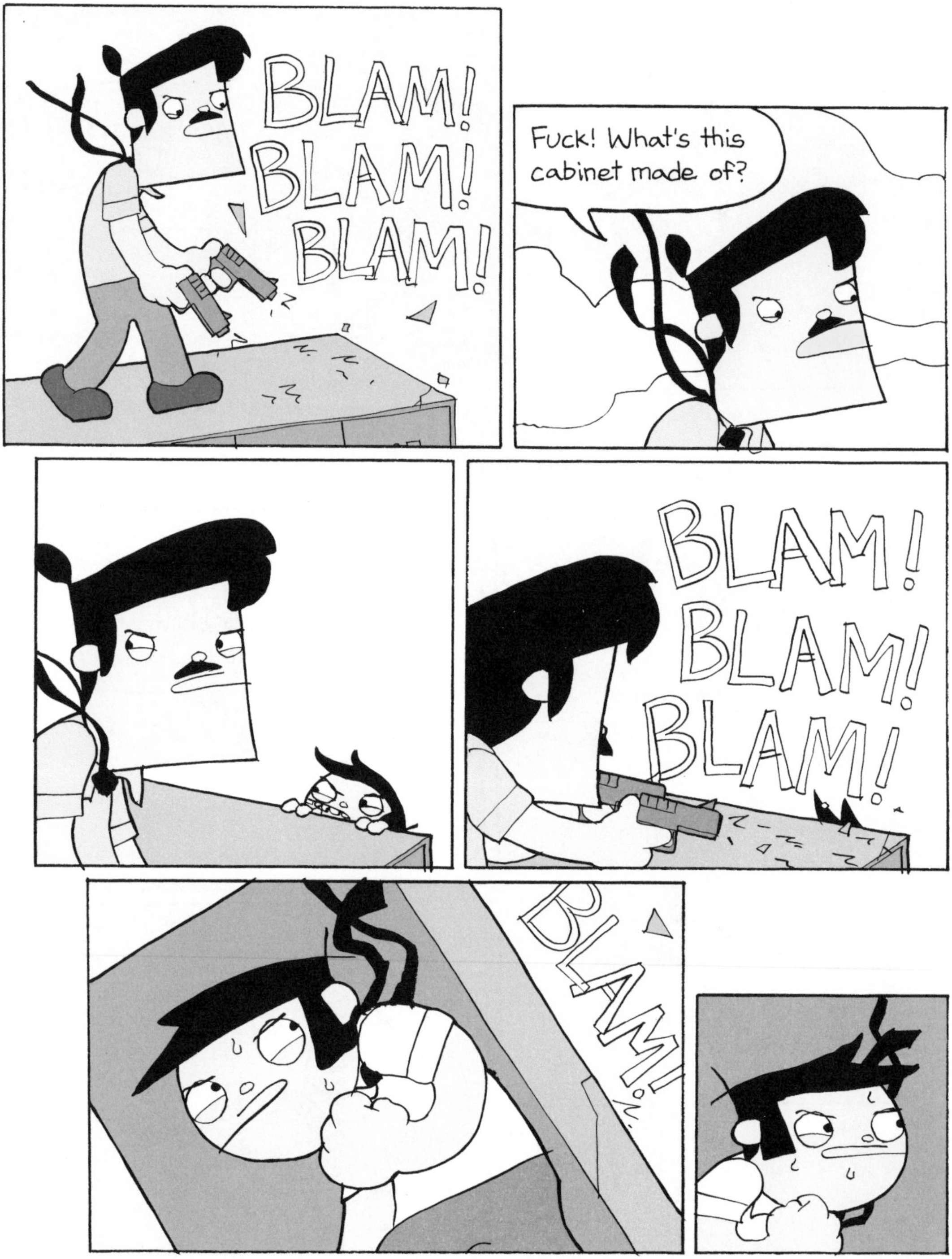
BLAM!
BLAM!
BLAM!
Fuck! What's this cabinet made of?
BLAM!
BLAM!
BLAM!
BLAM!

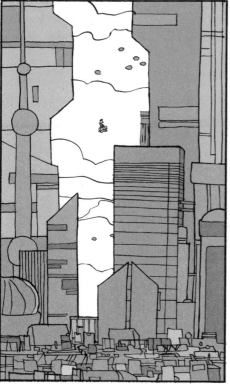

Shit! I'm running out of altitude.

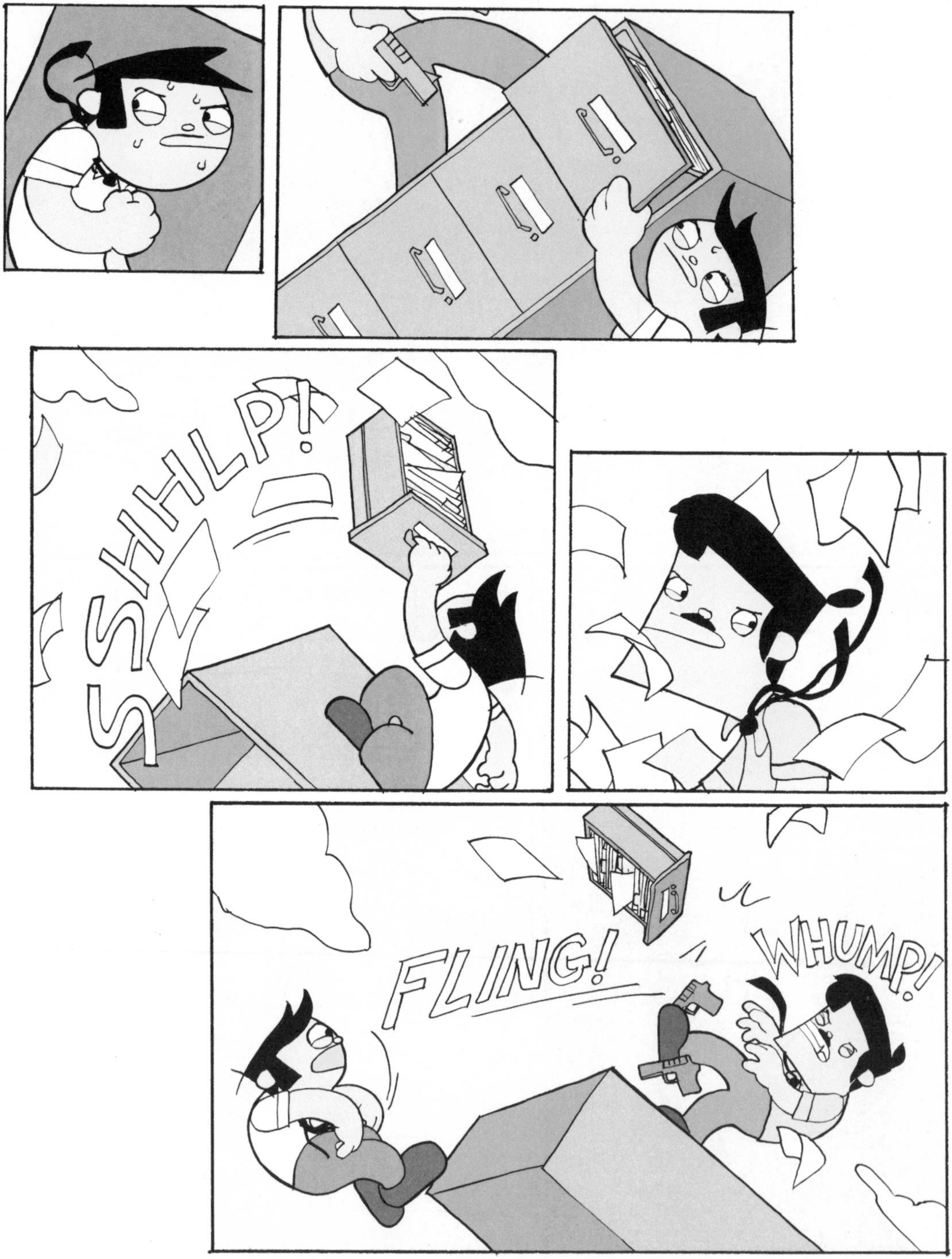
SHHLP!
FLING!
WHUMP!

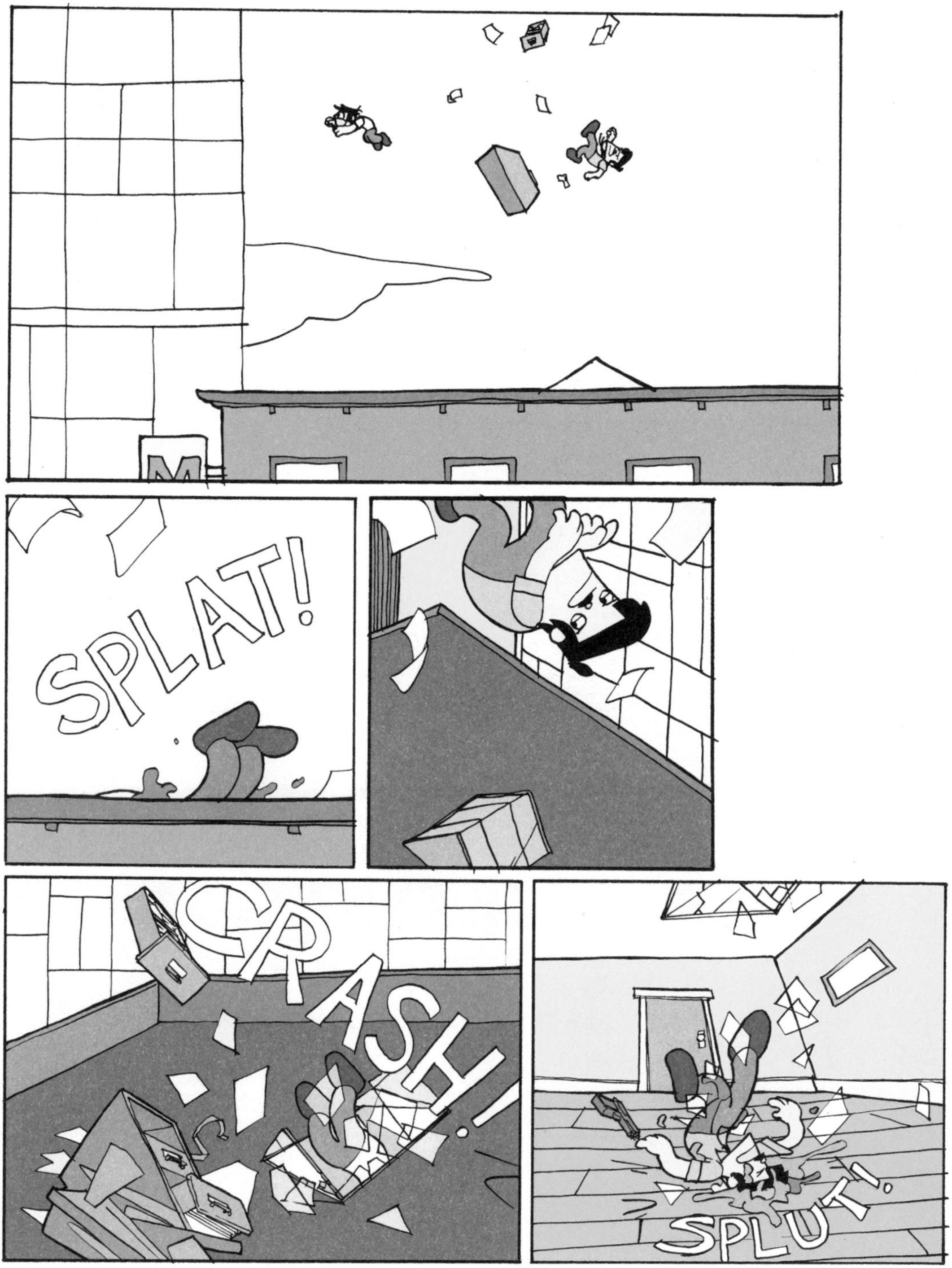
SPLAT!
CRASH!
SPLUT!

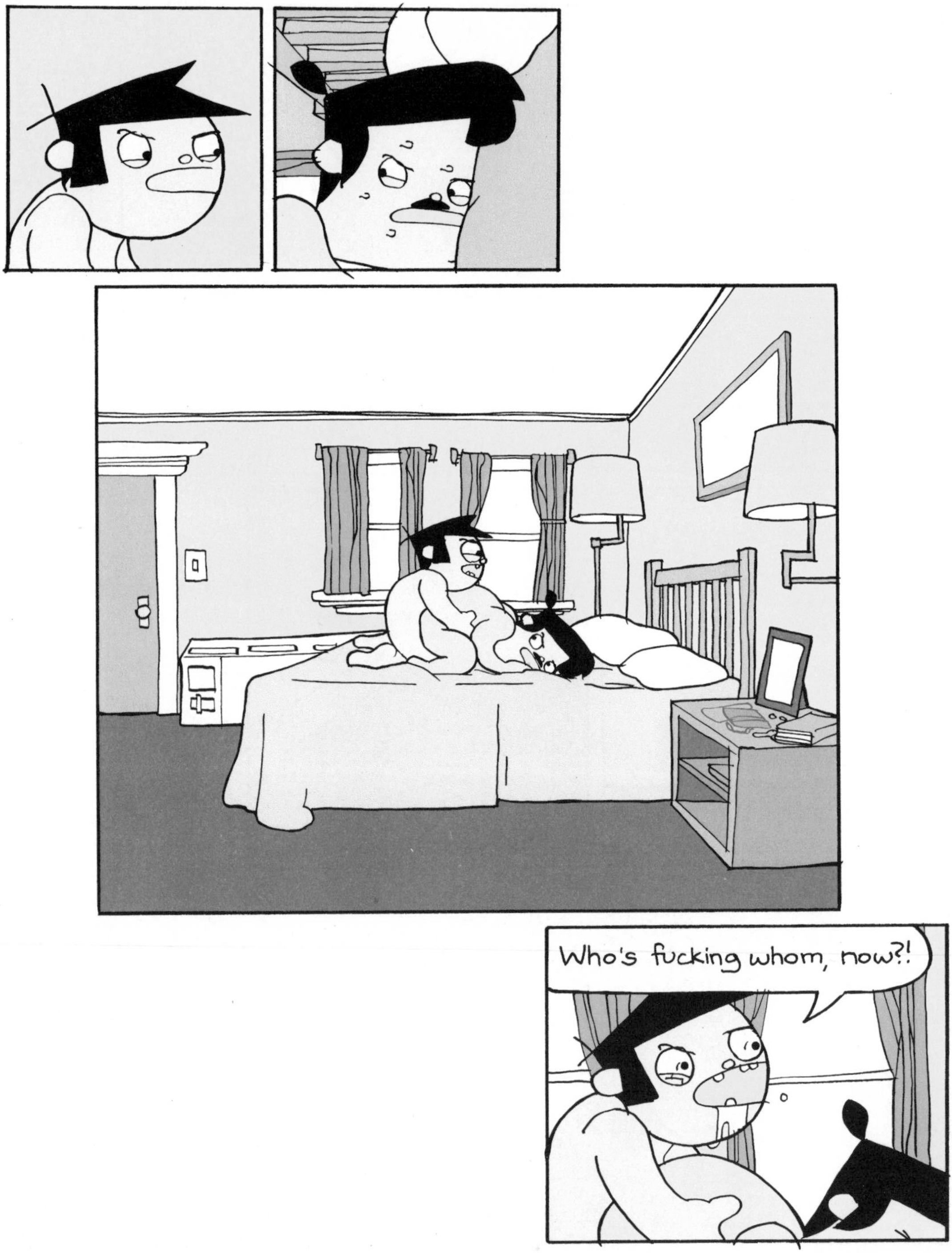
Who's fucking whom, now?!

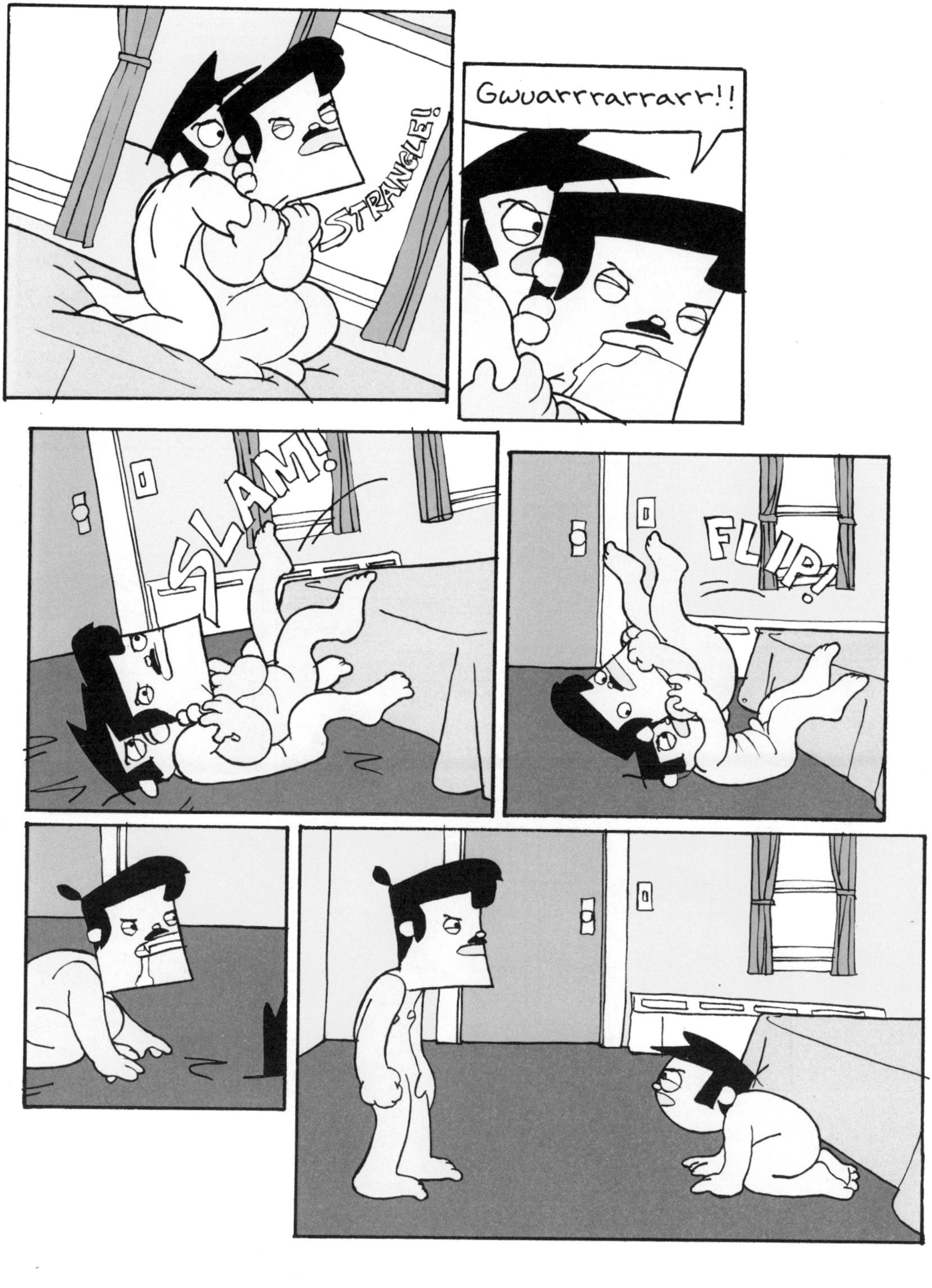
STRANGLE!
Gwuarrrarrarr!!
SLAM!
FLIP!

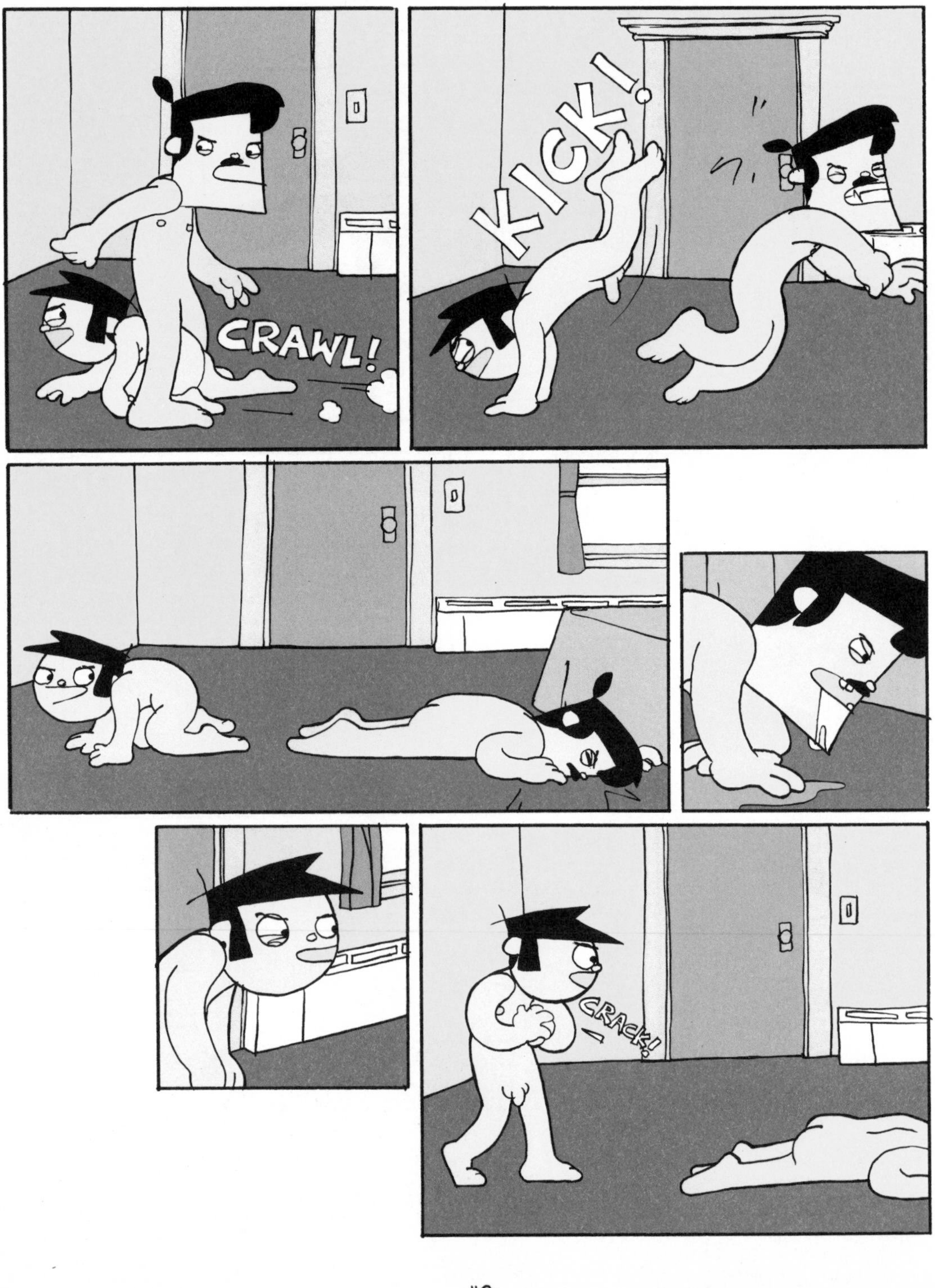
CRAWL!
KICK!
CRACK!

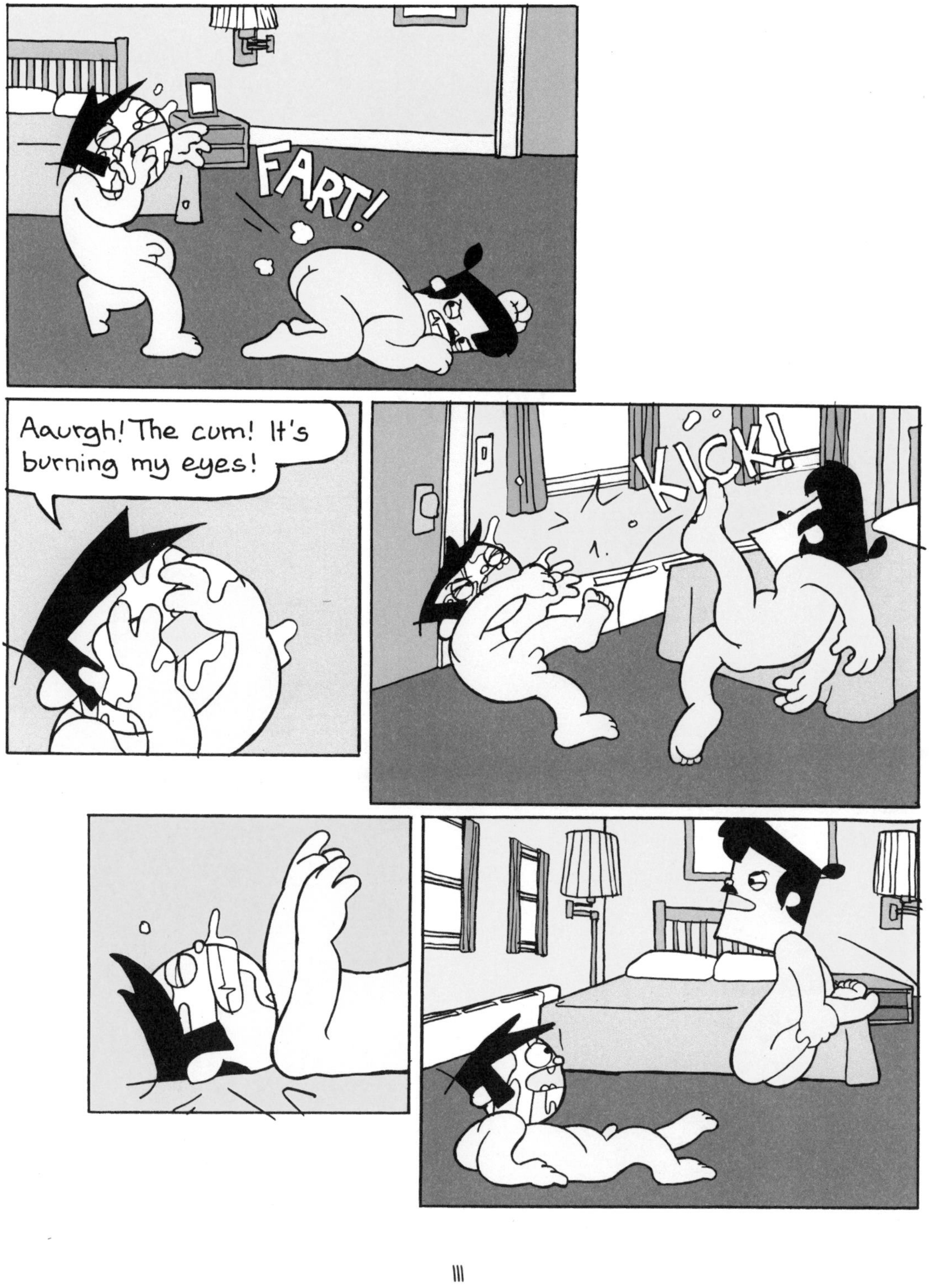
FART!
Aaurgh! The cum! It's burning my eyes!
KICK!

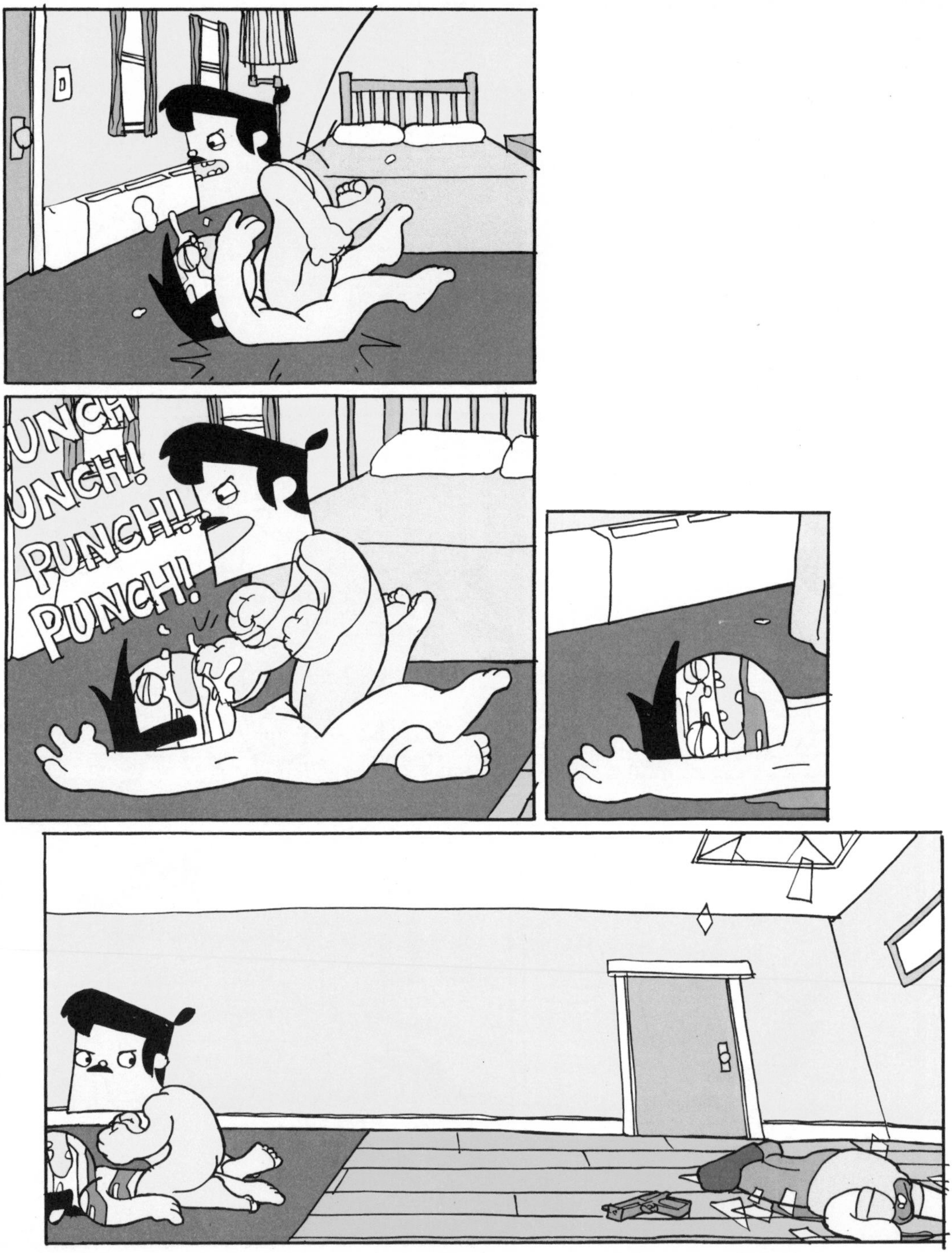
UNCH
UNCH!
PUNCH!
PUNCH!

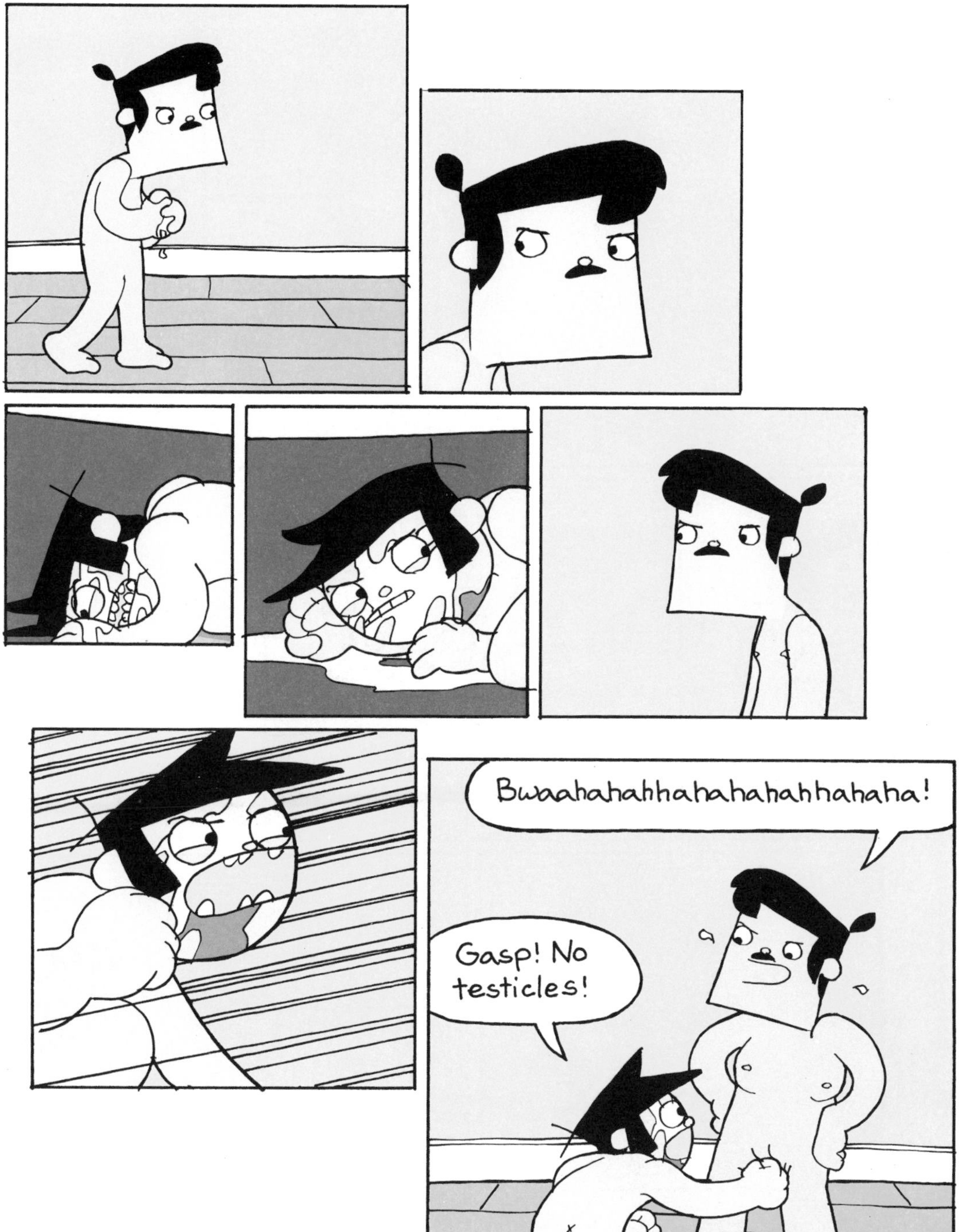
Bwaahahahhahahahahhahaha!
Gasp! No testicles!

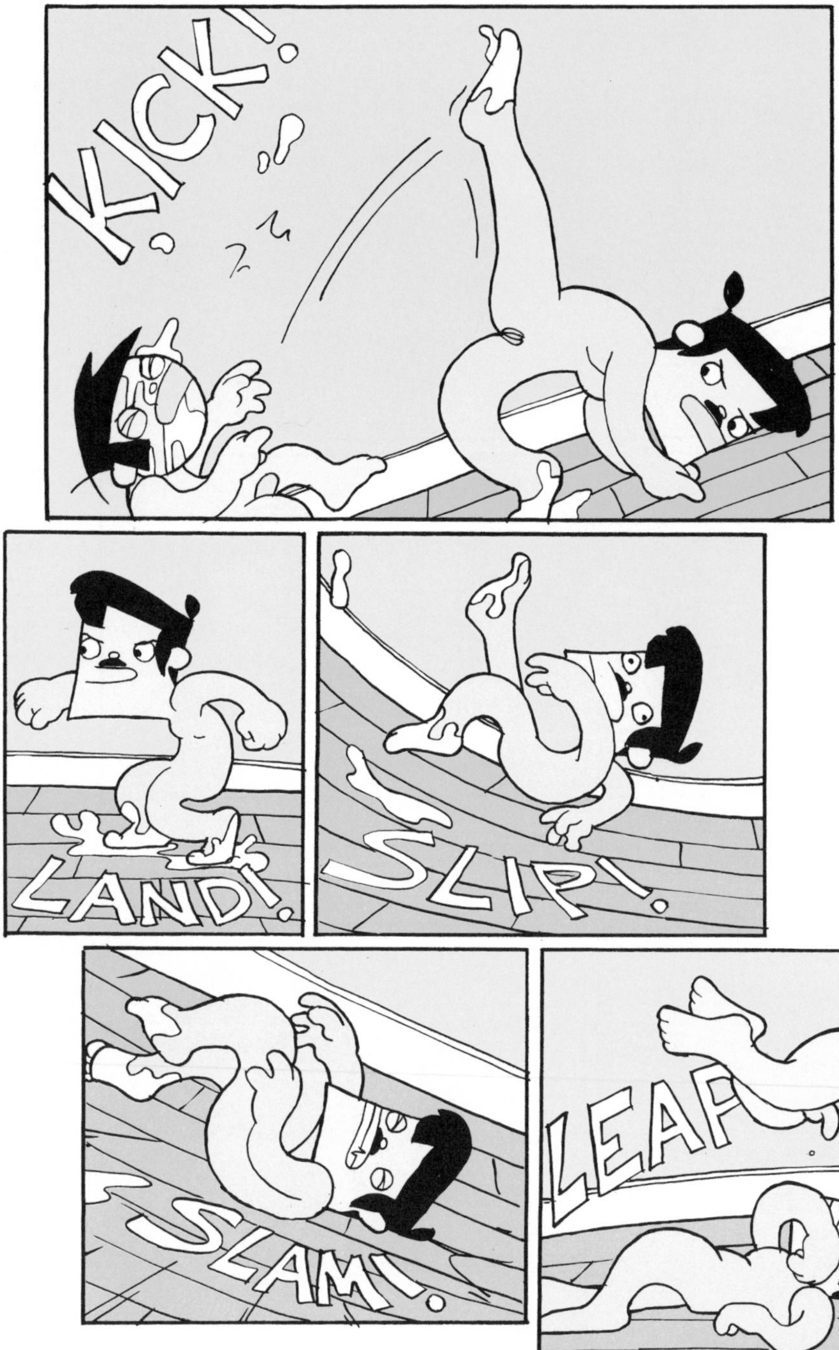
KICK!
LAND!
SLIP!
SLAM!
LEAP

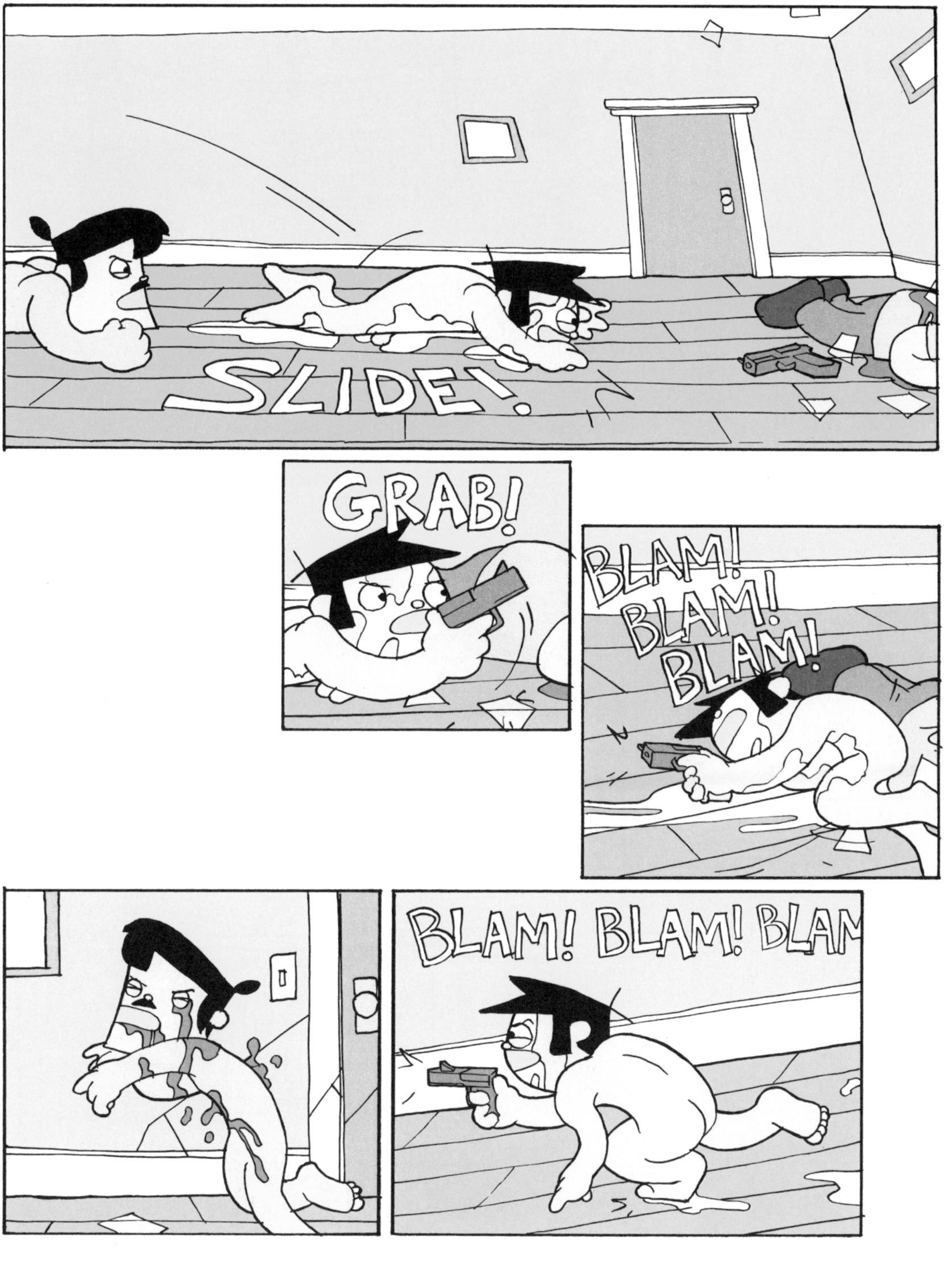
SLIDE!
GRAB!
BLAM!
BLAM!
BLAM!
BLAM! BLAM! BLAM

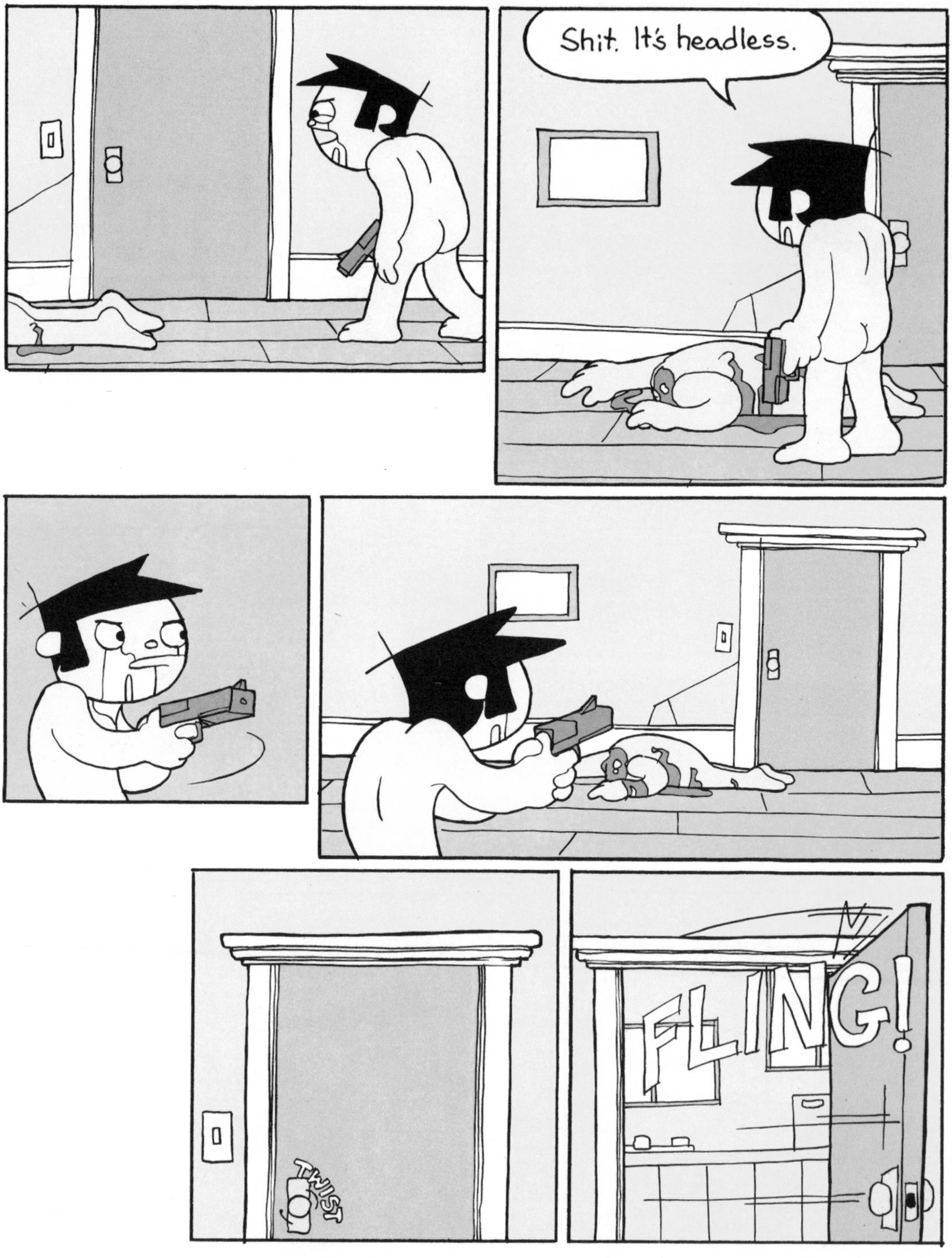
Shit. It's headless.
TWIST
FLING!

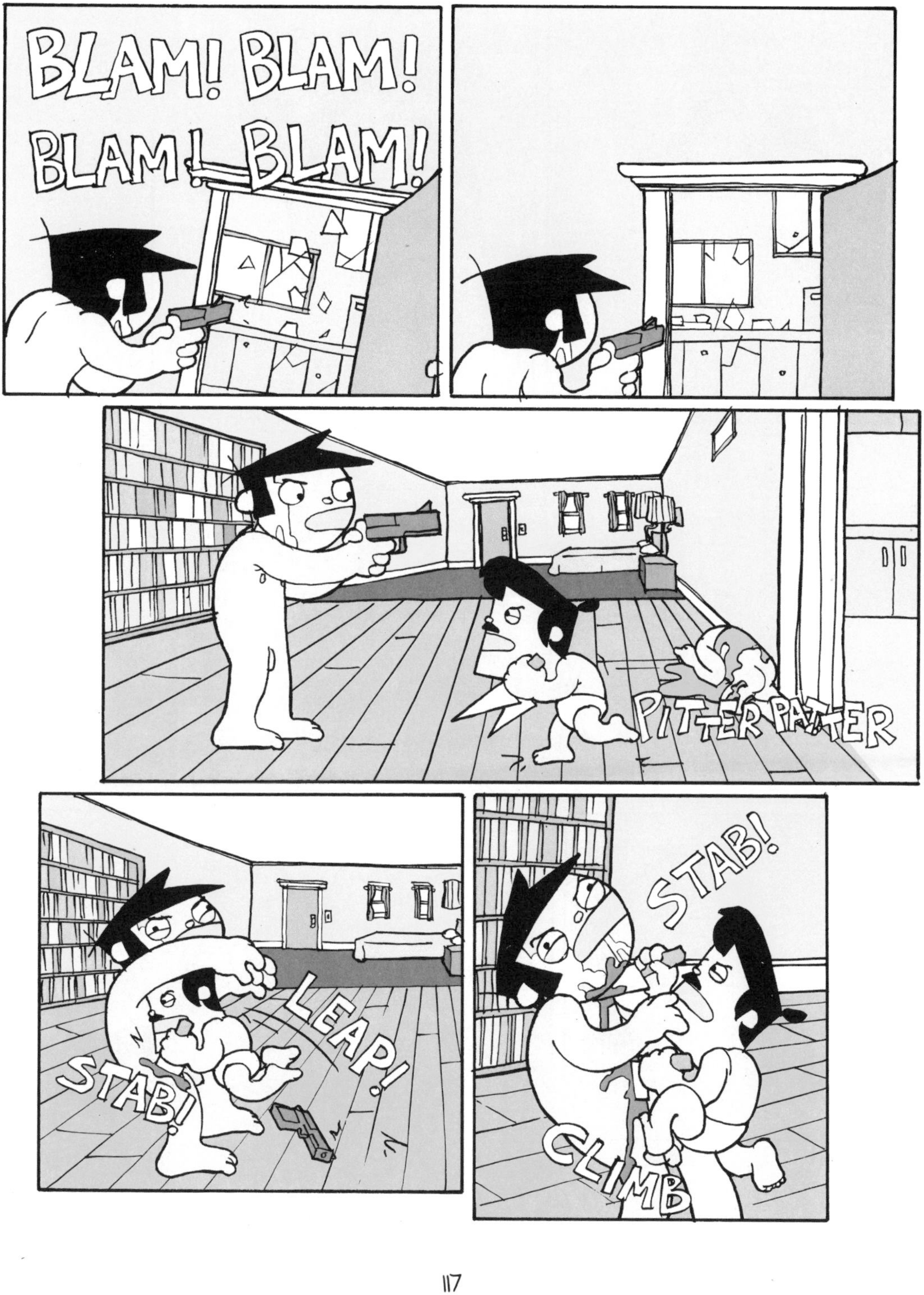
BLAM! BLAM!
BLAM! BLAM!
PITTER PATTER
LEAP!
STAB!
STAB!
CLIMB

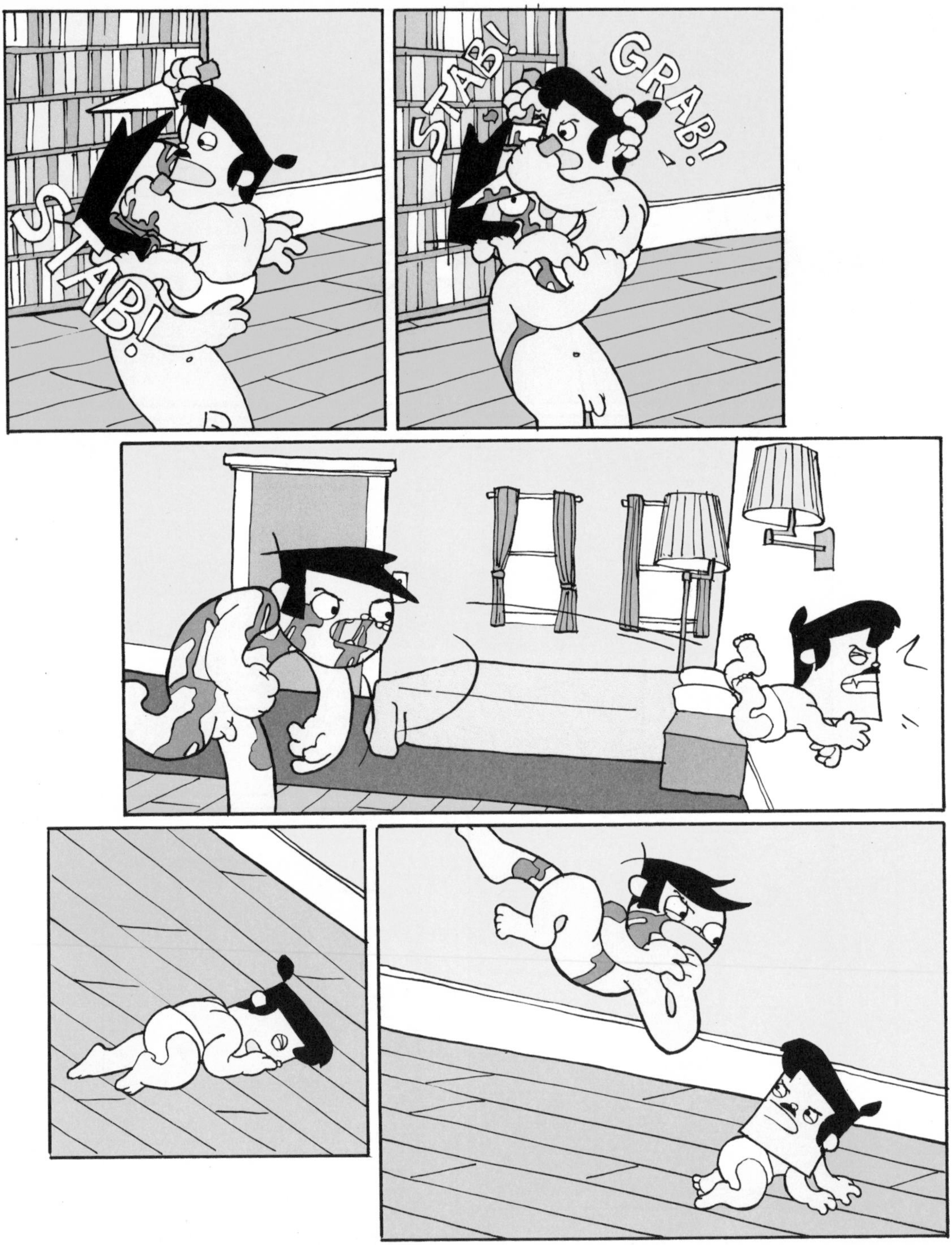
STAB!
STAB!
GRAB!

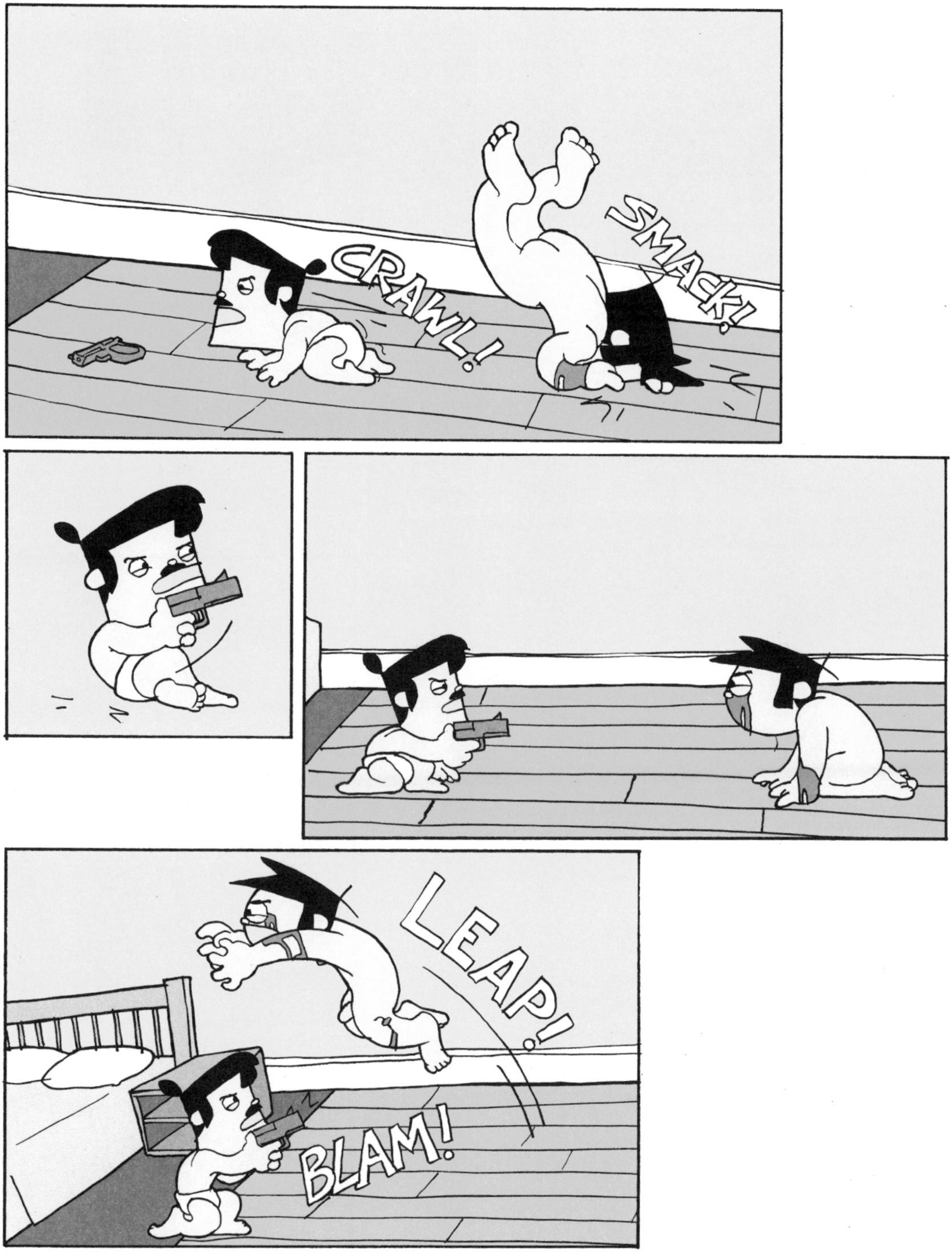
CRAWL!
SMACK!
LEAP!
BLAM!

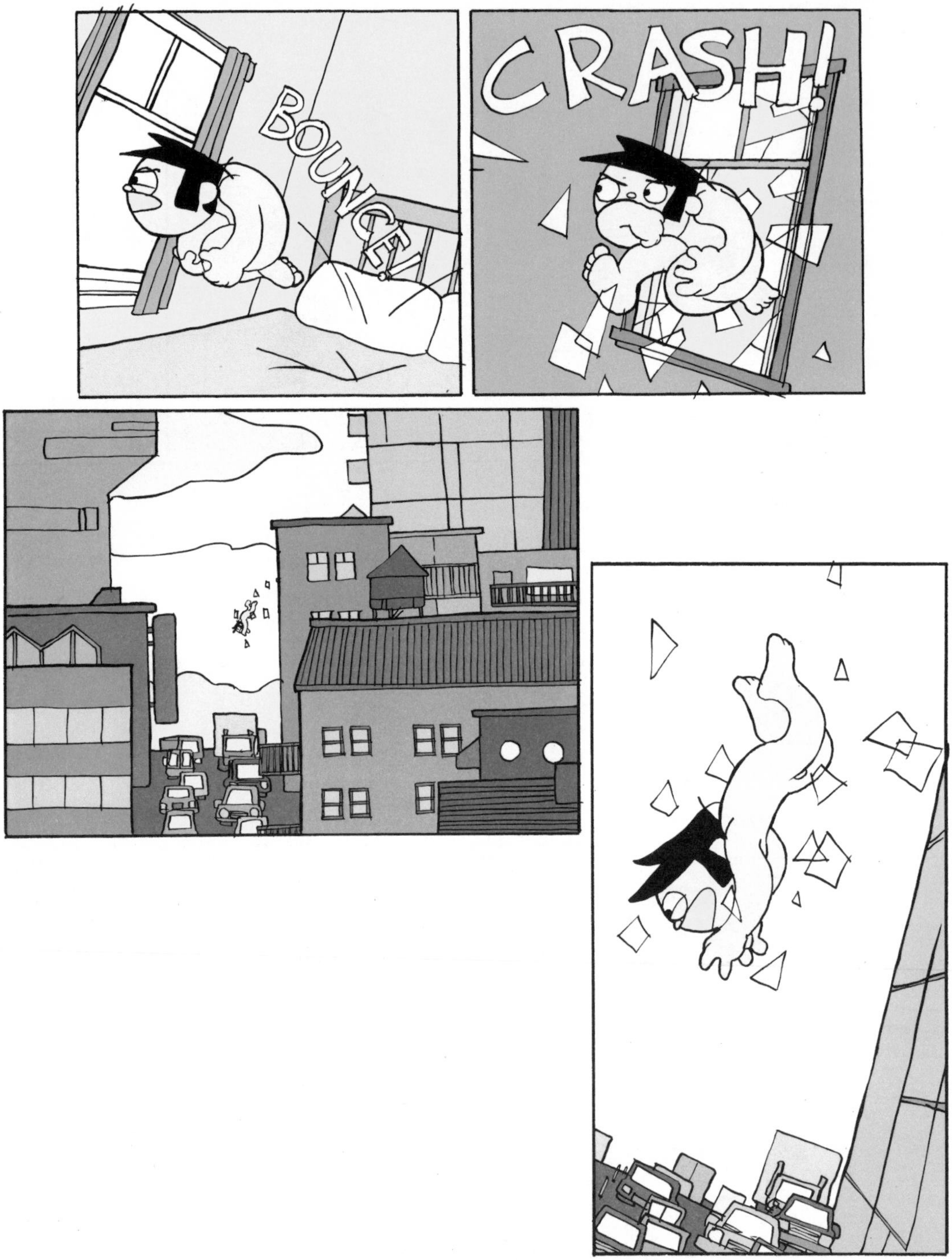
BOUNCE!
CRASH!

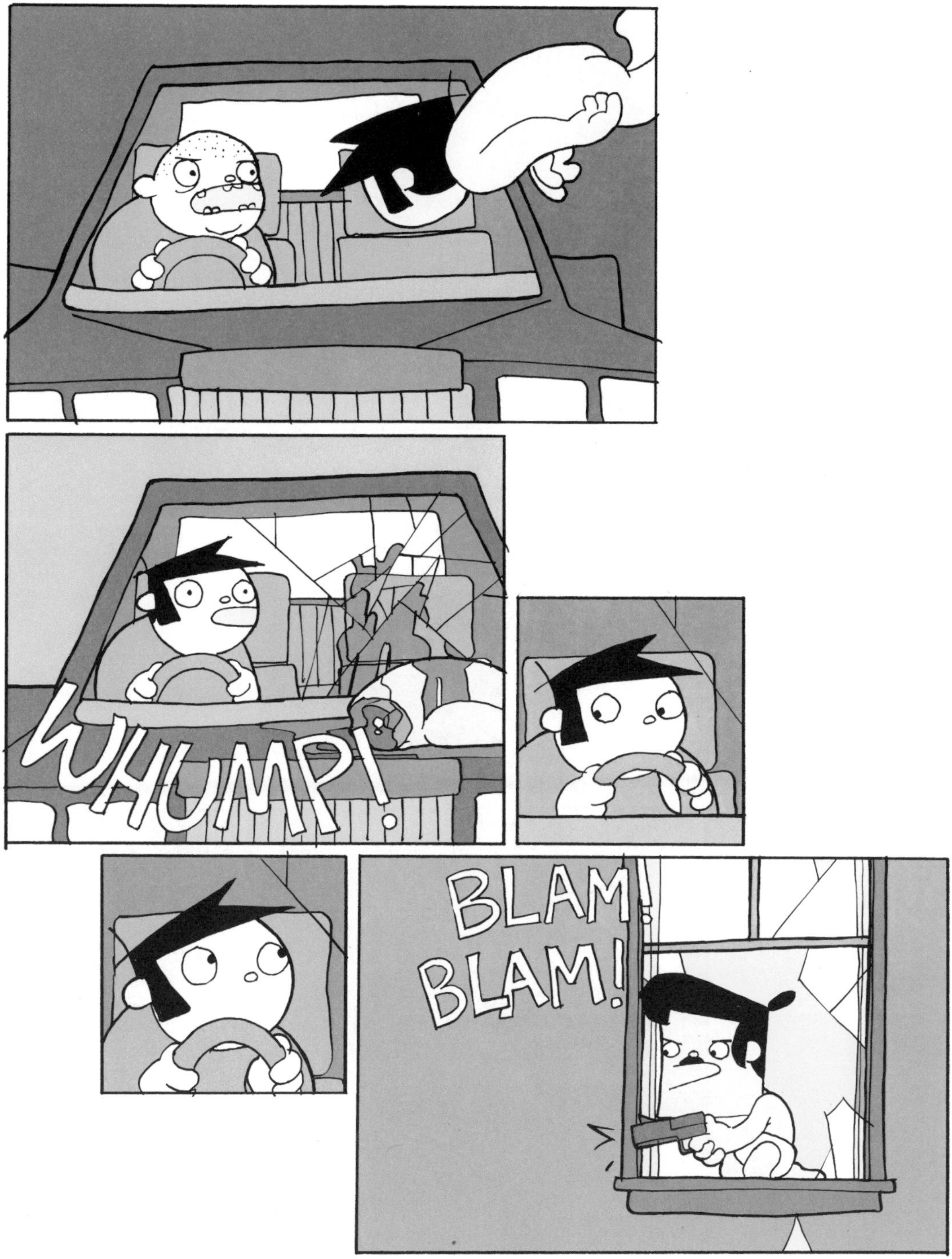
WHUMP!
BLAM!
BLAM!

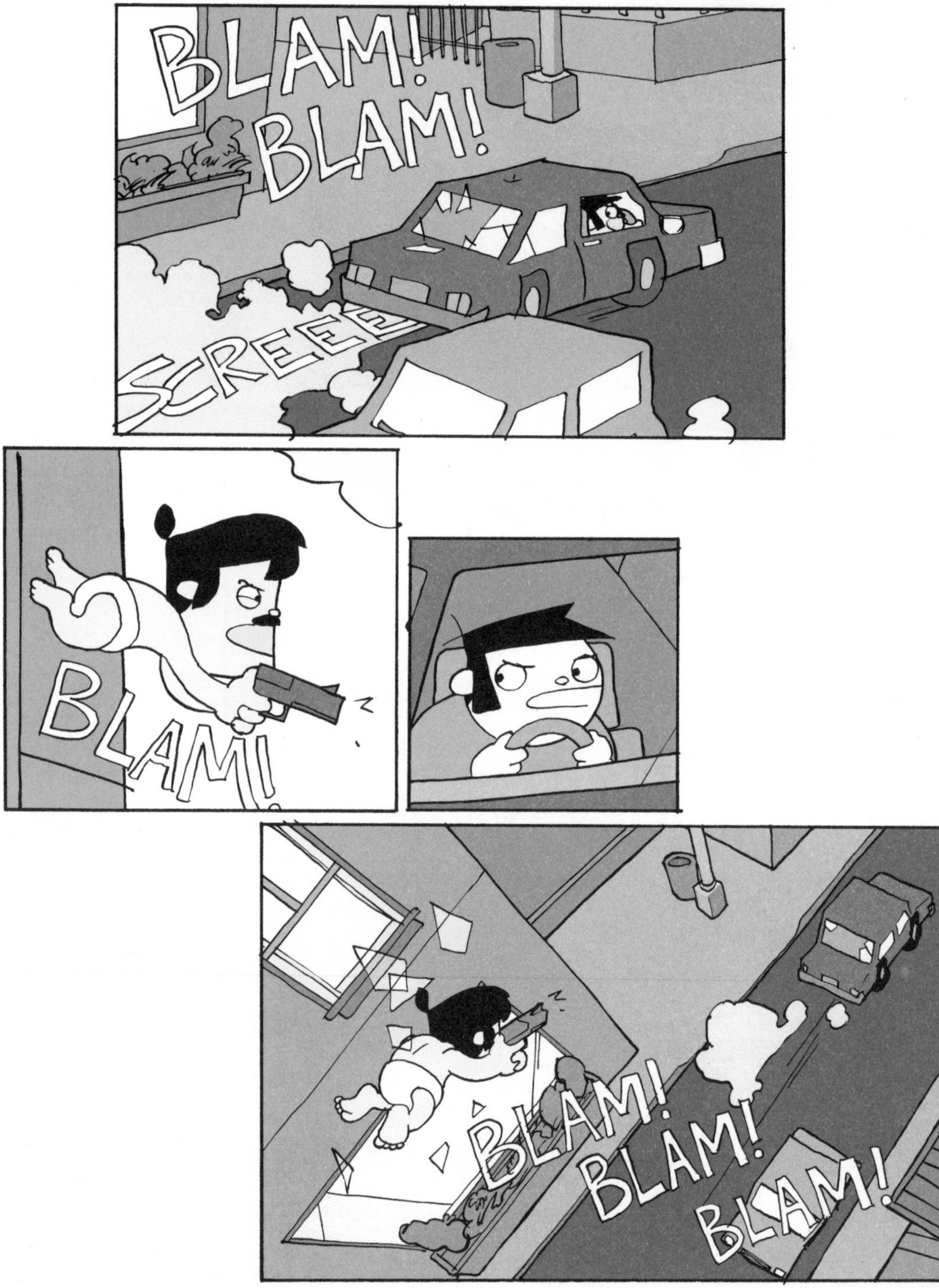

BLAM!
BLAM!
SCREEEE
BLAM!
BLAM!
BLAM!
BLAM!

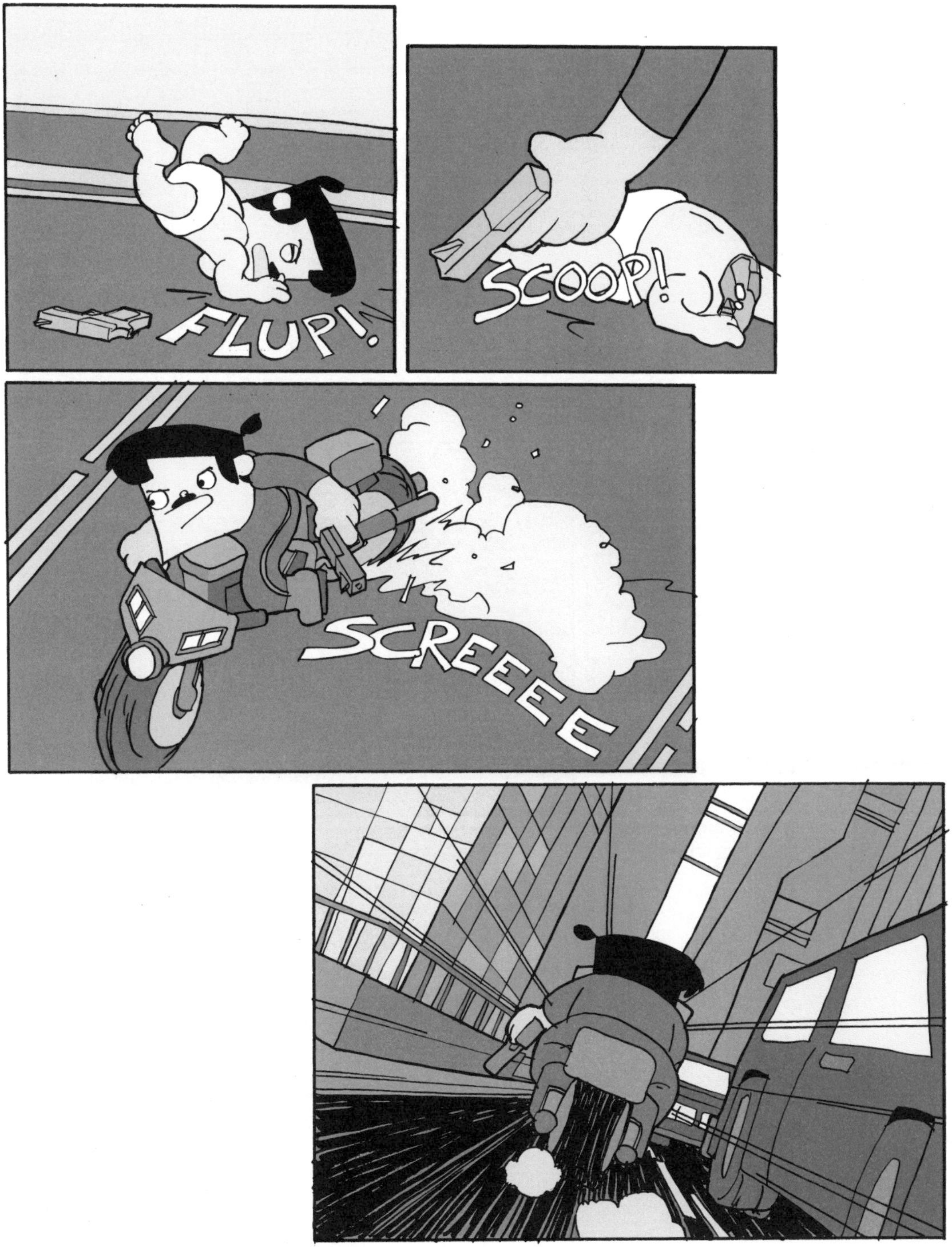
FLUP!
SCOOP!
SCREEEEE

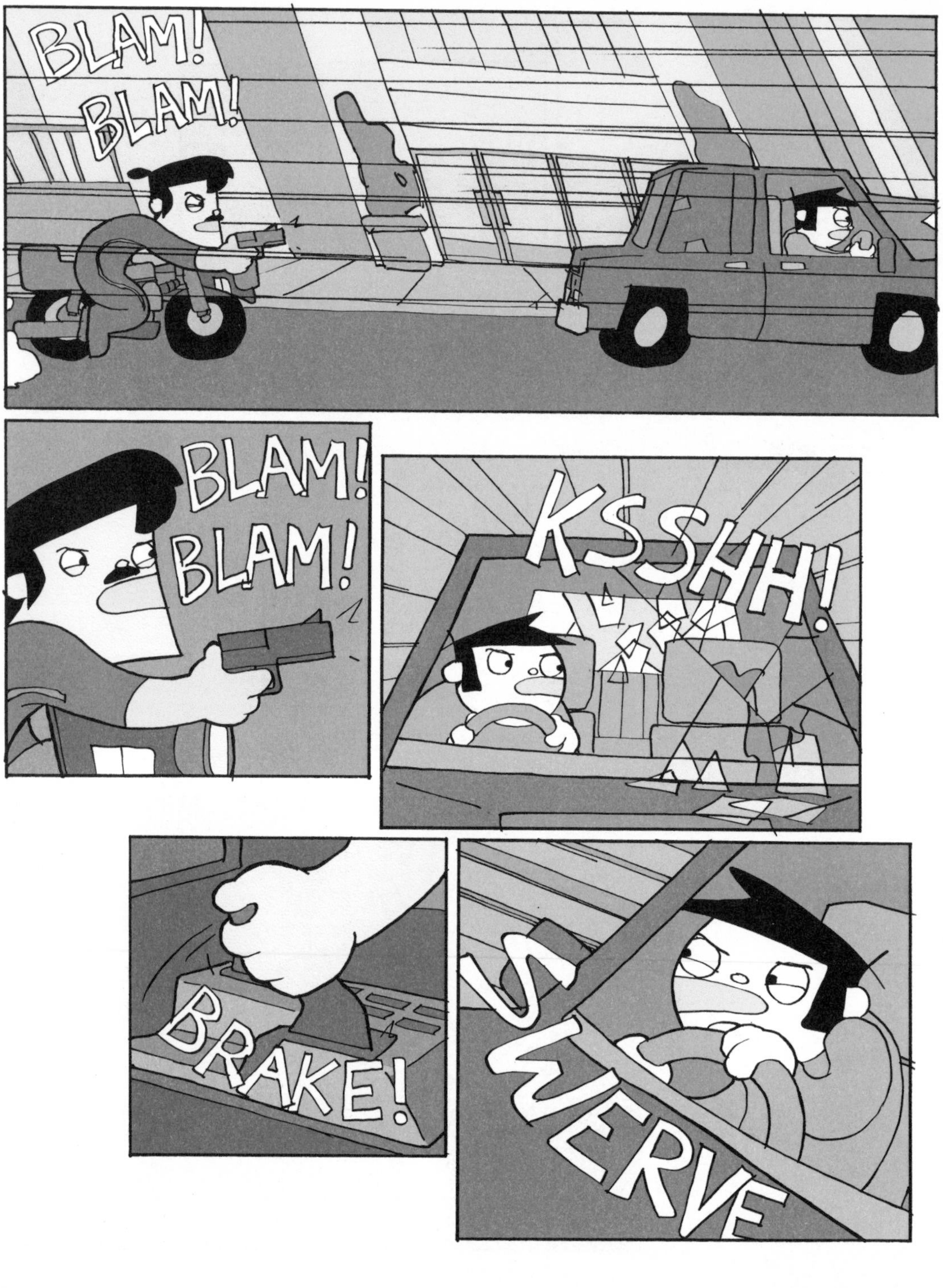
BLAM!
BLAM!
BLAM!
BLAM!
KSSHH!
BRAKE!
SWERVE

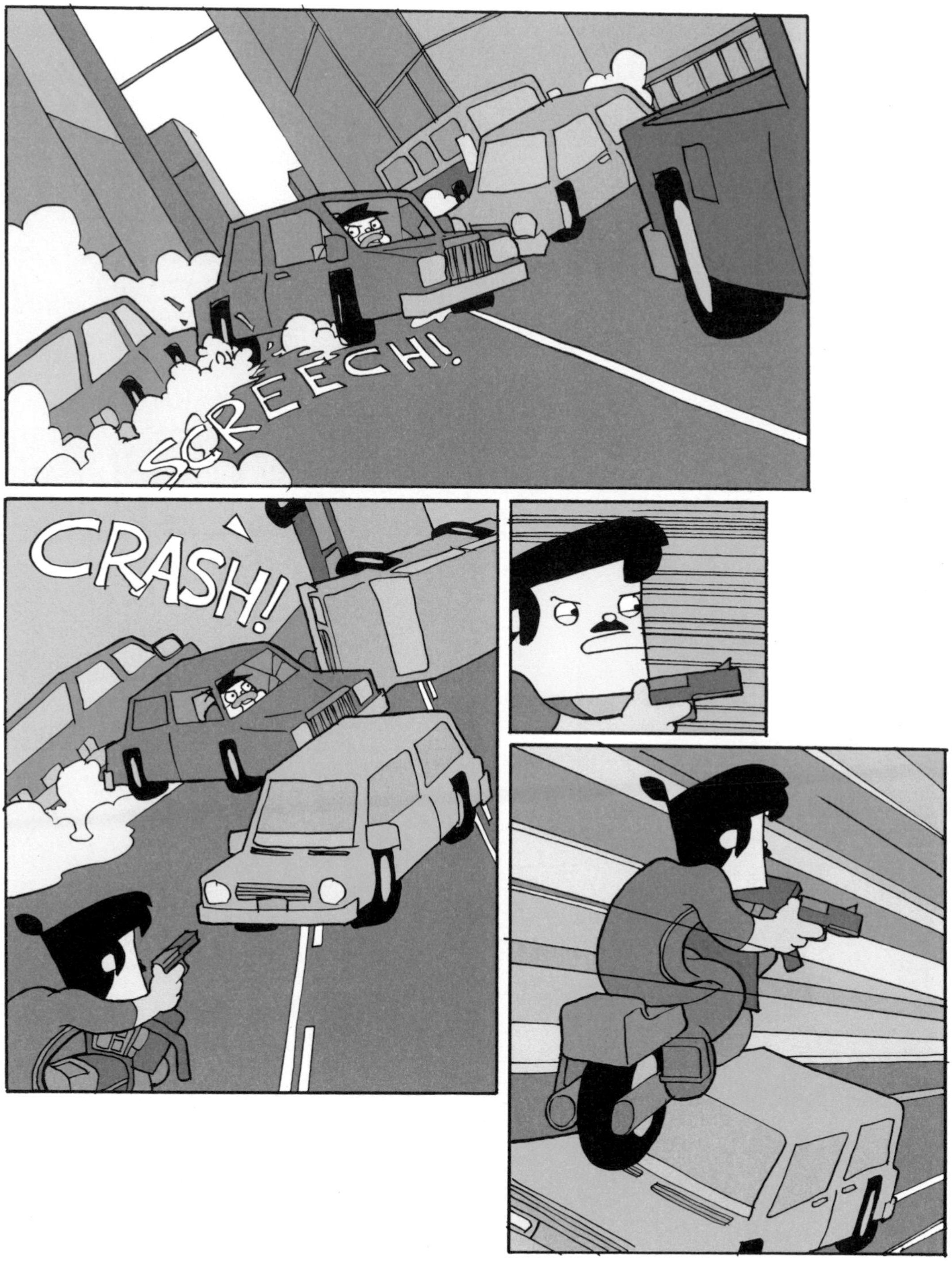
SCREECH!
CRASH!

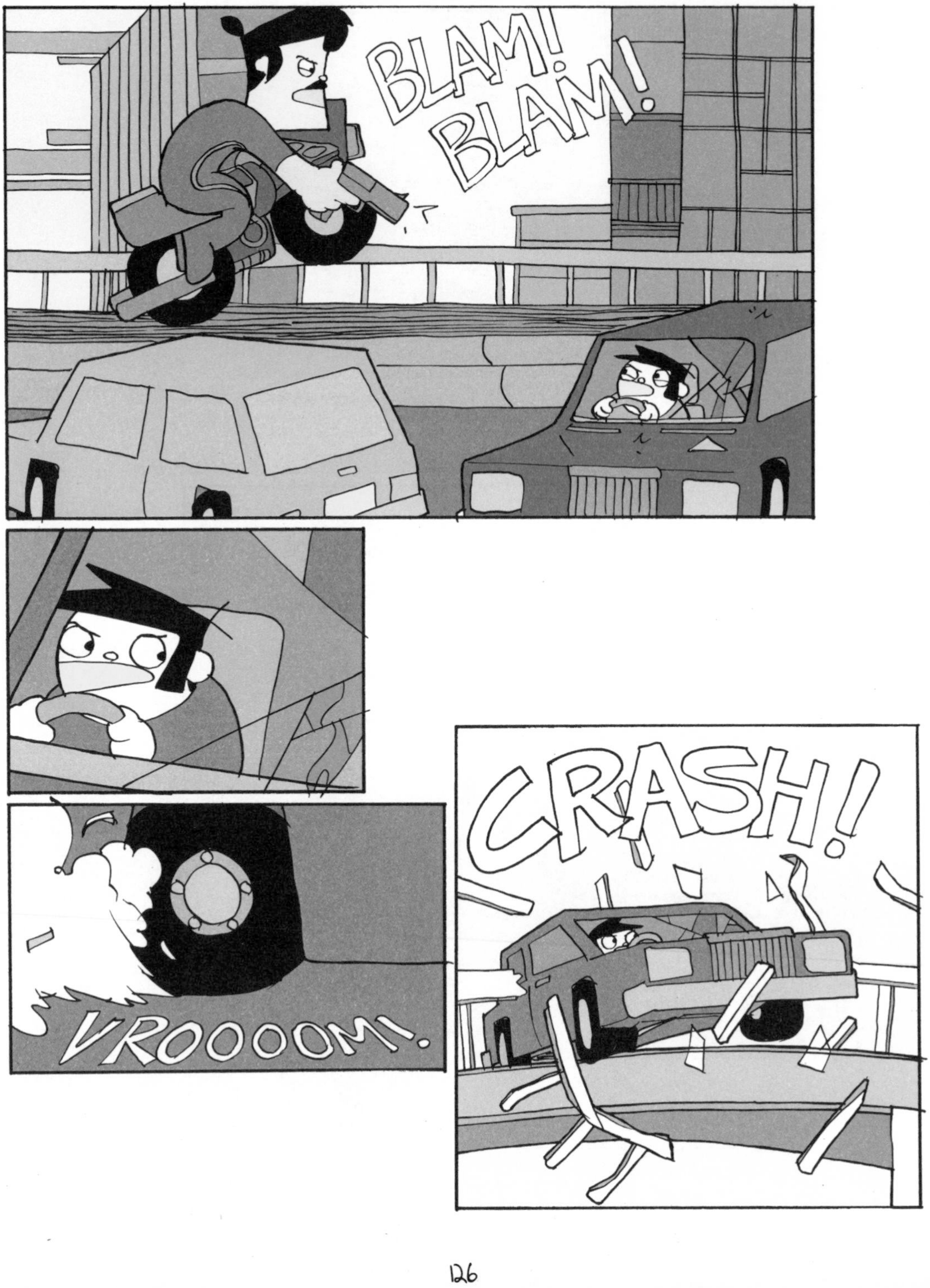
BLAM! BLAM!
VROOOOM!
CRASH!

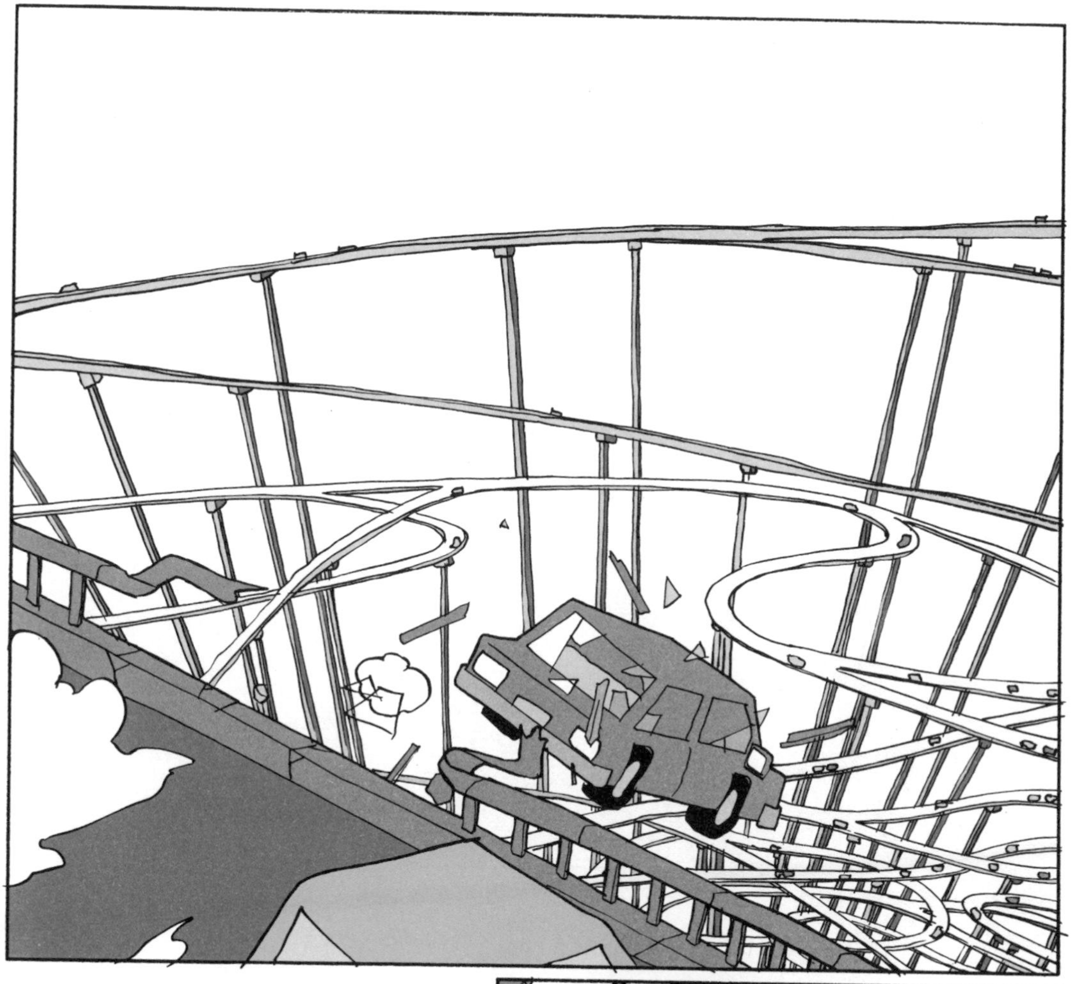

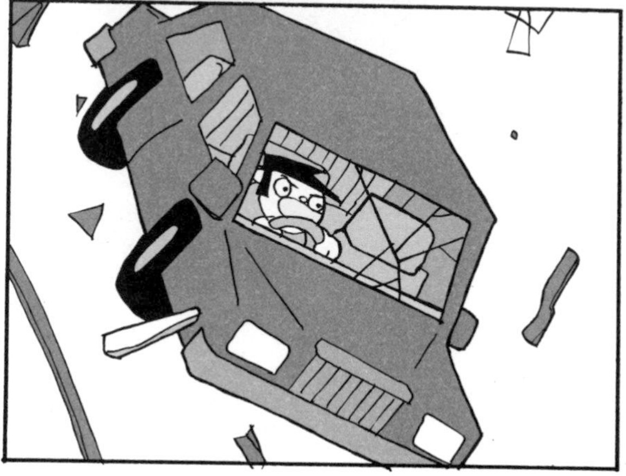

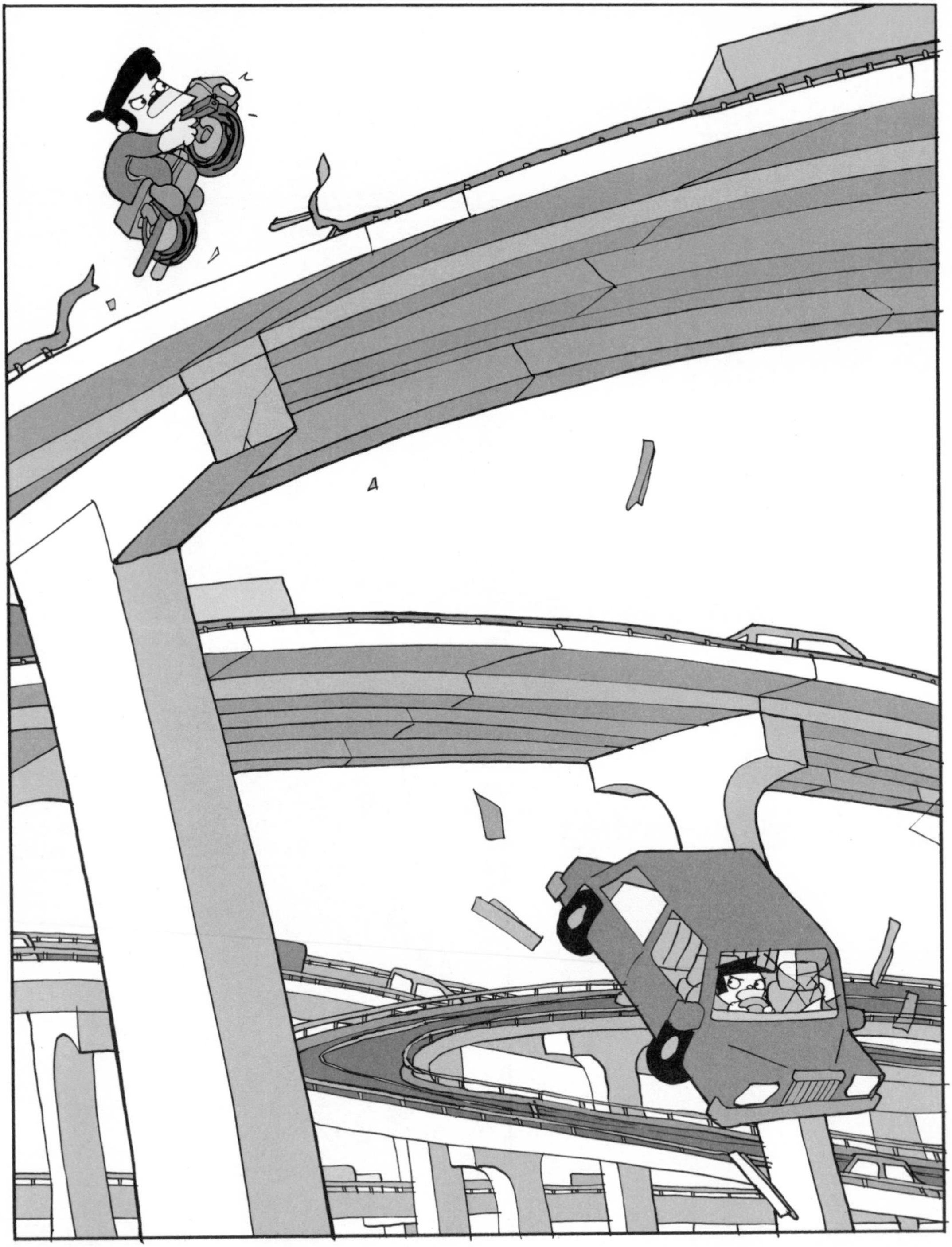

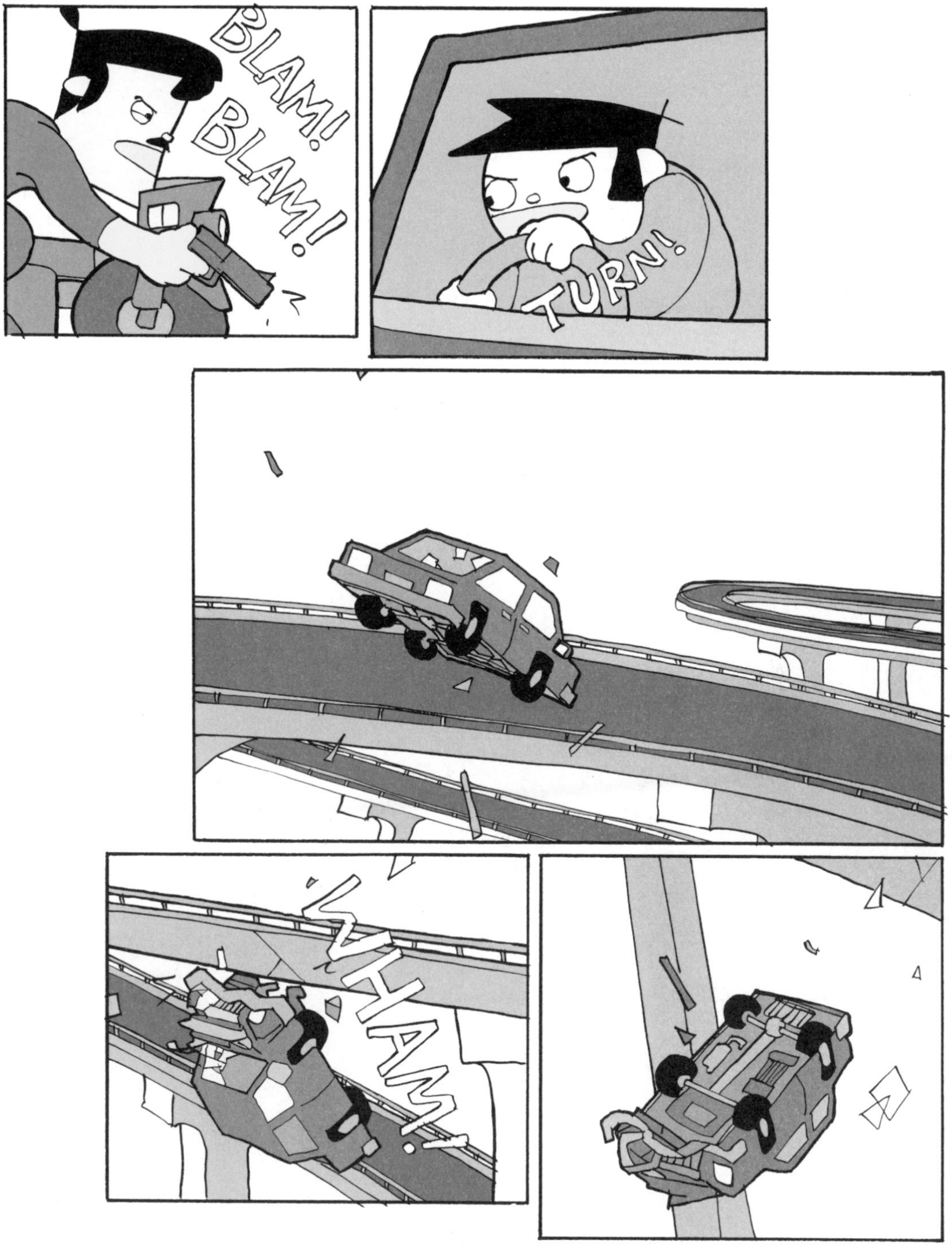

BLAM! BLAM! BLAM!
TURN!
WHAM!

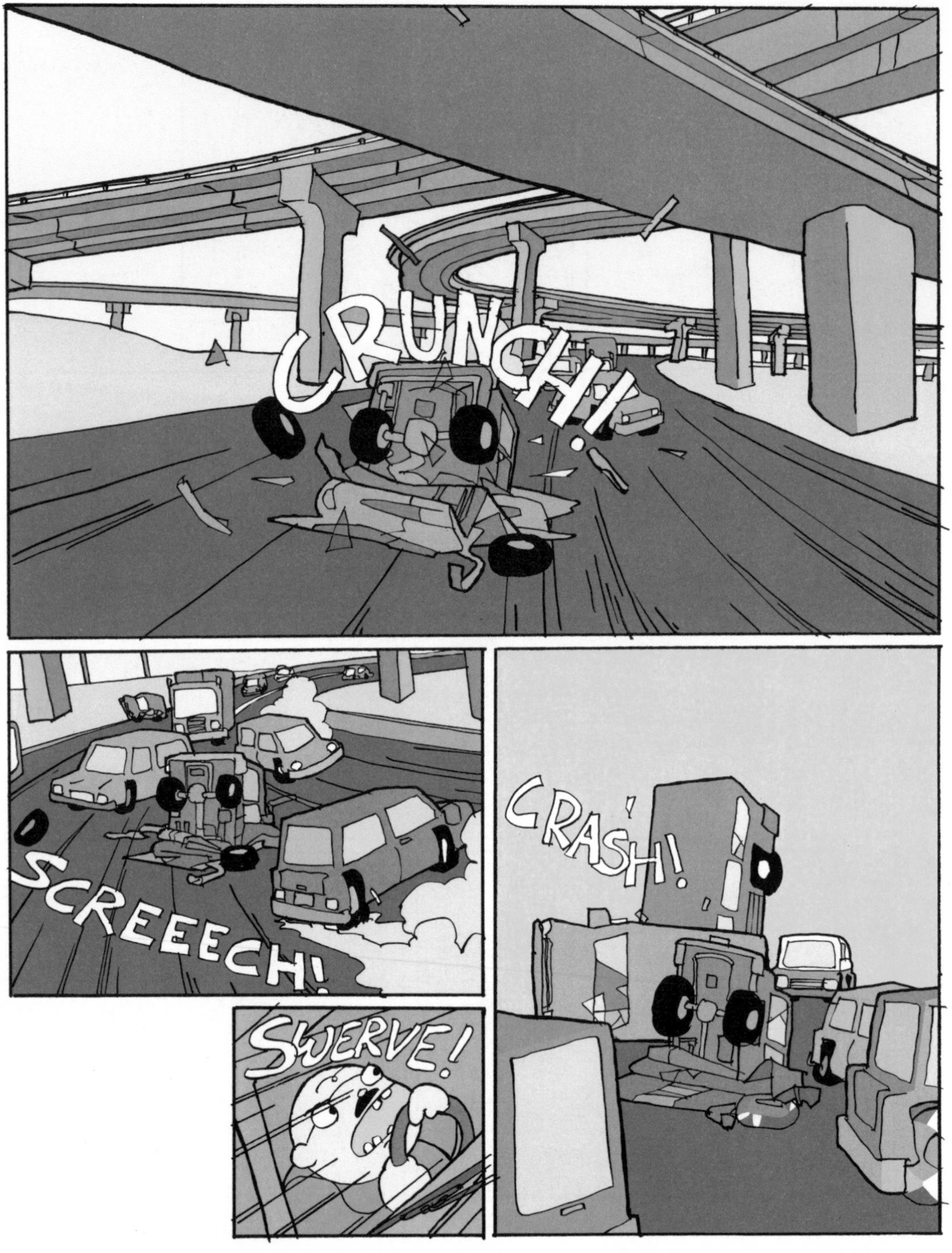
CRUNCH!
SCREEECH!
SWERVE!
CRASH!

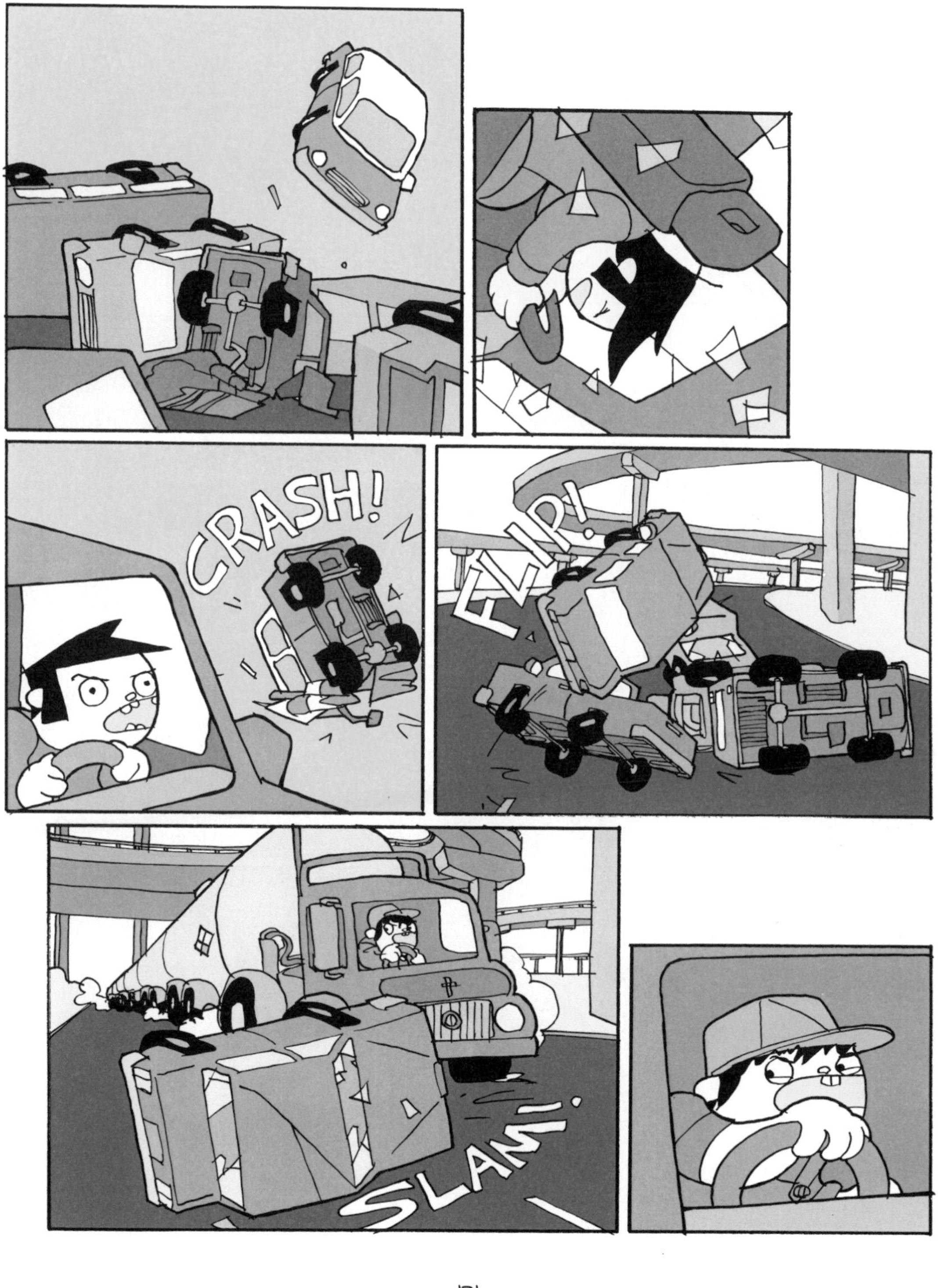
CRASH!
FLIP!
SLAM!

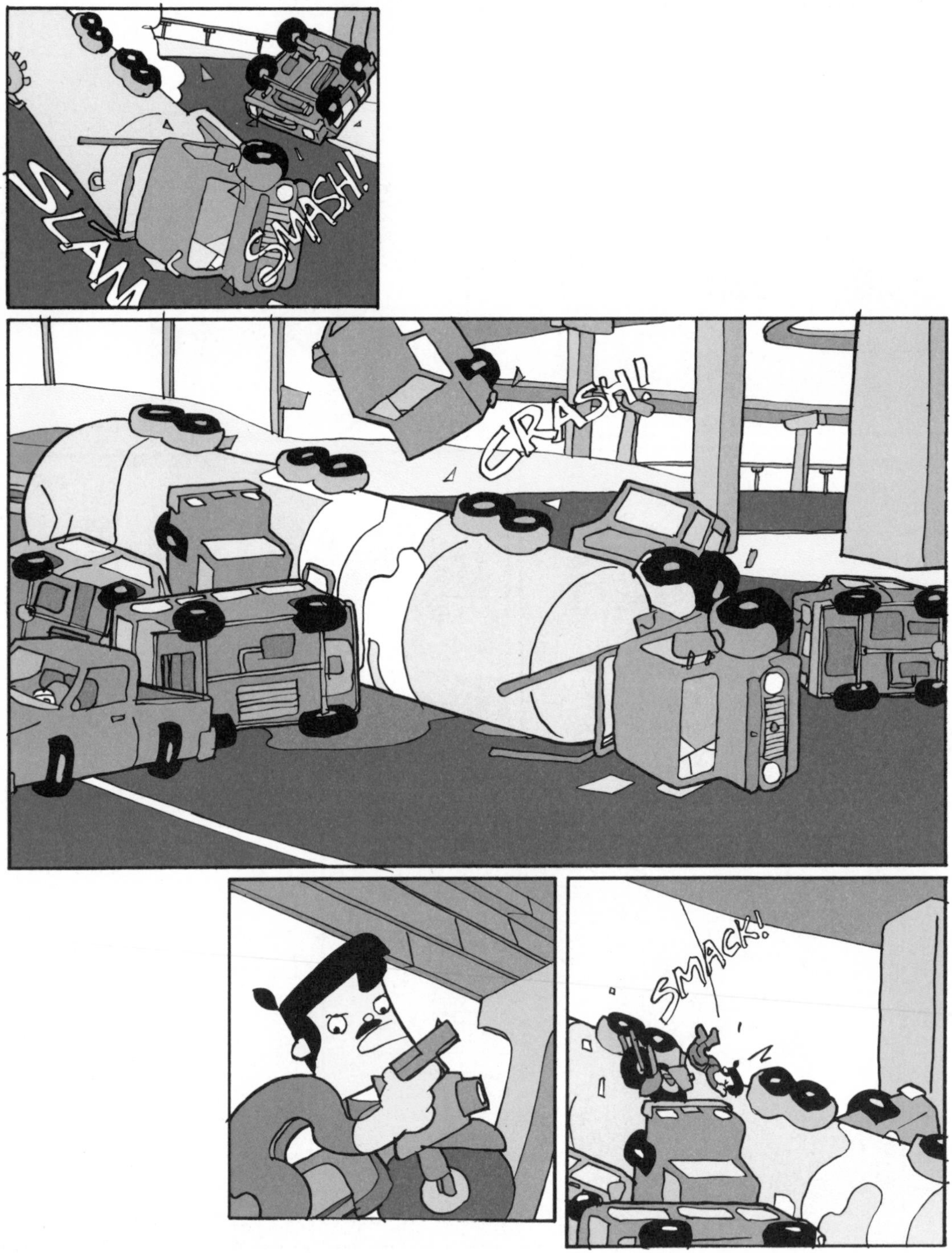
SLAM
SMASH!
CRASH!
SMACK!

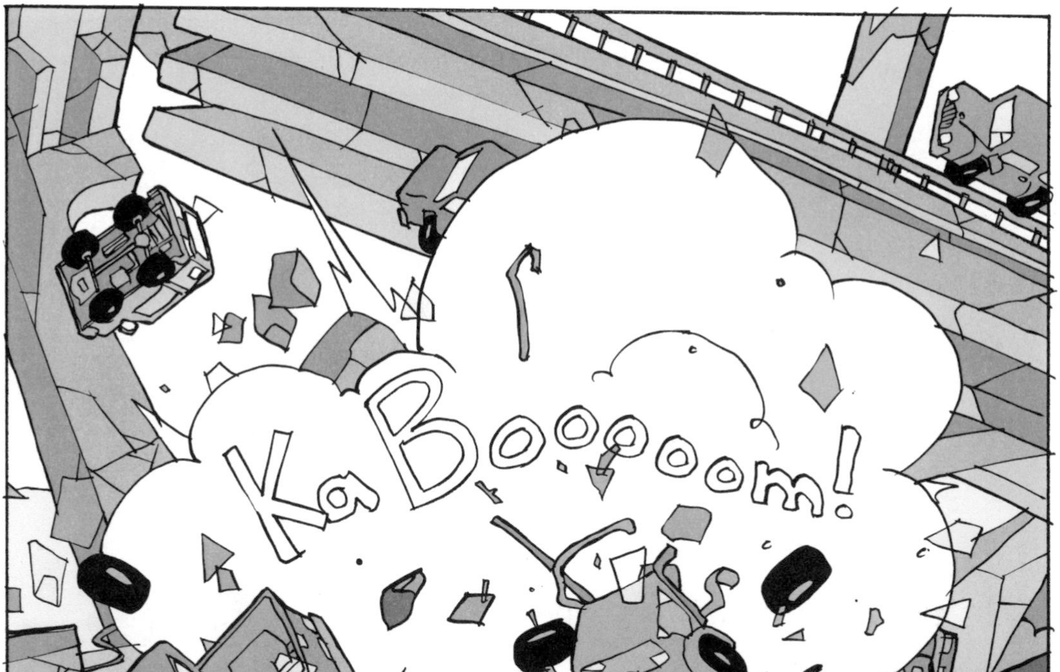
KaBooooom!
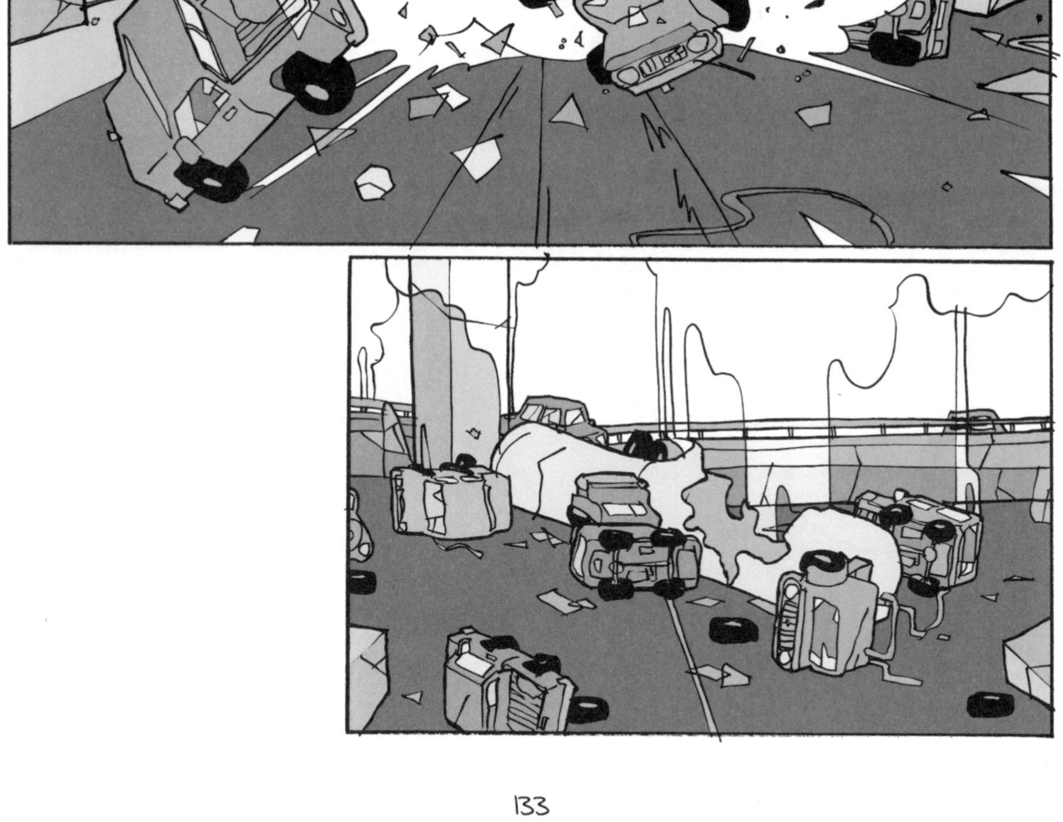

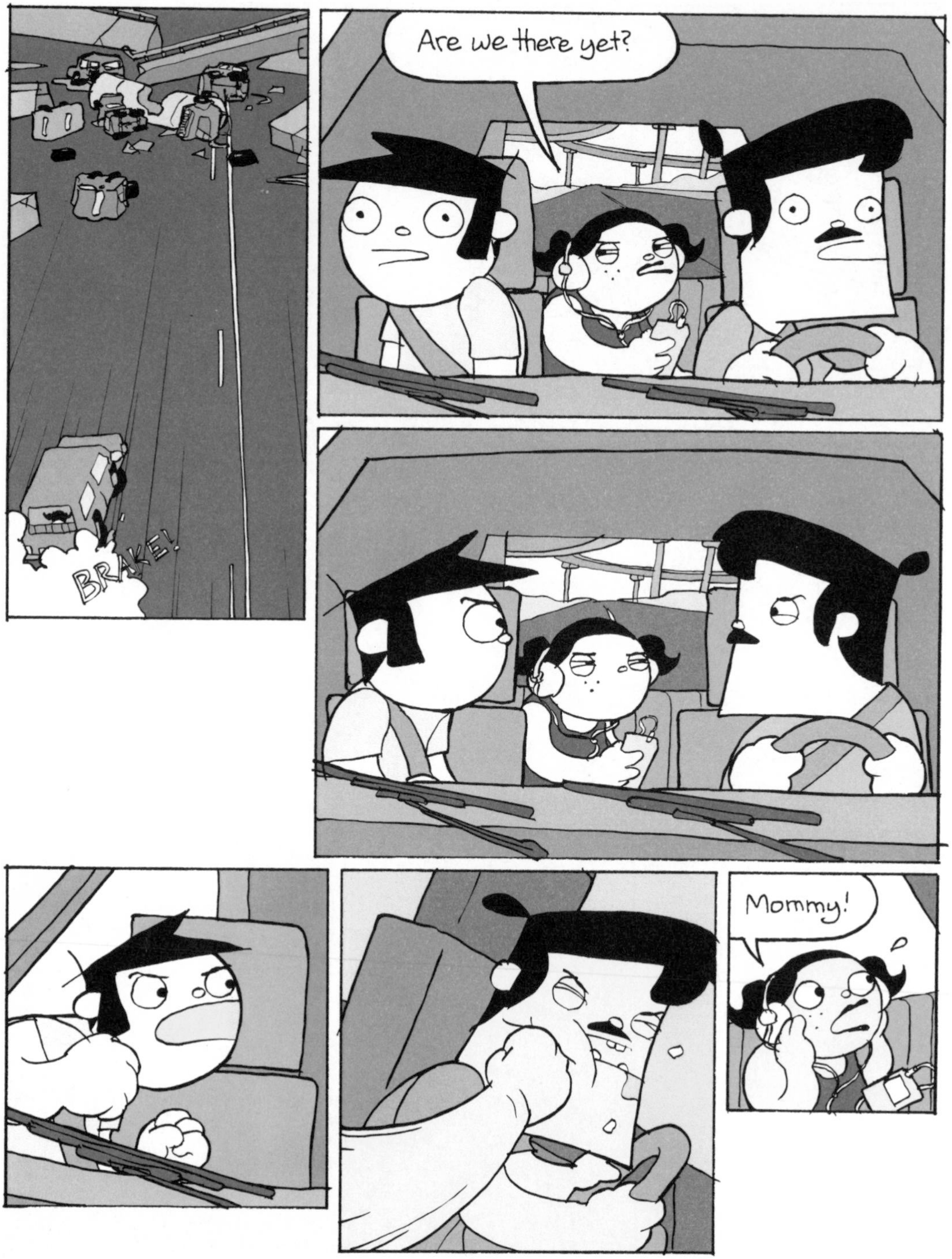
BRAKE!
Are we there yet?
Mommy!

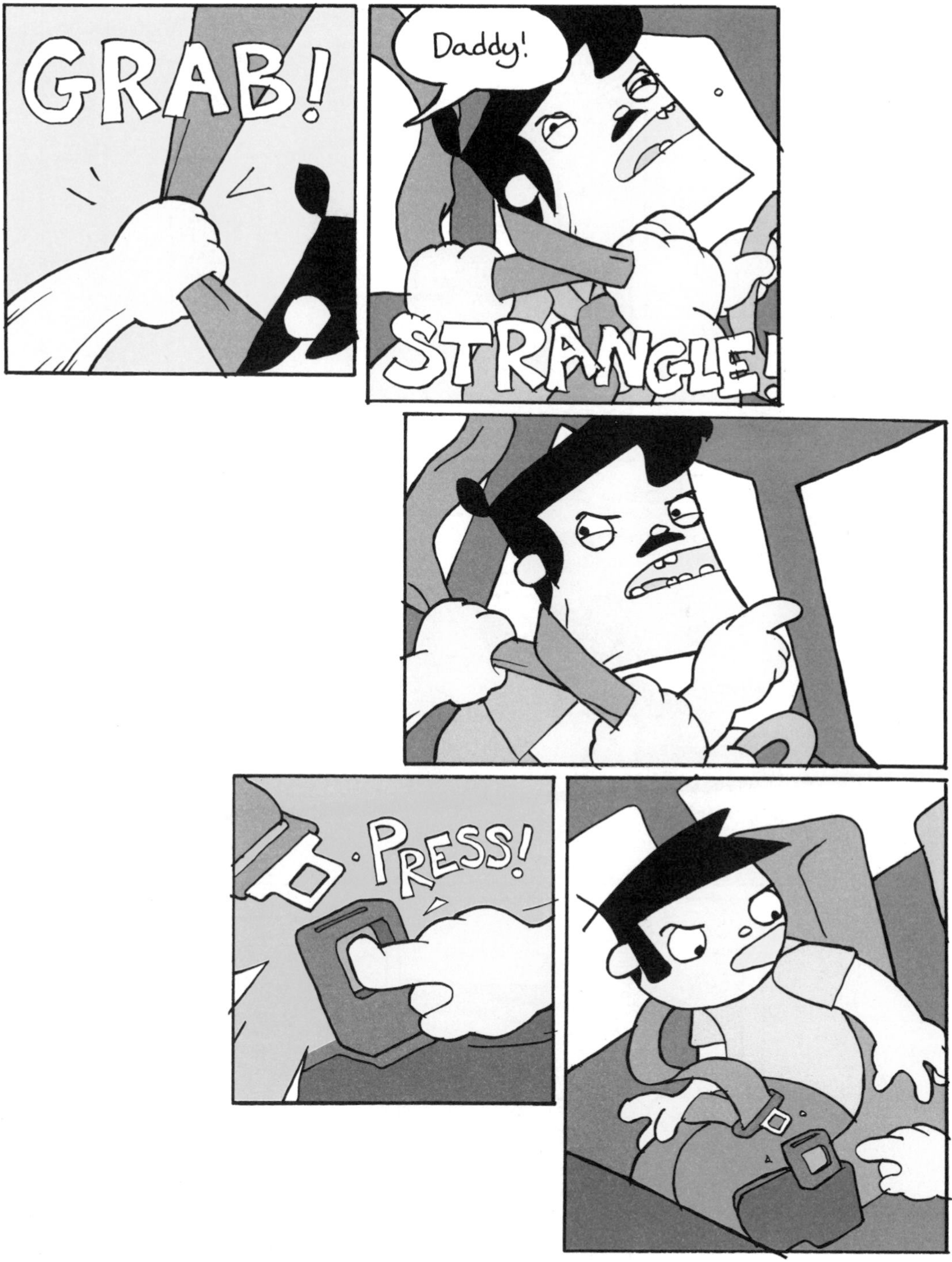
GRAB!
Daddy!
STRANGLE!
PRESS!

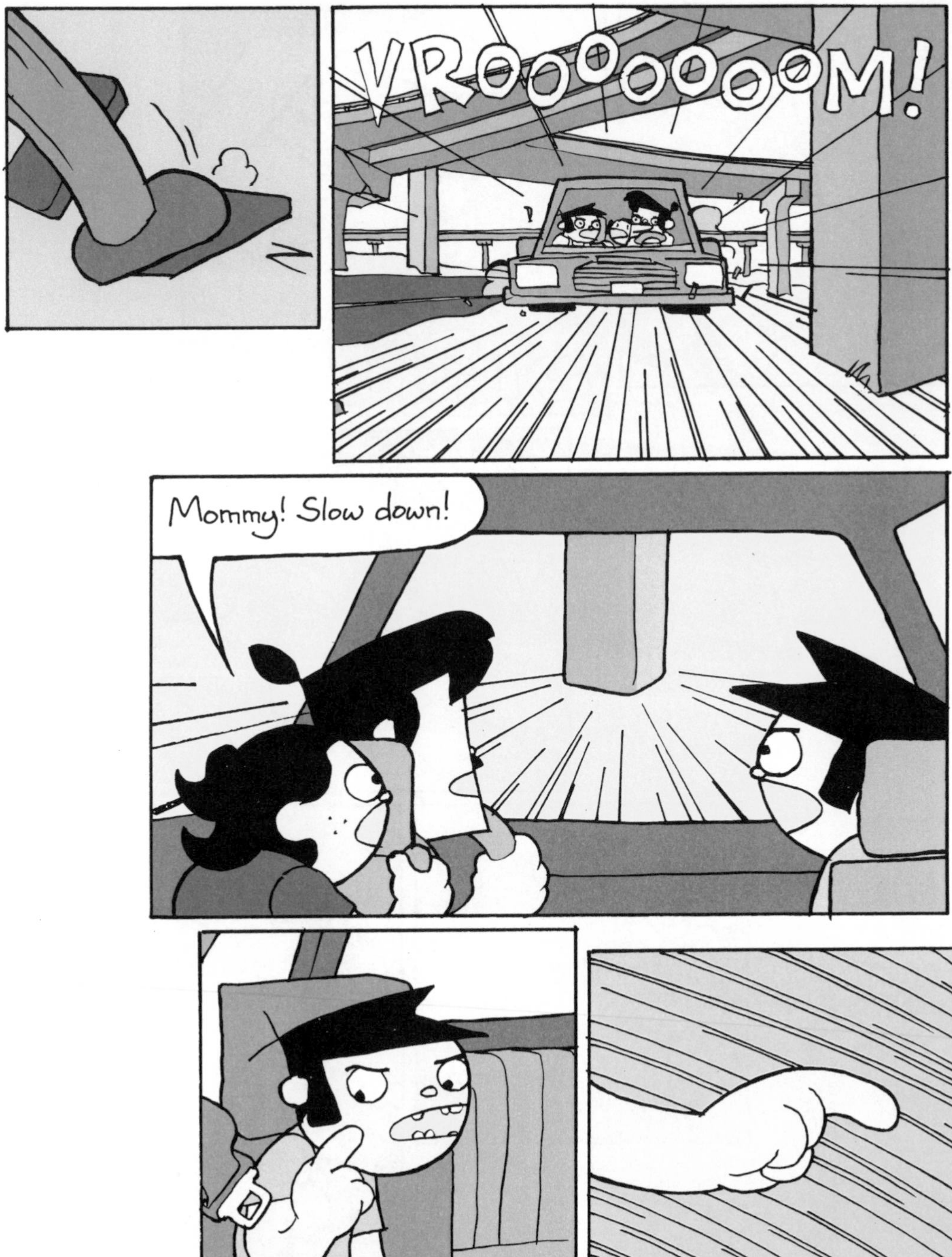
VROOOOOOOM!
Mommy! Slow down!

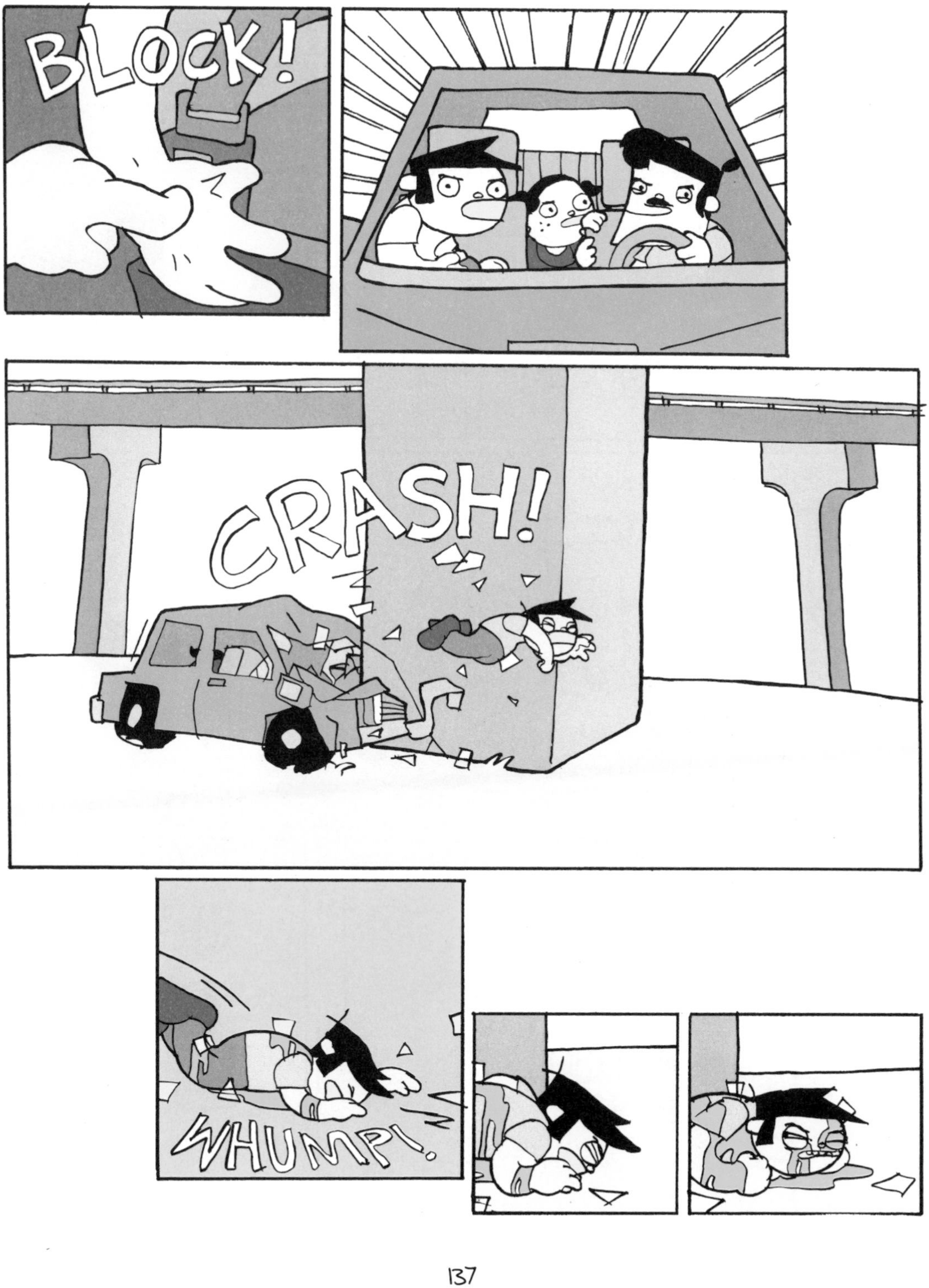
BLOCK!
CRASH!
WHUMP!

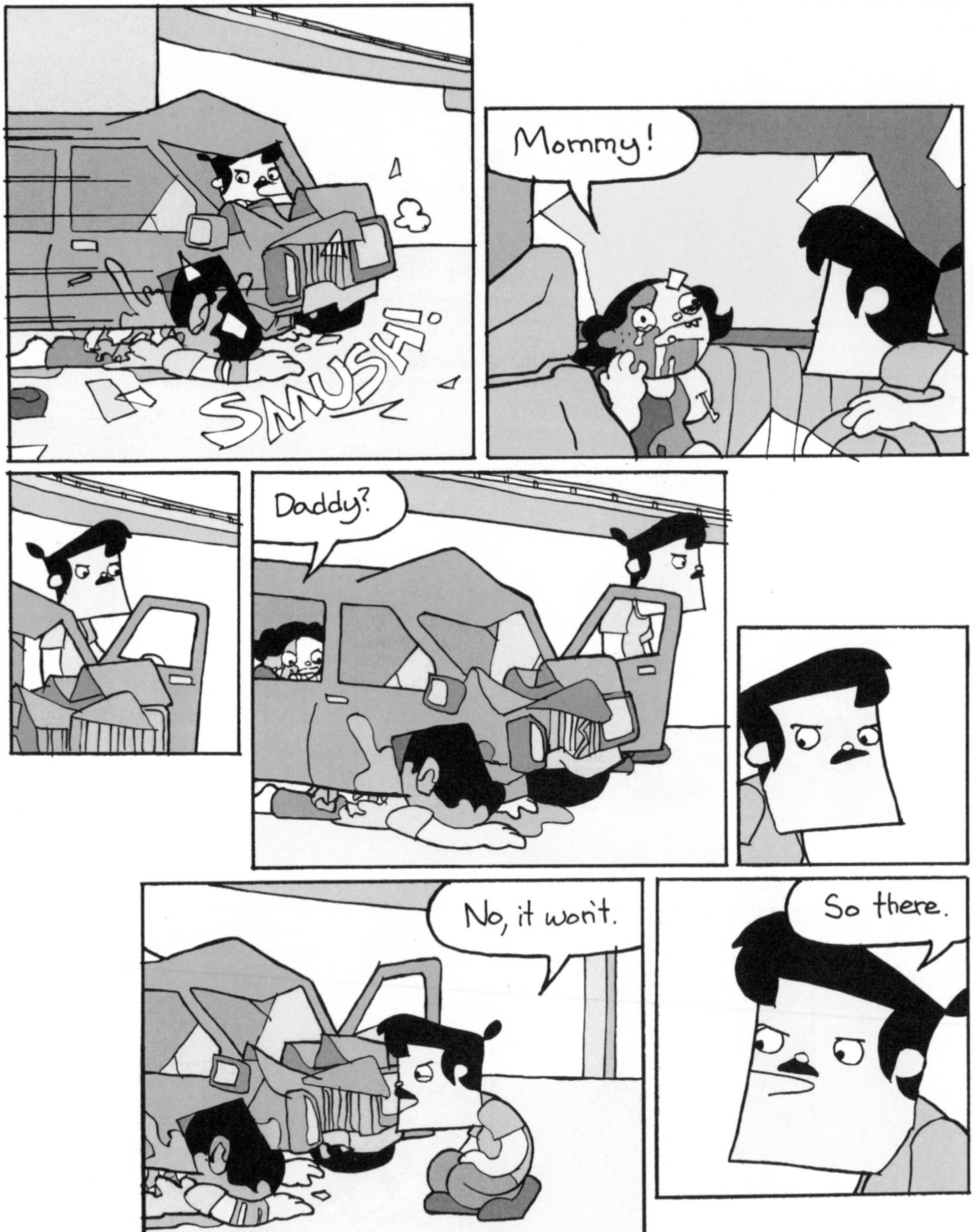
SMUSH!
Mommy!
Daddy?
No, it won't.
So there.

CHAPTER 16

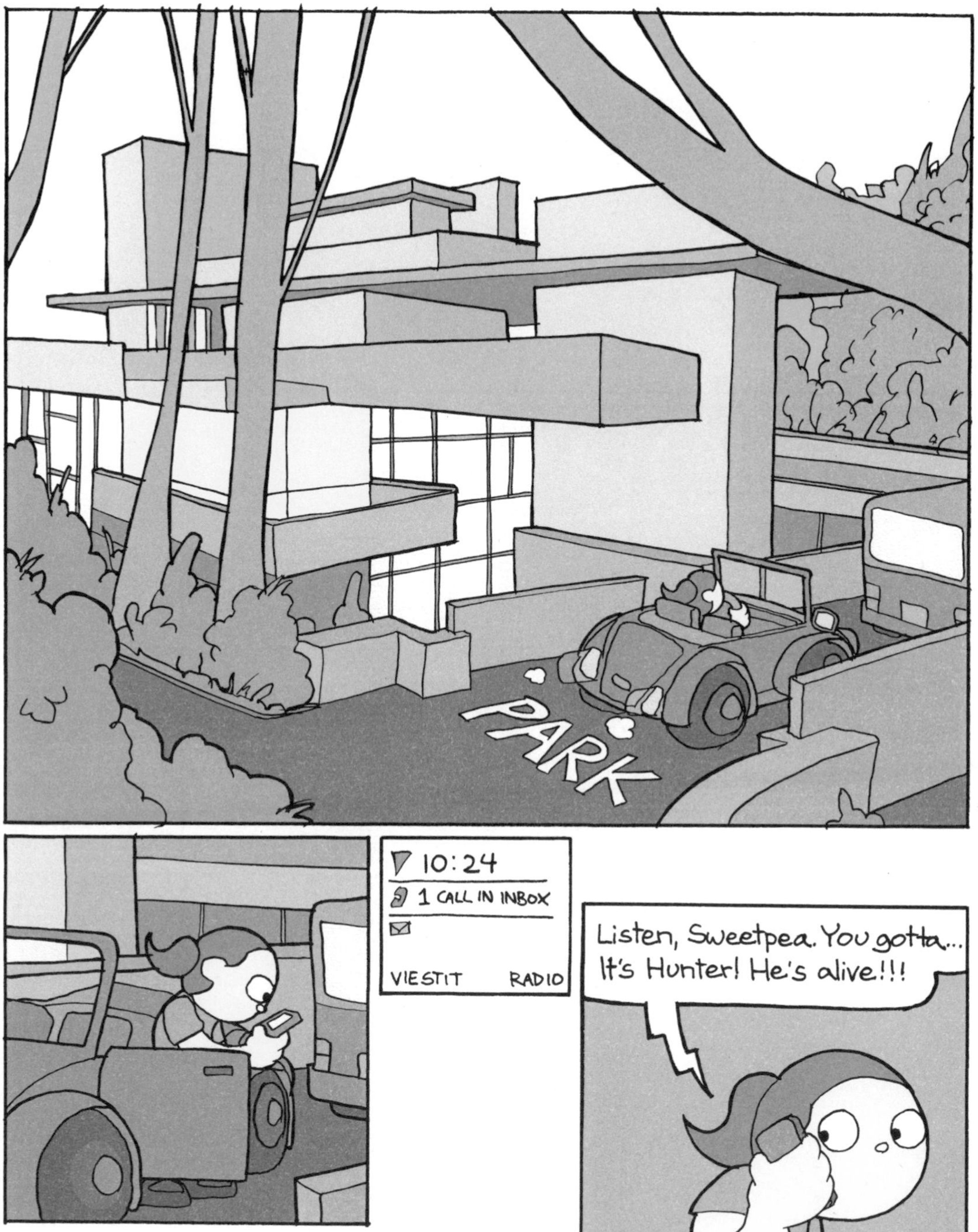
PARK
10:24
1 CALL IN INBOX
VIESTIT
RADIO
Listen, Sweetpea. You gotta... It's Hunter! He's alive!!!

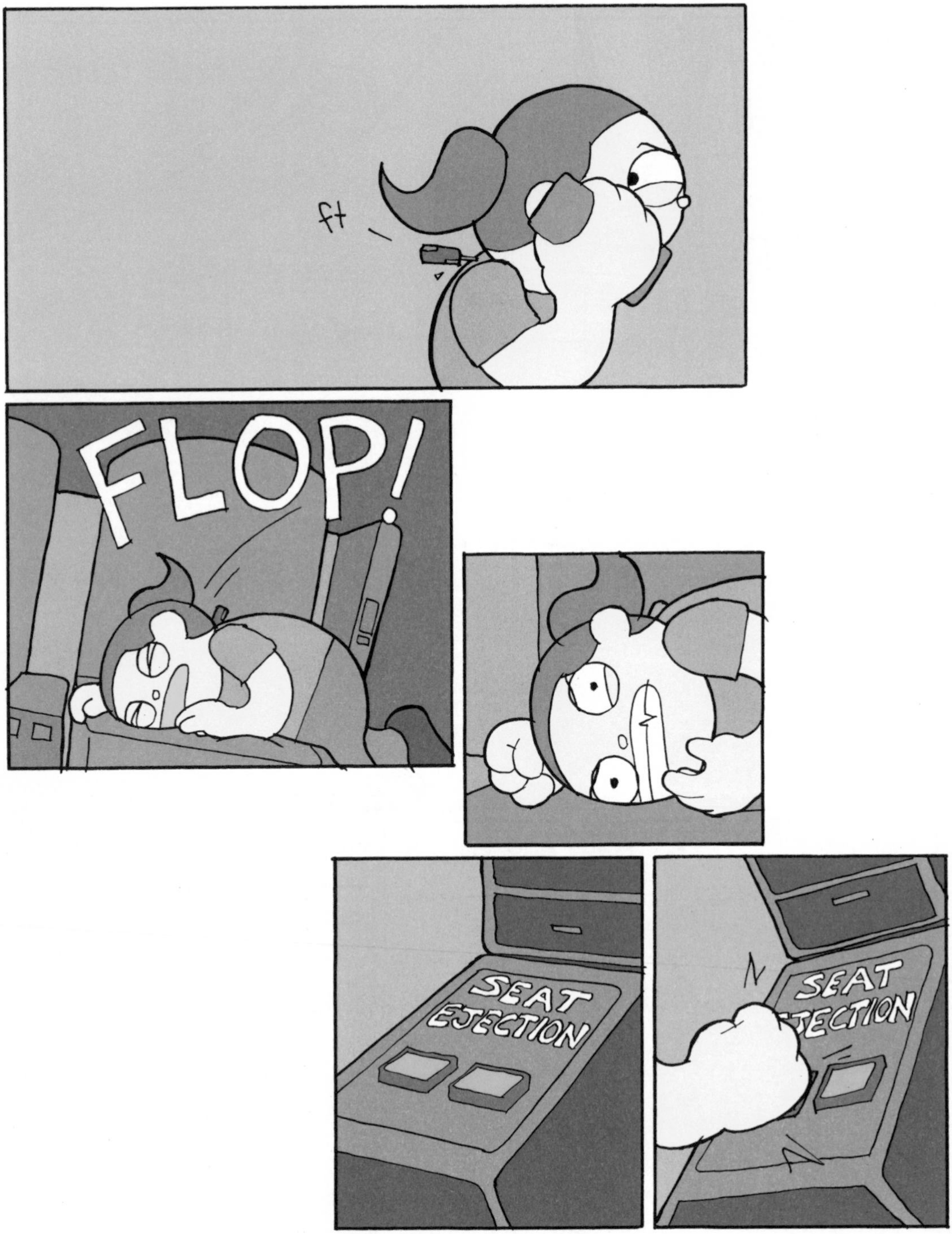
ft
FLOP!
SEAT EJECTION
SEAT EJECTION

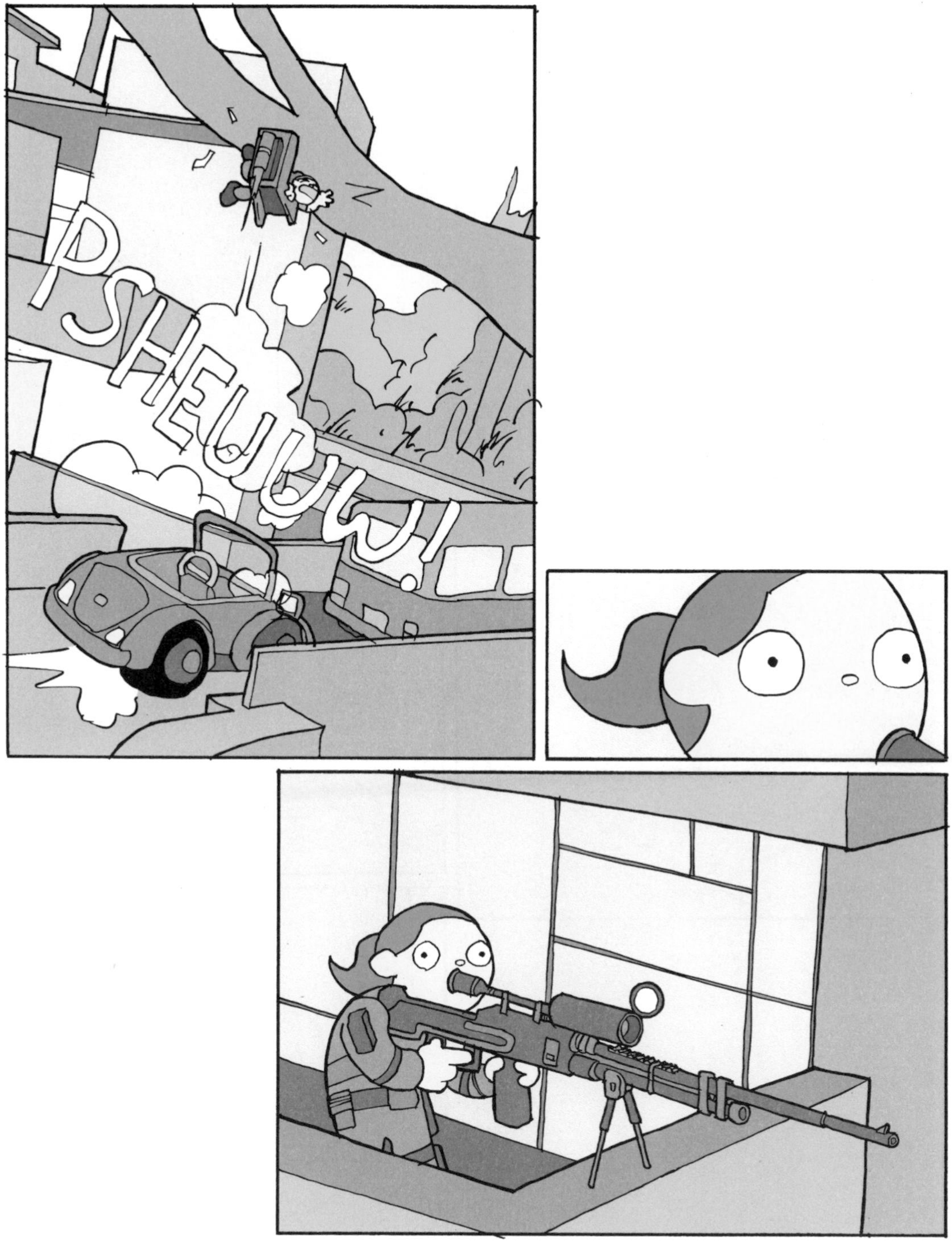
PSHEUUUW!

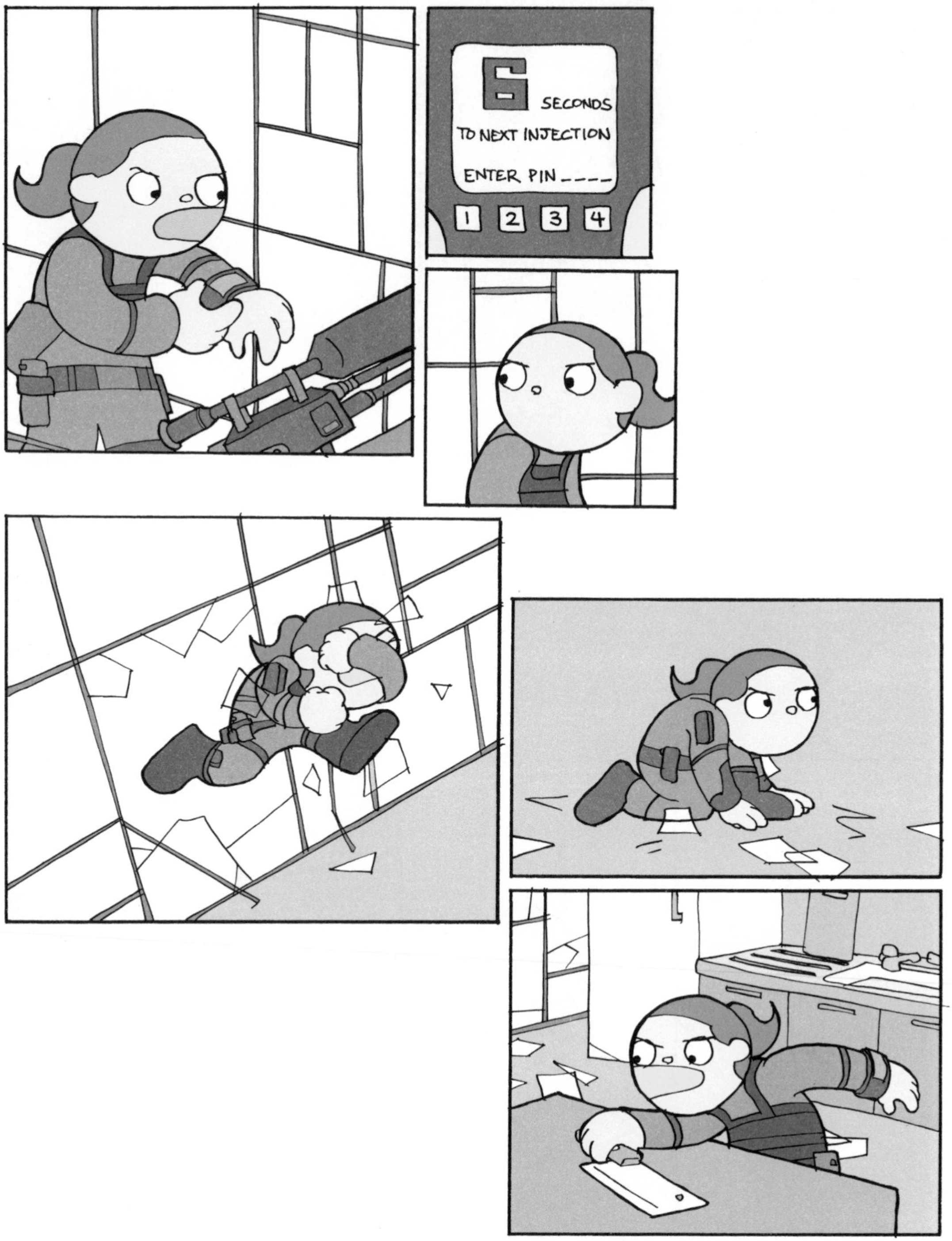

6 SECONDS
TO NEXT INJECTION
ENTER PIN ----
1 2 3 4

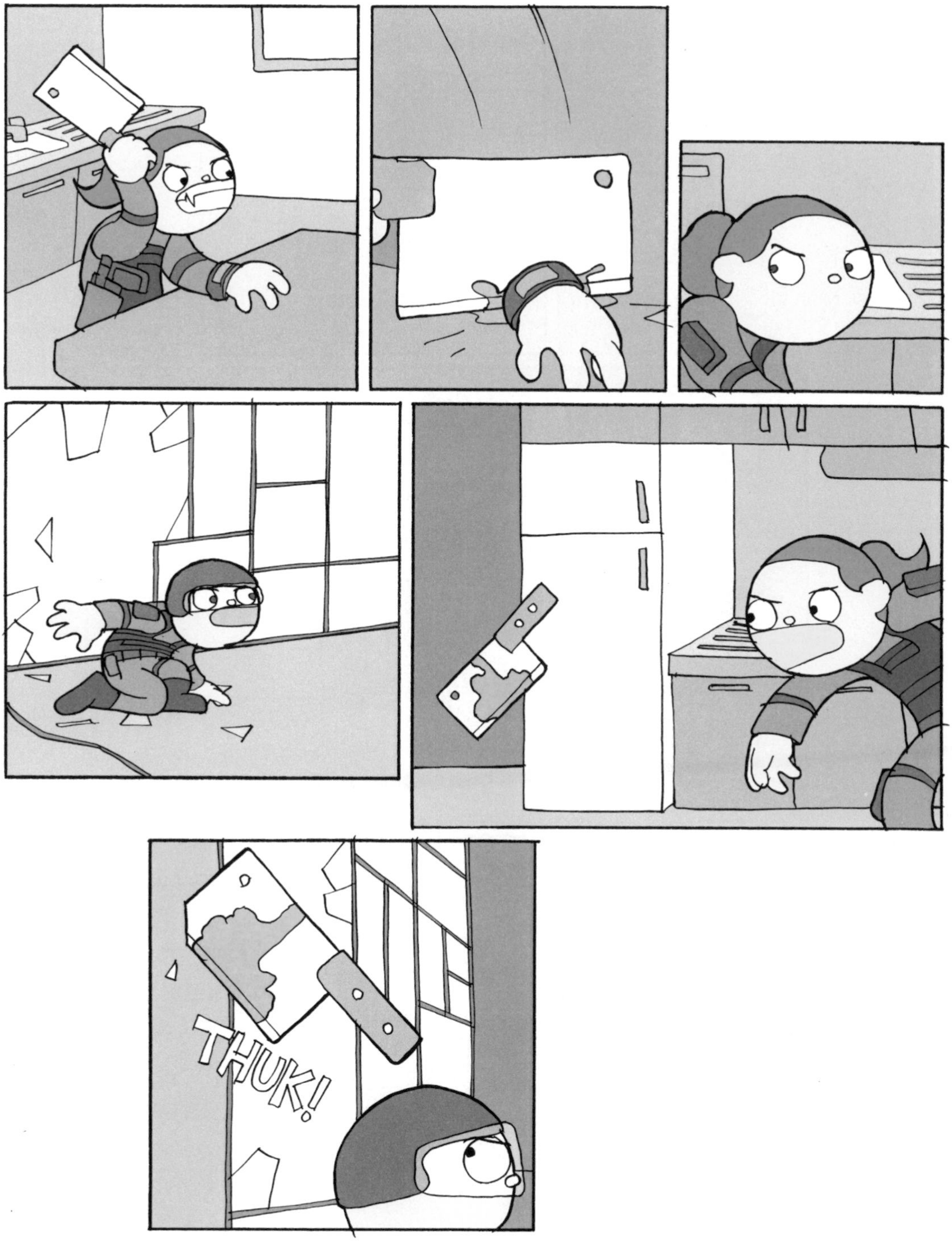
THUK!

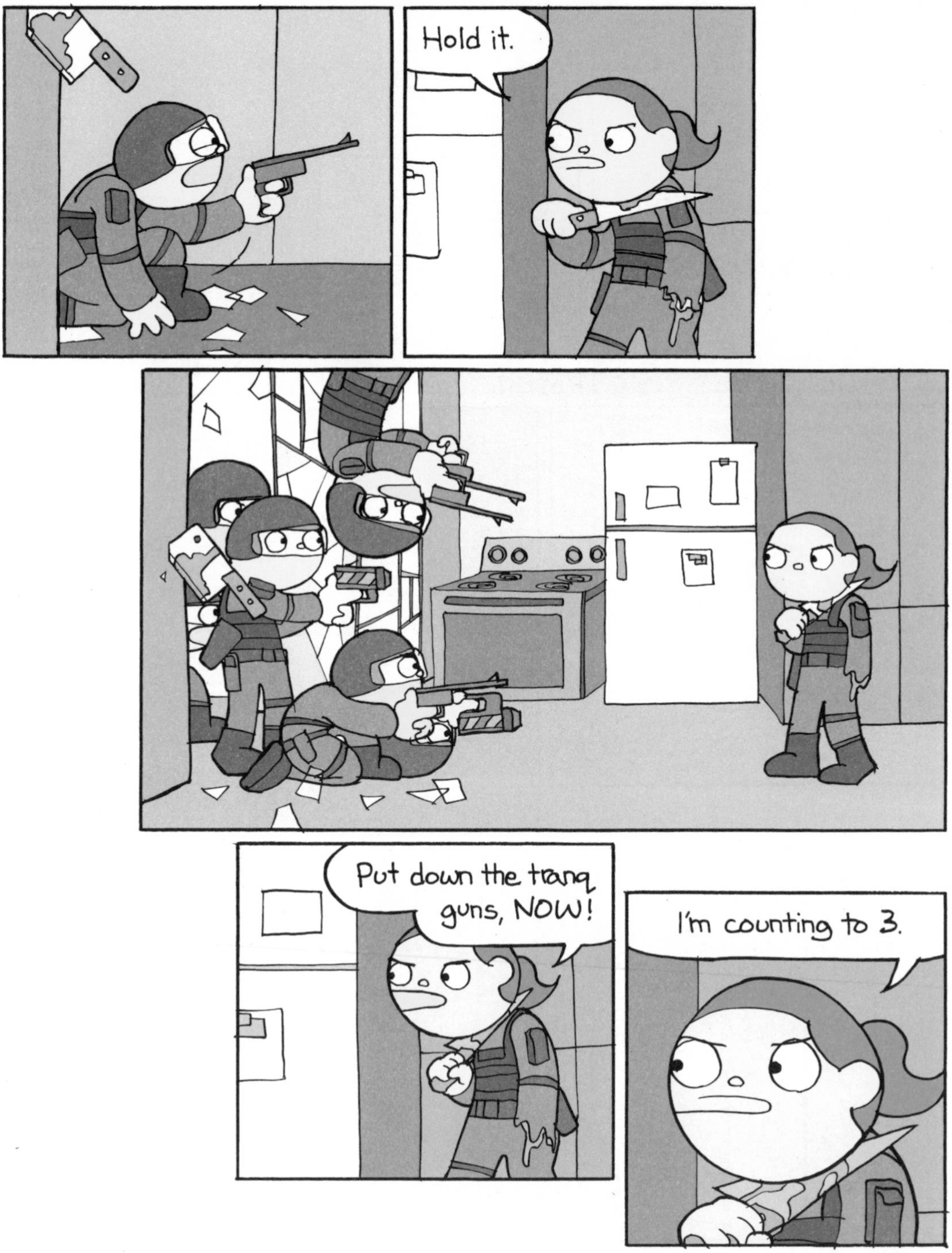
Hold it.
Put down the tranq guns, NOW!
I'm counting to 3.

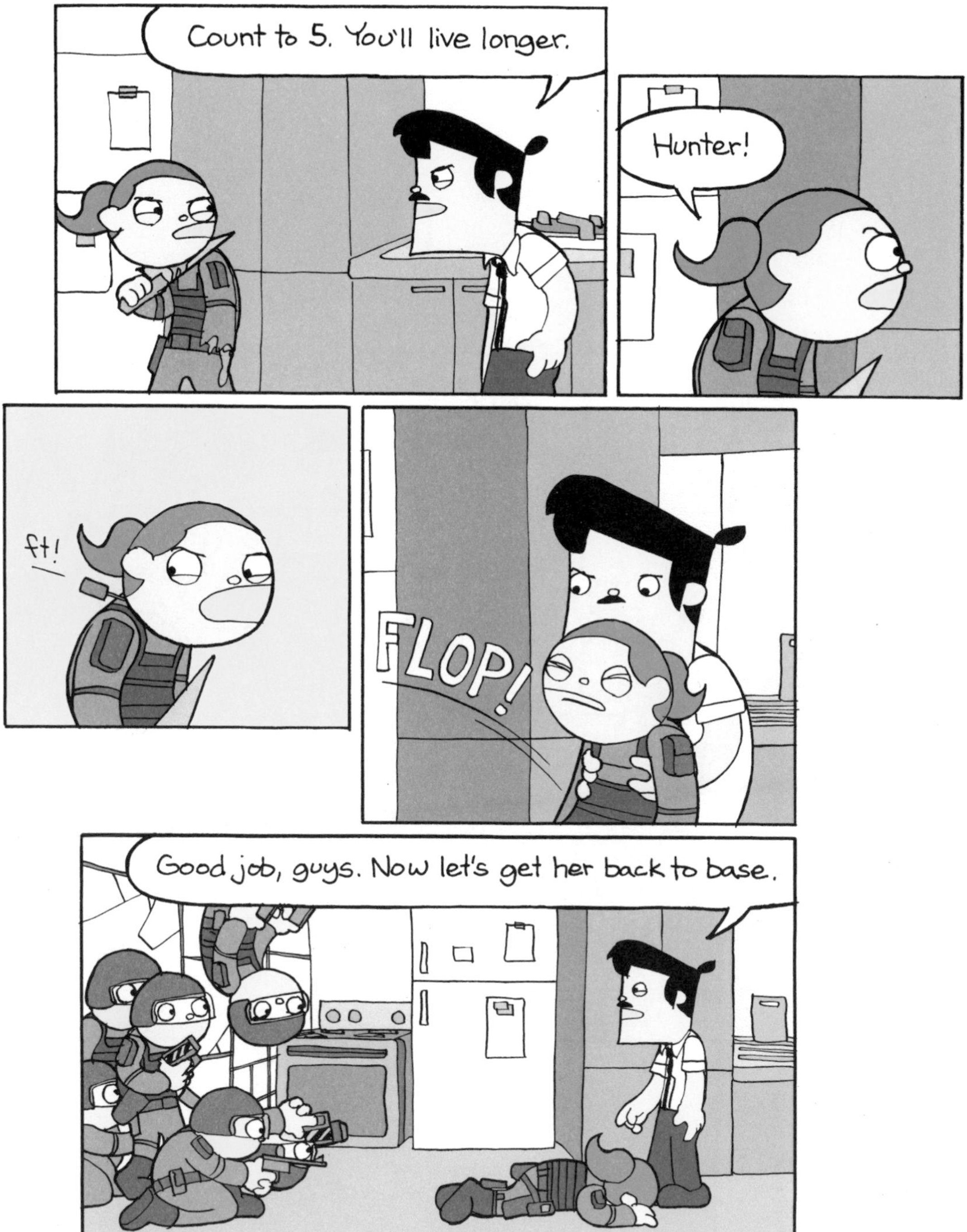
Count to 5. You'll live longer.
Hunter!
ft!
FLOP!
Good job, guys. Now let's get her back to base.

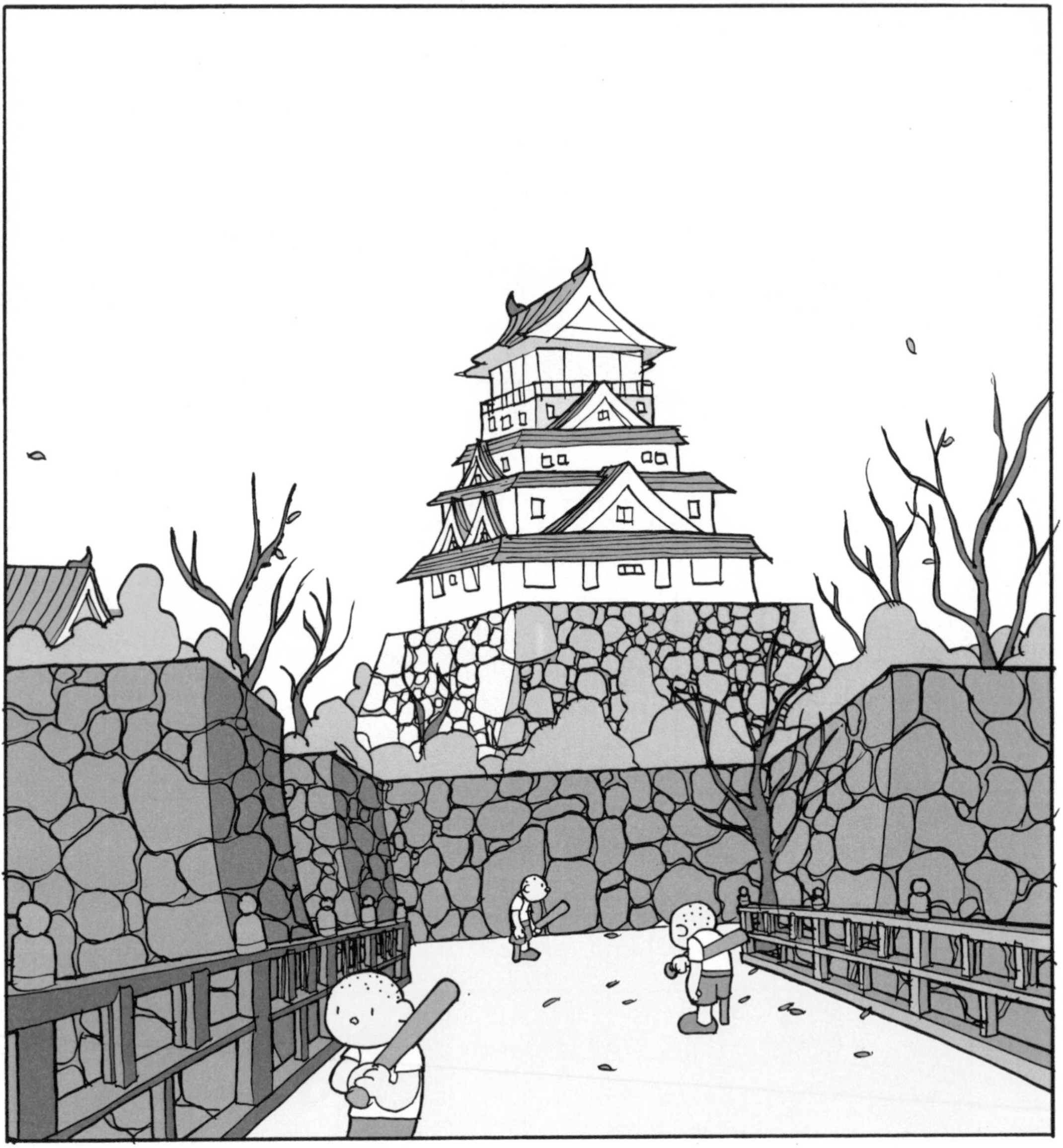

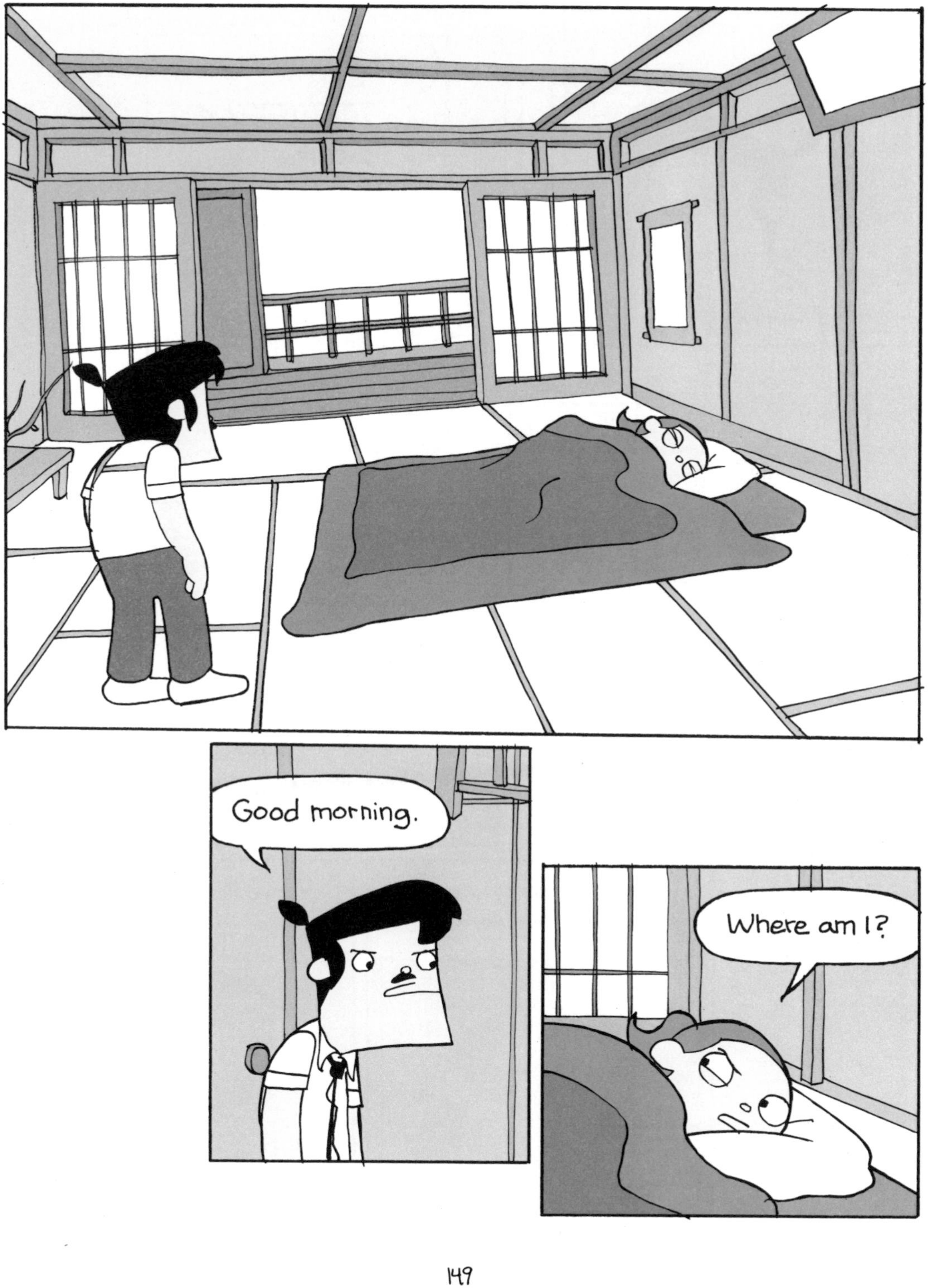
Good morning.
Where am I?

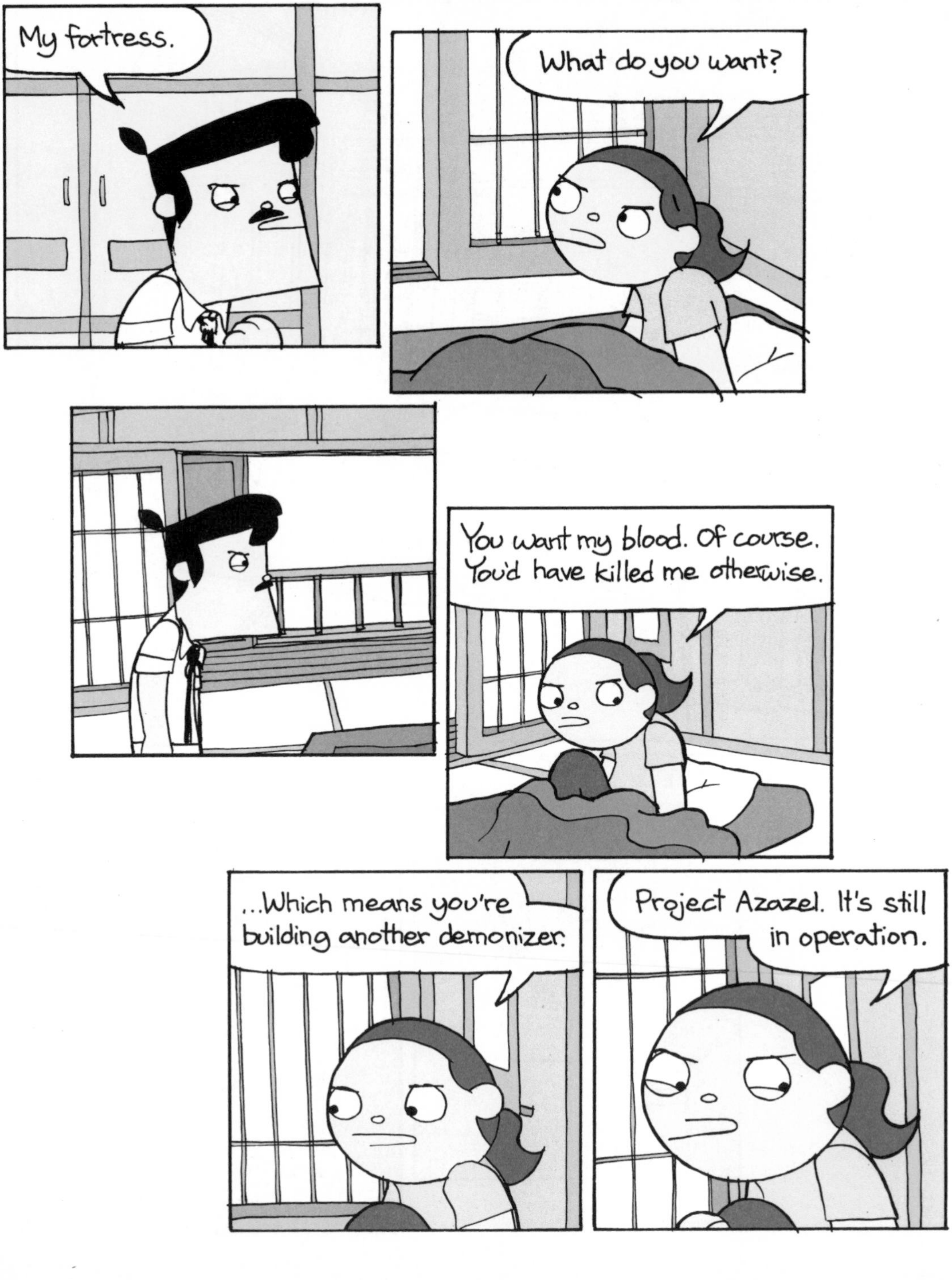
My fortress.
What do you want?
You want my blood. Of course. You'd have killed me otherwise.
...Which means you're building another demonizer.
Project Azazel. It's still in operation.

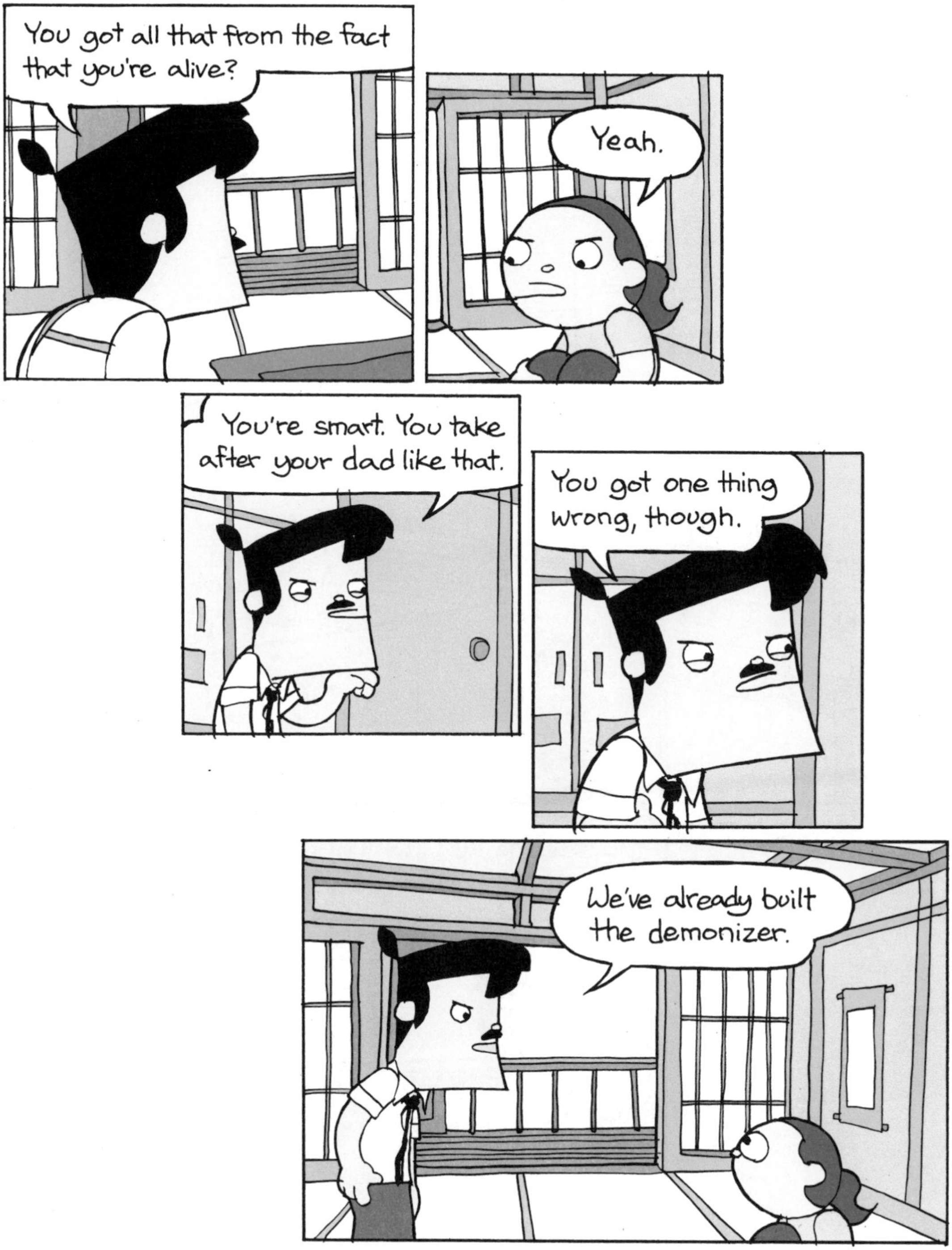
You got all that from the fact that you're alive?
Yeah.
You're smart. You take after your dad like that.
You got one thing wrong, though.
We've already built the demonizer.

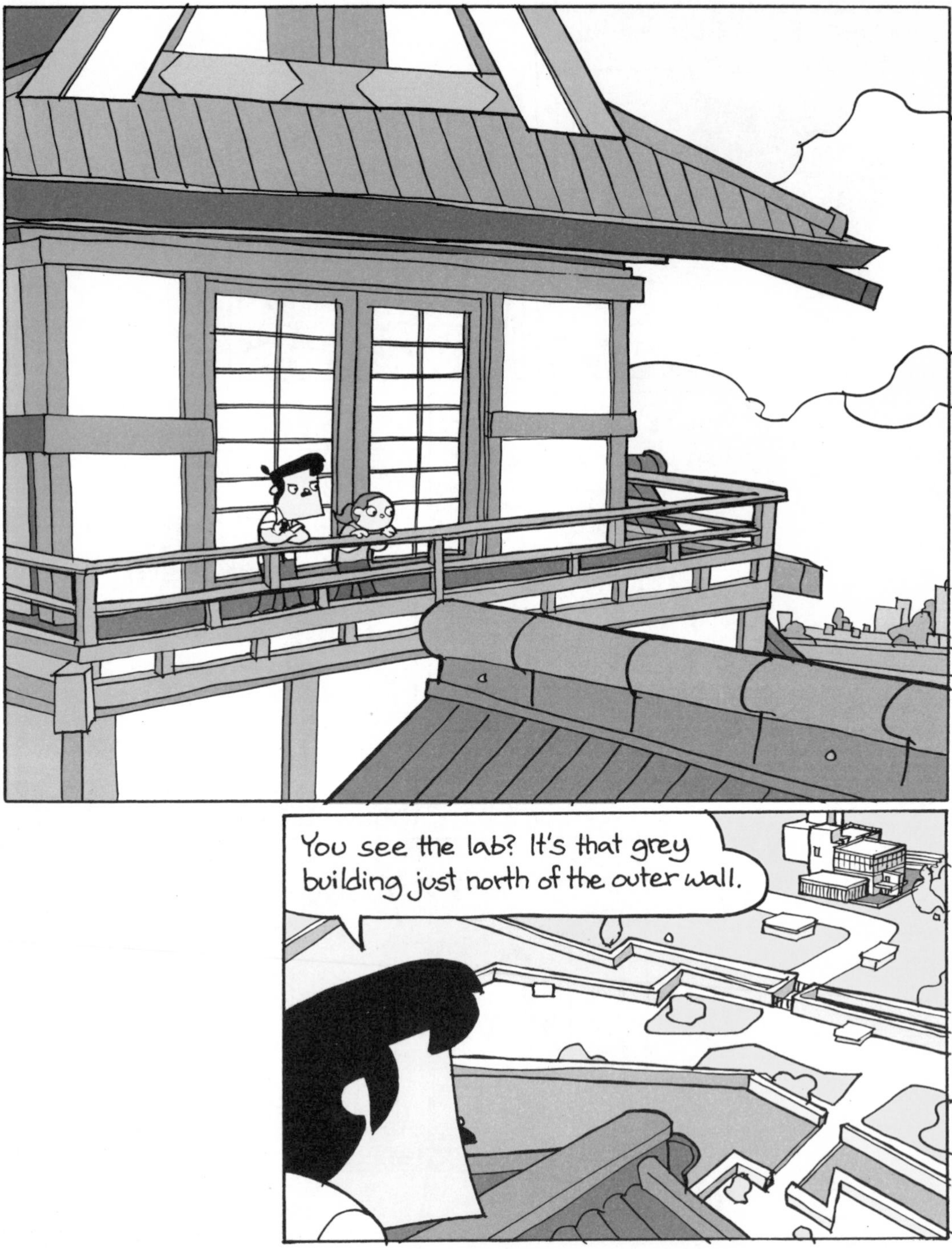
You see the lab? It's that grey building just north of the outer wall.

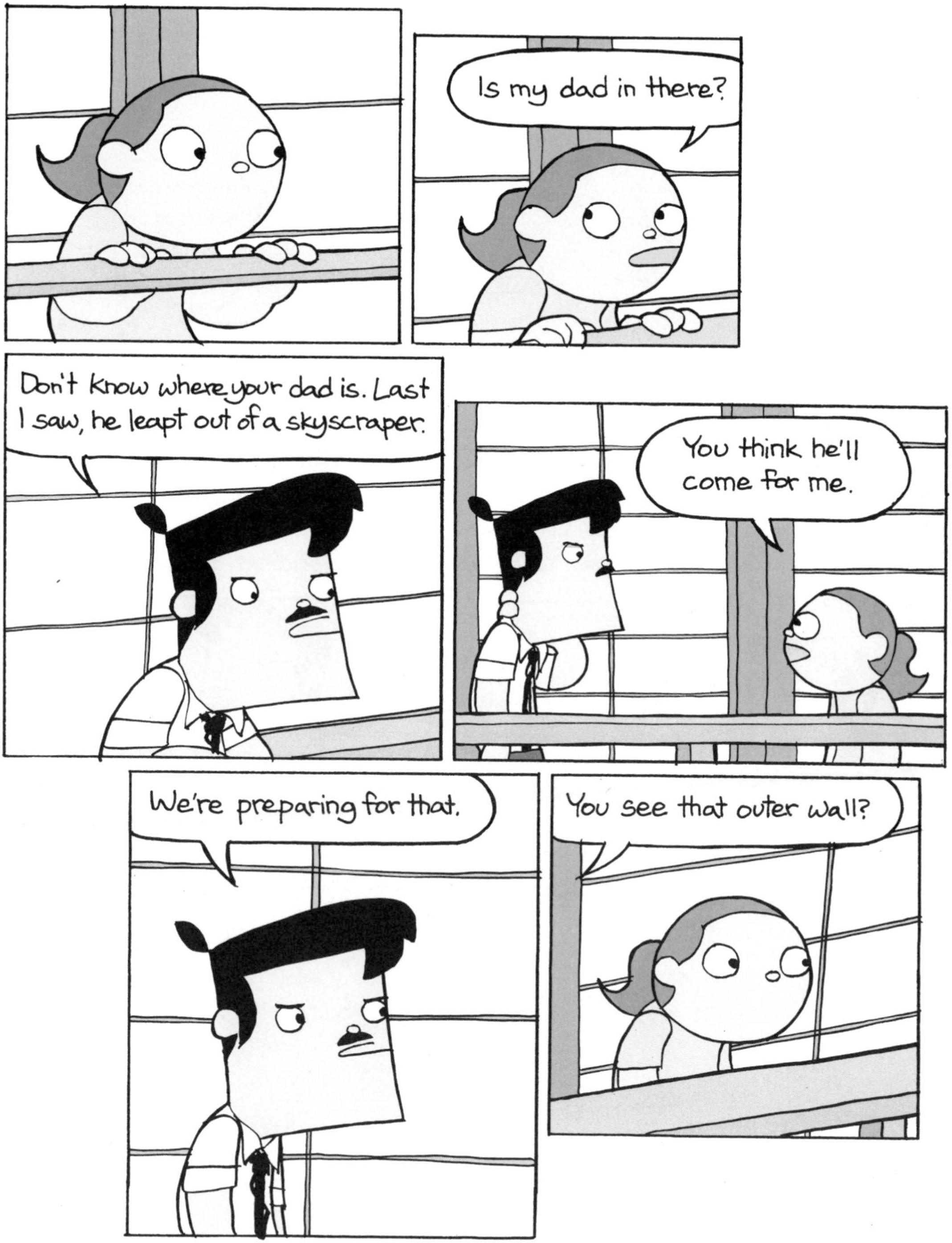
Is my dad in there?
Don't know where your dad is. Last I saw, he leapt out of a skyscraper.
You think he'll come for me.
We're preparing for that.
You see that outer wall?

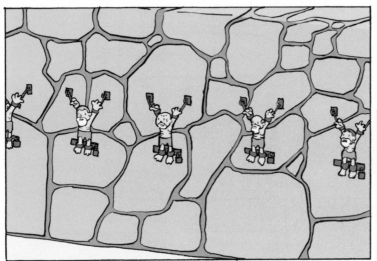

It's lined with prisoners.

Death row inmates. Your dad tries to get into the compound by killing himself on the far side of the wall, he'll just possess one of them.

I imagine he'll try and make another possession from there.

They've all had glossectomies so I'm not sure how, but suppose your dad manages to kill himself again.

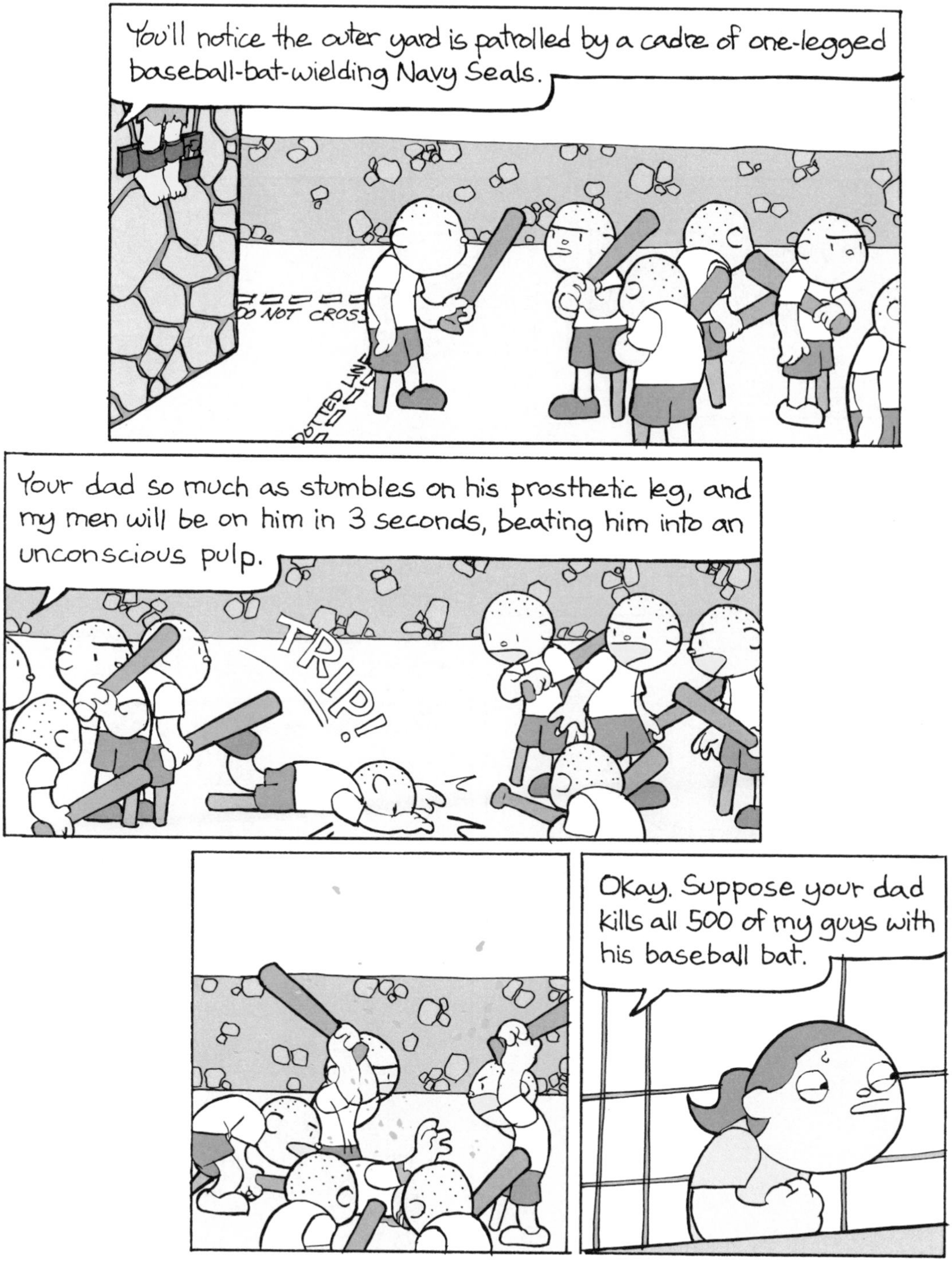
You'll notice the outer yard is patrolled by a cadre of one-legged baseball-bat-wielding Navy Seals.
DO NOT CROSS
DOTTED LINE
Your dad so much as stumbles on his prosthetic leg, and my men will be on him in 3 seconds, beating him into an unconscious pulp.
TRIP!
Okay. Suppose your dad kills all 500 of my guys with his baseball bat.

Suppose he turns that bat on himself and manages to possess his way over the 30-foot inner wall.

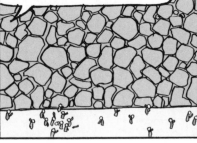

A lot of good that'll do him. You notice the entire inner yard is filled with the world's largest assemblage of conjoined twins.

Now let's just say for the sake of argument that your dad can kill his twin and drag himself over to the main tower.

He'd still have to fight his way through 4 floors of demonized Israeli Commandos while lugging around his dead twin brother.

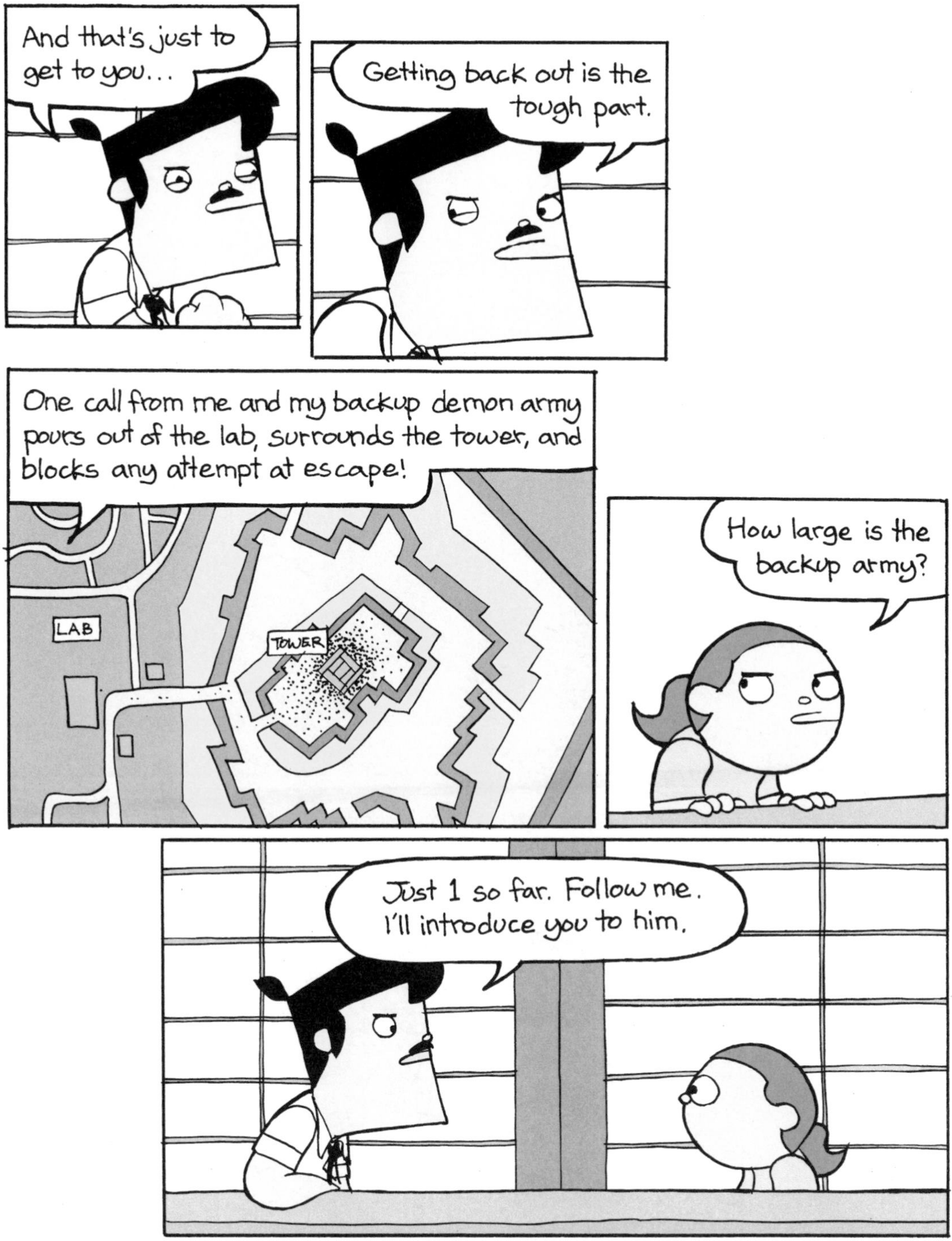
And that's just to get to you...
Getting back out is the tough part.
One call from me and my backup demon army pours out of the lab, surrounds the tower, and blocks any attempt at escape!
LAB
TOWER
How large is the backup army?
Just 1 so far. Follow me. I'll introduce you to him.

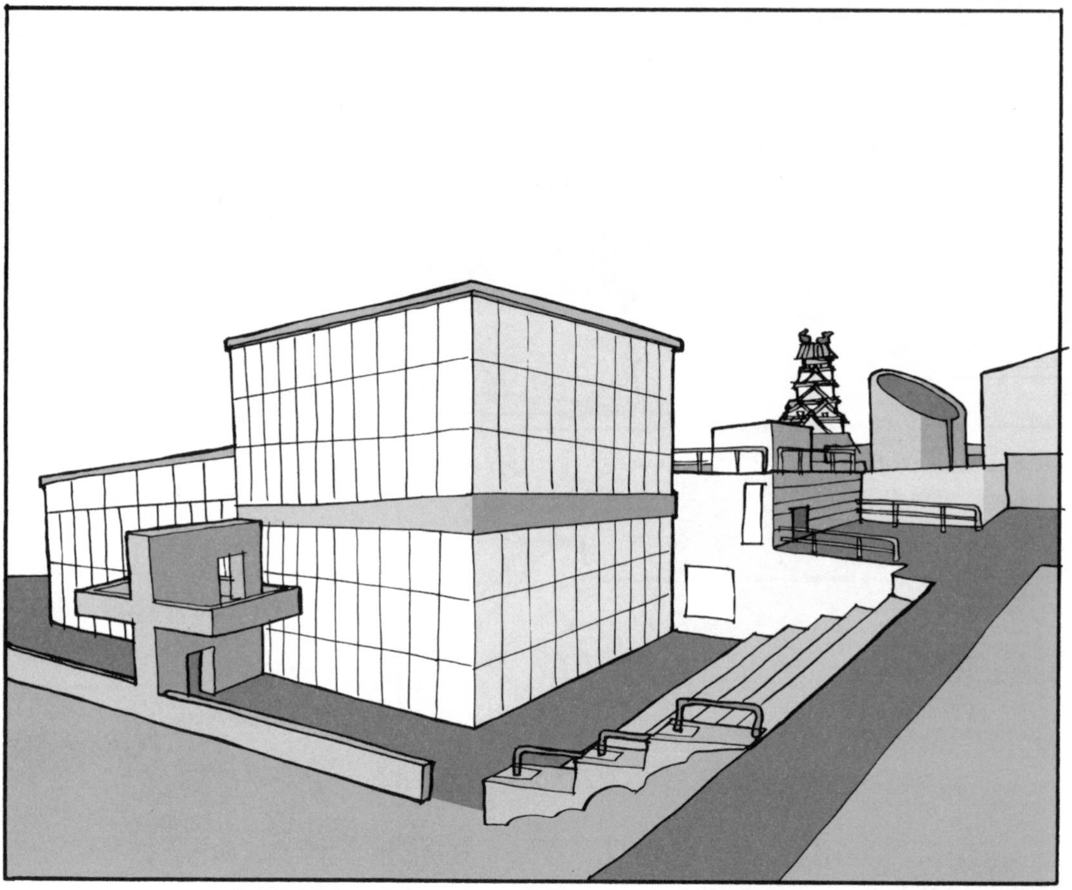

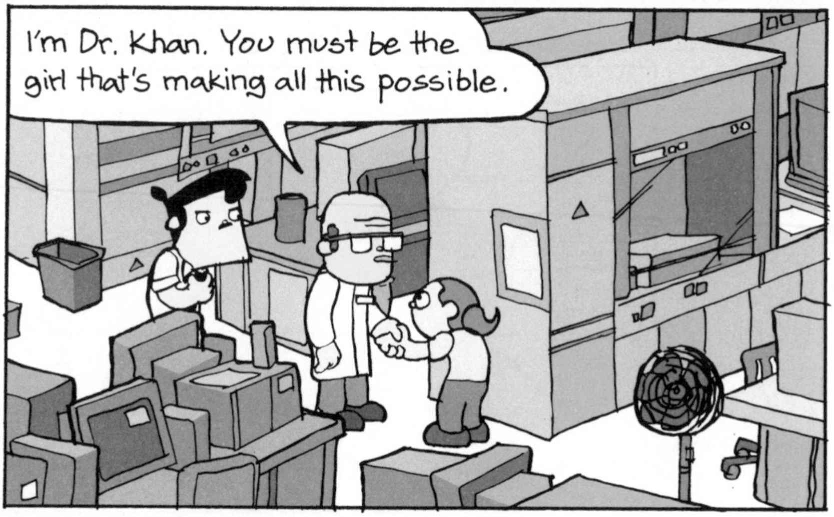
I'm Dr. Khan. You must be the girl that's making all this possible.

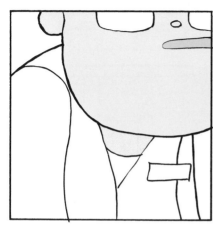

You're a demon. I can tell from the tan line on your neck.

How many others have you made?

You're new to this body so we can't squeeze out a whole lot.

But as you settle in, we're hoping to ramp up to 34 demons per unit of blood.

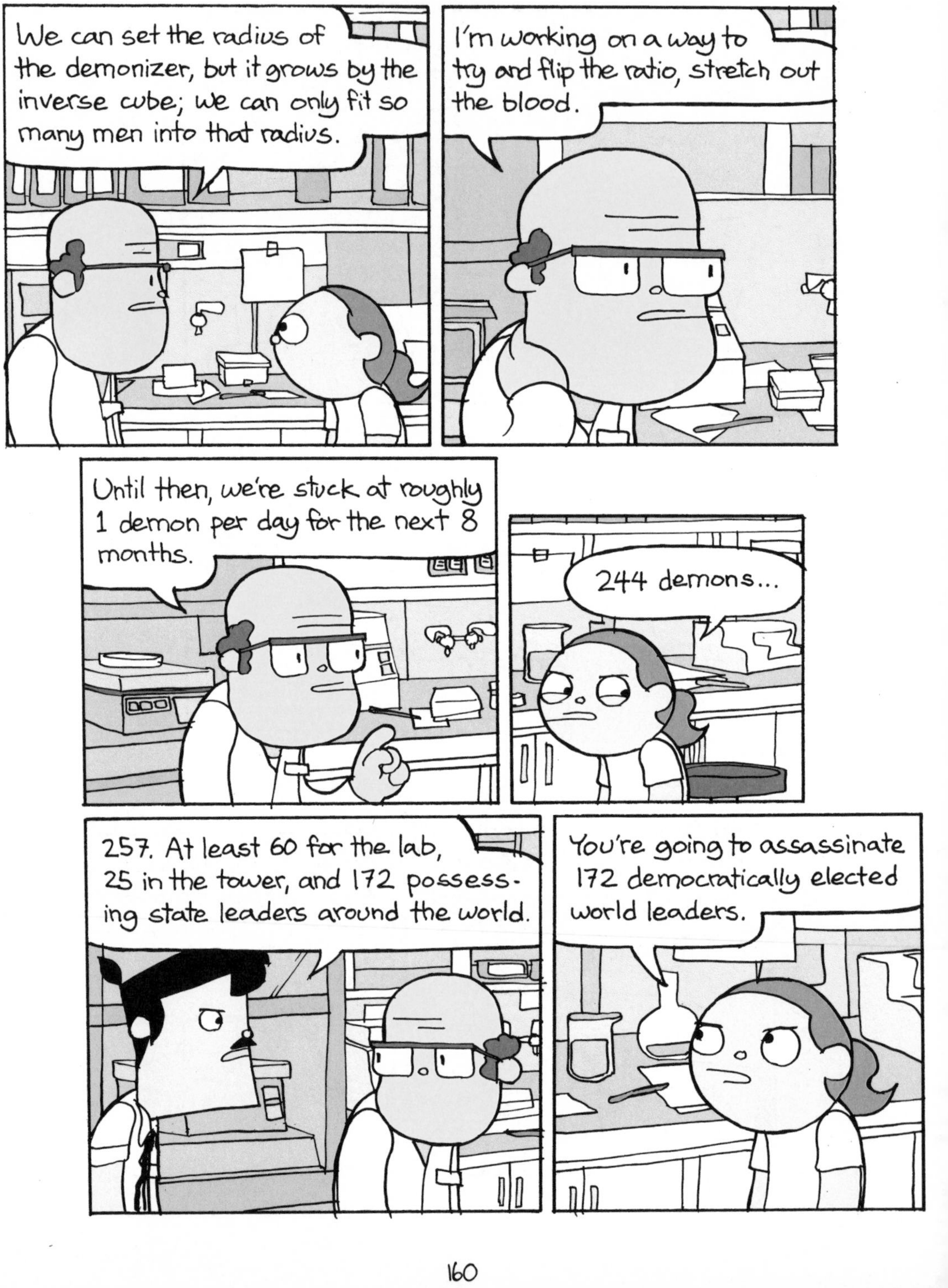
We can set the radius of the demonizer, but it grows by the inverse cube; we can only fit so many men into that radius.
I'm working on a way to try and flip the ratio, stretch out the blood.
Until then, we're stuck at roughly 1 demon per day for the next 8 months.
244 demons...
257. At least 60 for the lab, 25 in the tower, and 172 possess-ing state leaders around the world.
You're going to assassinate 172 democratically elected world leaders.

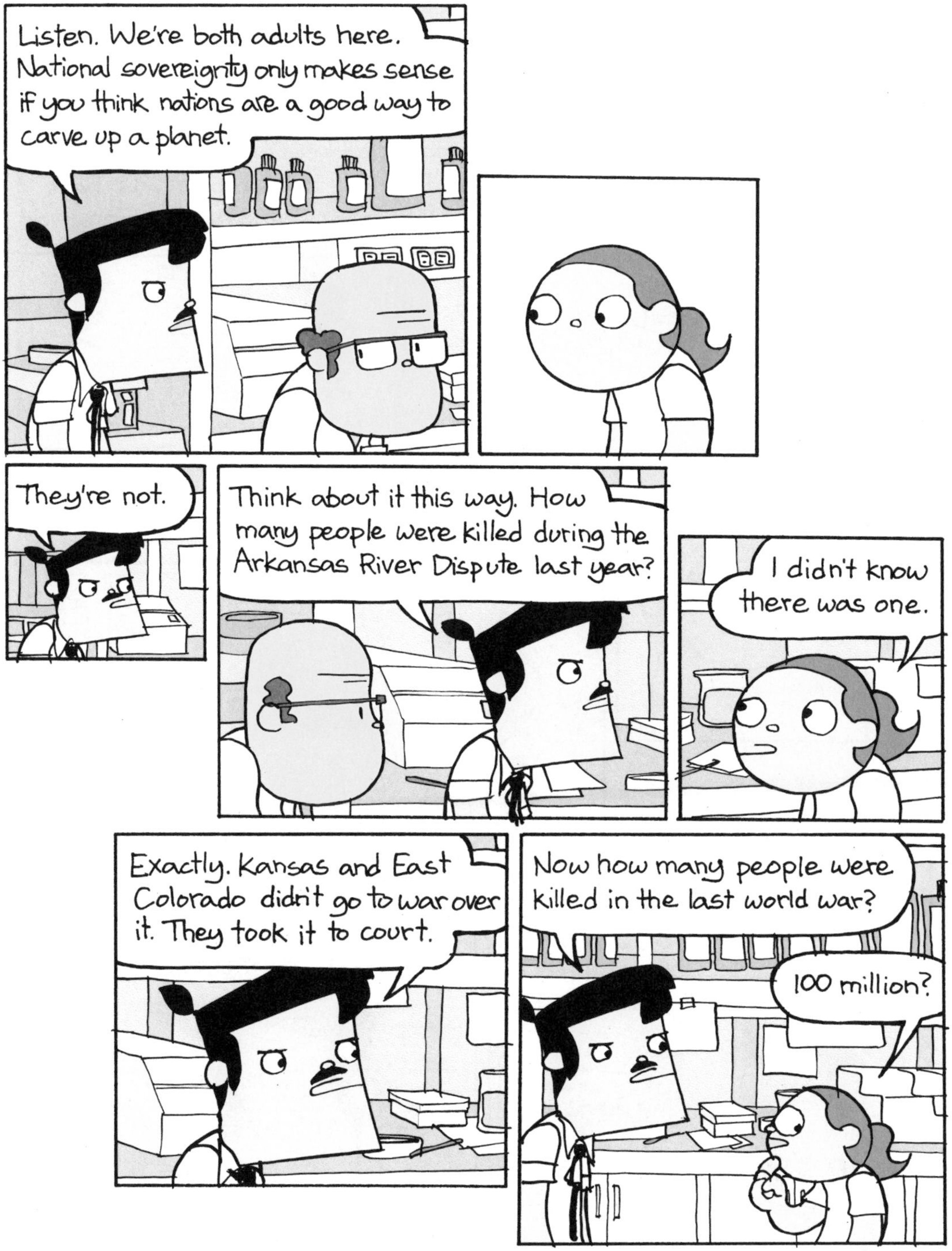
Listen. We're both adults here. National sovereignty only makes sense if you think nations are a good way to carve up a planet.
They're not.
Think about it this way. How many people were killed during the Arkansas River Dispute last year?
I didn't know there was one.
Exactly. Kansas and East Colorado didn't go to war over it. They took it to court.
Now how many people were killed in the last world war?
100 million?

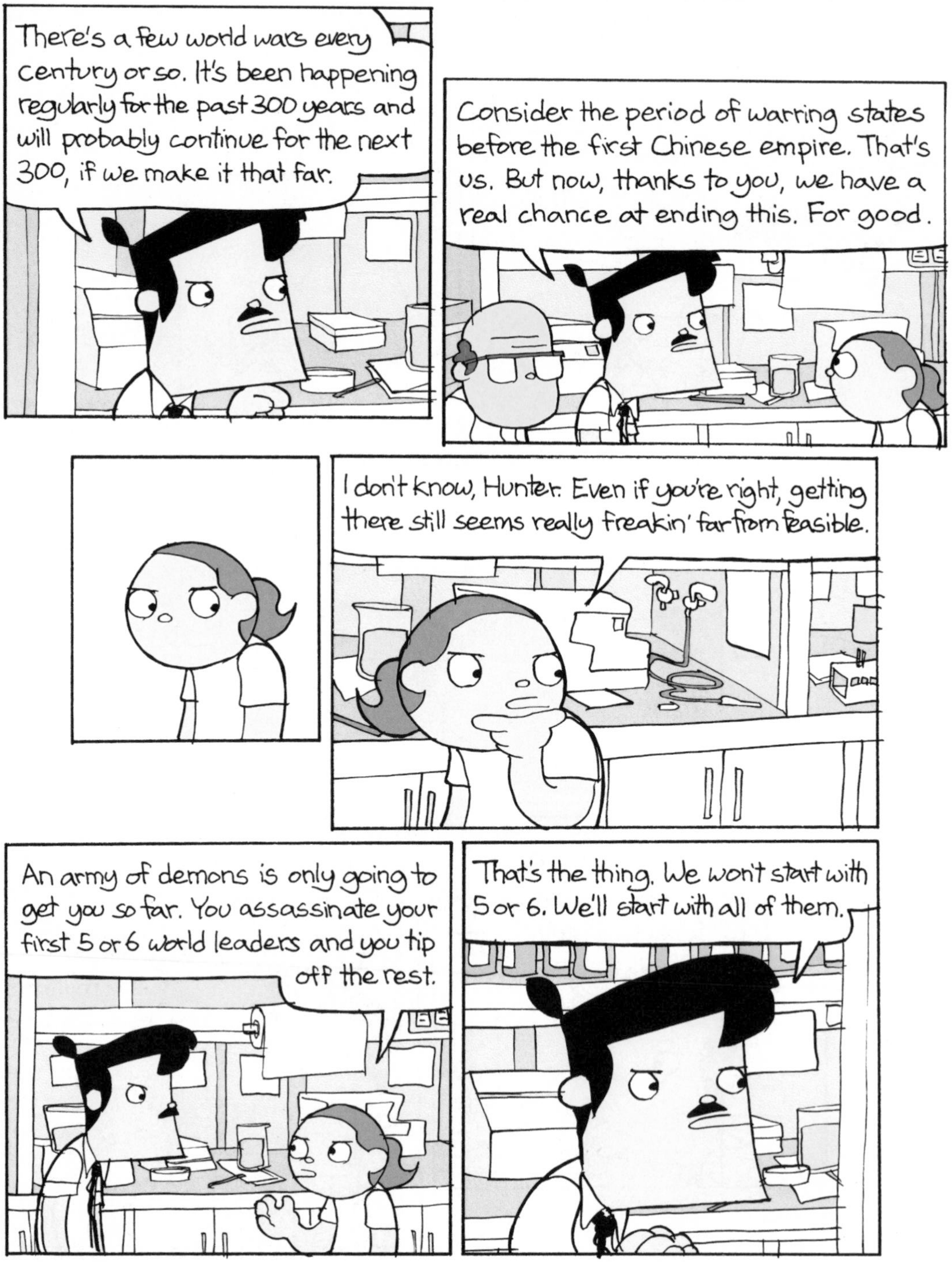
There's a few world wars every century or so. It's been happening regularly for the past 300 years and will probably continue for the next 300, if we make it that far.
Consider the period of warring states before the first Chinese empire. That's us. But now, thanks to you, we have a real chance at ending this. For good.
I don't know, Hunter. Even if you're right, getting there still seems really freakin' far from feasible.
An army of demons is only going to get you so far. You assassinate your first 5 or 6 world leaders and you tip off the rest.
That's the thing. We won't start with 5 or 6. We'll start with all of them.

July 4, 12am GMT: 172 possessions around the globe, all within 10 seconds of each other.

They'll start off possessing low-level cabinet members, relatives of secret service, and slowly work their way up the chain of command.

Every day, they'll get a little closer to their target. The president, prime minister, king, or tsar.

By the middle of the year, our men will have infiltrated every nation-state on the planet. One month after that, they'll all be in position.

And as soon as that clock hits midnight, it'll all be over.

The earth will be but one country and mankind its citizens.

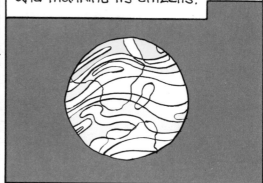

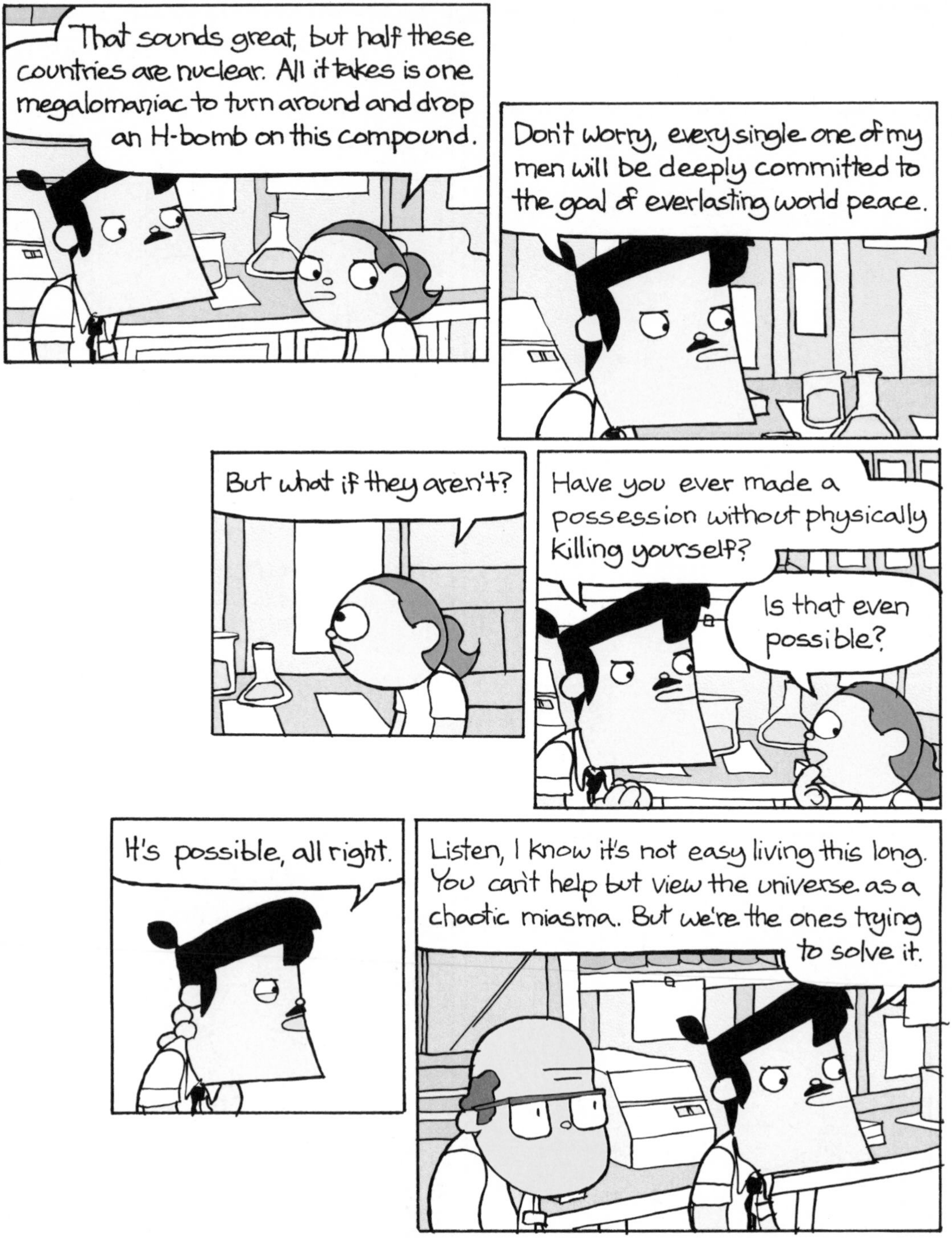
That sounds great, but half these countries are nuclear. All it takes is one megalomaniac to turn around and drop an H-bomb on this compound.
Don't worry, every single one of my men will be deeply committed to the goal of everlasting world peace.
But what if they aren't?
Have you ever made a possession without physically killing yourself?
Is that even possible?
It's possible, all right.
Listen, I know it's not easy living this long. You can't help but view the universe as a chaotic miasma. But we're the ones trying to solve it.

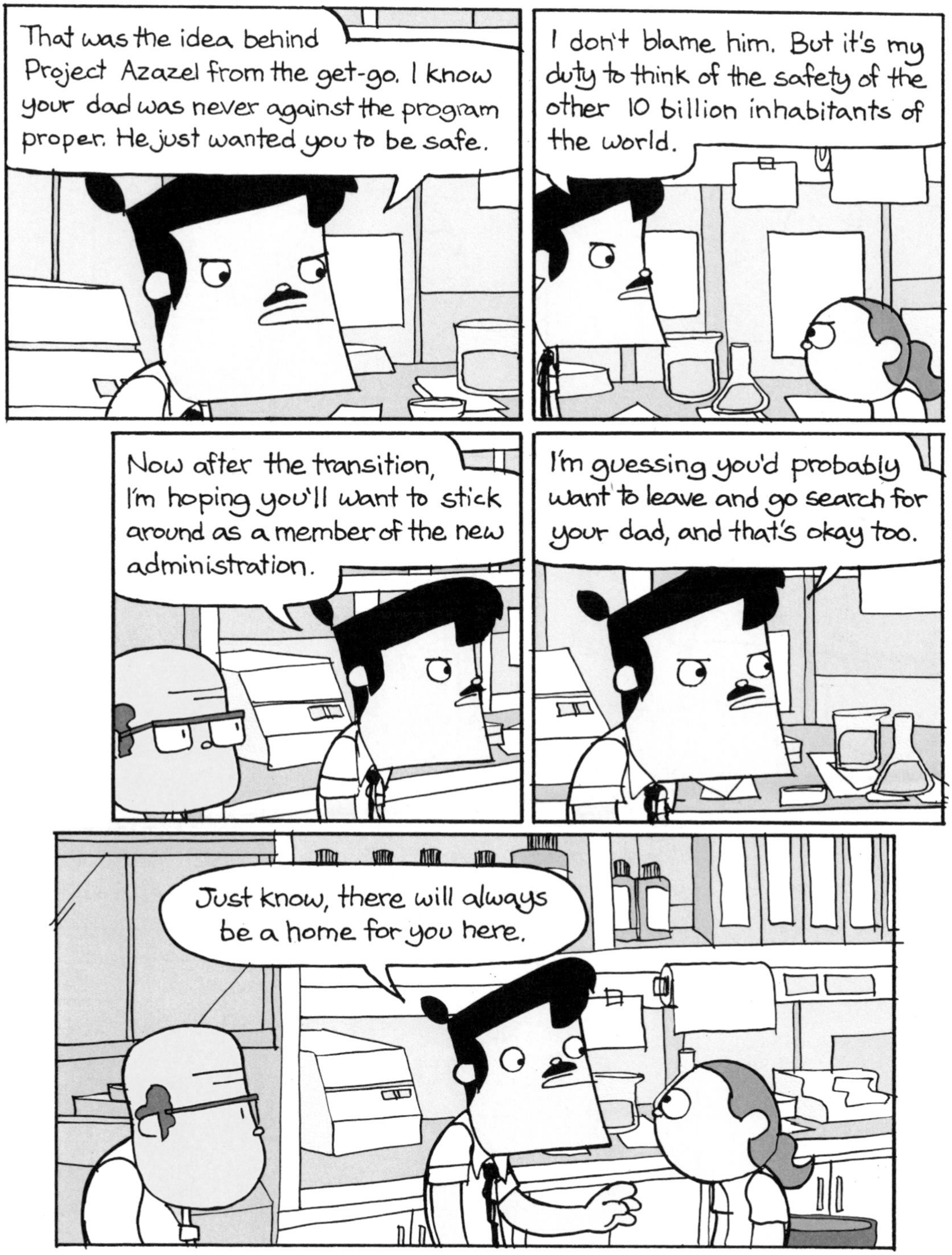
That was the idea behind Project Azazel from the get-go. I know your dad was never against the program proper. He just wanted you to be safe.
I don't blame him. But it's my duty to think of the safety of the other 10 billion inhabitants of the world.
Now after the transition, I'm hoping you'll want to stick around as a member of the new administration.
I'm guessing you'd probably want to leave and go search for your dad, and that's okay too.
Just know, there will always be a home for you here.

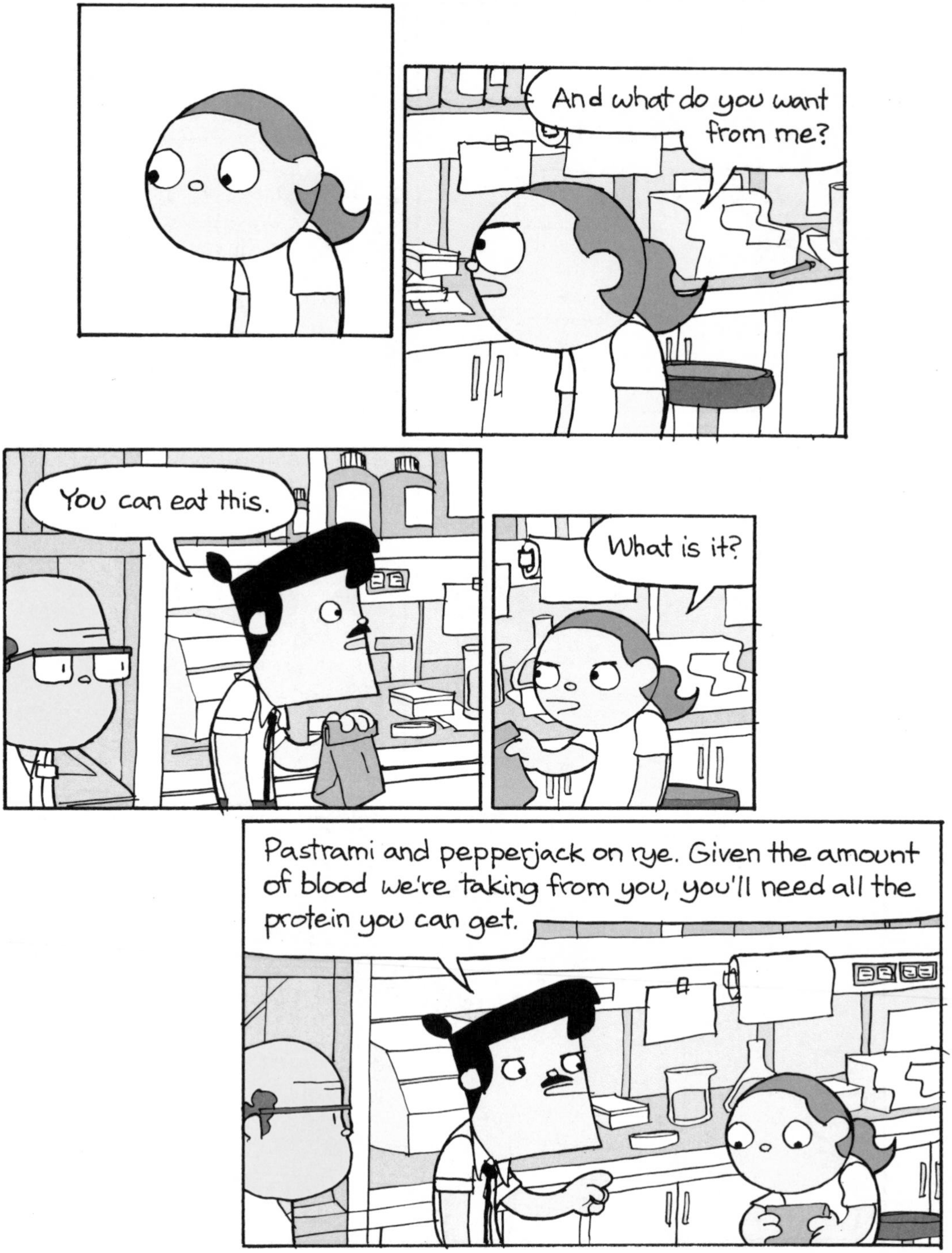
And what do you want from me?
You can eat this.
What is it?
Pastrami and pepperjack on rye. Given the amount of blood we're taking from you, you'll need all the protein you can get.

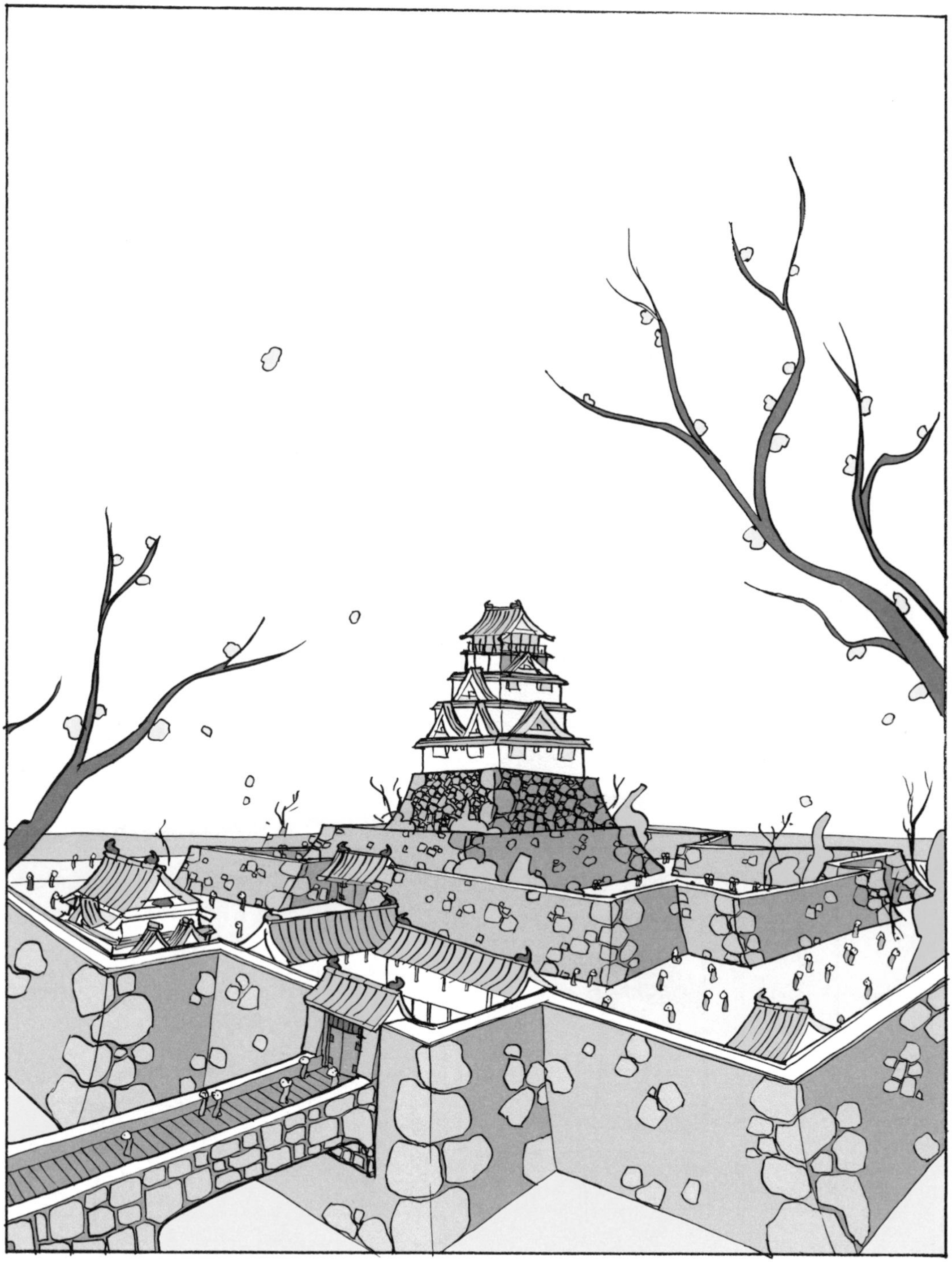

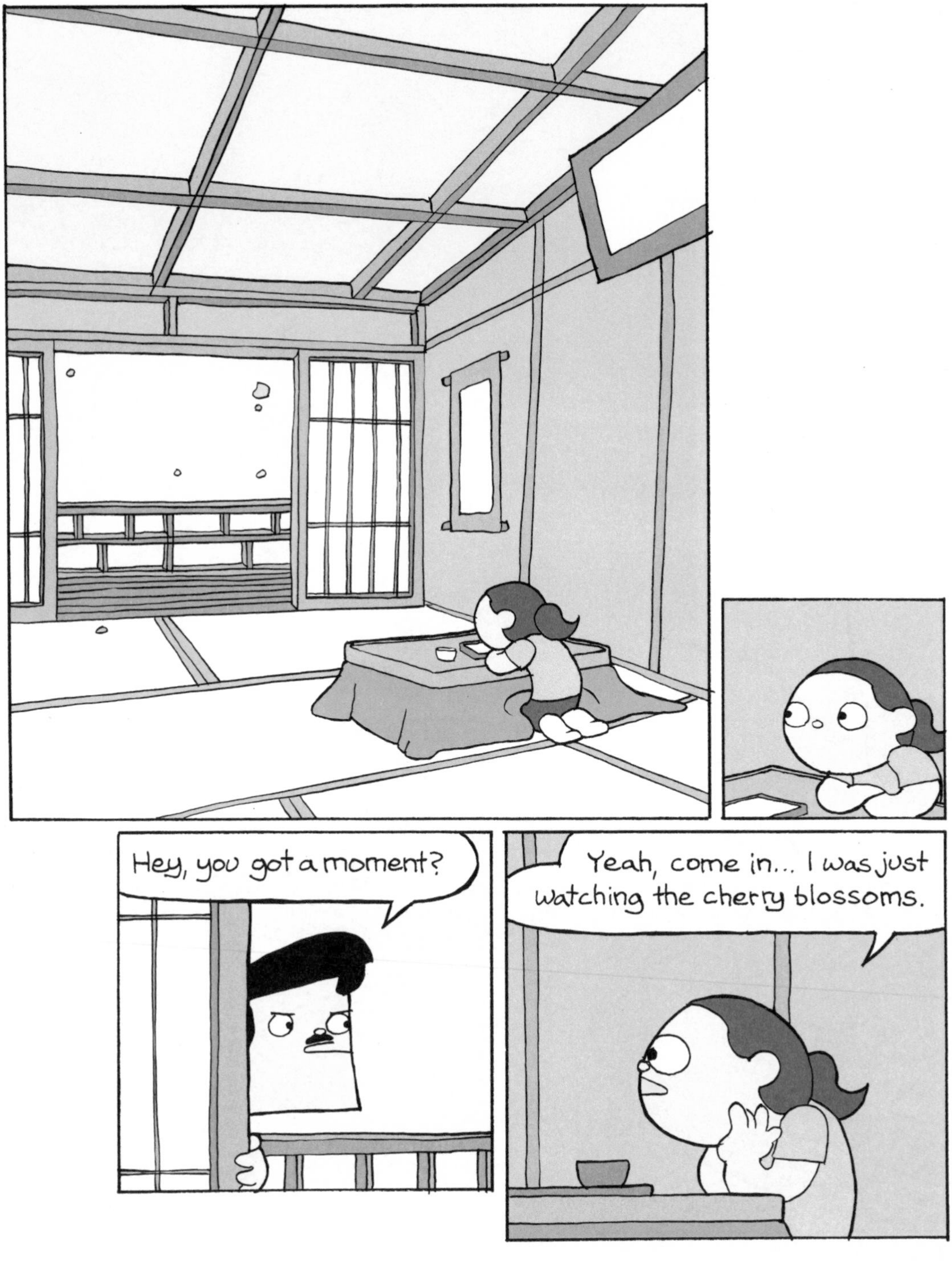
Hey, you got a moment?
Yeah, come in... I was just watching the cherry blossoms.

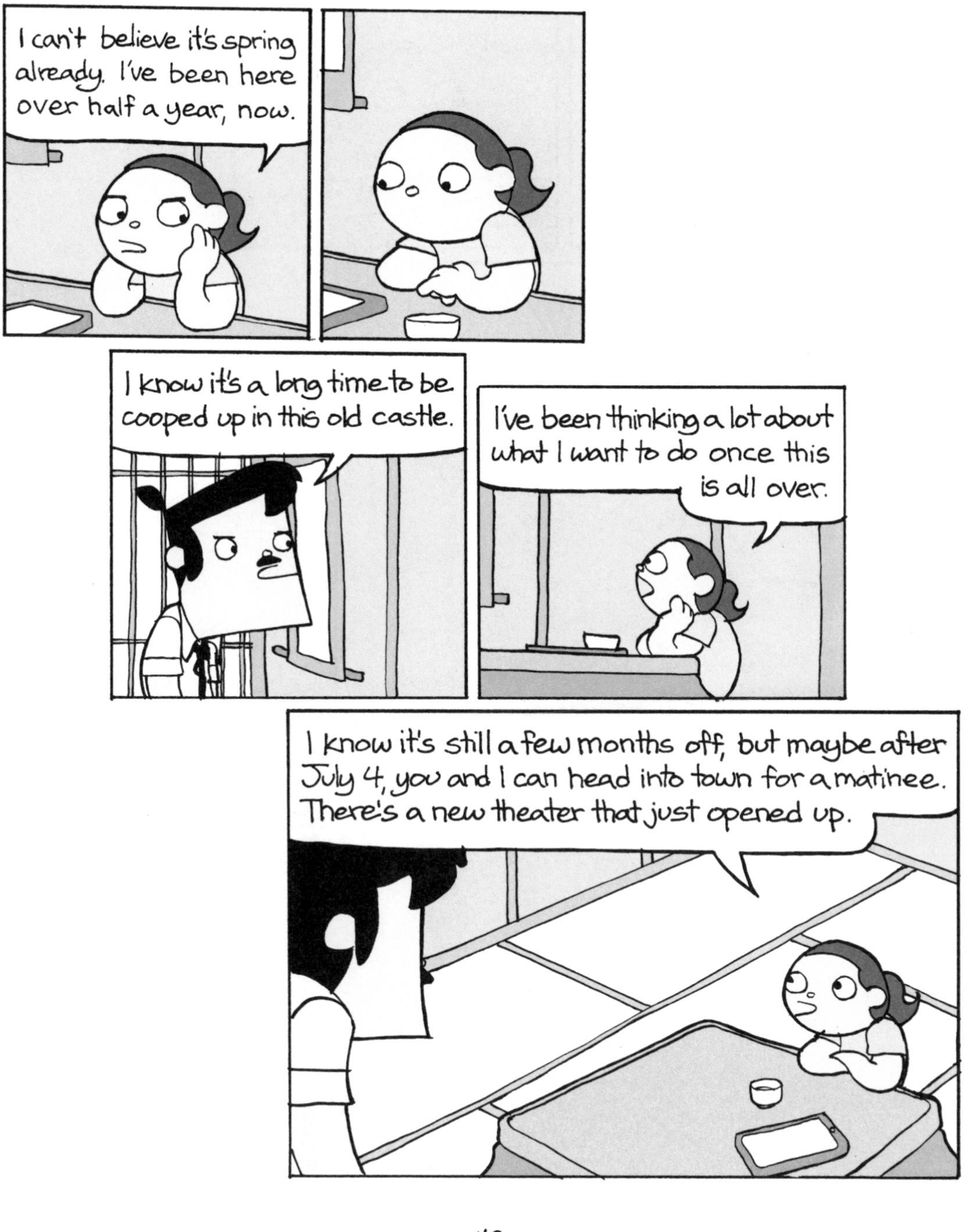
I can't believe it's spring already. I've been here over half a year, now.
I know it's a long time to be cooped up in this old castle.
I've been thinking a lot about what I want to do once this is all over.
I know it's still a few months off, but maybe after July 4, you and I can head into town for a matinee. There's a new theater that just opened up.

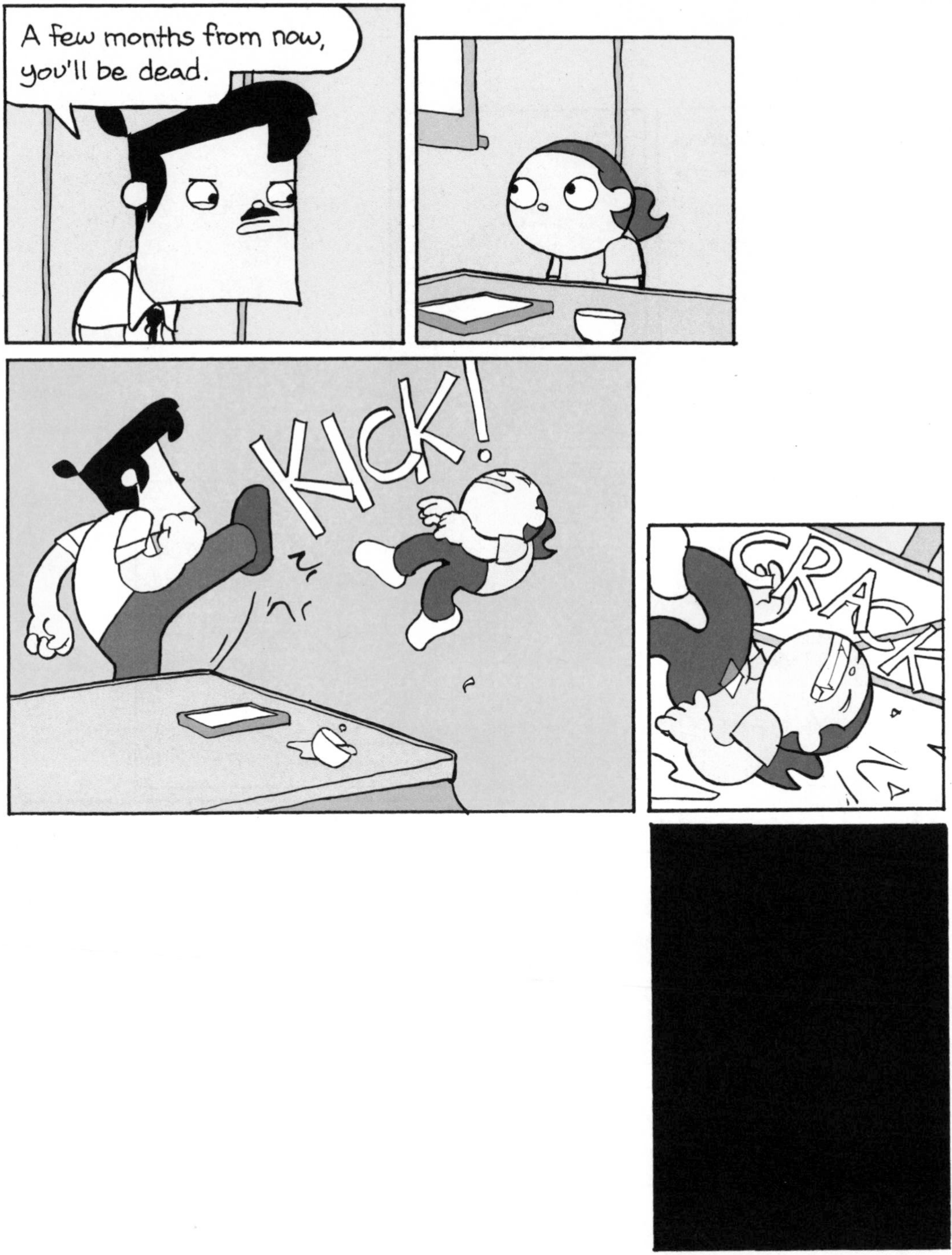
A few months from now, you'll be dead.
KICK!
CRACK

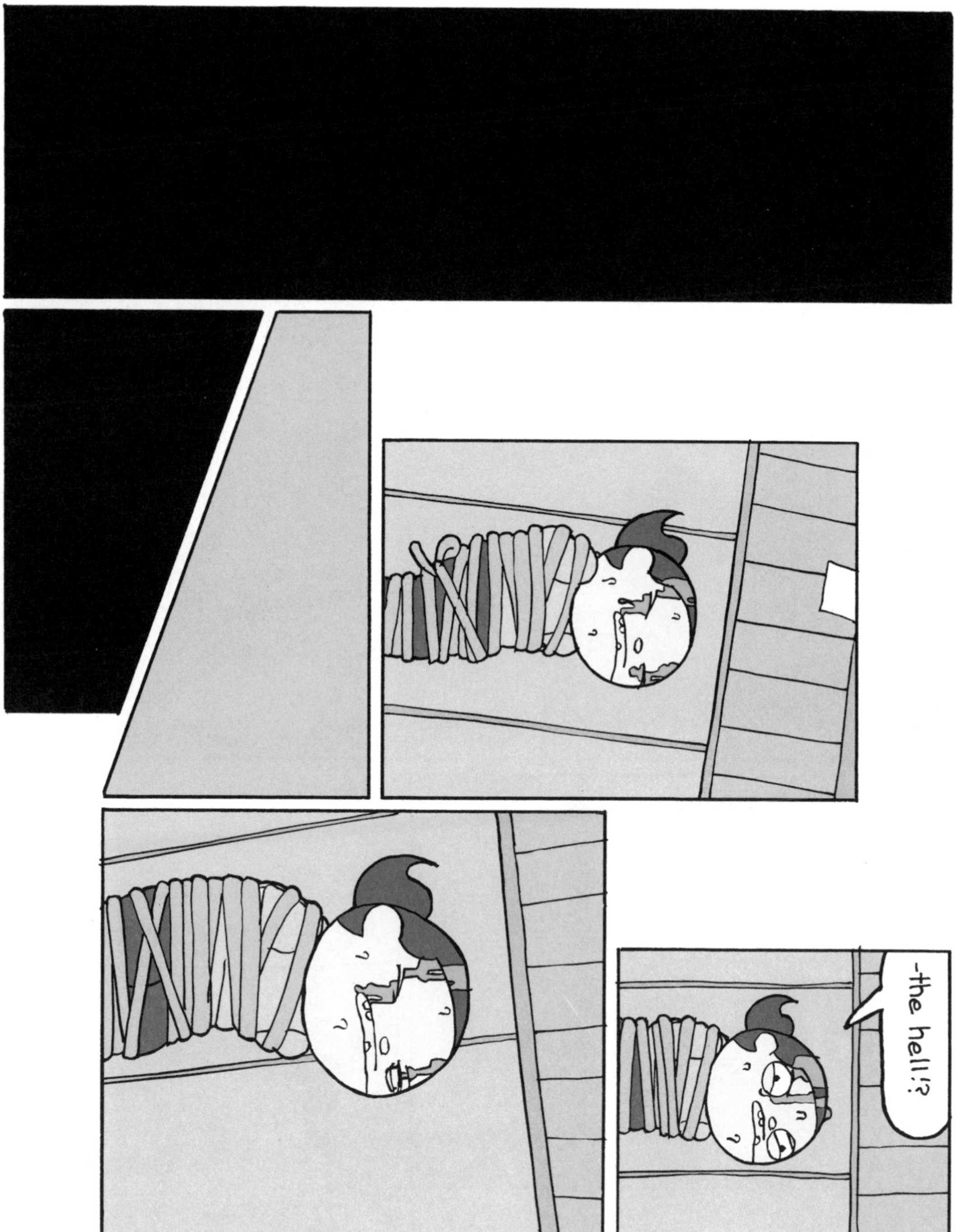
-the hell!?

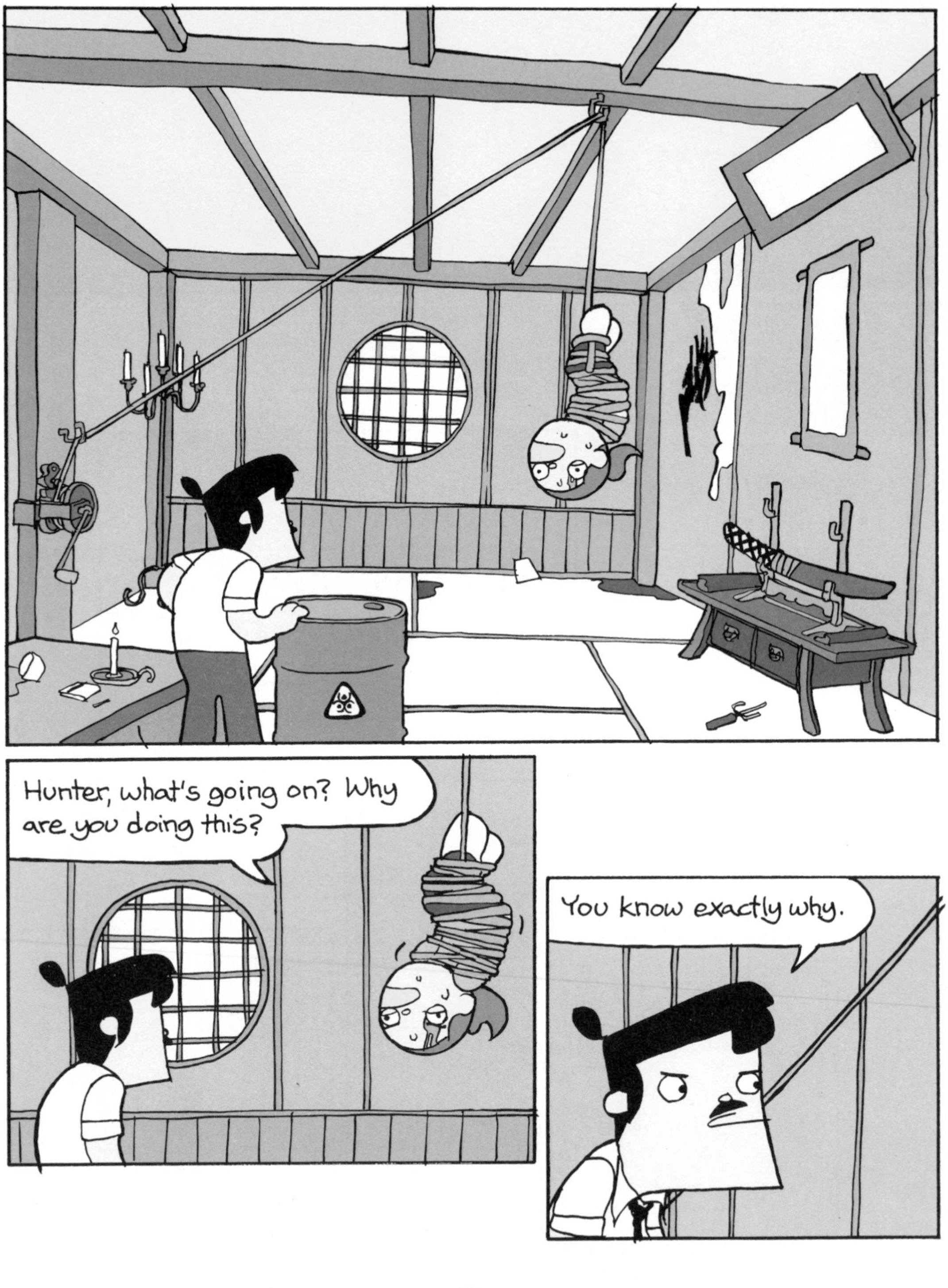
Hunter, what's going on? Why are you doing this?
You know exactly why.

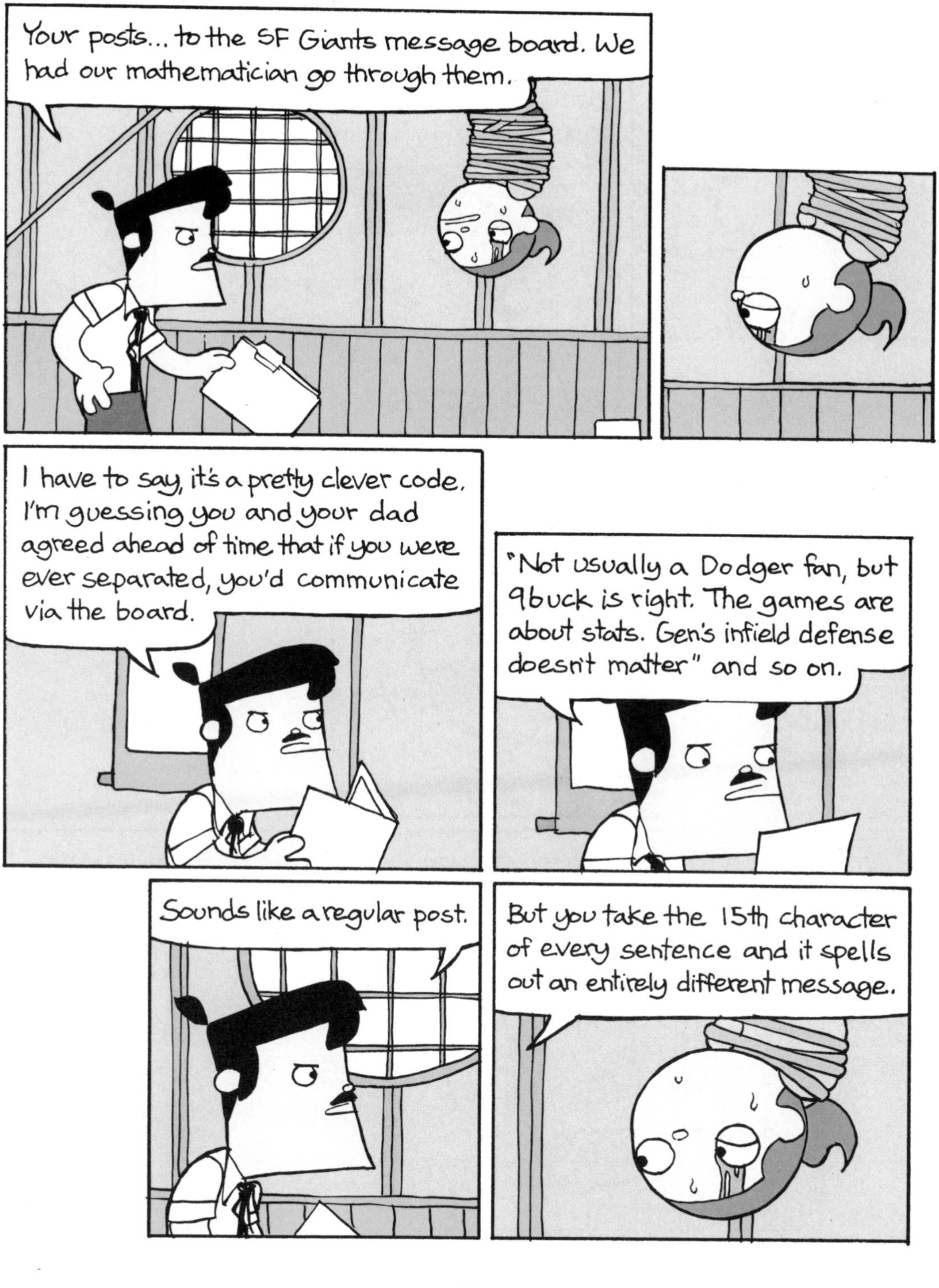

Your posts... to the SF Giants message board. We had our mathematician go through them.
I have to say, it's a pretty clever code. I'm guessing you and your dad agreed ahead of time that if you were ever separated, you'd communicate via the board.
"Not usually a Dodger fan, but 9buck is right. The games are about stats. Gen's infield defense doesn't matter" and so on.
Sounds like a regular post.
But you take the 15th character of every sentence and it spells out an entirely different message.

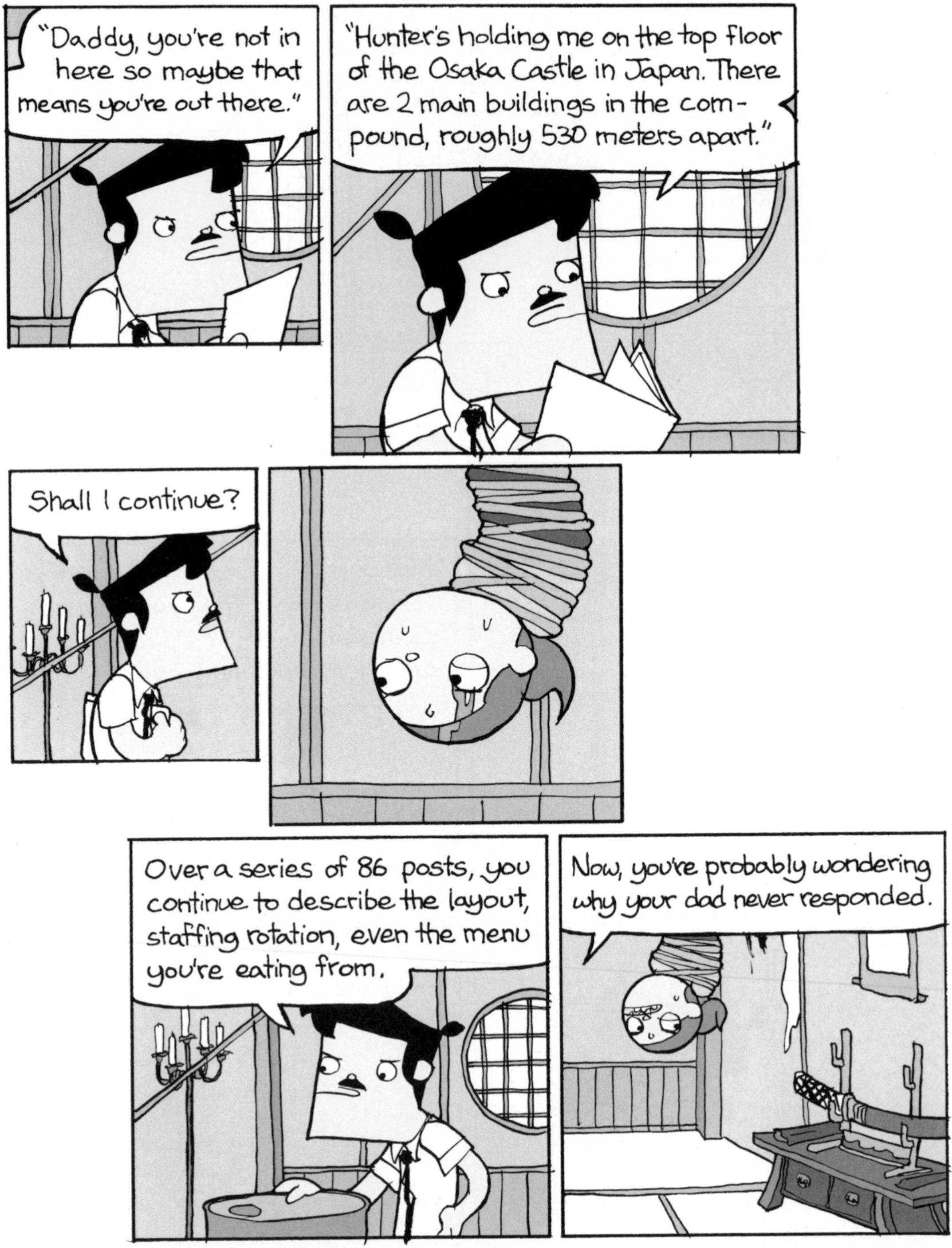
"Daddy, you're not in here so maybe that means you're out there."
"Hunter's holding me on the top floor of the Osaka Castle in Japan. There are 2 main buildings in the compound, roughly 530 meters apart."
Shall I continue?
Over a series of 86 posts, you continue to describe the layout, staffing rotation, even the menu you're eating from.
Now, you're probably wondering why your dad never responded.

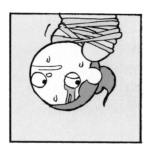

The security measures here. They were never meant to keep my dad out, were they?

Your dad is dead. I killed him last year. The security measures were always meant to keep you in.

Let me guess, you're already plotting your escape.

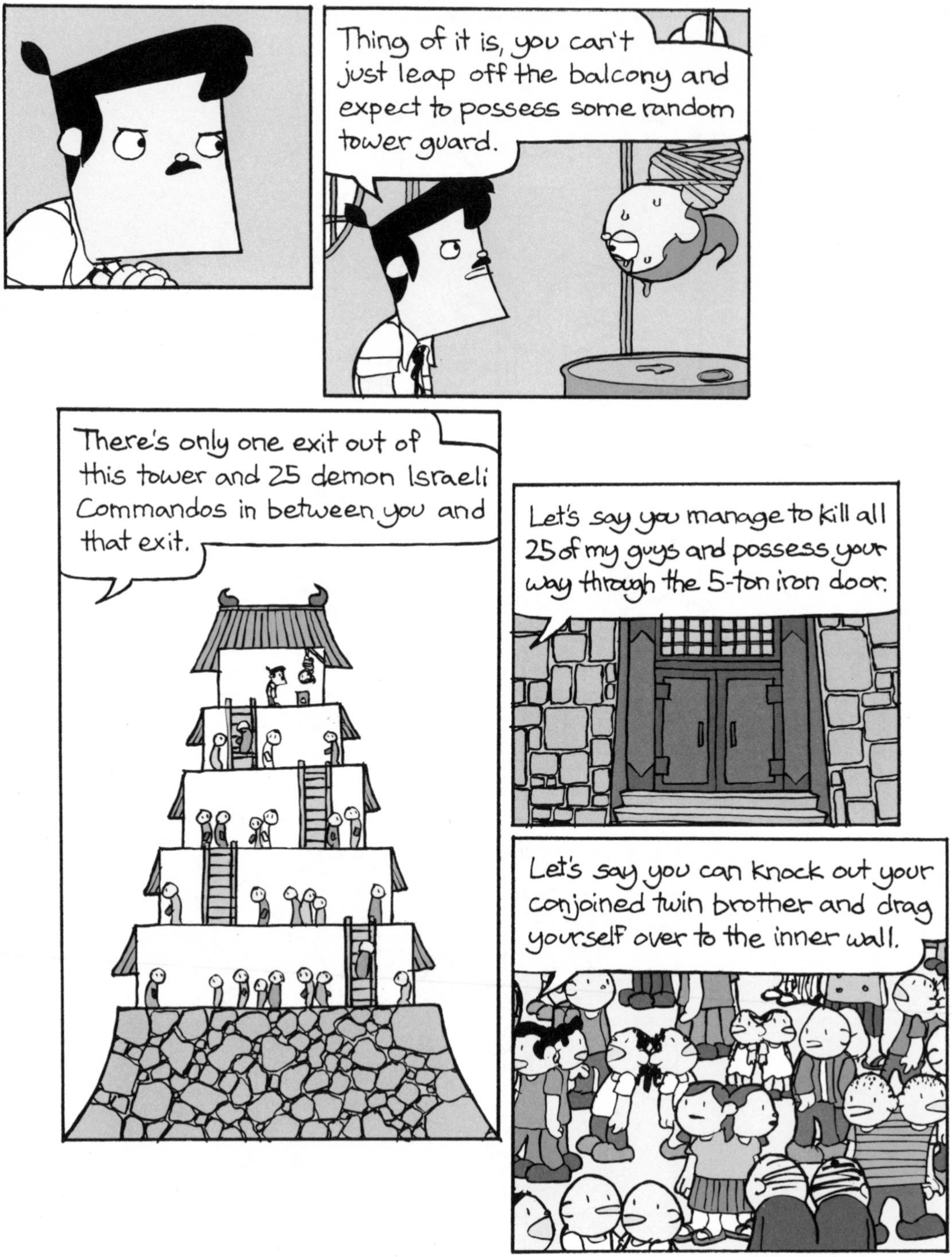
Thing of it is, you can't just leap off the balcony and expect to possess some random tower guard.
There's only one exit out of this tower and 25 demon Israeli Commandos in between you and that exit.
Let's say you manage to kill all 25 of my guys and possess your way through the 5-ton iron door.
Let's say you can knock out your conjoined twin brother and drag yourself over to the inner wall.

Let's say you possess yourself across the inner wall, walk up casually to the outer wall on one leg, kill yourself with a baseball bat, kill yourself again with all 4 limbs manacled, on the off chance that someone just happens to be on the other side of that wall.

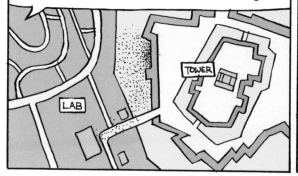

There's still the matter of the backup army of 1000 demons that have just run down from the lab and surrounded you.

LAB

TOWER

And let me guess. This is all presuming I can wriggle out of these knots before that candle burns through this rope and drops me into this vat of gastric acid.

Oh no. This vat isn't filled with acid.

it!us yo

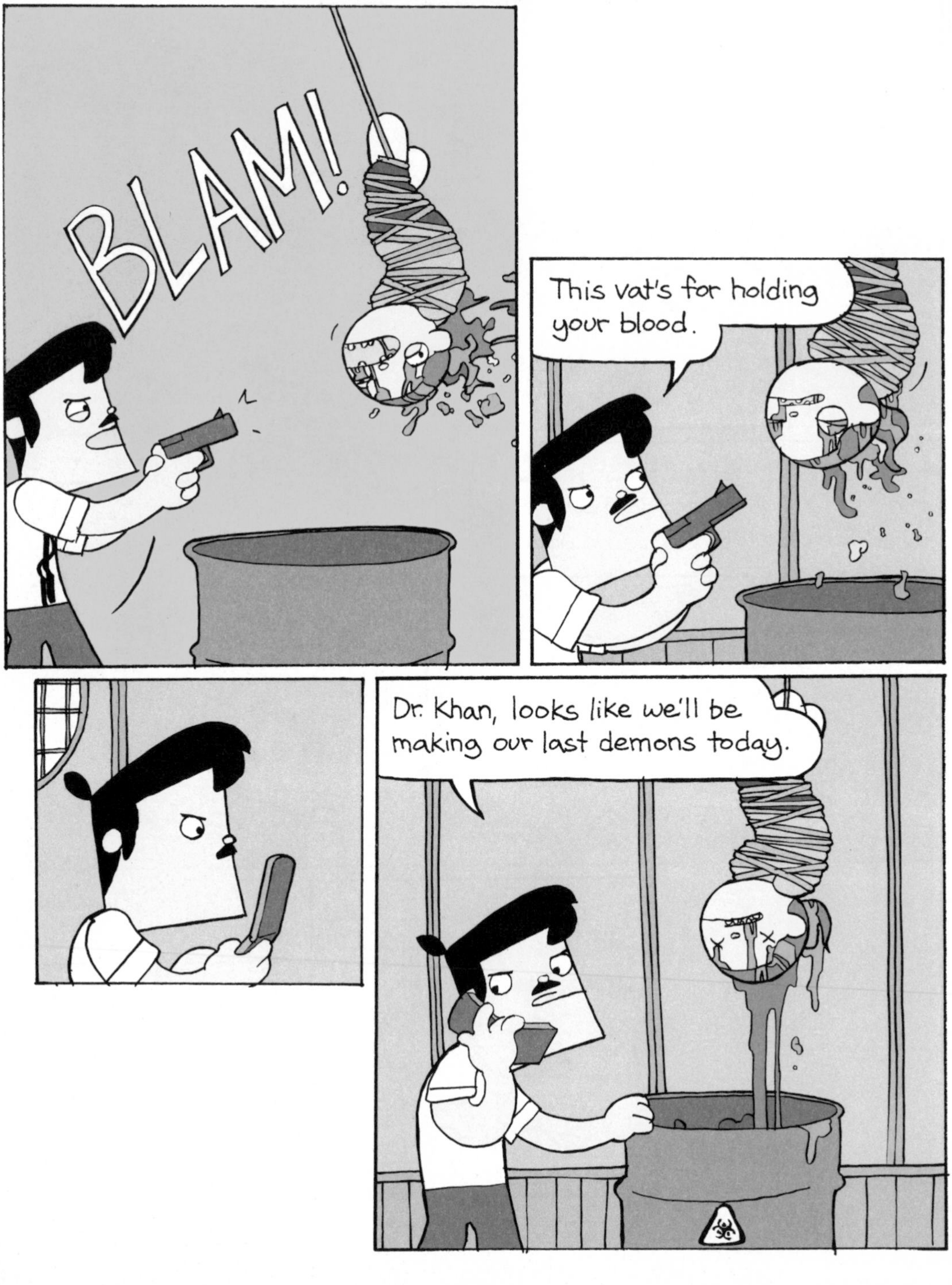
BLAM!
This vat's for holding your blood.
Dr. Khan, looks like we'll be making our last demons today.

CHAPTER 17

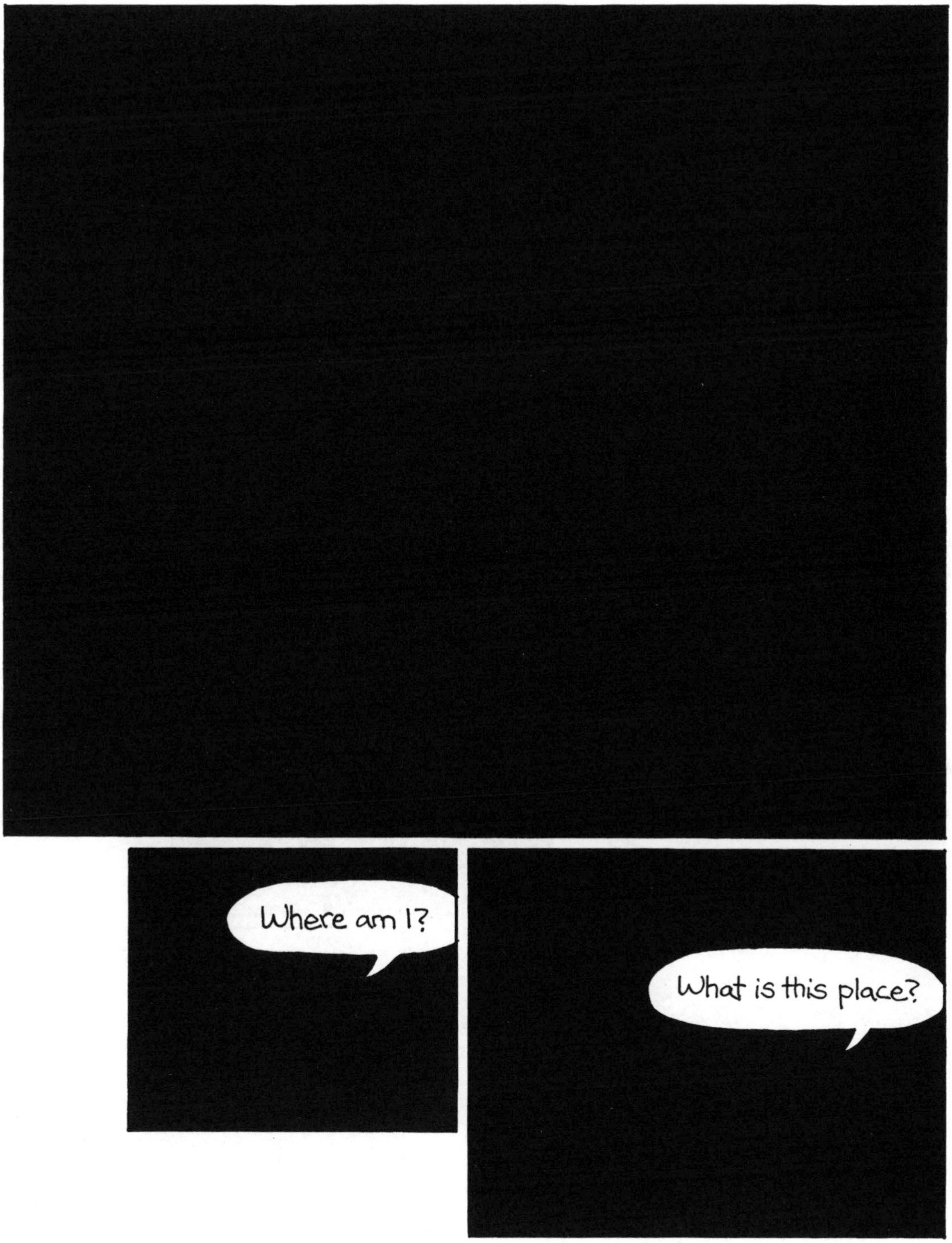
Where am I?
What is this place?

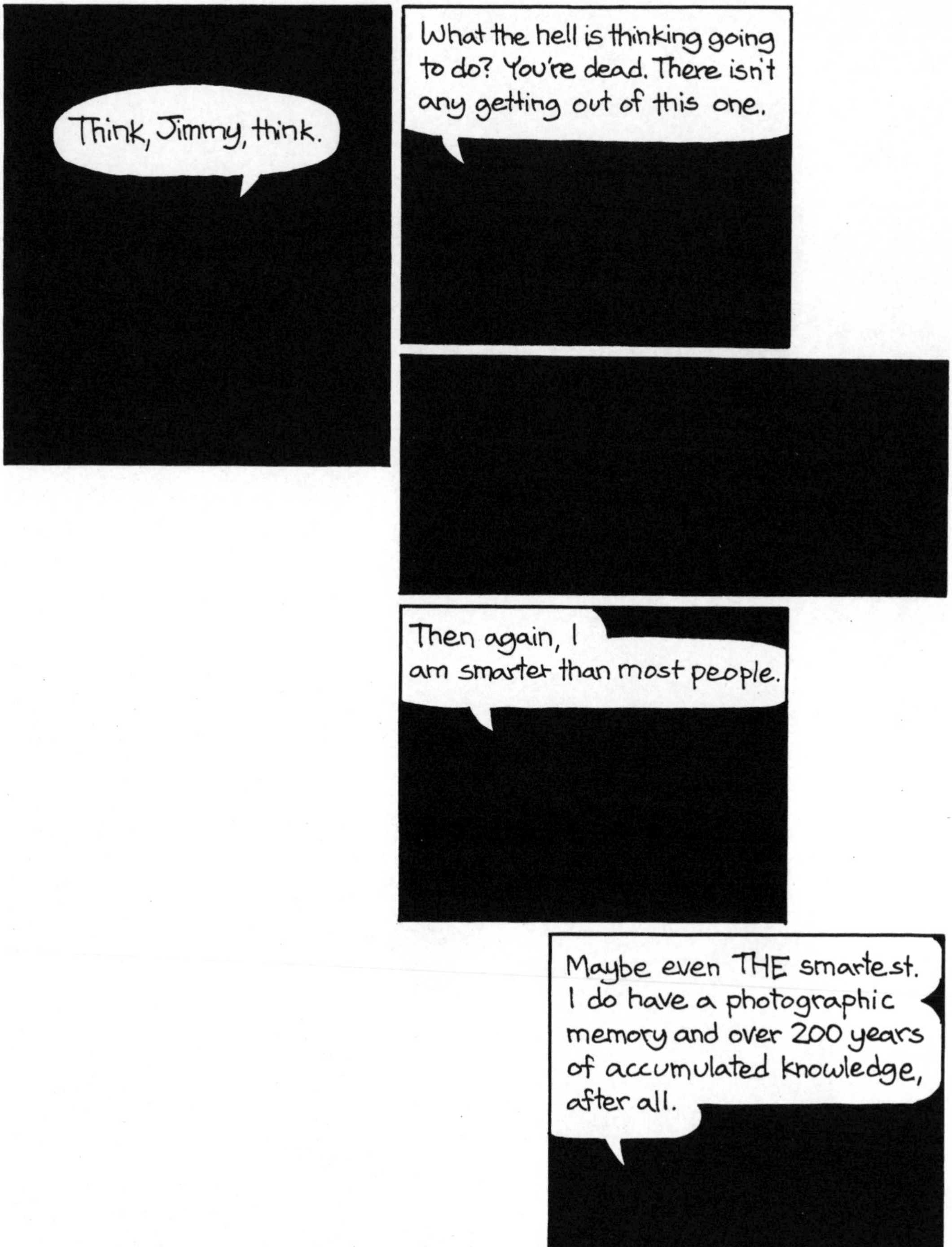
Think, Jimmy, think.
What the hell is thinking going to do? You're dead. There isn't any getting out of this one.
Then again, I am smarter than most people.
Maybe even THE smartest. I do have a photographic memory and over 200 years of accumulated knowledge, after all.

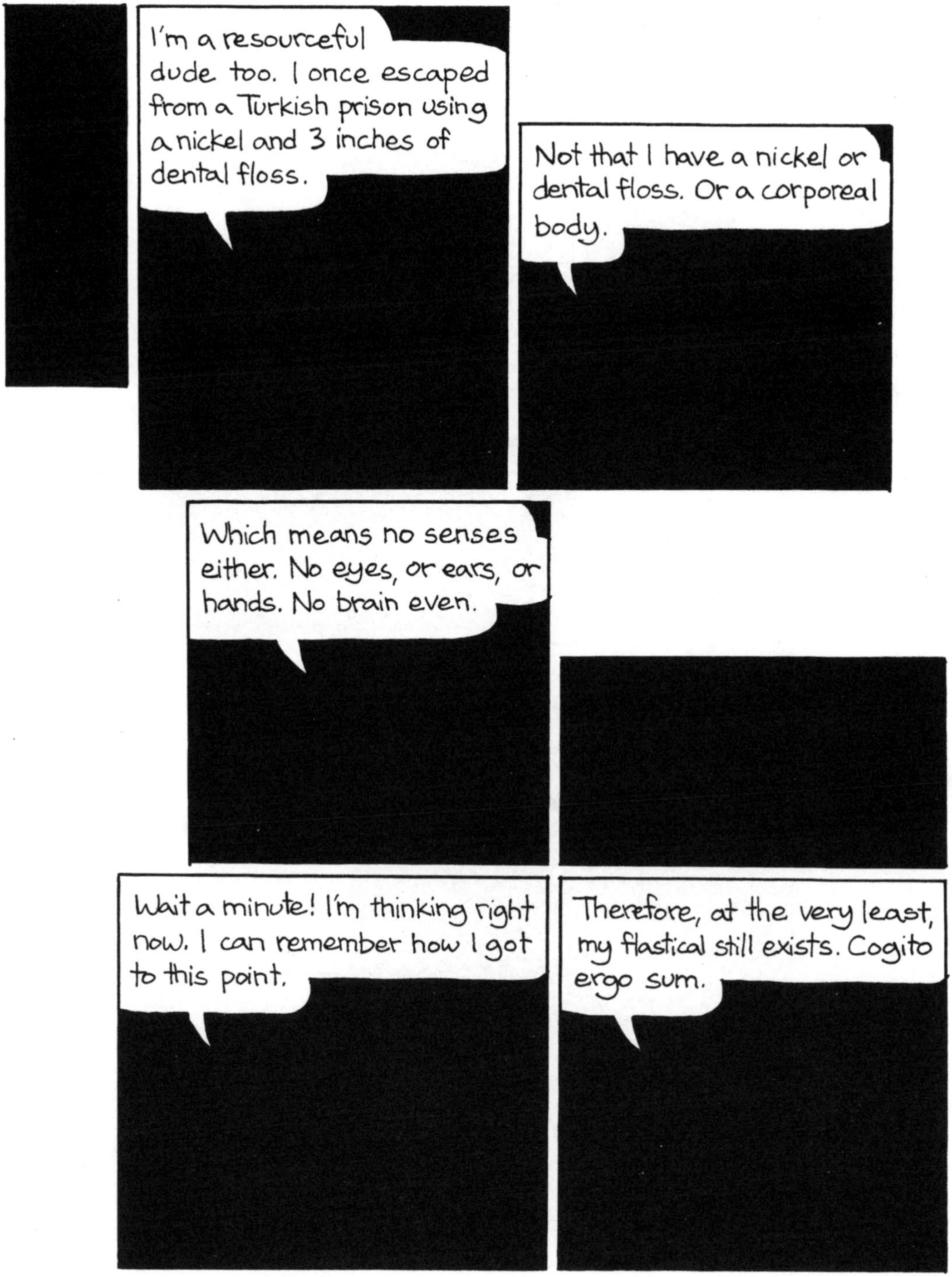
I'm a resourceful dude too. I once escaped from a Turkish prison using a nickel and 3 inches of dental floss.
Not that I have a nickel or dental floss. Or a corporeal body.
Which means no senses either. No eyes, or ears, or hands. No brain even.
Wait a minute! I'm thinking right now. I can remember how I got to this point.
Therefore, at the very least, my flastical still exists. Cogito ergo sum.

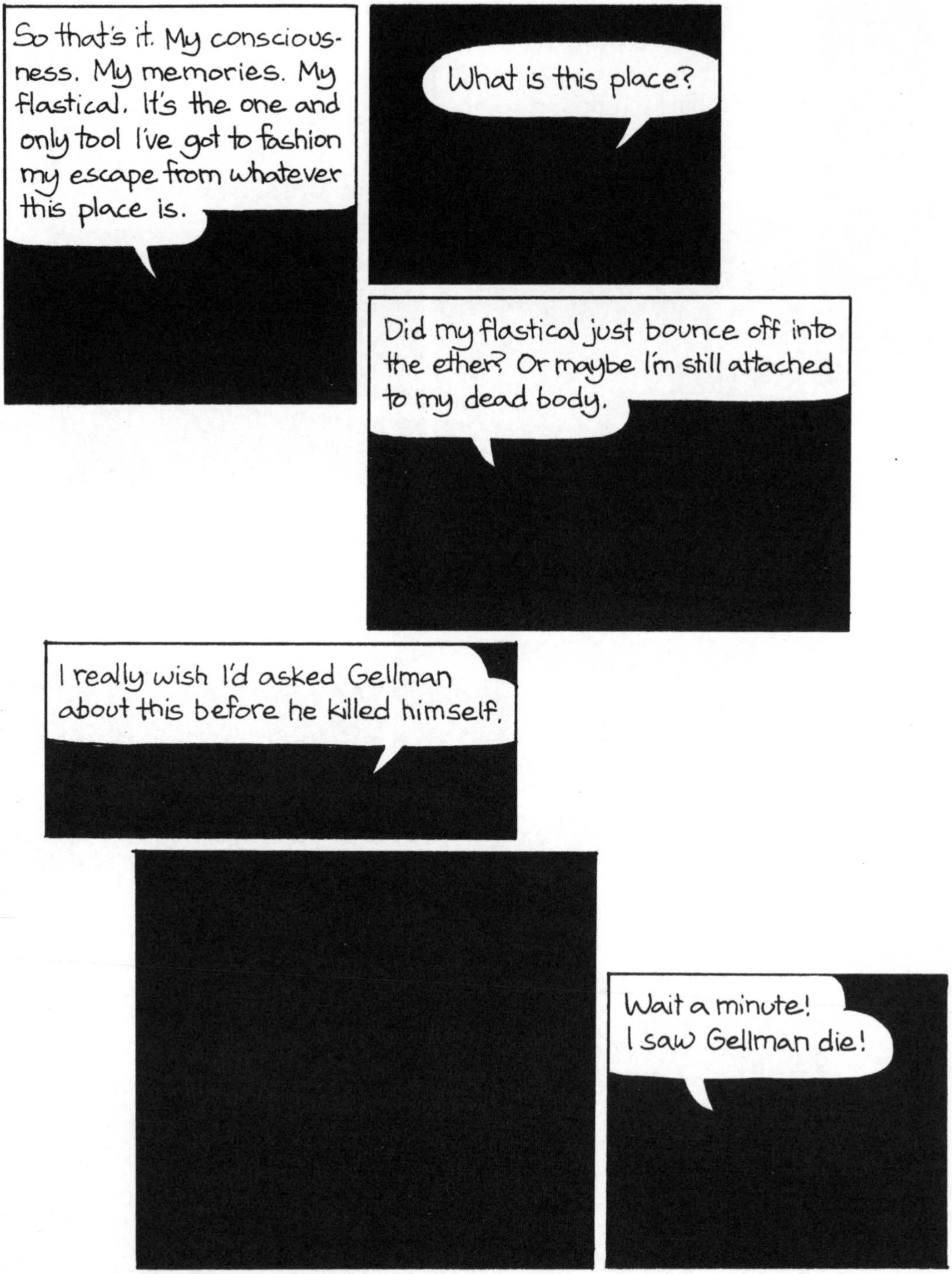
So that's it. My consciousness. My memories. My flastical. It's the one and only tool I've got to fashion my escape from whatever this place is.
What is this place?
Did my flastical just bounce off into the ether? Or maybe I'm still attached to my dead body.
I really wish I'd asked Gellman about this before he killed himself.
Wait a minute! I saw Gellman die!

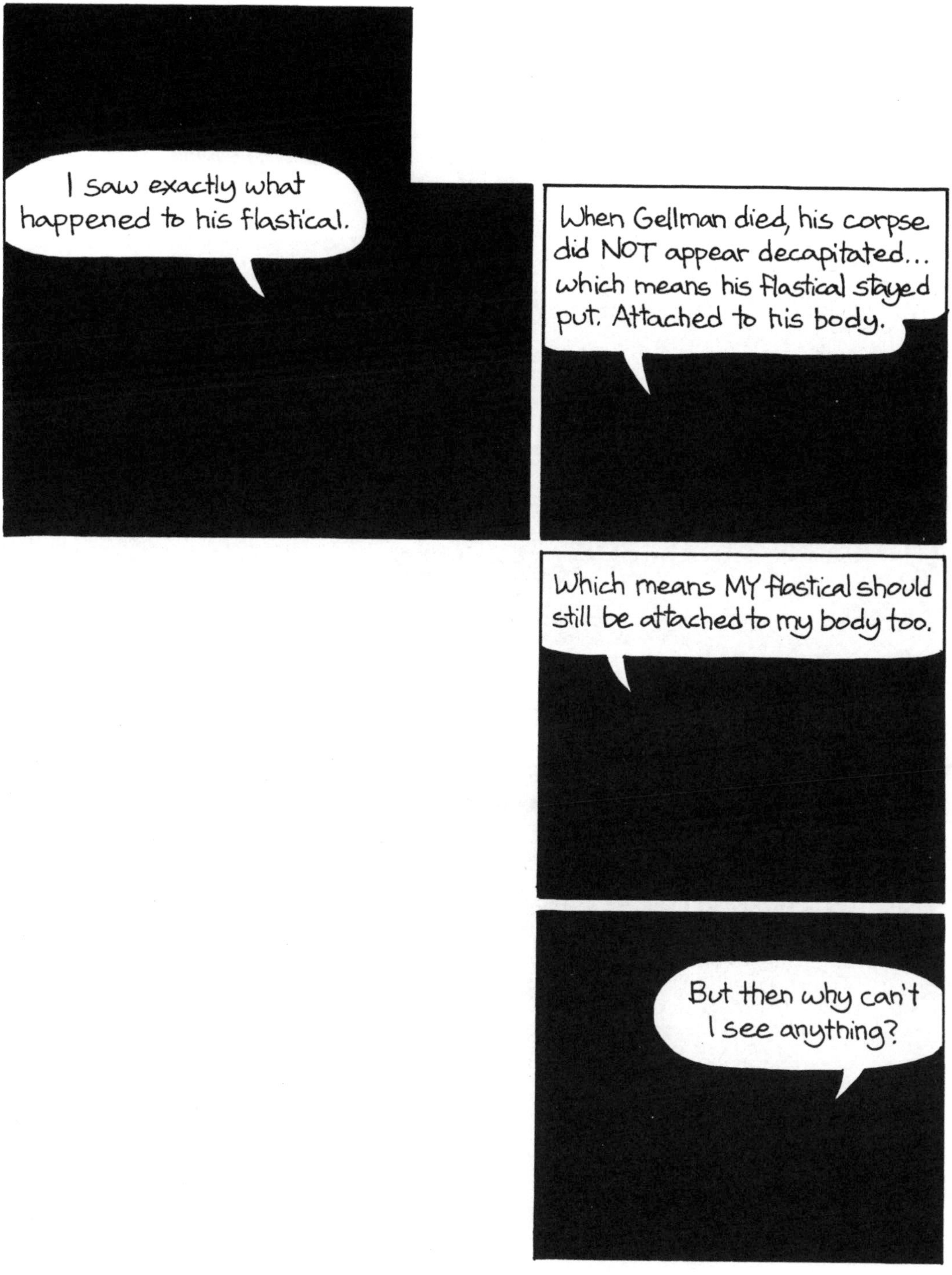
I saw exactly what happened to his flastical.
When Gellman died, his corpse did NOT appear decapitated... which means his flastical stayed put. Attached to his body.
Which means MY flastical should still be attached to my body too.
But then why can't I see anything?

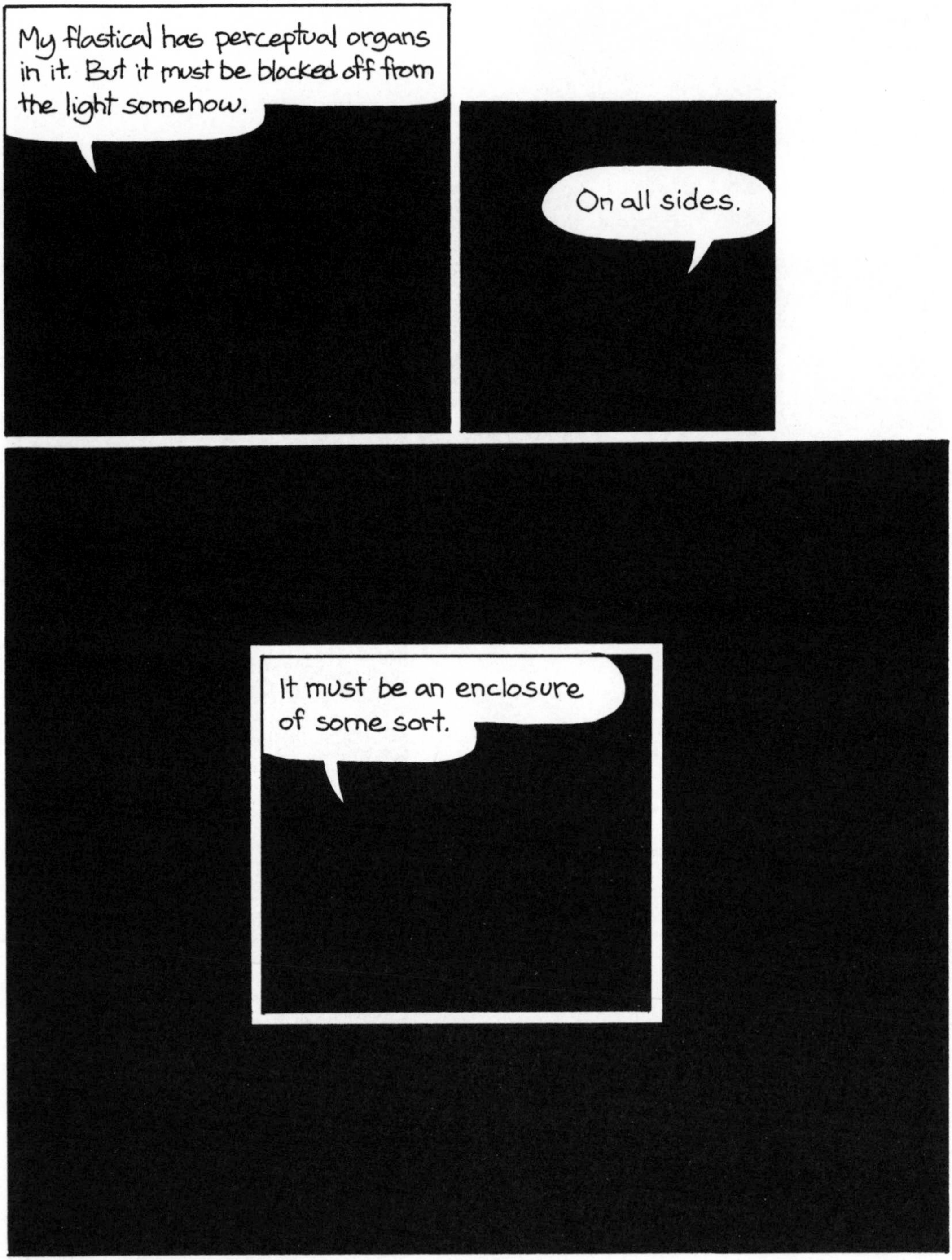
My flastical has perceptual organs in it. But it must be blocked off from the light somehow.
On all sides.
It must be an enclosure of some sort.

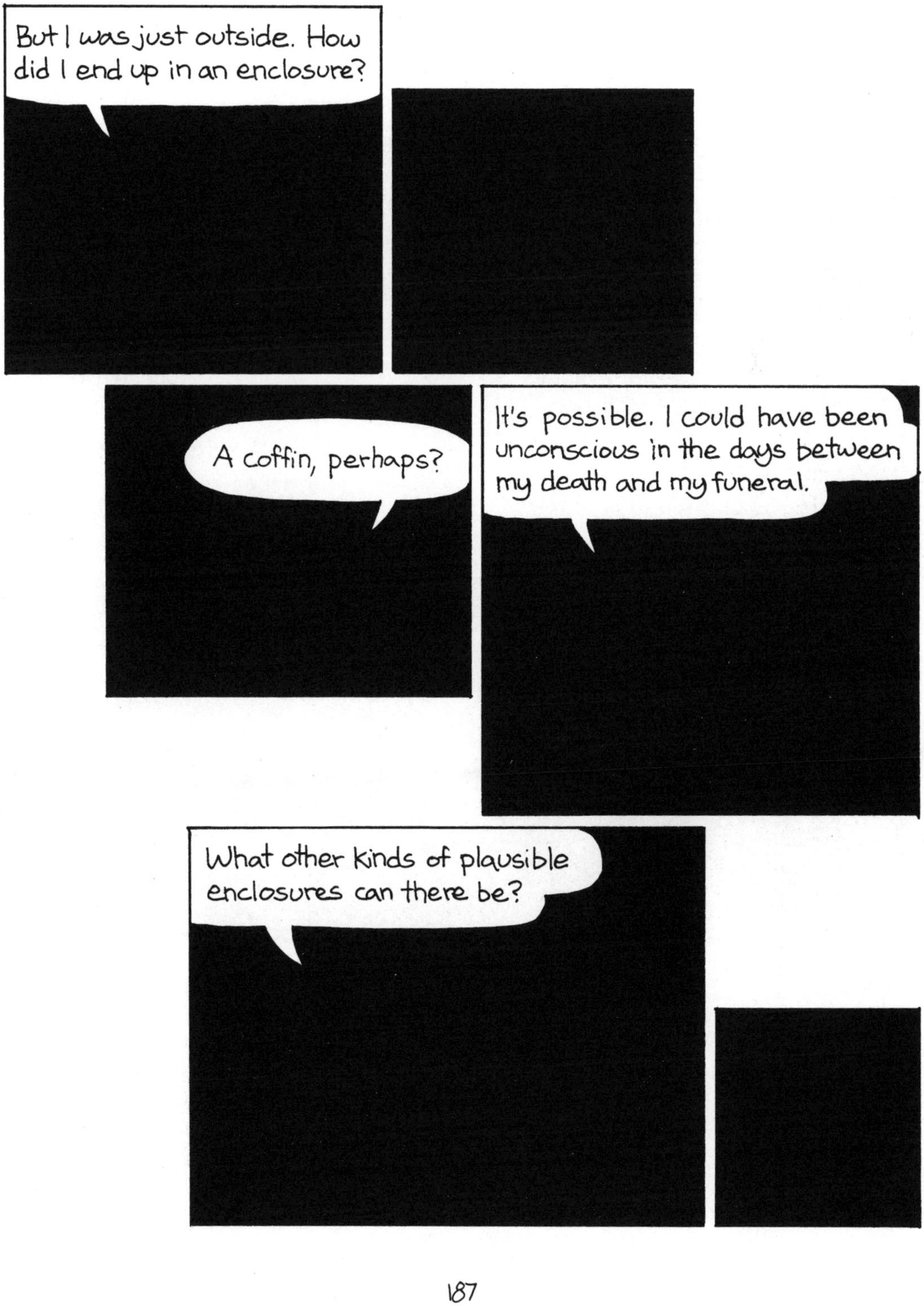
But I was just outside. How did I end up in an enclosure?
A coffin, perhaps?
It's possible. I could have been unconscious in the days between my death and my funeral.
What other kinds of plausible enclosures can there be?

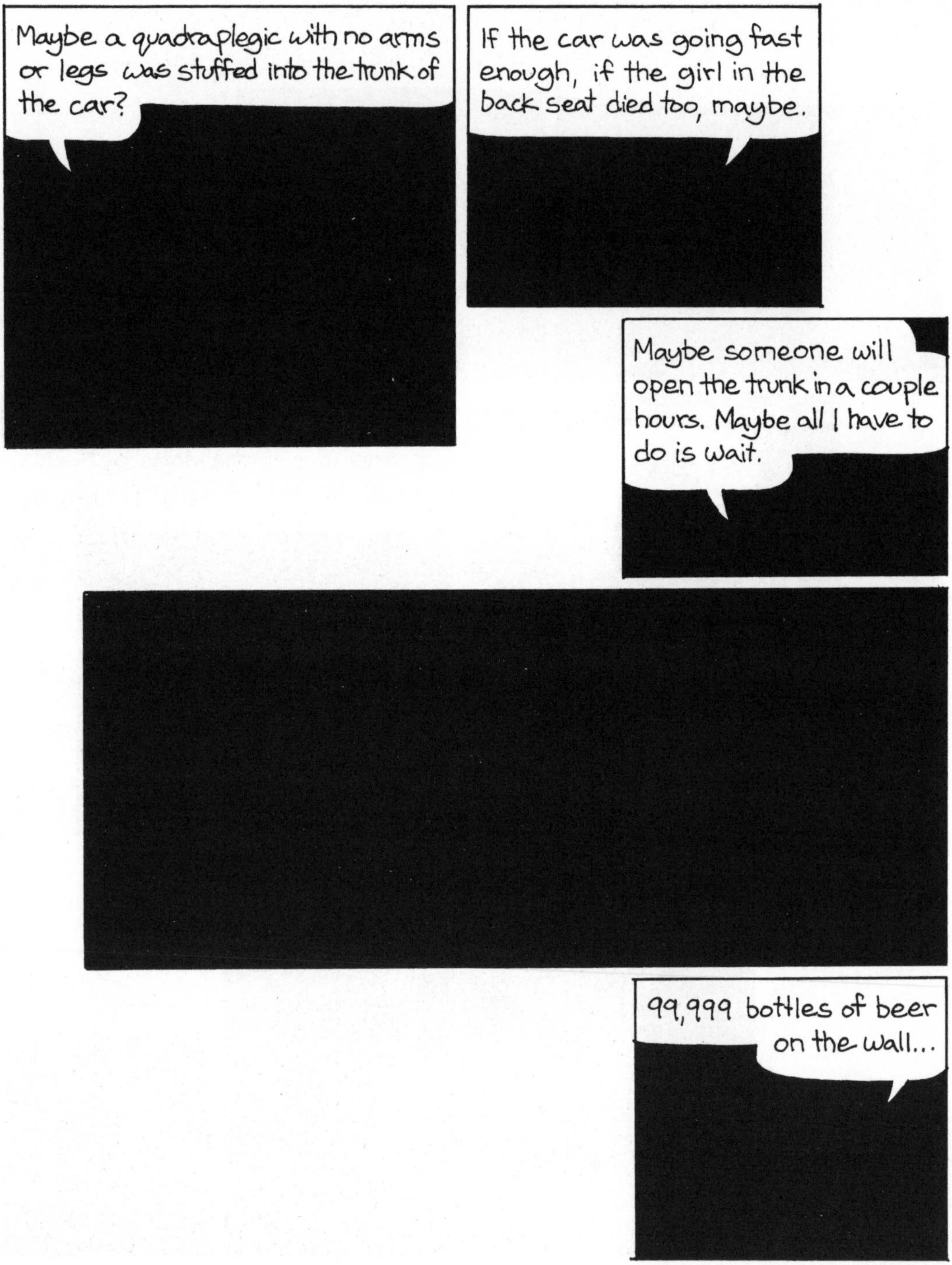
Maybe a quadraplegic with no arms or legs was stuffed into the trunk of the car?
If the car was going fast enough, if the girl in the back seat died too, maybe.
Maybe someone will open the trunk in a couple hours. Maybe all I have to do is wait.
99,999 bottles of beer on the wall...

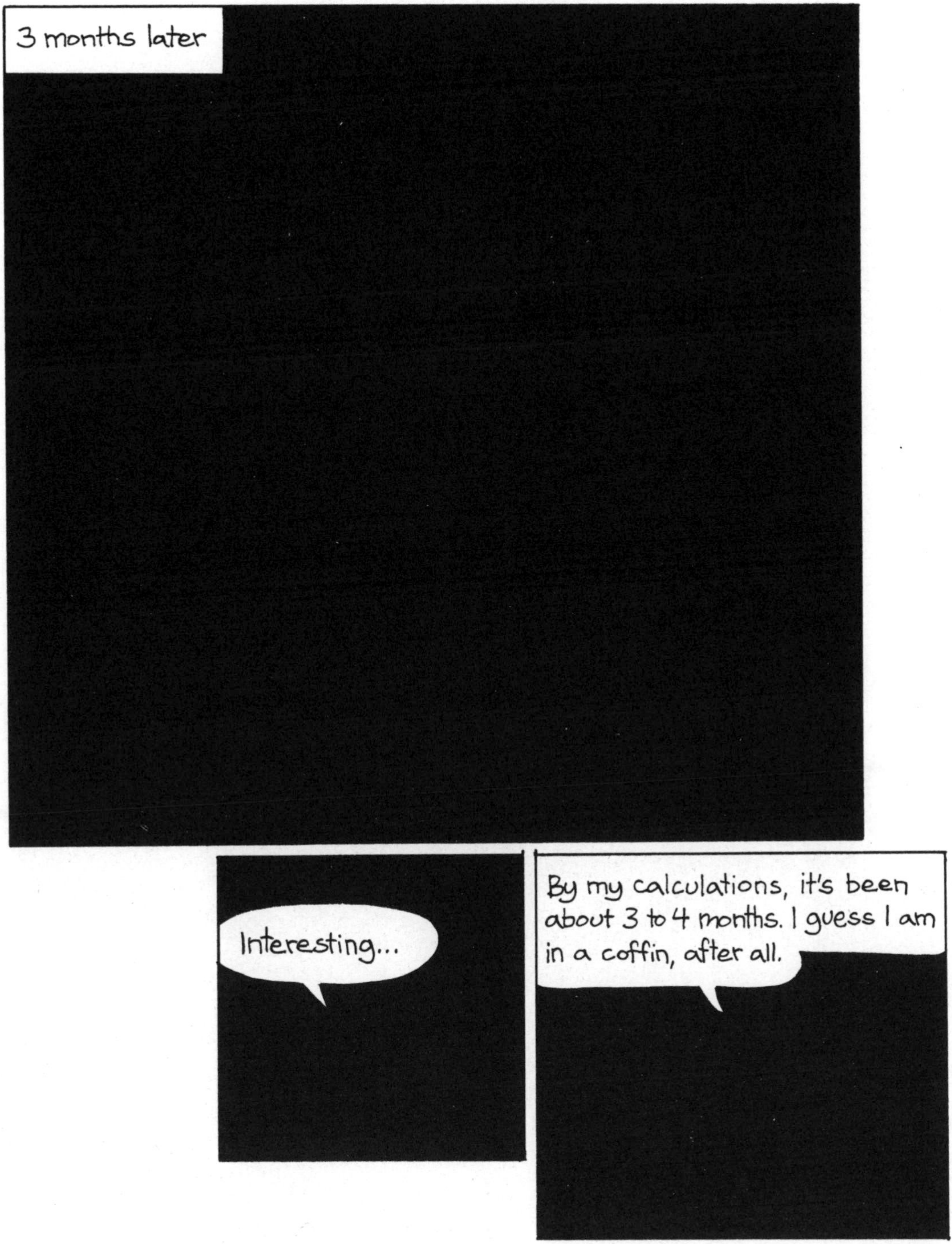
3 months later
Interesting...
By my calculations, it's been about 3 to 4 months. I guess I am in a coffin, after all.

Fuck.

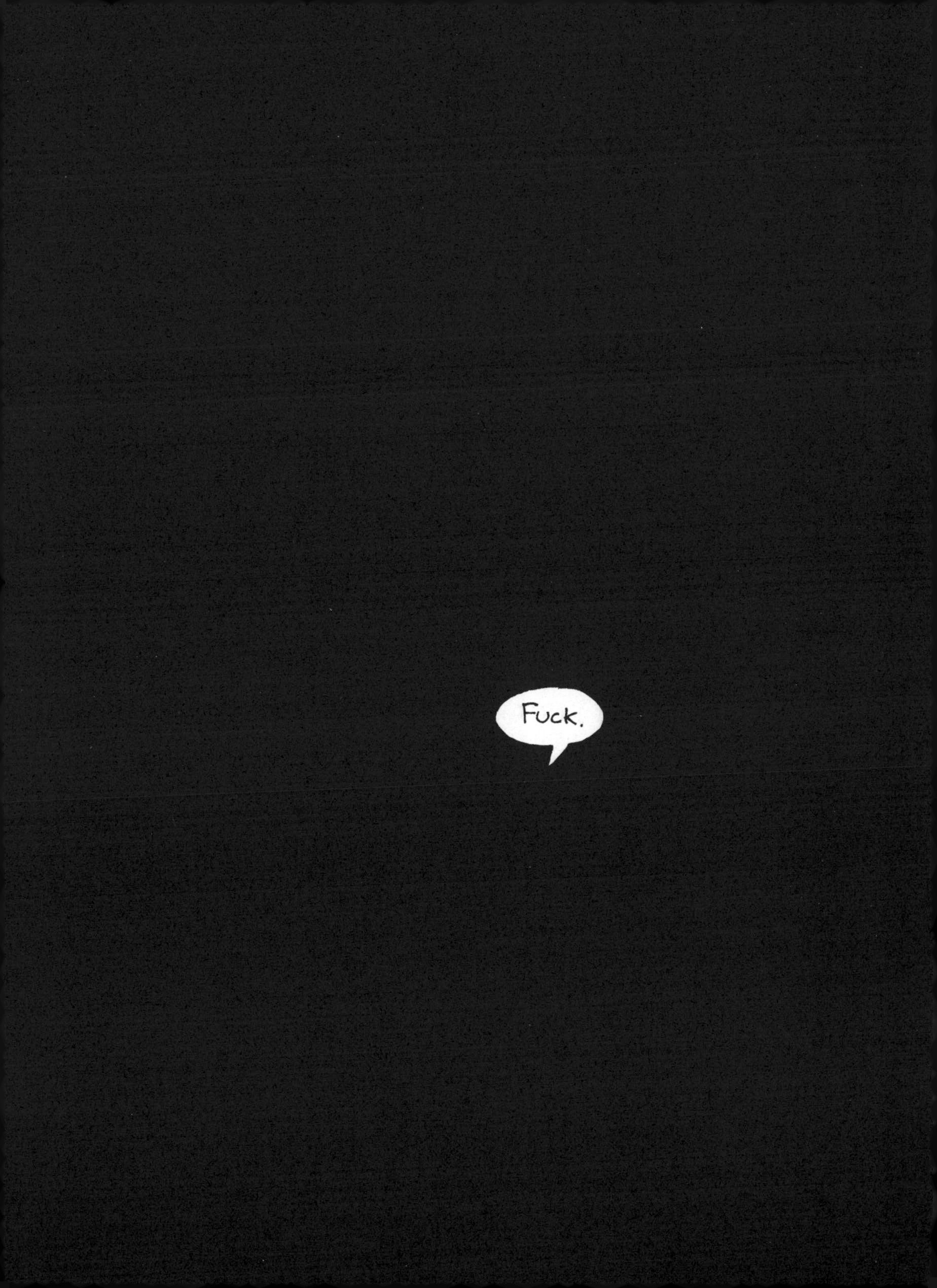

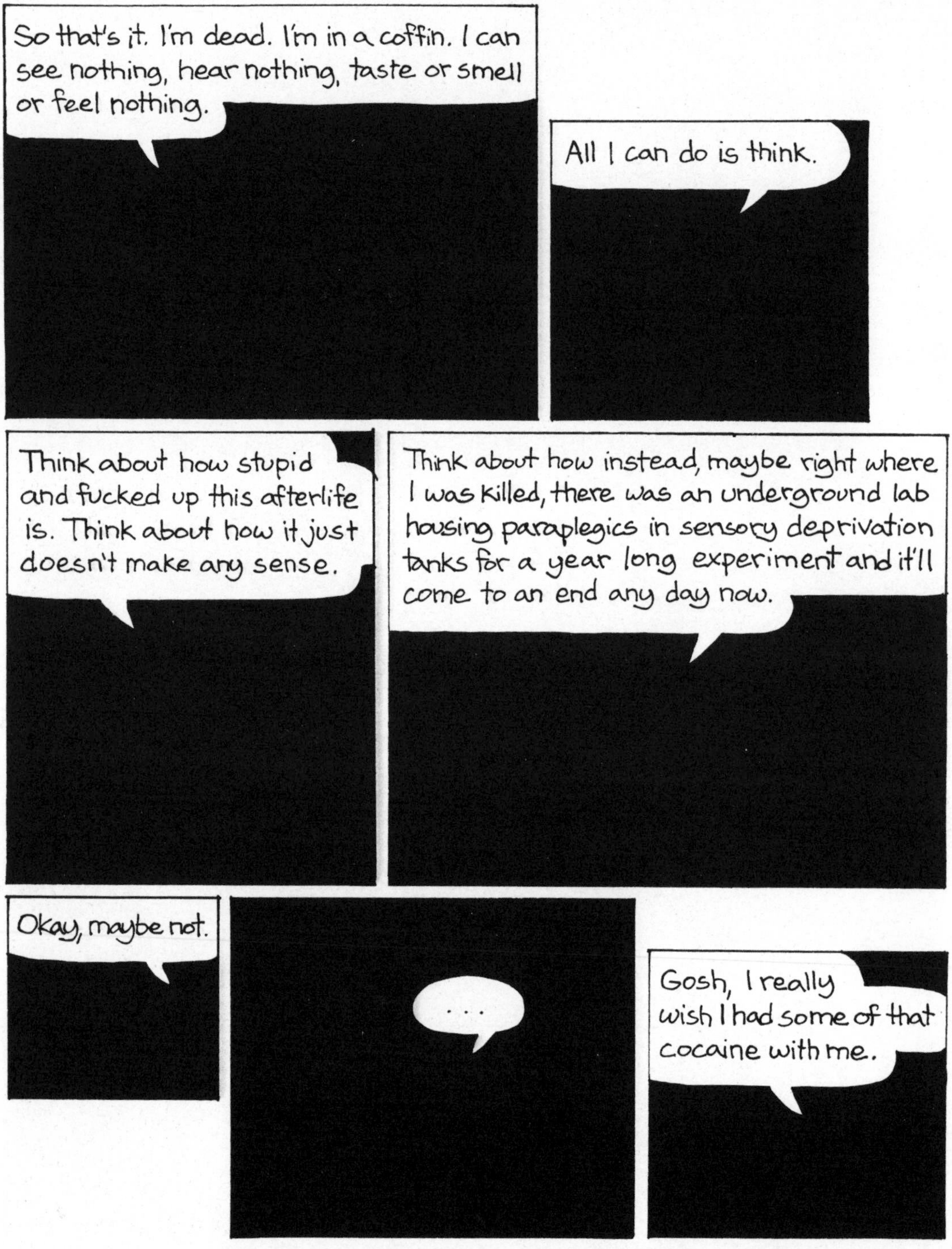
So that's it. I'm dead. I'm in a coffin. I can see nothing, hear nothing, taste or smell or feel nothing.
All I can do is think.
Think about how stupid and fucked up this afterlife is. Think about how it just doesn't make any sense.
Think about how instead, maybe right where I was killed, there was an underground lab housing paraplegics in sensory deprivation tanks for a year long experiment and it'll come to an end any day now.
Okay, maybe not.
. . .
Gosh, I really wish I had some of that cocaine with me.

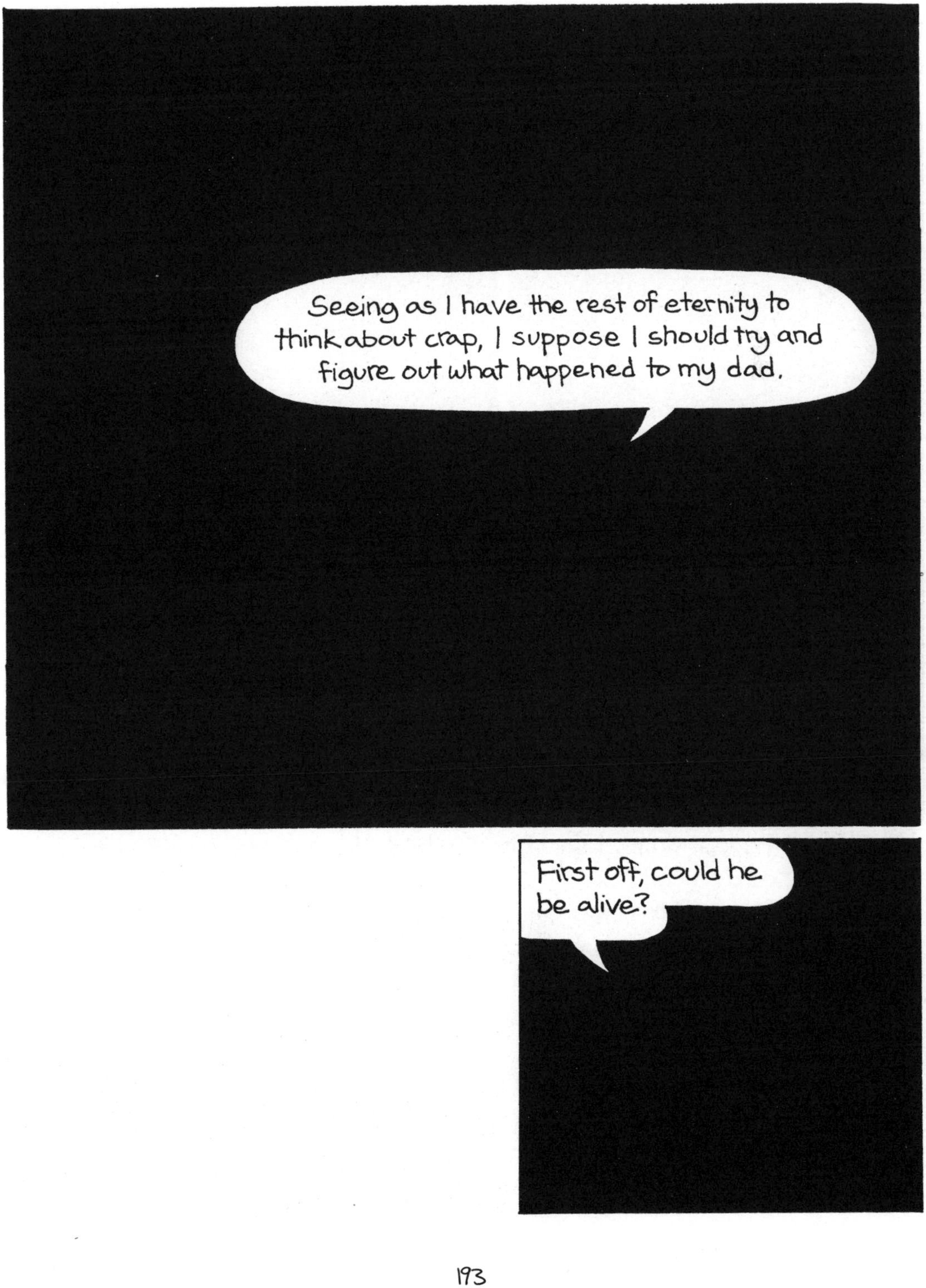
Seeing as I have the rest of eternity to think about crap, I suppose I should try and figure out what happened to my dad.
First off, could he be alive?

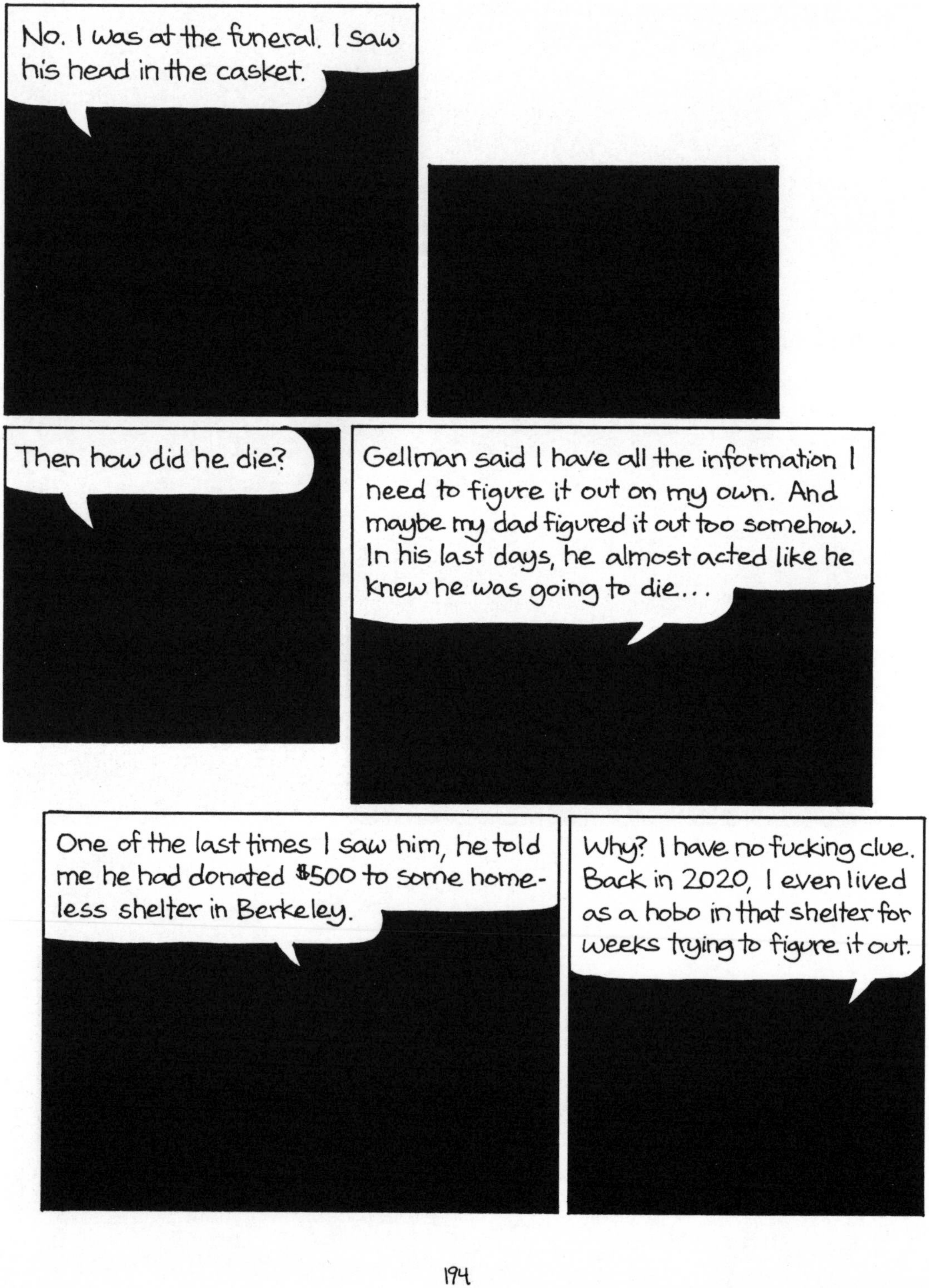
No. I was at the funeral. I saw his head in the casket.
Then how did he die?
Gellman said I have all the information I need to figure it out on my own. And maybe my dad figured it out too somehow. In his last days, he almost acted like he knew he was going to die...
One of the last times I saw him, he told me he had donated $500 to some homeless shelter in Berkeley.
Why? I have no fucking clue. Back in 2020, I even lived as a hobo in that shelter for weeks trying to figure it out.

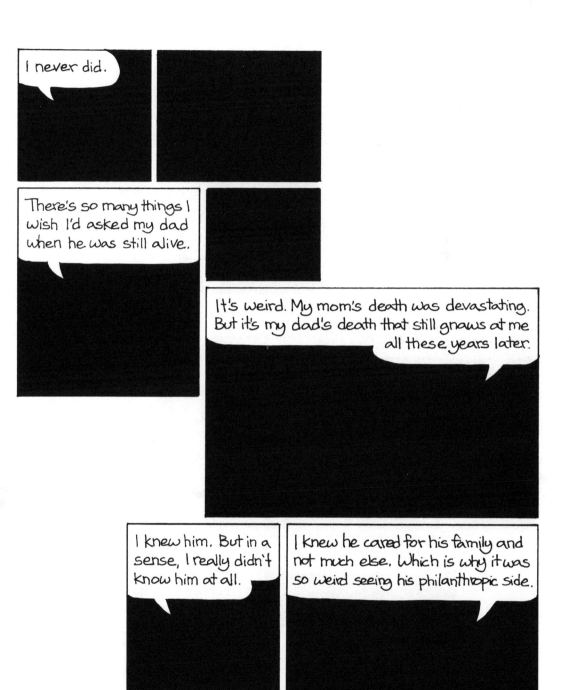

I never did.

There's so many things I wish I'd asked my dad when he was still alive.

It's weird. My mom's death was devastating. But it's my dad's death that still gnaws at me all these years later.

I knew him. But in a sense, I really didn't know him at all.

I knew he cared for his family and not much else. Which is why it was so weird seeing his philanthropic side.

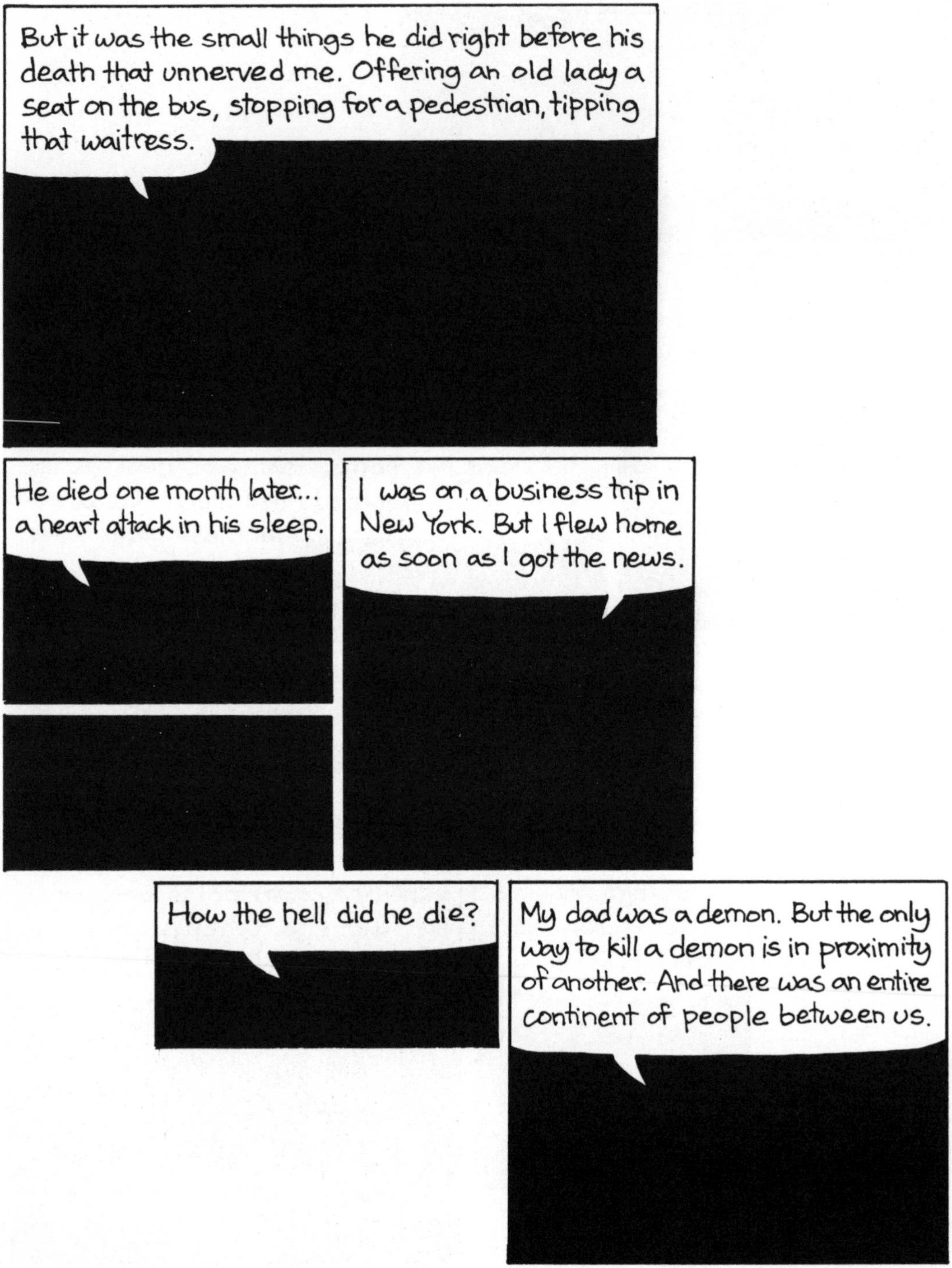
But it was the small things he did right before his death that unnerved me. Offering an old lady a seat on the bus, stopping for a pedestrian, tipping that waitress.
He died one month later... a heart attack in his sleep.
I was on a business trip in New York. But I flew home as soon as I got the news.
How the hell did he die?
My dad was a demon. But the only way to kill a demon is in proximity of another. And there was an entire continent of people between us.

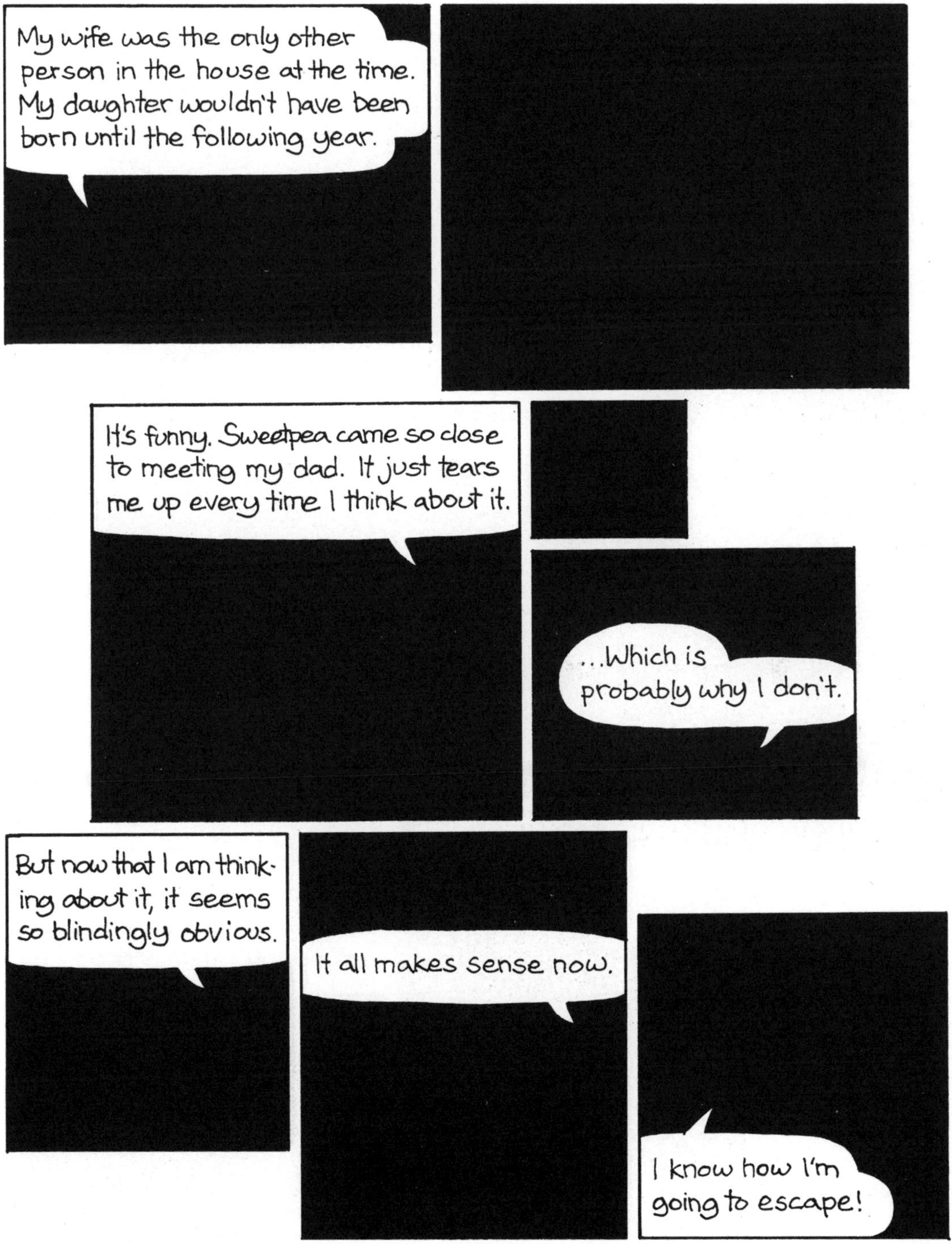
My wife was the only other person in the house at the time. My daughter wouldn't have been born until the following year.
It's funny. Sweetpea came so close to meeting my dad. It just tears me up every time I think about it.
...Which is probably why I don't.
But now that I am think-ing about it, it seems so blindingly obvious.
It all makes sense now.
I know how I'm going to escape!

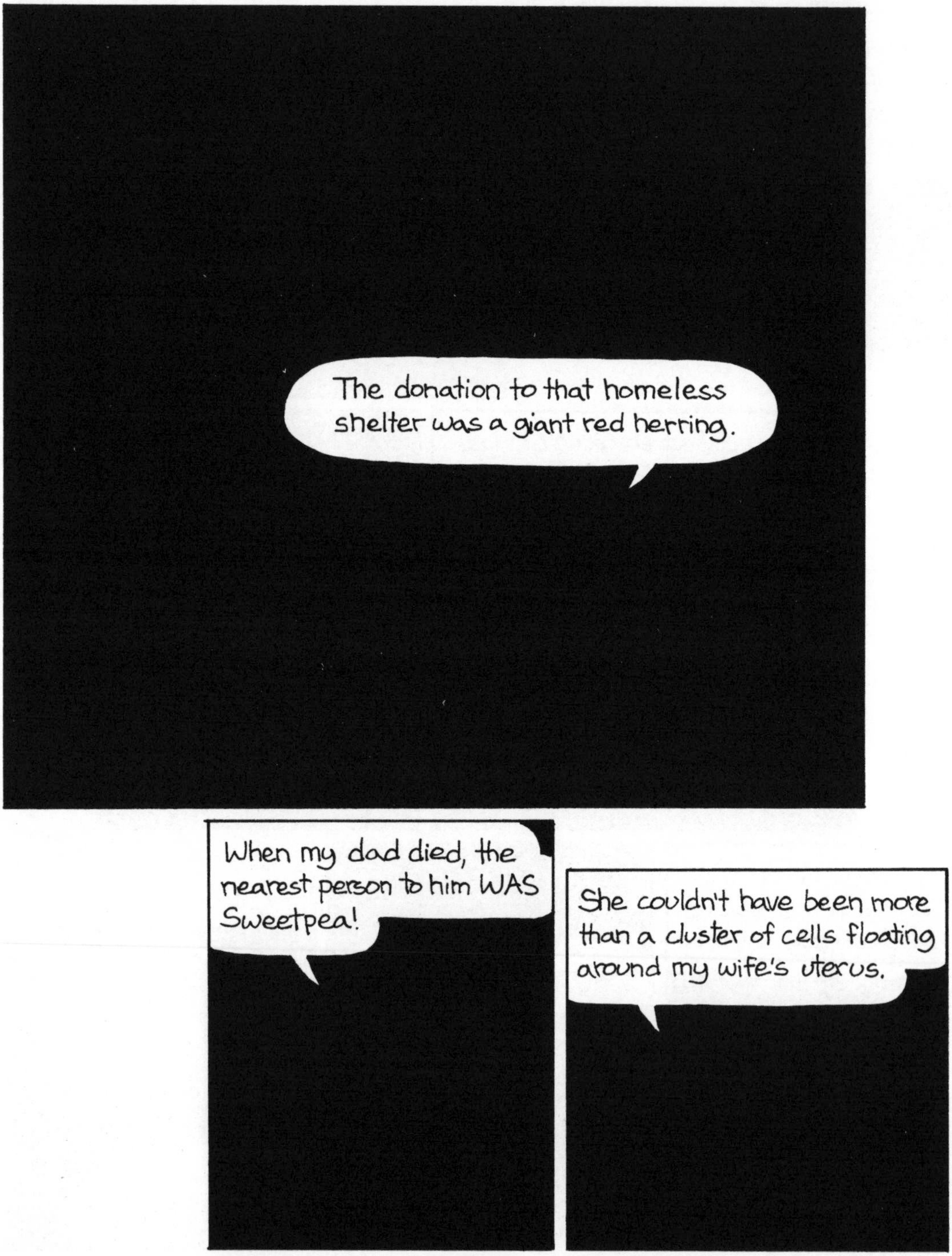
The donation to that homeless shelter was a giant red herring.
When my dad died, the nearest person to him WAS Sweetpea!
She couldn't have been more than a cluster of cells floating around my wife's uterus.

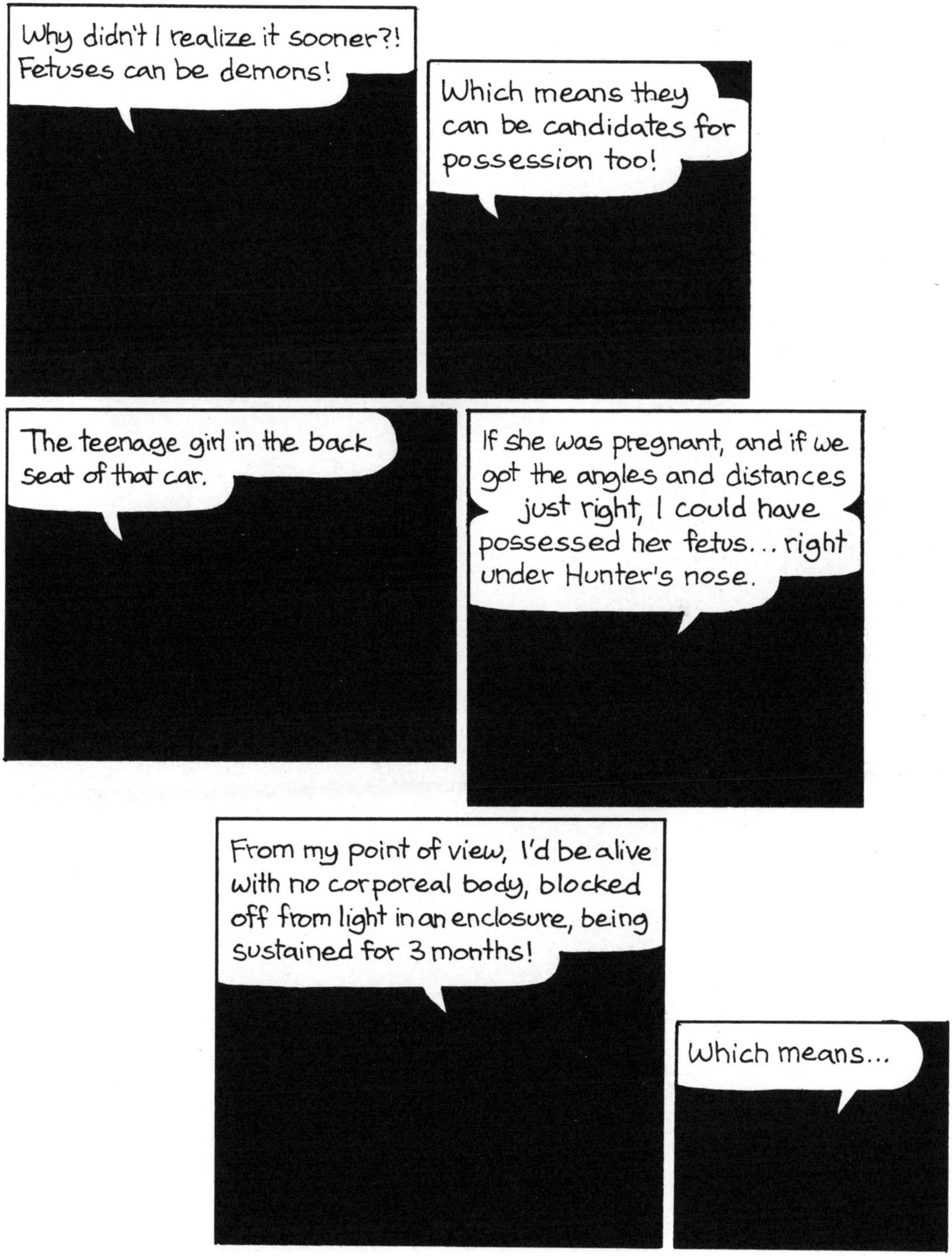
Why didn't I realize it sooner?! Fetuses can be demons!
Which means they can be candidates for possession too!
The teenage girl in the back seat of that car.
If she was pregnant, and if we got the angles and distances just right, I could have possessed her fetus... right under Hunter's nose.
From my point of view, I'd be alive with no corporeal body, blocked off from light in an enclosure, being sustained for 3 months!
Which means...

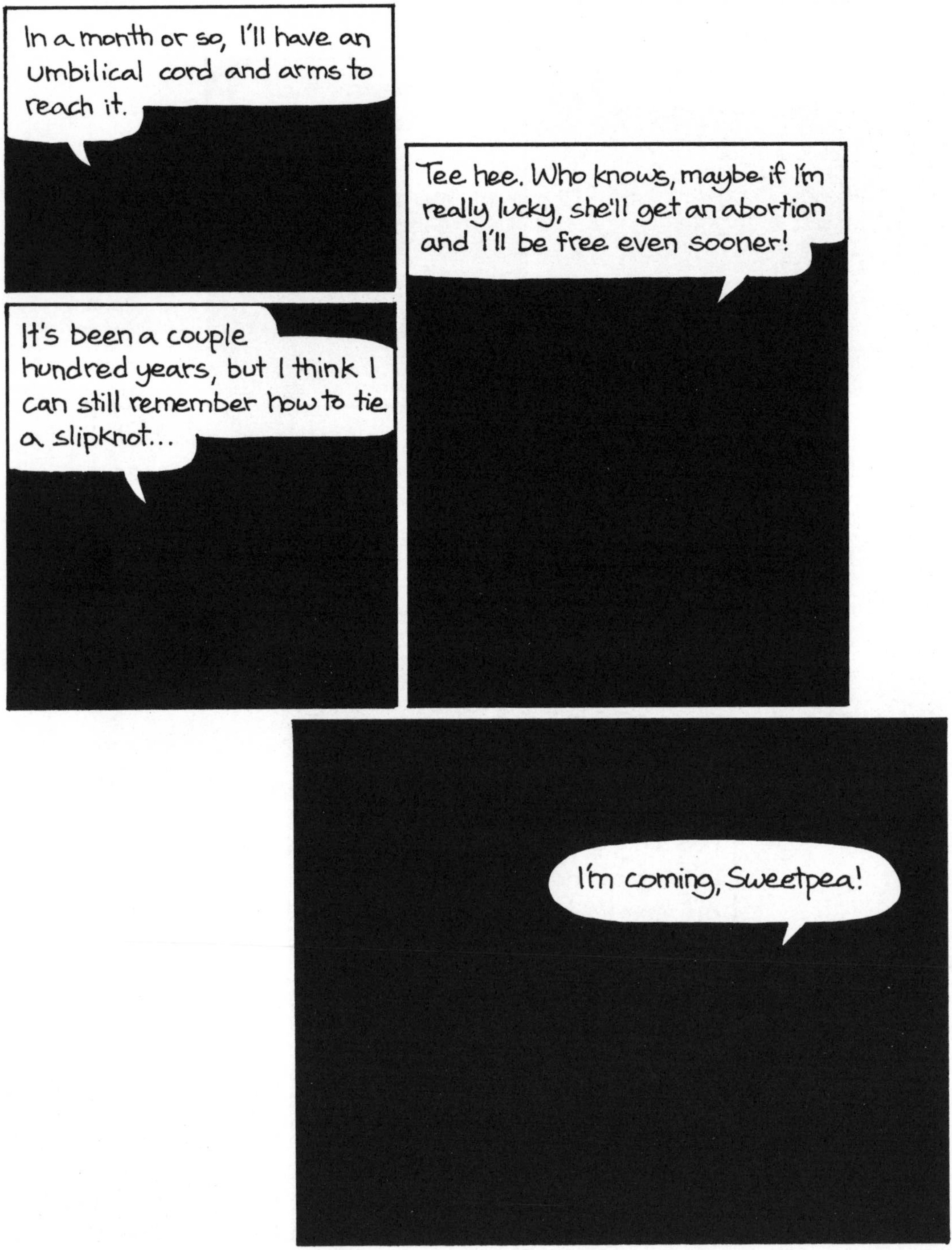
In a month or so, I'll have an umbilical cord and arms to reach it.
It's been a couple hundred years, but I think I can still remember how to tie a slipknot...
Tee hee. Who knows, maybe if I'm really lucky, she'll get an abortion and I'll be free even sooner!
I'm coming, Sweetpea!

CONCLUDED IN

DEM●N

VOLUME 4

PRAISE FOR JASON SHIGA AND DEMON:

"Deeply uncomfortable and utterly brilliant."

—Gene Luen Yang, author of *American Born Chinese*, *Boxers & Saints*, and the Secret Coders series

"Crazy + Genius = Shiga!"

—Scott McCloud, author of *The Sculptor*

"I truly think Demon is one of the best comics that has come out in the last few years. It's surprising, unique, and insanely well crafted."

—Brian Michael Bendis, author of the Ultimate Spider-Man series

"I respect Jason so much for following his audacious, wild, insane muse. Demon is raw, explosive fun."

—Chester Brown, author of *Paying For It*

"Awesome! And horrifying. But mostly awesome!"

—Zach Weinersmith, author of *Saturday Morning Breakfast Cereal*

"Demon reaches unparalleled heights in terms of storytelling and the use of bodily fluids as a narrative device. It's a masterpiece."

—Derek Kirk Kim, author of *Same Difference* and *Tune*